The Promise
of the Future

The Promise of the Future

CORNELIS P. VENEMA

THE BANNER OF TRUTH TRUST

THE BANNER OF TRUTH TRUST

3 Murrayfield Road, Edinburgh EH12 6EL, UK
P. O. Box 621, Carlisle, PA 17013, USA

*

© Cornelis P. Venema 2000

First published 2000
Reprinted 2009
Reprinted 2014

ISBN

Print: 978 0 85151 793 3
EPUB: 98 1 84871 500 4
Kindle: 978 1 84871 501 1

*

Typeset in 11.5/13 pt Sabon MT at
The Banner of Truth Trust

Printed in the USA by
Versa Press Inc.,
East Peoria, IL

*

Unless otherwise indicated, all Scripture quotations
are taken from the New American Standard Bible,
1979 edition, © The Lockman Foundation

Contents

Contents

Foreword

IT IS A PLEASURE to introduce Cornelis Venema's exceptional book *The Promise of the Future*. Dr Venema is Professor of Doctrinal Studies at Mid-America Reformed Seminary. For some time now his acumen as a theologian and skill as a teacher and author have been recognized and deeply appreciated in the circles in which he has been known in the United States. I hope that the publication of *The Promise of the Future* will bring his work to the notice of a wider public on both sides of the Atlantic (and, indeed, the Pacific!). It is a model of what systematic theological exposition should be.

Doctrinal or (as it is frequently called) Systematic Theology has fallen into disfavour in the modern age and also into a kind of self-created decline. Much that is taught in universities and seminaries under this heading is now little more than the study of the religious opinions of scholars. The views of various theologians are clarified, compared, contrasted and critiqued. While this is a legitimate enough exercise in itself, its net effect has been that Systematic Theology is no longer viewed as a systematic presentation of what divine revelation teaches on any given subject. Rather it has become a kind of religious anthropology. The vision is downwards, sideways and inwards. To tinker a little with the well-known Latin proverb, the voice of the theologians is the voice of God. The voice of God in Scripture has come to be treated with scepticism, even with disdain; allusions to it (often by those who are most critical of 'proof-text' theology) have been little more than occasional proof texts which buttress views held on other grounds.

In this atmosphere, charged as it is with a kind of theological carbon monoxide poisoning, Cornelis Venema's work can be safely inhaled. It provides us with a healthy injection of doctrinal oxygen. He stands in the august tradition of biblical theologians like Herman Bavinck, Geerhardus Vos and John Murray who, with John Calvin and Johannes Cocceius in an earlier age, sought to quarry doctrine from the rich and varied seams of biblical revelation.

The Promise of the Future is thus the fruit of long and patient study of the Bible. That is why it is such a satisfying, unfrustrating book for a Christian to read. In its pages the voice of God is not muffled by the philosophies of man but allowed to speak for itself. Here the reader will find that there is always the solid ground of Scripture under his or her feet.

This does not mean that Dr Venema ignores the history of theology or is not well abreast of intellectual developments. Those more familiar with historical theology will recognize his sensitivity to the Christian tradition in the whole warp and woof of the tapestry of instruction he has woven here. In this respect, his footnotes are but the tip of the iceberg.

The Promise of the Future introduces us to the full range of biblical teaching on eschatology (the study of the last things). It rightly stresses that in Scripture the eschatological dimension is never relegated to 'the end'. Rather, from the beginning God's purposes have had an eschatological perspective. Moreover, as Simon Peter pointed out on the Day of Pentecost, the resurrection of Christ and the gift of the Spirit mean that the future has invaded the present, so that we are already living in 'the last days'. This helps to explain the sense of thrill and vibrancy that characterized the first Christian disciples. They realized that the new, long-awaited age of God's kingdom had already dawned in the advent of the Lord Jesus Christ.

Dr Venema's fine study is both comprehensive and careful. He is thoroughly biblical; he is also honest and fair in dealing with the variety of eschatological positions that are current in the Christian church. He does not shrink from tackling the hard questions which arise. Nor is he intimidated by the heavy artillery behind some of the views which he believes to be unbiblical. Furthermore, his commitment to serve the church, coupled with his background in pastoral ministry, guarantees that his exposition even of complex issues is expressed in a way that the average Christian should be able to follow.

For these reasons and others, I believe that you will find the study on which you are about to embark both intellectually satisfying and spiritually enriching. It will certainly inform you; more than that it will help you to sense what a glorious thing it is to be a Christian. For this, above all, I believe you will share my gratitude to Cornelis Venema for the labour of love for Christ's people which this book represents.

SINCLAIR B. FERGUSON
St George's-Tron Church
Glasgow, Scotland

Preface

Blessed be the God and Father of our Lord Jesus Christ,
who according to His great mercy has caused us to be
born again to a living hope through the resurrection of
Jesus Christ from the dead, to obtain an inheritance
which is imperishable and undefiled and will not fade
away, reserved in heaven for you, who are protected by
the power of God through faith for a salvation ready to
be revealed in the last time.

1 PETER 1:3–5

As the clock wound down to midnight, 31 December
1999, much of the world was captivated by the prospect
of the dawn of a new millennium. With the assistance of
modern technology, many were able to join in the countdown
and witness the remarkable celebrations that marked the
passage of the second millennium and the beginning of
the third. In those countries whose economies and means of
communication have become largely dependent upon
modern computers, expectation for the future included a
considerable dose of apprehension and uncertainty. The 'Y2K'
computer bug threatened to wreak havoc throughout the

world economy. For a brief moment, it seemed everyone's attention was fixed upon the future and what it would bring. The time was ripe for foretellers to offer their predictions regarding what the new century and millennium would bring. And, as if to confirm the truth of the adage, 'a fool is born every minute', there was no shortage of articles, books and media presentations purporting to predict what the coming future would entail.

Now that this moment has passed, however, it is remarkable to witness how quickly the subject of the future has receded from view. Since nothing out of the ordinary occurred at the stroke of midnight, 31 December 1999, and since the dreaded 'Y2K' computer bug proved to be a toothless tiger, many people have returned to business as usual. The topic of the future is no longer the centre of attention. Life in the present is once again the pre-occupation.

If you were to ask why modern men and women so quickly lose interest in the future – the passing of a millennium getting so much attention one day and forgotten the next – the simplest answer would have to be: *despair*. Our English term 'despair' is formed from a Latin root whose original meaning suggests the idea of a loss or absence of hope. Because it has lost faith in the Triune God of the Bible, the secularised West profoundly witnesses to this loss of hope. When a culture trumpets the 'death of God' it must inevitably also succumb to despair, to the loss of any real sense of expectation for the future. Though Alexander Pope may have declared that 'hope springs eternal in the human breast', those who reject the Triune God of the Scripture – 'who is, and who was, and who is to come' – will inevitably experience the death of hope. Consequently, even when the world finds itself captivated for a passing moment with the subject of the future, its attention span is limited and its expectation for the future empty of anything ultimately satisfying.

This absence of hope which marks the worldview of so many modern people contrasts sharply with Christianity, which is nothing if not a hope-filled faith. Every Easter, orthodox Christians throughout the world gather to commemorate and celebrate the resurrection of Jesus Christ from the dead. They find themselves joining the Apostle Peter in saying, 'Blessed be the God and Father of our Lord Jesus Christ, who according to His great mercy has caused us to be born again to a living hope through the resurrection of Jesus Christ from the dead.' In the resurrection of Christ, the 'firstfruits of them that sleep', the future has been revealed to faith. Christ's resurrection is the great event in history that fuels the hope of every Christian – hope for victory over sin and death, for triumph over the grave, for new life in fellowship with God that will have no end, for a new heaven and earth. Christians believe that the first rays of the light of the new creation began to shine on Easter morning, when the angels announced, 'He is not here, He is risen.'

The following study aims to describe the contours and content of this Christian hope. It is written in the awareness that many people no longer have a clear understanding or conviction about the future. Ironically, many recent celebrants of the dawn of a new millennium did not even realize that the calendar which most parts of the world use to date the passing of years, centuries, and millennia, itself testifies to the kingship of Jesus Christ. We mark every year as *Anno Domini*, as a 'year of the Lord'. This growing ignorance of the Christian hope for the future may be due in part to the neglect of many churches to teach what the Scriptures tell us about the future. Since they have often rejected the authority and truth of the Scriptures, they find themselves unable to echo their teaching or affirm what the Christian church has generally taught about this subject throughout its history. But likely it is also due to the excessive curiosity and often even strange teaching of more conservative and fundamentalist Christians on this subject. One does not have to browse long in Christian bookshops before discovering that the subject of the future continues to fascinate conservative Christians. However, many of these studies of the future are plagued by a concentration upon one or two controversial issues. Often attempts are made to predict the future, including the return of Christ, in terms that go beyond the testimony of Scripture. Contemporary events are correlated with biblical prophecy in a way that is sensationalistic and attention grabbing, despite the Scriptural reminders that no one knows or can know the day or hour of Christ's return.

For this reason it is an advantage that this study appears in the aftermath of the excitement of the passing of a millennium. Unlike many studies of the subject of the future, this one offers no detailed predictions regarding the future course of events. Nor does it attempt to correlate recent events with biblical prophecy. Rather, the following study seeks to present a comprehensive survey of the Bible's teaching regarding the future following the traditional sequence of topics in eschatology.

Several features of the following study require brief comment. First, the approach and method of the study is primarily one of biblical exposition. One of the burdens of my argument is that the canon of the Old and New Testament Scriptures constitutes the primary source and basis for our knowledge of the future. The shape of the Christian hope for the future can be determined only on the basis of a careful study of the Scripture's teaching regarding its various facets. Admittedly, this will seem naïve to those who regard the Scriptures as little more than the distilled wisdom of human authors who wrote in the distant past. It will also seem inadequate to those who insist upon subordinating the teaching of the text of Scripture to the worldview and perspectives of the contemporary reader. However, as I argue in the opening chapter, I am writing from the settled conviction that only the Holy Spirit speaking in the Scriptures can ultimately teach us with certainty what we need to know about the promise of the future.

Second, the approach of the following study as an extended biblical exposition upon the subject of biblical eschatology reflects the occasion for its writing. Much of the following material first appeared in a lengthy series of articles in the Christian periodical *The Outlook*. Though this material has been considerably revised and rewritten at points, it retains something of its original character as a study aimed at the biblically and theologically informed lay person. This accounts for the relative absence of any extended treatments of more technical aspects of the subject. References to the original languages of the biblical text, for example, are kept to a minimum and occur only where it relates to a significant point in the argument. Similarly, though a knowledge of history and theological treatments of the subject of biblical eschatology will prove helpful to any reader of this book, I have deliberately avoided presuming more than is appropriate among a general readership. This does not mean that more technical issues of language, history, and theology, have been ignored. The footnotes serve to alert the reader to the more important literature for further study.

Third, one of the most controversial issues in modern treatments of biblical eschatology is the subject of the millennium of Revelation 20. Due to the predominance of Premillennialism, especially Dispensational Premillennialism, among many contemporary evangelicals, the biblical case for Amillennialism has seldom been made very forcefully or comprehensively. In some ways, recent debates regarding the subject of the millennium have been dominated by voices advocating Premillennialism on the one hand and Postmillennialism on the other. One distinctive feature of the following study is its defence of an amillennialist eschatology and its extended critique of Premillennialism. Though not postmillennialist in the narrower sense of that term, the Amillennialism defended is one which embraces a strong conception of the present lordship of Jesus Christ in history prior to his coming at the end of the age.

Last, the Bible version used in this study is the 1979 edition of the New American Standard Bible. Though this version is not the most readable of modern English translations, it reflects a principle of formal equivalence to the original languages that makes it useful for my purpose. The principle of formal equivalence in translation, though a weakness from the standpoint of readability, makes it especially useful for the purpose of biblical exposition and study. Unfortunately, the English-speaking church continues to suffer from a proliferation of new English versions based upon different text traditions. Readers are encouraged, accordingly, to make use of several of the better translations as a companion to their reading and study.

There are several people whom I would like to thank for their encouragement and help in the preparation of this study. I am grateful to the publishers of *The Outlook* for granting me permission to revise and rewrite the following material for publication in book form. In particular, I want to thank my colleagues, Mark Vander Hart and J. Mark Beach, for the different ways, sometimes unknown to them, in which they have contributed to my thinking and writing on this subject. I am also deeply grateful to the Banner of Truth Trust for their willingness to undertake the publication of this volume. When I first wrote to the Trust regarding their possible interest in this project, it was with the advice and encouragement of a former colleague, Raymond O. Zorn. Ray, shortly before he died and went home to be with the Lord, directed me to Hywel Jones, who proved to be unfailingly kind and helpful at every step along the way and who undertook the difficult work of editing my manuscript. I am deeply indebted to Hywel Jones and Mrs Danielle Plant for their work in preparing the manuscript for publication. I also want to thank those who assisted with the work of preparing the indices, including my son, Joseph.

When I was a graduate student at Princeton Theological Seminary, one of my fellow students quipped that when he acknowledged his wife's contribution to his dissertation, he was going to write, 'without whom I would have finished three years earlier'! As I recall that dubious attempt at humour, I am reminded of something closer to the truth, namely, how much I am indebted to my wife, Nancy, without whose encouragement and joyful presence, this study could not have been written. In gratitude to God, the giver of every good and perfect gift, I dedicate this book to her.

CORNELIS P. VENEMA
Dyer, Indiana
Easter Monday,
24 April 2000

ABBREVIATIONS

The following abbreviations occur in the references and Selected Bibliography:

ICC:	International Critical Commentary
NICNT:	New International Commentary on the New Testament
NIGTC:	New International Greek Testament Commentary
NTC:	William Hendricksen's New Testament Commentary

PART ONE

The Future Is Now

I

Hope Nurtured by the Word

M OST PEOPLE generally have a keen interest in the future. Curiosity about the events that lie on the horizon of life is difficult to suppress. Everybody wants to know what is coming around the corner. Nobody likes to be taken by surprise. Consequently, many 'itching ears' are ready to listen to anyone boldly claiming to be a prophet or seer (2 *Tim.* 4:3). Such prophets are more than ready to claim knowledge of what the future will bring. Witness, for example, the popularity of psychic hotlines, fortune tellers and prognosticators of the future. Similarly, there is the prevalent temptation to support the political candidate who can make the most compelling case for what the future holds, should he or she be elected. 'Campaign promises' are really little more than attempts to predict a future that will captivate the electorate and ensure a candidate's election.

This general interest in the future has become especially pronounced in North American culture. An American who visits Europe cannot help but notice the greater attention Europeans pay to the past. Traditions shaped over centuries continue to influence the patterns of their lives. By contrast 'New World' North Americans are more oriented to the future, not so impressed by ancient traditions. Interpreters of American cultural traits have noted this characteristic of American culture. Whether these interpreters attempt to describe the future by determining the 'megatrends' of our day or by noting the 'future shock' that many people are experiencing,[1] they generally agree that North Americans today are far more preoccupied with the future than were many previous generations.[2]

Christians share this heightened interest in the question of the future, but are confused as to what to believe. This may reflect in part the confusion and uncertainty of our culture. However, it also reflects the myriad of voices from within the Christian community whose pronouncements about the future differ so radically. Often, these pronouncements are born out of a certain construction of the Bible's teaching about the future commonly known as Dispensationalism.[3] Authors who write from a dispensationalist perspective have been especially adept at seizing upon the uncertainty many people experience with respect to the future.[4] Fuelled by the

[1] See John Naisbitt, *Megatrends. Ten New Directions Transforming Our Lives* (New York: Warner Books, 1982); and Alvin Toffler, *Future Shock* (New York: Random House, 1970). Naisbitt and Toffler's books convincingly illustrate and document the tendency to focus upon the future that is such a characteristic feature of modern times.

[2] For a recent study that documents past and more recent apocalyptic speculation about the end times, see Richard Kyle, *The Last Days Are Here Again: A History of the End Times* (Grand Rapids: Baker, 1998). Kyle argues that recent end-times interest represents the latest chapter in a long history of such interest.

[3] Dispensationalism and its construction of the Bible's teaching about the future will be the particular focus of Chapters 8 and 10 of this study.

[4] Two examples of this adeptness are illustrative, the one of an earlier and the other of more recent times. The first is the best-selling book by Hal Lindsey, *The Late Great Planet Earth* (Grand Rapids: Zondervan, 1970), which argued, as its provocative title indicates, that the end was near for planet Earth. The second is a recent series of best-selling novels, *Left Behind*, written by Jerry B. Jenkins, purporting to

uncertainty and anxiety that accompanies the closing of the twentieth century and the approach of a new millennium, interest regarding what the future may bring has never been more pronounced.[1]

This confusion, uncertainty, and heightened interest in the future call for careful study and reflection upon what the Bible teaches. Especially on the subject of the future, we need to study the Word of God so as to become wise unto salvation in Jesus Christ. We need to examine the Scriptures to determine what we can know and believe regarding the future. The only reliable antidote to much of the speculation and fear that attend modern approaches to the future is a disciplined listening to what the Bible reveals to us. Thus, as we approach the subject of the promise of the future, we should bear several things in mind.

Staying within the Boundaries of God's Word

The most important rule believers must observe is to stay within the boundaries of God's Word, the Scriptures. Much of the confusion and uncertainty that abounds on this subject nowadays is due to a failure to abide by this rule.

When we contemplate the future, we are considering something that in the strictest sense might be termed a 'mystery'. Though we may have many reminders of the past, this is not the case with respect to the future. We can consult a scrapbook, examine historical documents, or search out the historical evidence to determine the past, but this procedure cannot be followed in determining the future. The

---

describe the end times in the light of biblical prophecies. The interest in this series of novels was heightened by the approach of a new millennium.

[1] The 'Y2K' computer problem, as it is popularly termed, has made its own contribution to the heightening of interest in the coming of a new century. I use the term 'century' rather than 'millennium' because the new millennium will not actually begin until 1 January 2001.

future is, from our vantage point, hidden. It is shrouded from our view. Even though we can conjecture what it might bring, we cannot predict with any certainty what will occur.

This needs to be qualified, however. Though we cannot know or predict the future, the Triune God who created the world and all things in it, who providentially superintends the life and history of the creation – he is able to do so, for in his Word he reveals the things we need to know for our salvation, including those things which pertain to the future. He reveals precisely what we need to know about the shape of things to come.

This is the only antidote available to counteract the speculation that abounds today about the future: we need to listen carefully to the Word of God, taking notice of what it promises regarding the future and disciplining ourselves not to go beyond what it warrants. It is the only safe course available to us in this otherwise confused and disputed terrain. We must therefore be both grateful and humble – grateful to receive what God has been pleased to teach us in his Word about the future, and humble to remain within the limits of this revelation.

Christ, the Lord of History

God's Word also teaches us that Christ is the Lord and centre of history.[1]

One of the common mistakes believers make when they consider the future is to become disoriented by focusing upon a variety of themes, without seeing any biblical connections

---

[1] I do not use the usual language of 'redemptive history', because it is not just redemptive history that is in view here. Christ's lordship is not limited to a particular current of history, the redemptive as contrasted with the non-redemptive. The language of redemptive history may not be used to permit an unbiblical separation between Christ's lordship in the redemption of his church in history, and the remainder of 'secular' history. All history finds its meaning in Christ (cf. *Eph*. 1:10).

between them. For example, we think of such things as the millennium, the signs of the times, the return of Christ, the resurrection of the dead, and the like. But our vision is unfocused. It is as though we see a whole complex of disconnected events looming large upon the horizon. The whole picture remains confused. We do not see what joins these events together.

This disorientation about the future occurs whenever we fail to see that all of God's ways in history are centred upon Jesus Christ, who is 'the same yesterday, today and forever'. He is the One through whom we are given to know the meaning and purpose of all history. This can be illustrated from the Scriptures in a number of ways.

In the Old Testament, the Lord's dealings with his people continually pointed to the future and particularly to One in whom his promises to them would be fulfilled. Already in the 'mother promise' of Genesis 3:15, the focus falls upon the 'seed of the woman' through whom God promises to crush the head of the serpent and bring triumph for his people. The promises of God's gracious covenant communion with his people constantly find their basis and fulfilment in Christ. Christ is the seed of Abraham through whom all the families of the earth will be blessed (*Gen.* 17:7; cf. *Gal.* 3:16). He is the promised Son of David who will be established upon his father's throne forever, reigning in righteousness and peace over the people of God (2 *Sam.* 7:12–13, *Psa.* 89:3–4). Accordingly, when Luke describes the risen Christ's conversation with the two men on the road to Emmaus, he notes that 'beginning with Moses and with all the prophets, [Christ] explained to them the things concerning himself in all the Scriptures' (*Luke* 24:27).

Similarly, the New Testament treats the history of the Lord's previous dealings with his people as a preparation for the coming of Christ in the 'fulness of the time' (*Gal.* 4:4). In the genealogies of Matthew and Luke, for example, Christ's birth is traced back through the centuries to Abraham

(*Matt.* 1:1) and ultimately to Adam (*Luke* 3:38). Matthew, by crafting his account of Christ's genealogy in terms of three sets of fourteen generations (the number fourteen being the numerical equivalent of the name of David in Hebrew), clearly wants to reveal that history has been moving forward under God's faithful superintendence to its great and decisive events, namely, Christ's birth, life, death, resurrection, ascension and anticipated return at the 'end of the age' (*Matt.* 28:20).

The central place of Christ, as the Author, Governor and Goal of history within the will and purpose of God, is explicitly affirmed as well in several New Testament passages. In Ephesians 1:9–11 the Apostle Paul describes the 'mystery of God's will' revealed in Jesus Christ as 'the summing up of all things in Christ, things in the heavens and things upon the earth'. In Colossians 1:16–17, we read, 'For by Him [Christ] all things were created, both in the heavens and on the earth, visible and invisible, whether thrones or dominions or rulers or authorities – all things have been created by Him and for Him. And He is before all things, and in Him all things hold together.' The Apostle John's visions on the isle of Patmos, recorded in the book of Revelation, describe Christ as the 'the faithful witness, the firstborn of the dead, and the ruler of the kings of the earth' (*Rev.* 1:5). Only Jesus Christ, the Lamb of God, has the power and authority to 'open the book and its seven seals', signifying his power to administer God's sovereign purposes in all of history (*Rev.* 5).

Just as Christ fulfils all of the Old Testament promises (*2 Cor.* 1:20), Christ also guarantees the future consummation of all God's promises by his resurrection from the dead, session at the Father's right hand, and outpouring of the Spirit at Pentecost. These events are disclosed in the New Testament as end-time events, that is, events which mark a decisive turning point in history. These events signal that Christ has been given all authority in heaven and on earth and will reign until all things have been subjected to him, including death, the last enemy (*1 Cor.* 15:25–26). By his resurrection from the dead, Christ has become a 'first fruits' of all who will through union with him share in his victory. By his session at the Father's right hand, Christ has been given the keys to unlock God's plan for history until he is revealed at the 'last day'. And by his outpouring of the Holy Spirit, he has entered into the last and most decisive epoch in his church-gathering work which, once completed, will serve to prepare all things for his coming again.

The biblical revelation regarding the future, therefore, always fixes our attention upon Christ. Just as God's ways with his people in history in times past have all met in Christ, so all of his ways in the future will meet in Christ. The great event on the horizon of the future, in biblical perspective, is accordingly the event of Christ's return or 'Second Coming'. This event is the great future toward which all history is moving. It is the event that gives meaning to present history and which will consummate God's work of redemption. The entirety of the biblical teaching about the future is intimately linked to the coming of Christ at the end of the present age.

Paradise Lost, Paradise Regained

Another theme in the biblical revelation regarding the future is that of 'paradise lost, paradise regained'. To understand the biblical promises for the future, it is necessary to go back to the beginning, to the circumstances of God's original covenant fellowship with Adam and Eve, our first parents, in the Garden of Eden. For in these circumstances we see something of that communion of life with God for which humankind was created, and which will be restored in the new heavens and the new earth.

It is striking, for example, how closely the vision of the new heavens and the new earth in Revelation 22 resembles the original circumstances of paradise. In Revelation 22, the last chapter of the Bible, the new heaven and earth is described, not only as a city, the new Jerusalem come down out of heaven to earth, but also as a renewed garden of life: 'And he showed me', says John, 'a river of the water of life, clear as crystal, coming from the throne of God and of the Lamb, in the middle of its street. And on either side of the river was the tree of life, bearing twelve kinds of fruit, yielding its fruit every month; and the leaves of the tree were for the healing of the nations' (verses 1–2). The 'first things' of creation are thus prophetic of the 'last things' of the new creation. The fullness of redemption for God's people in the new heavens and the new earth is reminiscent of the life Adam and Eve (and in them, all people) enjoyed at creation.

This does not mean that the future, in which paradise is regained, will bring nothing more than was humankind's at creation. This would be to deny the progress of history and the greater glory that is given in redemption through Christ. The Christian church has understood that the new heavens and the new earth will surpass the old in glory. Not only will God be acknowledged throughout the whole of his creation as the Most Holy One, but he will also suffer no further prospect of the sinner's rebellion against his dominion or covenant unfaithfulness by his people. The covenant communion which God's people will enjoy before the face of God will be an unbroken and unbreakable friendship. It will not be threatened by a 'fall from grace' or defection among those who constitute the new humanity, the company of the redeemed from every tribe and language and people and nation.

A Living and Certain Hope

The Bible's promises and expectation for the future are not to be confused with the modern practice of 'fortune telling', consulting a horoscope, or predictions of the precise timetable for the future. There is much in the future that God does not give us to know in his Word. But what he has given us to know kindles in the believer a living and certain hope, a confidence that the redeeming work of God in Christ will not fail to be fully accomplished in God's own time. Through the resurrection of Jesus Christ from the dead, 'we have been born anew to a living hope' (*1 Pet.* 1:3). Such hope will not die.

This is the pattern of the believer's expectation for the future: it is characterized by a hope nurtured by the Word. It is marked out by a lively expectation of the accomplishment of God's purpose in Christ. The future does not loom darkly on the horizon as something to be feared. It is something eagerly expected and anticipated, something which the believer is convinced is bright with the promise of the completion and perfection of God's saving work.

It is true that many of the biblical exhortations relating to the future call God's people to watchfulness and sobriety, warning them against being found unprepared at Christ's coming (*1 Pet.* 4:7, *1 Thess.* 5:6, *Matt.* 24:42–45). They often warn the church to remain faithful and steadfast in holding to the apostolic teachings and Word of God (*2 Thess.* 2:15, *Heb.* 10:23). In addition, the biblical descriptions of Christ's coming starkly describe its frightening and terrible consequences for the wicked (*2 Thess.* 2:8, *2 Pet.* 3:12, *Rev.* 18:10).

But the chief note sounded in God's revelation regarding the future is one of hope. God's people eagerly await Christ's return because it promises the completion of God's work of redemption for them and for the whole creation. The Christian's approach to the future is always one of hope nurtured by the Word. The future is bright because it is full of promise, the promise of God's Word.

2

The First Coming of the Lord

IN HIS *INSTITUTES OF THE CHRISTIAN RELIGION*, John Calvin declares that the Old Testament was given to the people of Israel as a means to 'foster hope of salvation in Christ until his coming'.[1] All of the Lord's redemptive dealings with his covenant people, prior to the birth of Christ in the 'fullness of time', were aimed at kindling in them an expectation and anticipation of the coming Saviour. Whatever initial fulfilments of God's covenant promises they may have received, these were only a down payment and pledge of a fuller, richer fulfilment yet to come.

Consequently, a restlessness characterizes the Old Testament's view of history, even when the children of Israel enjoyed a provisional rest in the land of Canaan. Each new chapter in the history of the Lord's gracious acts on behalf of his people only heightened their anticipation of the consummation of that history in the future. The fullness of salvation in fellowship with God which the covenant promised, awaited its realization, when the redeeming work of the Lord

---

[1] Ed. by John T. McNeill (Philadelphia: The Westminster Press, 1960), I.vii. This language is part of the heading for the chapter dealing with the 'Law' or the Old Testament revelation. I will refer to Calvin's *Institutes* by book, chapter, and section (for example I.i.1).

would have reached its goal. There is a dynamic to the history of the covenant in the Old Testament that would not permit the believer to look only to the past, in the remembrance of what the Lord had already done, but demanded that he or she also look to the future, in the hope of even better things to come.

Before treating the New Testament's understanding of the importance of Christ's coming into the world for the Christian's understanding of history, and particularly the future, it is necessary that we consider in a general way the Old Testament's view of the future. This is because the New Testament teaching concerning the coming of Christ and the unfolding of God's redemptive purpose can only be understood within the context of the preceding history of redemption in the Old Testament. The first words of the New Testament – 'The book of the genealogy of Jesus Christ, the son of David, the son of Abraham' (*Matt.* 1:1) – tell us that the story of redemption does not begin with Christ, but many centuries earlier. They remind us that all of the hopes of the Old Testament believer met in the birth and coming of Jesus Christ.

Preparing the Way in the Old Testament

To set the stage for our consideration of the New Testament's understanding of the future, therefore, we will begin with a sketch of the Old Testament background. What, from the perspective of the Old Testament, was the outlook for the future?[1]

[1] In my discussion of the Old Testament expectation or outlook upon the future, I am following the outline of Anthony Hoekema's discussion in his *The Bible and the Future* (Grand Rapids: Eerdmans, 1979), pp. 3–22. Throughout this study, I will indicate where appropriate my indebtedness to Hoekema's fine study of biblical eschatology, as well as those areas where my interpretation of the biblical data differs from his. My study of the Bible's teaching regarding the future is more exegetical than Hoekema's and interacts with more recent literature on the subject, particularly the debates respecting the millennium of Revelation 20.

THE PROMISE OF THE FUTURE

I. THE COMING SAVIOUR OR MESSIAH

The great centre of Old Testament expectation, undoubtedly, is the expectation of a coming Saviour, the Messiah. This expectation is the seedbed for all of the other dimensions of the Old Testament's teaching about the future.

The first Word of the Lord, spoken to our first parents after the Fall into sin in Genesis 3, announces the future birth of a Redeemer who will crush the head of the serpent and vindicate God's gracious rule within his creation. In Genesis 3:15, we find this so-called 'mother promise' in the history of redemption, the *protevangelium,* the 'first gospel' announcement: 'And I [the Lord God] will put enmity between you and the woman, and between your seed and her seed; he shall crush you on the head, and you shall bruise him on the heel.' In this first gospel promise, the Lord announces that he will establish an antithesis between two kinds of seeds, the seed of the serpent and the seed of the woman, representing the people at enmity with God and the people whom he befriends. This antithesis between these two peoples will serve God's gracious purpose for his people whom he will deliver and save through One born of a woman. In the seed of the woman the people of God will find their deliverance and salvation from the power and dominion of the evil one. This 'mother promise' is the fundamental promise in the old covenant, fixing the eye of faith of God's people upon the Person of the coming Saviour.

Subsequent to this first announcement and promise of a coming Saviour, the Lord renews and specifies this promise in his Word to Abraham, the father of believers. Promising to make Abraham one through whom 'all the families of the earth' would be blessed (*Gen.* 12:3), the Lord assured Abraham that in his seed this promise would be fulfilled. Through the birth of a son, Isaac, Sarah would become the mother of nations (*Gen.* 17:16); from him would be born the seed in whom all the nations would enter into the blessing of the covenant (*Gen.* 22:18; cf. 26:4; 28:14). Now the promise of a Saviour becomes focused upon the seed of Abraham, the son in whom the promise of redemption will be realized. Later in the history of Old Testament revelation, we learn that this son in the line of promise will be born of the tribe of Judah (*Gen.* 49:10) and of the family of David (2 *Sam.* 7:12–13).

With the progressive unfolding of the revelation of the Lord to his covenant people, the expectation of this coming Saviour, the seed of promise, becomes further refined in the three special offices ordained by the Lord – of prophet, priest, and king. The children of Israel were thus taught to expect One in whom these offices would be fulfilled. The Messiah or 'Anointed One' would be called of God and empowered by his Spirit to speak the Word of the Lord, offer sacrifice and intercession on behalf of his own people, and rule in righteousness in the Lord's name.   The great prophet of the old covenant, Moses, was a 'type' of an even greater prophet, like Moses, who was to come. So we read in Deuteronomy 18:15, 'The Lord God will raise up for you a prophet like me [Moses] from among you, from your countrymen, you shall listen to him' (cf. *Acts* 3:22). The Aaronic priests who ministered daily at the altar were only a 'shadow' of an eternal priest, after the order of Melchizedek, who would offer himself once for all a perfect sacrifice for his people (*Psa.* 110:4, *Heb.* 5). Furthermore, the Lord promised King David that he would establish the throne of his son forever (2 *Sam.* 7:12–13, *Isa.* 9:7). In the offices of prophet, priest and king, Israel was given the promise of the Messiah who, commissioned and empowered by the Lord, would reveal the Word of the Lord, make atonement for the sins of the people, and rule in righteousness over an eternal kingdom.

---

[1] We are apt to forget that when the New Testament describes the Saviour as 'the Christ', it is using an official title, 'Anointed One' (from the Hebrew, *mashiach*), not a personal name. It designates him as One called and anointed of God to a particular task or work. The 'anointing' refers to both a divine commission and empowerment.

THE PROMISE OF THE FUTURE

The person and work of the coming Messiah are also described in the Old Testament as the coming of the Lord himself to be with his people. In the person of the Messiah, God himself would dwell among his people, just as he had in the Old Testament tabernacle and temple. The Messiah's name will be Immanuel, 'God with us' (*Isa.* 7:14). He will also be the suffering servant of the Lord, who will take upon himself the sin of his people, providing atonement for them. In the well-known words of Isaiah 53, the prophet Isaiah strikingly foresees the suffering of the Messiah, by which he will accomplish his people's redemption: 'But he was pierced through for our transgressions, he was crushed for our iniquities; the chastening for our well-being fell upon him, and by his scourging we are healed' (verse 5). But the Messiah will not only be Immanuel and the suffering servant, he will also be the heavenly Son of Man to whom God will give the dominion and power to establish his kingdom and destroy every enemy who would resist God's rule (*Dan.* 7:13–14).[1]

In all of these ways and more, the Old Testament prepares the way for the future coming of the Lord to his people in the person of a Saviour. To this central promise the Old Testament adds a variety of alternative expressions to reveal the shape of the future, as the Lord realizes his covenant promises and re-establishes his kingdom on the earth. None of these is to be separated from the one great expectation of a coming Saviour; they are only alternative, and related, aspects of the salvation which this Saviour will bring with him. But they do enrich and deepen our appreciation of the Old Testament's view of the future.

II. THE FUTURE KINGDOM

Though the Old Testament clearly reveals God to be the King over all (*Psa.* 103:19), the majestic Lord of heaven and earth

---

[1] It is interesting that the most common New Testament designation of the Messiah is 'Son of Man'. Though we traditionally think of this title as emphasising Christ's humanity, it actually speaks as much of his heavenly power and majesty (see, e.g. *Matt.* 24:29–31).

whose will cannot be frustrated in any corner of his creation-kingdom, it also acknowledges that sin has disrupted it. Sin is rooted in rebellion against God's righteous rule. Whole nations and peoples are under the dominion of darkness and sin, captive to the kingdoms of this world and at enmity with God. Only Israel was given to know and confess the kingdom of the true and living God.

One of the ways in which the Old Testament portrays the future is in terms of the final victory and (re-)establishment of God's kingdom over all creation. Not only will the Lord continue to reign in majesty from heaven, the place of his dwelling and throne, but he will also come to be acknowledged as King in the whole realm of the creation. All who have rebelled against him, all the kingdoms of humankind which have resisted his rule and dominion, will be brought into subjection. One of the most powerful and dramatic prophecies of the future establishment of the Kingdom of God is found in Daniel 2, which speaks of a kingdom that God will set up in the 'latter days', that will never be destroyed and that will come to fill the whole earth. Interestingly, this kingdom is depicted as being like a 'little stone' that will crush the kingdoms of this world and grow until it fills the whole earth, a depiction that associates the realization of this kingdom with the coming of the Messiah, the Son of Man.

III. THE NEW COVENANT

In the Old Testament, it becomes increasingly clear that what the covenant of grace promised the people of God did not come to full flowering, because of the unfaithfulness and disobedience of the covenant people. The history of the covenant is marked by a striking contrast between the faithfulness of the Lord and the unfaithfulness of his people. As a result, the children of Israel are finally sent away into exile under the covenant wrath and judgement of the Lord. In this darkest period of redemptive or covenant history, it almost seems as though the Lord's way of grace with his people has ended in failure.

But the Lord remains forever faithful to his promises! The disobedience of the children of Israel will not frustrate his redeeming purpose for and on behalf of his chosen people. Hence, we find, even in their exile and subsequent restoration to the land of promise, that the people of God are given further promises of a new and better covenant. The day will come, the Lord promises, when he will gather his people to himself and establish a new covenant with them, based upon better promises! This means that the old covenant failed, partly because its promises were less rich than those of the new covenant, and partly because of the stubborn refusal of the children of Israel to live according to the covenant's stipulations (cf. *Heb.* 8). However, in the new covenant the Lord promised to write his law upon the hearts of the people: "'But this is the covenant which I will make with the house of Israel after those days," declares the Lord, "I will put My law within them, and on their heart I will write it; and I will be their God, and they shall be My people"' (*Jer.* 31:33).

IV. THE GATHERING OF A RESTORED ISRAEL

Still another aspect of the expectation for the future found in the Old Testament, is that of the restoration of the people of God. With the dispersion of the people of Israel before and during the exile, the unity and future of the people of God seemed imperilled. Would there be a return to the land of promise and, if so, under what circumstances? What did the future hold for them as the peculiar possession of the Lord?

In this setting, the Lord reveals to his people a future in which there will be a new exodus (*Isa.* 11:11), a return to the land of promise and restoration of the people of God. A remnant of the people would return to the Lord in renewed faithfulness and repentance. As the Lord spoke through Jeremiah, "'Then I Myself shall gather the remnant of My flock out of all the countries where I have driven them and

shall bring them back to their pasture; and they will be fruitful and multiply"' (*Jer.* 23:3). This restoration of a remnant
would not exclude, however, the fulfilment of the promise
that all the families of the earth would enter into the blessing
of the covenant through the seed of Abraham. Many of the
Old Testament promises concerning the restoration of Israel
also include the promise that the nations and peoples of the
earth will come to the light and enjoy, in fellowship with
Israel, the blessings of salvation (see, for example, *Jer.* 48:47;
49:39, *Isa.* 2:2, *Mic.* 4:1). The Lord would not fail to gather
his people, and through them, all the families of the earth.

v. The Outpouring of the Spirit
When the question is asked, On what basis could the Lord
assure the people of Israel of a future bright with promise,
a future that would bring a new and better covenant and
a new exodus?, the answer is to be found in the promise of a
new outpouring of the Spirit of God upon the people.

In Jeremiah 31, for example, the Lord's promise of a new
and better covenant, one in which his people will love him
according to his law even as he has loved them, is intimately
joined to the further promise of the Spirit who will write the
law of God, not upon tablets of stone, but upon the fleshly
hearts of his people (*Ezek.* 36:24–28). The new covenant will
be better than the old covenant, because in it the Spirit
will work in a new and powerful way, causing the people of
God to answer the Lord's faithfulness with a faithfulness of
their own. Similarly, in Ezekiel 37 the restoration of the
people of God is likened to the resurrection of a valley of
dead and dry bones, into which the Lord breathes new life by
his life-giving Spirit. Just at the time Israel's prospects for the
future seem bleakest, just then the Lord will graciously intervene in a mighty way by his Spirit, granting life from the
dead. As the Lord spoke through Ezekiel, "'And I will put My
Spirit within you, and you will come to life, and I will place
you on your land. Then you will know that I, the Lord, have

spoken and done it," declares the Lord' (*Ezek.* 37:14). This future work of pouring out his Spirit upon his people is most dramatically disclosed in *Joel* 2:28–29, a passage to which the Apostle Peter appealed in his sermon at Pentecost (*Acts* 2): "'And it will come about after this, that I will pour out My Spirit on all mankind; and your sons and daughters will prophesy, your old men will dream dreams, your young men will see visions.'"

VI. THE 'DAY OF THE LORD'

In the prophecies relating to the restoration of Israel, the outpouring of the Spirit, and the re-establishment of the covenant, references increasingly emerge to what is termed the 'day of the Lord'. This 'day of the Lord', whether understood to be in the near or more distant future, bespeaks a day of the Lord's final visitation of his people in grace and in judgement. Though it frequently emphasises the theme of God's wrath and judgement upon the wicked, it also promises salvation for the righteous.

Sometimes this day of the Lord is described as a fearsome day in the near future, when God will execute his judgement against Israel's enemies (*Obad.* 15–16). Sometimes it is disclosed to be a final day of the Lord's visitation, when he will deal once and for all with the world because of its sin (*Isa.* 13:9–11).

The prophet Amos warns the children of Israel that this day will mean destruction for the wicked, even as it brings vindication and salvation to the righteous (*Amos* 5:18). The prophets Isaiah (2:12, 17) and Zephaniah (1:14–15) sound similar notes of judgement and wrath falling upon the disobedient in that day. Though the note of the wrath of the Lord falling upon the wicked tends to predominate among the prophetic announcements of the coming of the Lord, some passages speak of the salvation for the Lord's people that will accompany it. Joel 2:32, for example, promises salvation to all who call upon the name of the Lord before the great and terrible day of his wrath which Malachi also predicted (cf. *Mal*. 4:2–5).

VII. A 'NEW HEAVENS AND NEW EARTH'

One of the grandest aspects of the Old Testament's expectation regarding the future is the promise that the Lord will establish a new heavens and earth. More than any other aspect of the future, this one reminds the believer of the beginning. Paradise lost will become paradise regained. What was in the beginning will become reality also in the future. But the future reality will even exceed the past.

When the redeeming work of the Lord has run its course and reached its goal, the whole of creation, ruined through the fall into sin, will be purged of sin and brought to a state of perfection. This hope is expressed particularly in the prophecies of Isaiah. In Isaiah 65:17, the Lord declares, 'For behold, I create new heavens and a new earth; and the former things shall not be remembered or come to mind.' Just as the Lord fashioned man from the dust of the earth, so in the day of the fullness of redemption, man will be restored to the fullness of life in the new heavens and earth.[1] When the earth is renewed, according to Isaiah, it will become an abundant and fruitful field, rather than a wilderness (32:15). The new earth will be one in which the former dry places have become springs of water (35:7). It will be a place where there will be no more conflict or disorder within the creation; all creatures will live together in harmony and peace. As the prophet so beautifully puts it, 'They will not hurt or destroy in all My holy mountain, for the earth will be full of the knowledge of the Lord, as the waters cover the sea' (11:6–9).

---

[1] It is important to notice, in the account of creation in Genesis 2, a play on words between the name given to man, *Adham*, and the term used for the earth from which he was taken, *adhamah*. Though man is distinguished from all other creatures as an image-bearer of God, he is taken from the earth and finds his life and calling in relation to it. So also in redemption: salvation without a new earth is inconceivable in the biblical perspective.

VIII. THE 'LATTER DAYS'

Though many more things could be said about any one of these aspects of the Old Testament's expectation for the future, this sketch will be concluded by considering the phrase 'the latter days'. This phrase captures well the whole thrust of the Old Testament revelation regarding the future. To the extent that Old Testament believers were nurtured by the Word of the Lord in their view of the future, they came to fix their gaze upon the latter days which would introduce the age to come, in distinction from their own day which was the present age.

The use of the expression 'the latter days' varies considerably in the Old Testament. However, it does have some characteristic features. Typically, this language draws into focus the future destiny, not only of individuals, but of all peoples and nations. It is language which encompasses the Lord's purpose and intention to bring salvation as well as judgement upon all peoples, depending upon their response to his Word. In Daniel 2:28, for example, the 'latter days' encompass the entire history in which the stone will destroy the kingdoms of this world and inaugurate God's eternal kingdom. Not only does this reference include a period of history of some duration leading to the 'end' of history as we now know it, but it also includes the realizing of God's purpose for all the nations and kingdoms of the earth.

The latter days are also consistently days both of blessing for the people of God and tribulation for the enemies of God. Often the theme of blessing and peace for the people of God is prominent (*Isa.* 2:2, *Mic.* 4:1, *Hos.* 3:4–5). However, this is also balanced by the theme of tribulation and judgement upon those who reject God and who oppress his people (*Dan.* 2:28). Furthermore, the blessing which will come to the children of Israel will also mean blessing for all the nations who will come to Jerusalem and be given a share in the salvation of the Lord (*Jer.* 48:47; 49:39).

This revelation regarding the latter days is a fitting place, therefore, to conclude our sketch of the Old Testament's view of the future. Though it is important not to read more into this expectation than is present in the Old Testament, a clear outline does emerge from it.

All of these dimensions and aspects of the Old Testament outlook upon the future are accumulative. Together they form a single mosaic of anticipation and expectation for the day, on the furthest horizon of history, the great future, when the Lord would visit his people in grace and his enemies in judgement. All of the promises we have discussed – the coming of the Saviour, the establishment of the kingdom of God, the granting of a new and better covenant, the restoration of the people of God, the day of the Lord – point to a time in history when the Lord will bring to fruition and realize in perfection all of his gracious purposes and covenantal ways with his people.

'In the Fullness of Time' – the New Testament

To the Old Testament believer, peering over the immediate present toward the horizon of the future, a new and better day was approaching. Thus, when this glorious future dawned at the birth and coming of Jesus Christ, we should not be surprised to find believers rejoicing like Simeon. Simeon, Luke tells us, was 'righteous and devout, looking for the consolation of Israel'. When Joseph and Mary presented Jesus at the temple, Simeon took him in his arms and blessed God and said: 'Sovereign Lord, as you have promised, you now dismiss your servant in peace. For my eyes have seen your salvation, which you have prepared in the sight of all people, a light for revelation to the Gentiles and for glory to your people Israel' (*Luke* 2:29–32, NIV). This event, recorded early in the Gospels of the New Testament, indicates that the future of Old Testament expectation has become the now of New Testament fulfilment in the birth of the Saviour.

Similarly, songs of Mary and Zacharias celebrate and praise God for his faithfulness in bringing to pass what he had declared formerly. Notice how the Song of Mary, the

Magnificat, links the birth of Christ with the promises of the covenant: 'My soul exalts the Lord, and my spirit has rejoiced in God my Saviour . . . He has given help to Israel his servant, in remembrance of his mercy; as he spoke to our fathers, to Abraham and his offspring forever' (*Luke* 1:46–47; 54–55). Similarly, Zacharias views the coming of Christ in the light of all that had come before:

> Blessed be the Lord God of Israel, for He has visited us and accomplished redemption for His people, and has raised up a horn of salvation for us in the house of David His servant – as He spoke by the mouth of His holy prophets from of old . . . to show mercy toward our fathers, and to remember His holy covenant, the oath which He swore to Abraham our father . . . (*Luke* 1:68–70, 72–73).

With these familiar songs celebrating the Lord's fulfilment of his Old Testament promises in the coming and birth of the Saviour, we confront the new and altered situation of New Testament believers. Whereas the typical look of the Old Testament believer was forward, into the future, the New Testament believer now looks backward and forward, back to the coming of Christ in the fullness of time, forward to the expected coming of Christ at the end of time.

The New Testament clearly trumpets the good news that with the coming of Christ, the history of redemption has entered a new and decisive epoch. The 'latter days' of Old Testament expectation are now upon us.

I. THE FUTURE INAUGURATED

Thus, the first and most fundamental dimension of the New Testament's outlook upon the future is, ironically, that the future is now.[1] What Old Testament believers anticipated on the furthest horizon of redemptive history has become a

---

[1] Hence the title of George Eldon Ladd's study of New Testament eschatology: *The Presence of the Future* (Grand Rapids: Eerdmans, 1974), a revised and updated version of an earlier work, *Jesus and the Kingdom* (New York: Harper and Row, 1964). I will evaluate Ladd's view of the millennial kingdom in Chapters 8, 10 and 11.

reality, has 'drawn near', in the person and work of Jesus Christ.

One does not have to read far in the New Testament Scriptures to discover the language of fulfilment. Christ's coming fulfils many of the promises of the Old Testament Scriptures. In Matthew's Gospel, Jesus' birth of the virgin Mary is set forth as a fulfilment of the prophecy of Isaiah (*Matt.* 1:20–23). Among other events in Christ's life that fulfil Old Testament prophecy, the following are only a sampling: Christ's birth in Bethlehem (*Matt.* 2:5–6; cf. *Mic.* 5:2); his rejection by his people (*John* 1:11; cf. *Isa.* 53:3); his flight into Egypt (*Matt.* 2:14–15; cf. *Hos.* 11:1); his triumphal entry into Jerusalem (*Matt.* 21:4–5; cf. *Zech.* 9:9); his being sold for thirty pieces of silver (*Matt.* 26:15, *Zech.* 11:12); his being pierced on the cross (*John* 19:34; cf. *Zech.* 12:10); the soldiers' casting lots for his clothing (*Mark* 15:24; cf. *Psa.* 22:18); the fact that none of his bones were broken (*John* 19:33; cf. *Psa.* 34:20); his burial with the rich (*Matt.* 27:57–60; cf. *Isa.* 53:9); his resurrection (*Acts* 2:24–32; cf. *Psa.* 16:10); and his ascension (*Acts* 1:9; cf. *Psa.* 68:18). Surely nothing is more emphatically taught in the New Testament than that Christ is the heir of the Old Testament prophecies concerning the Saviour to come.

Because the coming of Christ marks the beginning of the fulfilment of so many Old Testament promises, it is also described in terms which bespeak the finality and epochal significance of his coming for the history of redemption. Implicitly contrasting Christ's work with the priestly ministry of the old covenant, the Apostle Peter declares, 'For Christ also died for sins once for all, the just for the unjust, in order that he might bring us to God, having been put to death in the flesh, but made alive in the spirit' (*1 Pet.* 3:18). The writer to the Hebrews makes this a major theme in his comparison and contrast of the old and new covenants. Comparing the daily sacrifices offered by the Old Testament priesthood with the sacrifice of Christ, he notes that Christ 'does not need daily, like those high priests, to offer up sacrifices, first for his own sins, and then for the sins of the people, because this he did once for all when he offered up himself' (*Heb.* 7:27).

In the coming of Christ, the long-awaited coming of God's kingdom on earth is inaugurated. In the Gospels, both John the Baptist and Jesus announce in their preaching that the kingdom of God 'is at hand' (literally, 'has drawn near', *Matt.* 3:2, *Mark* 1:15). When Christ cast out demons, he testified to the Pharisees that this was evidence that the kingdom of God 'had come upon them' (*Matt.* 12:28). Similarly, the Gospel accounts of Christ's miracles and the authority with which he commissioned the disciples to preach the gospel of the kingdom serve to confirm that, with his coming, the Old Testament promise regarding the future coming of the kingdom was being fulfilled. Though this kingdom has not yet come in all of its fullness, it has come in the person and work of Christ, in his life, death, resurrection and ascension to the Father's right hand, whence he presently reigns until all of his enemies have been subdued beneath his feet (*1 Cor.* 15:25).[1]

Another way in which the New Testament emphasizes the presence of the future of Old Testament expectation is by means of the language of the 'last days', the 'fullness of time', or the 'end of the ages'. In Peter's sermon at Pentecost, the

[1] See Herman Ridderbos, *The Coming of the Kingdom*, trans. H. de Jonste, ed. Raymond O. Zorn (Philadelphia: Presbyterian and Reformed, 1962), for a comprehensive and outstanding treatment of the present and future aspects of the coming of the kingdom in the New Testament Gospel accounts. For similar treatments of the Apostle Paul's understanding of the presence of the future in the person and work of Christ, see Herman Ridderbos, *Paul. An Outline of His Theology*, trans. J. R. de Witt (Grand Rapids: Eerdmans, 1975); Geerhardus Vos, *The Pauline Eschatology* (Princeton: The University Press, 1930); and Raymond O. Zorn, *Christ Triumphant: Biblical Perspectives on His Church and Kingdom* (Edinburgh: Banner of Truth, 1997), a revised and updated version of *Church and Kingdom* (Philadelphia: Presbyterian and Reformed, 1962).

apostle cites the prophecy of Joel in Acts 2:17, '"And it shall be in the last days", God says, "that I will pour forth of My Spirit upon all mankind."' When the Apostle Paul describes the birth of Jesus Christ, he declares, 'But when the fulness of the time came, God sent forth His Son, born of a woman, born under the Law' (*Gal.* 4:4). This language, 'the fulness of the time', speaks of the moment in God's appointment which marks the completion and fulfilment of his promise and saving purpose. In 1 Corinthians 10:11 the Apostle Paul remarks that the history of Israel's disobedience under the old covenant has been recorded for the benefit of believers, 'upon whom the end of the ages have come'. Elsewhere the sacrifice of Christ is described as having been offered 'once at the end of the ages' (*Heb.* 9:26). The Apostle John also speaks, in his warning to beware the coming of anti-Christ, of this being 'the last hour' (*1 John* 2:18).

All of these passages only serve to confirm the New Testament teaching that the times in which we now live are the times of fulfilment, the times which mark out the beginning of the end of history, the times in which Christ has begun to establish and ultimately will fully usher in the glorious future of promise.

II. THE FUTURE ANTICIPATED

However, we must be careful not to draw too sharp a line of distinction between the Old Testament and the New Testament. Though the New Testament resoundingly declares that the great complex of events in redemptive history has occurred, it also still teaches that something further lies on the horizon of history. One great event on the horizon of history still remains to be accomplished: the coming again or return of the glorified and reigning Jesus Christ at the close of the present age.[1] Only with Christ's

---

[1] The differences among premillennialists, dispensationalists and postmillennialists on the subject of Christ's return are discussed in Chapters 8–12. Here I am only interested in sketching the main lines of the New Testament's perspective on the future.

coming again will the curtain be drawn on redemptive history and the consummation of God's kingdom achieved.

What from the vantage point of Old Testament expectation appeared to be a single movement has now in the New Testament become a two-stage movement. Whereas the Old Testament saw only one great, future Messianic age, coinciding with the coming of the Messiah, the New Testament further reveals that the present Messianic age awaits its consummation at Christ's coming again.

Though, as we noted in the preceding, the New Testament speaks of the present age as the 'last days', we often find in the New Testament writings a distinction drawn between this age and the age to come. These passages clearly indicate that though the future has drawn near in Christ, there remains an even greater future, a consummate future at the end of the age.

In the Gospels, Christ contrasts the present age and the future age in several passages. In Luke 20:34–35, responding to a question of the Sadducees about the resurrection, Jesus answers, 'The sons of this age marry and are given in marriage, but those who are considered worthy to attain to that age and the resurrection from the dead, neither marry, nor are given in marriage.' In Matthew 12:32, a similar contrast is drawn between the two ages, when Christ announces, 'And whoever shall speak a word against the Son of Man, it shall be forgiven him; but whoever shall speak against the Holy Spirit, it shall not be forgiven him, either in this age, or in the age to come.' In a passage in which Christ encourages the disciples with the promise of kingdom blessings for those who follow him, a similar point is made about these two ages: 'Truly I say to you, there is no one who has left house or wife or brothers or parents or children, for the sake of the kingdom of God, who shall not receive many times as much at this time and in the age to come, eternal life' (*Luke* 18:29–30).

It is interesting to observe that this same contrast is drawn in the New Testament in terms of the contrast between 'the last days' (plural) and 'the last day' (singular), or between the 'end of the ages' (plural) and 'the end of the age' (singular). Though we live presently in the last days, these days are not identical with the final termination and end of redemptive history, marking the point of transition to God's eternal kingdom. In John 6:40, accordingly, Jesus promises that 'everyone who beholds the Son and believes in him, may have eternal life; and I Myself will raise him up on the last day'. Clearly, here Jesus means to refer to an event in the future, an event still anticipated. Using similar language, Martha in John 11:24 speaks of the resurrection of her brother, Lazarus, 'at the last day'. Jesus also speaks in John 12:48 of the judgement that will befall those who reject his Word 'at the last day'. These passages suggest that, though we are living in the 'last days', *the* last day is yet to come. An alternative expression, 'the end of the age', is used in several places in the New Testament (e.g., *Matt.* 13:39; 24:3; 28:20) to designate the great and definitive day which will mark the closure of redemptive history at the return of Christ.

III. THE 'PLEDGE' OF THINGS TO COME

Since Christ's first coming inaugurates the future and points, with his resurrection from the dead and ascension to the Father's right hand, to his glorious coming at the end of the age, believers who are joined to Christ by faith already share in his victory. The blessings of salvation that come to the believer in this present age are so many tokens of the fullness of salvation in the age to come. This can be seen in two outstanding ways: first, in the resurrection of Jesus Christ; and second, in the outpouring of the Spirit upon the church at Pentecost. Both of these events are end-time events, events that are prophetic of the future of which they are a pledge and guarantee.

The familiar description of the resurrection of Jesus Christ in 1 Corinthians 15 is sufficient to illustrate that Christ's resurrection is an end-time event, pledging to believers the certainty of their own resurrection. The Apostle Paul illustrates the relation between Christ's resurrection and the believer's resurrection in terms of the metaphor of 'harvest'. Just as the harvest encompasses the gathering of the first fruits and the remainder of the harvest, so it is with the resurrection: the one, end-time harvest is a two-staged event, encompassing the period between Christ's resurrection and the resurrection of believers at the end of the age. These are not two, separate events; these are two aspects of one great eschatological harvest. As the Apostle Paul describes it, 'But now Christ has been raised from the dead, the first fruits of those who are asleep. For since by a man came death, by a man also came the resurrection of the dead. For as in Adam all die, so also in Christ all shall be made alive. But each in his own order: Christ the first fruits, after that those who are Christ's at his coming' (*1 Cor.* 15:20–23).[1]

We have already noted that the outpouring of the Spirit at Pentecost was understood by the apostle Peter to be a fulfilment of Joel's prophecy of what would occur 'in the latter days'. However, in the New Testament the work of the Spirit in joining the believer to Christ is also regarded as a work which pledges the fullness of salvation in the future.

This can be seen in a number of passages. In Romans 8:23, the apostle Paul, echoing the language of 1 Corinthians 15 regarding the resurrection of Christ, speaks of the 'first-fruits of the Spirit', which promise the full harvest in the future: '[we] have the first-fruits of the Spirit . . . waiting for our adoption, to wit, the redemption of our body.' On several occasions, the Spirit is termed a 'pledge' of the fullness of salvation that awaits the believer in the future (*Eph.* 1:13–14,

---

[1] See Richard B. Gaffin, Jr., *Resurrection and Redemption. A Study in Paul's Soteriology*, 2nd ed. (formerly *The Centrality of the Resurrection* [Grand Rapids: Baker, 1978]; Phillipsburg, NJ: Presbyterian and Reformed, 1987), for an extended treatment of the Apostle Paul's understanding of the resurrection of Christ as an end-time event and the focal point of redemption.

2 Cor. 1:22; 5:5; cf. *Eph.* 4:30). This language suggests that believers have in the Spirit a promissory, though partial, participation in the fullness of salvation that will be theirs at Christ's return. In the Spirit believers enjoy a provisional experience of what will be a consummate experience in the age to come; life in the Spirit for believers is a foretaste of the life to come. The teaching of Ephesians 1:13–14 is typical of this emphasis: 'You were sealed with the Holy Spirit of promise, who is an earnest or pledge of our inheritance, unto the redemption of God's own possession, unto the praise of His glory.'

On the basis of these and other passages, it can be said that the believer's experience of salvation in the present age is an anticipation of saving benefits that will only be fully received in the age to come. Through union with Christ by faith the believer already experiences a foretaste of the life which is still to come, a life of unbroken communion with God through Christ, a resurrection life in a glorified body which will be a fit dwelling-place of God in the Spirit.

IV. LIVING 'BETWEEN THE TIMES'

Though we have only provided a sketch of some of the main lines of the New Testament's teaching about the future, enough has been said to characterize the life of the believer in this present age as a living 'between the times'. What gives spirit and shape to the Christian life is the relation between salvation already experienced and yet still anticipated for the future. Christians live out of the reality of Christ's first coming, resurrection, and ascension to the Father's right hand. They also live in fervent expectation of Christ's return at the close of the age, when the work already begun and secured by his resurrection and ascension is consummated.

This accounts for the frequent New Testament exhortations to believers to walk by faith and to live in hope. Believers embrace Christ 'clothed in his promises',[1] knowing

[1] The expression is Calvin's (*Institutes* II.ix.3).

that the future of God's consummated kingdom has been guaranteed in the great events of Christ's resurrection and the outpouring of the Spirit at Pentecost.

The Apostle Paul well summarizes the quality of the Christian's life in this time 'between the times':

> If then you have been raised with Christ, keep seeking the things above, where Christ is, seated at the right hand of God. Set your mind on the things above, not on the things that are on earth. For you have died and your life is hidden with Christ in God. When Christ, who is our life, is revealed, then you also will be revealed with Him in glory (*Col.* 3:1–4).

The promised future is already a reality in the person and work of Jesus Christ, the crucified, resurrected and ascended Lord, but it is not yet present to the believer who must walk by faith not sight. However, the certainty of the Lord's coming strengthens believers' confidence that it will come and quickens their desire for it.

PART TWO

---

*The Future Between
Death and
Resurrection*

3

The Intermediate State

IT HAS BEEN CUSTOMARY in the study of theology to divide the Bible's teaching about the future into two parts, the first dealing with the future of the individual believer and the second dealing with that of the creation. These two divisions are sometimes termed 'individual eschatology' and 'general eschatology'.[1] The first addresses such topics as physical death, immortality, and the state between death and the resurrection of the body – the 'intermediate state'. The second addresses such topics as the expectation of Christ's return or second advent, the 'signs of the times', the millennium, the resurrection of the body, the final judgement, and the final state.

Though this division of the Bible's teaching is somewhat artificial, it is nonetheless unavoidable because the question of what becomes of the individual believer at death, prior to the return of Christ and the resurrection of the body, cannot be escaped. This is true in part for pastoral reasons. Believers

[1] The term 'eschatology' is a combination of two words, *eschatos*, meaning 'last' or 'end', and *logos*, meaning 'word'. Eschatology, then, is the study of (word about) the last things or end times in the light of Scripture. Anthony Hoekema, *The Bible and the Future*, p. 77, uses the language of 'cosmic' eschatology rather than 'general eschatology', to emphasize that it deals with the future of the cosmos or the world rather than only of the individual.

are anxious to know what the Bible teaches about their condition following death and prior to Christ's return. Pastors and elders who minister the Word of God to the people cannot escape the obligation to provide biblical answers to questions about death and what it brings. But it is also true for biblical reasons. The Bible does speak of the intermediate state or of what becomes of believers upon death. Any attempt to summarize the Bible's teaching about the future will have to reckon with what it says.

Consequently, we take up in this chapter the subjects of individual eschatology, namely, physical death, immortality, and the intermediate state. Afterwards we will move on to the questions of general eschatology.

Two Biblical Themes

Before we can consider the question of the intermediate state, it is necessary to review what the Bible teaches about death, immortality, and the ultimate victory over death that the believer anticipates through union with Christ. For unless we do this, we will not keep to the path marked out for us in the Bible.

I. PHYSICAL DEATH AS THE 'WAGES OF SIN'

Contrary to many modern myths about death – that death is a 'natural' part of life, that it marks the cessation of existence, that there is a natural 'dignity' in dying well – the Bible paints its portrait of death with the most stark and sobering of colours. Nowhere in the Bible is death treated as something natural, as something that can easily be domesticated or treated as 'a part of life'.[1] No encouragement is given us in

---

[1] In the history of the Christian church, a small minority of theologians have tried to argue that death is, at least in some respects, a 'natural' part of life and not exclusively the consequence of sin. In the early church, Celestius, a disciple of the British monk Pelagius, taught this view. The Socinians, a radical branch of the Reformation, also taught it. In recent centuries, theologians who have sought to accommodate their views to evolution, have simply taken it as a given that death is a natural feature of human life.

the Bible to minimize the terror and fearfulness of death our 'last enemy' (*1 Cor.* 15:26).

The biblical understanding of death begins with the Fall into sin. Death is the divinely appointed punishment of humankind's disobedience. In Genesis 2:17, as part of the stipulation and probation of obedience, Adam was forewarned, 'You must not eat from the tree of the knowledge of good and evil, for when you eat of it you shall surely die.' Adam, formed from the dust of the earth and made a 'living soul' through the in-breathing of his Creator (*Gen.* 2:7), became liable to death through his act of disobedience, a liability which now falls to all whom he represented as their covenant head. One does not have to read far in the biblical record to discover that the curse of God extends to all. Because of Adam's sin and disobedience, he and his posterity must now return to the dust whence they were formed (*Gen.* 3:19).

This is the ruling theme throughout the Scriptures when it comes to the subject of death. Dissolution of the body (*2 Cor.* 5:1) brings separation from God in the normal creaturely form of human existence. Created life for human beings is bodily life. Accordingly, the Psalmist fears death because it will cut him off from the opportunity to praise and serve the Lord on earth (*Psa.* 30:9). Physical death, the loss of that fullness of communion and fellowship with God in the sphere of creation for which human beings were originally created, is a picture of spiritual death.

One of the more prominent passages in Scripture on the subject of sin and death is Romans 5:12–21. In this passage the inseparability of sin and death is underscored. This is clear in the opening verse of this portion of Scripture, 'Therefore, just as through one man sin entered into the world, and death through sin, and so death spread to all men, because all sinned' (*Rom.* 5:12; cf. *1 Cor.* 15:21). Through the sin of the first Adam, all have become sinners and are subject to the reign of death. This reign of death is the consequence of sin and condemnation. It has spiritual meaning, signifying humankind's being cut off from God's favour and blessing. Death is even described as the 'wages of sin' (*Rom.* 6:23). Thus, the sin of the first Adam which leads to condemnation and death finds its remedy only in the obedience of the second Adam, which leads to righteousness and life for all who believe (*Rom.* 5:17–21).

It is this biblical understanding of death as the consequence and punishment of sin that forms the background for the gospel message of salvation and life through Jesus Christ. Christ has come into the world to 'render powerless him who had the power of death' and to 'deliver those who through fear of death were subject to slavery all their lives' (*Heb.* 2:14–15). By means of Christ's resurrection from the dead, the death which results from the sin of the first Adam is overcome (*1 Cor.* 15:21). In this respect it can be said that Christ has 'abolished death and brought life and immortality to light through the gospel' (*2 Tim.* 1:10). Even as death is the 'wages of sin', so 'the free gift of God is eternal life in Christ Jesus our Lord' (*Rom.* 6:23).

This does not mean that believers no longer have to die. Though their death is not a satisfaction for sin nor something that can separate them from God's love in Christ Jesus (*Rom.* 8:39), it remains inevitable. The saying 'there is nothing so certain as death and taxes' needs to be amended in more biblical form to say, 'there is nothing so certain as death' – taxes can be avoided, death cannot! But for the believer this certainty does not occasion fear or dread, for it brings a more intimate fellowship with the Lord than that capable of being known in this life (*Phil.* 1:21, *2 Cor.* 5:8). As the *Heidelberg Catechism*, a popular confession of the Reformation, concisely puts it, 'Our death is not a satisfaction for our sins, but only a dying to sins and entering into eternal life' (Question 42).[1]

[1] Quoted from *Ecumenical and Reformed Creeds and Confessions: Classroom Edition* (Orange City, Iowa: Mid-America Reformed

II. IMMORTALITY OF THE SOUL OR RESURRECTION OF THE BODY?

If death is inseparably joined in Scripture to the reality of sin and God's curse against it, it should not surprise us that the ultimate horizon of hope for the individual believer beyond this life and the grave is the resurrection of the body. The grace of God toward his people in Jesus Christ, saving them from the 'wages of sin', includes the promise of the future glorification of believers when they come to share in the power of Christ's resurrection. Christ, the 'first fruits', has been raised victorious from the dead, having suffered the curse on behalf of his people. Believers through faith anticipate that, when Christ finishes his work and vanquishes their 'last enemy', death, they will be given to share in the glory of his resurrection also (*1 Cor.* 15:20–23).

At this point, however, we must be wary of falling into a common error. This error is to minimize death and victory over it through the resurrection of the body by adopting an unbiblical view of what is sometimes called the 'immortality of the soul'.

Now, it has long been customary among Christians to use the expression 'the immortality of the soul'.[1] In part, it has been used to express (correctly) that believers, when they die, do not cease to exist, but continue to enjoy personal existence and communion with God in heaven prior to Christ's return and the resurrection of the body. In this sense, the immortality of the soul only means what will be advanced below as the biblical view of the believer's intermediate state.

But on the other hand, this expression is often used in an unbiblical way to minimize the reality of death and to render

---

Seminary, 1991). Unless otherwise indicated, here and hereafter quotations from the creeds and confessions are taken from the editions collected in this volume.

[1] This usage is sanctioned in part by the *Westminster Confession of Faith* which says that God 'created man, male and female, with reasonable and immortal souls' (IV. 2), and that men's souls have 'an immortal subsistence' (XXXII.1). See also the *Westminster Larger Catechism* Q. and A. 17.

almost superfluous any further hope for the resurrection of the body. In the history of the church, there has been a tendency at this point to read the Bible through the lens of Greek philosophical thought which commonly taught that each person is composed of two distinct substances, the one being the 'soul', the other being the 'body'. The first of these, the soul, as the higher aspect of the human person, was thought to be by nature indestructible or immortal. The second of these, the body, as the lower aspect of the human person, was thought to be by nature destructible and mortal. In some more extreme expressions of this kind of thinking, redemption is conceived of as a release of the soul from its imprisonment in the body. Not only are 'soul' and 'body' distinguishable and separable, but salvation actually comes through their separation in death.

However, this view threatens two clearly stated biblical truths. First, in the Bible God alone, in the strict sense of indestructible life, is immortal. Whatever immortality human beings may enjoy, it is always derived as a gift from God's creative hand. Only God as Creator has life of himself; human beings as creatures always owe to God whatever life they have. If we may speak at all of the immortality of the soul, then we must qualify our speaking to preserve this difference. We are not to speak of the inherent indestructibility of the soul, at least not in the sense in which God is indestructible. In 1 Timothy 6:16 God is spoken of as One 'who alone possesses immortality and dwells in unapproachable light'. Furthermore, in John 5:26 Jesus declares that 'just as the Father has life in himself, even so he gave to the Son also to have life in himself'. In this last passage, a clear contrast is drawn between the Father and the Son, who owe their life to nothing outside of themselves, and every creature, whose life is a gift from God.

But second, the Bible typically describes whatever immortality believers may enjoy as an immortality of the whole person, body and soul, which requires the resurrection of the body. Interestingly, when the Bible speaks of the believer's immortality, it normally refers to the immortality of the body. It is remarkable how in the Bible the language of 'immortality', when it is applied to human beings, typically refers to the believer in his or her perfected state, in the state of resurrection glory.

This can be illustrated from several New Testament passages. In 1 Corinthians 15:53–54, the Apostle Paul affirms, 'For the perishable must clothe itself with the imperishable, and the mortal with immortality. When the perishable has been clothed with the imperishable, and the mortal with immortality, then the saying will come true: 'Death has been swallowed up in victory" (NIV). Clearly this passage refers, not to the immortality of the soul, but to the immortality of the believer in the resurrection state of glory. This is consistent with other passages which speak of 'immortality' and 'imperishability', not to describe the disembodied state of believers in the interim between death and resurrection but to describe the future inheritance and blessedness of the redeemed in the kingdom of God (cf. *Rom. 2:7, 1 Cor. 9:25, 1 Pet. 1:4*). These passages suggest that it would be better to talk about the 'immortality of the believer' and understand that to include the resurrection of the body.

Why is it important to notice that, biblically speaking, we might better talk about 'the immortality of the resurrection body' of believers than of 'the immortality of the soul'? Certainly not in order to deny what most believers rightly affirm when they speak of the immortality of the soul: that believers, when their body and soul are separated through physical death, continue to enjoy communion with the Lord in the intermediate state.[1] As noted earlier, I shall in fact

---

[1] See Oscar Cullmann, *Immortality of the Soul or Resurrection of the Dead?* (New York: MacMillan, 1964), who argues from the biblical emphasis upon the resurrection of the body against the idea of the immortality of the soul. Cf. G. C. Berkouwer, *Man: The Image of*

argue in the following for precisely this understanding of the intermediate state. But I do mean to caution against any view of the believer's future that would minimize what remains central and primary in the biblical view: the resurrection of the body.

The work of the Triune God in the redemption of his people in Christ only reaches its perfection in the full participation of believers in Christ's resurrection from the dead. Until this mortal puts on immortality, even the believer's intermediate state of provisional joy in the Lord's presence upon death is incomplete. The hope of the believer for the future does not terminate with the intermediate state, but remains fixed upon the day of Christ's return and the resurrection of the dead.

This cannot be emphasized too much, particularly when the subject of the intermediate state is addressed, since an emphasis upon the intermediate state might easily distract us from the central hope of the believer which is the resurrection of the body. However, provided we remember that this hope is central, there is no reason to deny the biblical teaching about the intermediate state. Even the language used, 'intermediate', acknowledges that it is a provisional and incomplete form of communion with the Lord. It is precisely 'intermediate' because it falls between death and the resurrection of the body at the return of Christ. But though it is in this sense the penultimate, and the resurrection the ultimate, hope of the believer, this does not make it any less real.

God, trans. Dirk W. Jellema (Grand Rapids: Eerdmans, 1962), p. 276: 'Scripture is never concerned with an independent interest in immortality as such, let alone with the immortality of a part of man which defies and survives death under all circumstances, and on which we can reflect quite apart from man's relation to the living God.' Though I concur with the main point of Cullmann and Berkouwer's argument – that the resurrection is the primary focus of the biblical hope for the believer's future – they go too far in denying the intermediate state in which the soul or spirit enjoys continuing communion with the Lord.

The question of the intermediate state is, therefore, just this: What is the circumstance of the believer between death and resurrection? If we have to beware the idea of the 'immortality of the soul', especially when it diminishes the centrality of the resurrection of the body in the believer's hope for the future, does this prevent us from affirming that the believer enjoys a conscious fellowship with the Lord upon death and prior to the resurrection at the last day? Without falling prey to an unbiblical view of the immortality of the soul or denying the resurrection of the body, may we not still speak of a state intermediate between physical death and the final state in the resurrection?

Unbiblical Views of the Intermediate State

Though there has been a general unanimity in the historic Christian church that believers enjoy a provisional and intensified communion with Christ upon death, a communion which involves a conscious experience of fellowship with God through Christ, there have been minority opinions as well.

In the foregoing introduction to the subject of the intermediate state, we identified two great themes in the Scriptures which form the framework within which to approach this subject. The first of these themes is the biblical teaching that death is the 'wages of sin', and the second is that salvation brings victory over sin and death, a victory that includes and focuses ultimately upon the resurrection of the body. The biblical hope for the believer's future terminates, not upon the intermediate state, but upon the glorification the believer will experience in union with Christ and all other believers at the consummation of Christ's saving work. The believer does not place his or her confidence for the future in the 'immortality of the soul' but rather in the 'resurrection of the body'.

However, two minority opinions on the subject of the intermediate state distort this biblical focus on the resurrection of the body by denying the reality of an intermediate state in which believers enjoy conscious fellowship with the Lord. These views of the intermediate state wrongly conclude from the biblical teaching about death and the resurrection that there is no living fellowship with God in the state intermediate between death and resurrection. We must therefore examine these two viewpoints before stating positively the biblical teaching about the intermediate state. The first is annihilationism, and the second is soul-sleep.

I. ANNIHILATIONISM OR SOUL EXTINCTION

As this terminology suggests, annihilationism teaches that death brings about the annihilation of the whole person, body and soul, the cessation of human existence in any form whatsoever. There is no state between death and the resurrection. Until the resurrection of the body, the believer ceases to exist. In this respect, the resurrection of the body actually involves what amounts to the re-creation of the individual person.

The term 'annihilationism' is used in at least three different ways.[1] These diverging uses must be borne in mind in order to understand clearly the view we are considering here.

The first use refers to the view that all individuals, whether believers or unbelievers, cease to exist altogether at death and have no future prospect of life of any kind. This use reflects a materialistic world-view which is anti-Christian. This is not the view of annihilationism that is our interest at this point.

The second use refers to the view that all human beings are naturally mortal, but some (believers) are given immortality as a gift of God's grace. This view, sometimes called 'conditional immortality', can take one of two forms: either believers upon death cease to exist until the time of the

---

[1] See Benjamin B. Warfield, 'Annihilationism', in *Studies in Theology* (New York: Oxford University Press, 1932), pp. 447–500. Warfield termed these three kinds of annihilationism 'pure mortalism', 'conditional immortality', and 'annihilationism proper'.

resurrection or they enjoy a provisional state of fellowship with the Lord before the time of the resurrection.

The third use refers to the view that all individuals are created immortal, but God annihilates those whom he does not save (annihilationism proper). Those who do not believe in Jesus Christ and thereby receive the gift of eternal life are liable to annihilation or extinction by a direct act of God's judgement in death.

It should be clear enough from these different uses of the term 'annihilationism' that things can quickly become rather confused. They are mentioned here only to clarify the sense in which this terminology is being used. Annihilationism – so far as the question of the intermediate state is concerned – refers to any view that denies an intermediate state by teaching the non-existence of persons after death and prior to the resurrection. Obviously, there are several views of the intermediate state, corresponding to these forms of annihilationism: the materialist would deny any future existence whatever; the conditional-immortality advocate may or may not affirm an intermediate state;[1] and the annihilationism-proper advocate would affirm some view of an intermediate state, since only those whom God annihilates as an act of judgement cease to exist upon death. The only thing that interests us here, however, is the teaching, in whatever form, that there is no existence after death before the resurrection of the body.

Admittedly, this annihilationist view has had few advocates in the history of the church. However, it has increasingly gained advocates in the last century, primarily among two of the major cults, the Jehovah's Witnesses and the Seventh-Day Adventists,[2] and also among Christian

---

[1] I will be addressing the subject of conditional immortality in Chapter 15, 'The Doctrine of Eternal Punishment'.

[2] I am aware of the debate whether the Seventh-Day Adventists are a cult. In my judgement, they are probably best described as a seriously (doctrinally) deformed expression of evangelical Christian-

believers who have an exaggerated view of the importance of the resurrection of the body. Advocates of this view have in common the conviction that the biblical teaching of the integrity of each person's constitution as a 'living soul' (not a soul 'having' a body), requires the conclusion that death means annihilation.

The basic form of the argument for this view is, accordingly, quite simple. Because Adam was created from the dust of the earth and became, after the Creator breathed into him the breath of life, a 'living soul' (*Gen.* 2:7), in no meaningful sense could the 'soul' survive death and the dissolution of the body. The unity of soul and body is so intimate and necessary to each person's existence as a creature that they are inseparable, even at death. Typically, advocates of this annihilationist view of the intermediate state contend that to affirm the continued existence of the 'soul' between death and resurrection is to succumb to the influence of Greek thought and to teach an unbiblical view of our created unity. Because human beings do not 'have' a body, distinguishable from the soul, but are rather 'living souls', there can be no prospect of life apart from the body, even in the so-called intermediate state.[1]

---

ity, exhibiting several 'cult-like' features. Cf. Anthony A. Hoekema, 'Appendix E: The Teachings of Seventh-Day Adventists and Jehovah's Witnesses on the Life After Death', in his *The Four Major Cults* (Grand Rapids: Eerdmans, 1963), pp. 345–371, for a discussion of the teachings of these groups on the intermediate state.

[1] John Cooper, in his *Body, Soul, and Life Everlasting: Biblical Anthropology and the Monism-Dualism Debate* (Grand Rapids: Eerdmans, 1989), provides a good contemporary defence of the Bible's teaching that the soul is distinguishable from the body and able to experience an intermediate state. Cooper approaches the issue from a biblical, theological, and philosophical perspective, arguing that the Bible teaches a 'holistic dualism' (human beings were created as a psycho-somatic unity of body and soul, though these are distinguishable aspects of their constitution) that fits with its teaching of an intermediate state in which the 'soul' or 'inner self' goes to be with the Lord and enjoys continued, conscious existence.

In the following section, we will consider a number of biblical passages that clearly teach an intermediate state and that speak of the 'soul' or 'spirit' existing after death and apart from the resurrection of the body. These passages contradict annihilationism's main emphasis and show that it is based on an inference which, though drawn from the Bible's teaching of the unity of body and soul as well as the future resurrection of the body, is not itself supported by Scripture. They show that this view is based more upon arguments of a general nature than upon the teaching of specific biblical passages.

II. SOUL-SLEEP OR PSYCHOPANNYCHY

A second and, in terms of historical influence and advocacy, more important view of the intermediate state is what is often termed 'soul-sleep' or 'psychopannychy'. For some of the same reasons that lead to the advocacy of annihilationism, advocates of this view reject the doctrine of an intermediate state or the teaching that believers (and unbelievers) experience any conscious existence after death and before the resurrection. The state between death and resurrection is like that of sleep, an unconscious state with no experience of relationship to others or to the passage of time. Just as sleep is normally characterized by the non-experience of the passage of time, so it is with the intermediate state. The time between falling asleep and awaking is virtually non-existent – at least it is not experienced – so that upon awakening it is as though no time has elapsed.

In the history of the church, advocates of this view have included: an early, but small, sect of Christians in Arabia, whom Eusebius of Caesarea, the church historian, refers to in his writings;[1] a number of more radical sects among the

---

[1] Eusebius, *Church History*, VI.37, in *A Select Library of Nicene and Post-Nicene Fathers of the Christian Church*, eds. Philip Schaff and Henry Wace, second series, vol. 1 (repr. Grand Rapids: Eerdmans, 1976).

THE PROMISE OF THE FUTURE

Anabaptist movement of the sixteenth-century Reformation;[1] some of the 'Irvingites' in nineteenth-century England; and a number of contemporary Christians who dislike the doctrine of a conscious state of existence between death and the resurrection, fearing that it belittles the importance of the body to man's creaturely existence.

III. ARGUMENTS IN FAVOUR

The two most important arguments for this view of the intermediate state are, first, that the unity of body and soul is essential to human existence; and second, that the Bible often describes death as a 'falling asleep'.

The first of these arguments, that the unity of body and soul is essential to human existence, is reminiscent of the major argument of advocates of annihilationism. It runs like this: Because human beings are a psychosomatic unity (not souls 'having' a body, but 'living souls' or 'ensouled bodies'), death cuts them off from the possibility of any meaningful experience or continued conscious existence. It is therefore inconceivable that human beings, their bodies having dissolved, could enjoy an intermediate state of fellowship with the Lord or others apart from their bodies, which are indispensable to all meaningful human experience.[2]

---

[1] It is interesting to note that John Calvin, early in his reforming work, wrote a treatise against certain Anabaptist defenders of the doctrine of 'soul-sleep', entitled *Psychopannychia*. An English translation of this tract, still a worthwhile treatment of the arguments for and the biblical reasons against soul-sleep, can be found in: *Selected Works of John Calvin: Tracts and Letters*, eds. H. Beveridge and J. Bonnet, vol. 3 (1851; repr. Grand Rapids: Baker, 1983), pp. 414–490. The fortieth of King Edward VI's *Forty-Two Articles* (a precursor of the later *Thirty-Nine Articles* of the Anglican Church) also addressed these Anabaptist teachers of the doctrine of soul-sleep: 'They which say that the souls of those who depart hence do sleep being without all sense, feeling or perceiving till the Day of judgement, do utterly dissent from the right belief disclosed to us in Holy Scripture.'

[2] This raises one of the peculiar problems of the 'soul-sleep' position: if human experience requires the body, then does not death

The second argument is more substantial because it appeals to biblical passages that describe death as a 'falling asleep'. Passages already in the Old Testament describe the death of believers as a kind of sleep, in which that conscious experience that belongs to life in the body is presumably lost (for example, *Gen.* 47:30, *Deut.* 31:16, 2 *Sam.* 7:12, *Psa.* 30:9; 6:5; 115:17, *Eccles.* 9:10, *Isa.* 38:18–19). However, this is even more clearly affirmed in the New Testament. In 1 Corinthians 7:39, we read, 'A wife is bound as long as her husband lives; but if her husband has fallen asleep, she is free to be married to whom she wishes, only in the Lord.' Similarly, in a well-known passage regarding the future state of believers, the Apostle Paul declares in 1 Thessalonians 4:13, 'But we do not want you to be uninformed, brethren, about those who are asleep, that you may not grieve, as do the rest who have no hope.' Such language describing the death of believers as a falling sleep is found in many other New Testament passages (for example, *Matt.* 27:52, *John* 11:11–13, *1 Cor.* 11:30; 15:20; 15:51, *Acts* 7:60, *Luke* 8:52). Since sleep involves the loss of consciousness, advocates of the soul-sleep position argue that these texts clearly teach that believers are in a state of unconsciousness in the intermediate state.

In addition to these two primary arguments, advocates of the soul-sleep position suggest others. One is an argument from silence. Nowhere, it is noted, do we find in Scripture an account of anyone who had been subject to death and subsequently brought to life, whose experience in the interim is recounted in any way. The reason for this omission must be that the person who had died ceased to enjoy conscious

---

bring the end of all experience and existence, including the human experience known as 'sleeping'? Another way of putting the question would be this: if human existence is always bodily existence, does not death mark the termination of human existence, including that of the 'soul'? It seems odd to affirm the existence, including the 'sleeping' of something, namely, the human 'soul', when death is regarded as the end of any meaningful form of human existence.

experience in the interim period. Another argument is that the believer or unbeliever's experience of a provisional state of bliss or woe in the intermediate state would be an unwarranted and premature anticipation of the final judgement. Were believers and unbelievers to experience consciously the provisional form of their final state, the final judgement would be anticlimactic for them and serve no essential purpose.

IV. ARGUMENTS AGAINST

At first glance, these arguments for the soul-sleep position seem insuperable. However, upon closer scrutiny, they prove to be without much weight or cogency, especially if we consider them one at a time.

The first argument, that the unity of body and soul is essential to human experience, is partially true but overstated. The normal state of human beings as creatures is certainly one of the union of the 'inner' and 'outer' self, soul and body. Death is an abnormal condition, tearing apart what God created and joined together. Death does bring tremendous loss and deprivation; it precludes the fullness of creaturely existence for which humans were created. But this does not mean that it necessarily terminates any form of continued conscious experience and existence. What is more, this is not a conclusion warranted by the biblical evidence. For in the Bible, not only do angels experience conscious existence without bodily form, but believers are said to experience fellowship with the Lord, apart from their bodies, upon death (see *Heb.* 12:23, *Rev.* 6:9–11). Though we have yet to consider a number of biblical passages that speak of an intermediate state, it is sufficient now to say that the biblical teaching about the unity of soul and body, the importance of the future resurrection, and the deprivation that death brings, do not present an insuperable obstacle to the teaching of a conscious intermediate state.

Furthermore, the second argument which appeals to the biblical descriptions of death as a falling asleep, is not as formidable as it might first appear. Several observations about these biblical passages are in order. First, in none of them is it said that the 'soul' sleeps; it is the whole person, that is, body and soul, who sleeps. One might even argue that, because death results from the dissolution of the body, it is particularly the body that sleeps. Second, the imagery of sleeping means to describe death euphemistically, that is, in a way that shows how its sting and terror have been removed for the believer. Consequently, those passages that use this language only speak of the death of believers, never of unbelievers. Death is a 'falling asleep' only for those who are 'in Christ' (*1 Cor.* 15:18) or 'in Jesus' (*1 Thess.* 4:14), not for those who are outside of Christ. And third, the two ideas that predominate in this euphemism for the death of believers are resting from one's labours and involvement in the struggles and trials of this life, and entering into a state of peace and joy (cf. *Psa.* 37:37–39, *Isa.* 57:1–2, *Phil.* 1:23, 1 *Thess.* 5:10, 2 *Cor.* 5:8). The idea of a loss of consciousness or the absence of the experience of being in the presence of the Lord or fellow believers does not necessarily belong to it. It is a biblically unjustified pressing of the metaphor of sleep to insist that it means to deny consciousness to the believer upon death. This would in fact contradict the teaching of other biblical passages which do ascribe such conscious experience to believers in the intermediate state.

The other two arguments referred to are equally weak and invalid. The argument from silence, for example, has little to commend it. Only in a few instances mentioned in Scripture are the dead brought back to life. From these few instances, we are not permitted to establish the universal rule that all persons experience no conscious existence after death and before the resurrection of the body. It may well be for good reasons that such persons do not report their experience(s) in their disembodied state. Perhaps what the Apostle Paul declares in 2 Corinthians 12:4 holds also for them, when he speaks of having been 'caught up into Paradise, and [having] heard inexpressible things, things that man is not permitted to tell'.

Moreover, the other argument concerning the judgement day supposes that it serves the purpose of revealing for the first time the eternal destiny of believers and unbelievers. But this conflicts with the Scripture's teaching that believers have already the foretaste of 'eternal life' (cf. *1 John* 5:13, *John* 5:24, *Phil.* 1:28, *Rom.* 5:1; 8:1). It also confuses what is constitutive with what is declarative: the final judgement does not constitute or determine the destiny of believers and unbelievers, but only declares publicly, vindicating God's grace and justice, what that destiny is.

In the final analysis, the only antidote for these unbiblical views of the intermediate state is the positive teaching of Scripture itself about this state and its features. Neither annihilationism nor soul-sleep begin to do justice to the biblical teaching about this intermediate state. Both of them wrongly conclude from the Bible's emphasis upon the unity of body and soul and the future reality of the resurrection of the body, that there can be no conscious experience of communion with or separation from God in the intermediate state.

The comfort of every believer who 'falls asleep' in Jesus, according to the Scriptures, is that they go to be 'with the Lord'. They enter upon death into a new phase of unbroken and conscious fellowship with Christ and his people. This – not annihilation or soul-sleep – is the future prospect of believers in the intermediate state. To this positive biblical teaching and solid comfort we now turn.

The Intermediate State in Scripture

If the Bible rejects annihilationism or soul-sleep, what does become of the believer in the state intermediate between death and the resurrection?

Though the Bible is reticent on this subject and does not authorize undue speculation about what this state will be like, it does clearly teach that believers, in their 'soul' or 'spirit', will enjoy a state of conscious and unbroken (even intensified) communion with the Lord Jesus Christ. However provisional this state may be – awaiting the full redemption of the children of God, including their participation in the resurrection harvest of which Christ's resurrection was the 'first-fruits' (*1 Cor.* 15:20–23) – it will be a state of great joy in the presence of the Lord.

It is interesting to notice that the *Heidelberg Catechism*, a Protestant confession of the sixteenth century, in its answer to the question concerning the resurrection of the body, begins its answer by referring directly to this intermediate state. Even though this catechism does not elaborate upon the meaning of this state, it clearly affirms that the believer enjoys a continued and happy communion with the Lord after death and prior to the day of resurrection:

Q. 57. What comfort does the resurrection of the body afford you?
A. That not only my soul, after this life, shall immediately be taken up to Christ, its Head; but also that this my body, raised by the power of Christ, shall again be united with my soul, and made like unto the glorious body of Christ.

It will be my objective in what follows to show the biblical support for this beautiful confession and the comfort it affords believers in the Lord Jesus Christ.

I. OLD TESTAMENT FORESHADOWINGS
In the history of the church, the relation between the teaching of the Old Testament and the New Testament has often been described in terms of what is called progressive revelation. The Lord does not reveal everything to his people all at once. The history of redemption also brings a history of revelation, in which the Lord discloses his will and purpose to his people bit by bit. Some things that are fully and clearly revealed in the New Testament were only dimly seen and foreshadowed in the Old Testament.[1]

---

[1] John Calvin often employed the metaphor of a child maturing into adulthood to express this relation; the Old Testament is to the New

This is especially evident when it comes to the subject of the intermediate state. There is an evident progress in the history of revelation from the Old Testament to the New Testament. Things only foreshadowed in the Old Testament become clearly visible in the New Testament. For this reason, some have even gone so far as to argue that the Old Testament knows nothing of an intermediate state or an existence beyond death in the presence of God. They argue that this is revealed only in the New Testament. But this is going too far. There are, in fact, some interesting foreshadowings in the Old Testament of the teaching of the New Testament:

First, the Old Testament vigorously condemns the practice of necromancy or communicating with the dead (cf. *Deut.* 18:9–12, *Lev.* 20:6, *2 Kings* 21:6; 23:24, *Isa.* 8:19–20; 19:3; 29:4, *1 Sam.* 28:6ff). A number of passages condemn this practice, confirming at the very least a widespread conviction of continued conscious existence after death. This is particularly instructive since the Old Testament uniformly views death as the result of God's judgement curse upon humankind because of sin.

Second, in two outstanding instances in the Old Testament, godly believers did not die but were immediately ushered into the presence of God. Enoch 'was not, for God took him' (*Gen.* 5:24), and Elijah 'went up by a whirlwind into heaven' (*2 Kings* 2:11).

Third, there are passages, particularly in the Psalms, which express the confident hope of life for the believing child of God beyond the grave, in distinction from the wicked who go

---

Testament what the instruction of children is to that of adults. Warfield, the great Presbyterian theologian of the late nineteenth and early twentieth centuries, also compared the Old Testament to the New Testament by describing the first as a dimly lit and the second as a brightly lit room. Things that were only faintly visible in the Old Testament, in the light of the fuller revelation of the New Testament become more readily visible. Cf. B. B. Warfield, 'Biblical Doctrine of the Trinity', in *The Works of Benjamin B. Warfield, vol. 2, Biblical Doctrines* (1929; repr. Grand Rapids: Baker, 1981), pp. 141–2.

down into 'Sheol' under the wrath of God (*Job* 19:25–27; *Psa.* 73:24–26; 1:6; 7:10; 37:18). Despite the fact that the preponderance of references to 'Sheol' in the Old Testament simply refer to the 'grave' or to the 'place of the dead' (for example, *Gen.* 37:35, 1 *Sam.* 2:6), in some instances it connotes punishment and judgement upon the wicked, from which the righteous are ultimately delivered (*Psa.* 9:17; 55:15; 16:10; 49:14, *Prov.* 15:24).

Fourth, clearly expressed in the Old Testament is the expectation of the resurrection of the righteous and the wicked, respectively, unto weal and woe (*Hos.* 13:14, *Dan.* 12:2, *Isa.* 26:19).

And fifth, the covenant communion that the Lord establishes with his people, a communion which brings life out of death and redresses the consequences of sin and the curse, promises the fullness of life in unbroken communion with the Lord. It should not surprise us, therefore, that the Lord Jesus Christ, summarizing the promise of life in covenant with God, should say to the Sadducees, who denied the resurrection, 'have you not read that which was spoken to you by God, saying, "I am the God of Abraham, and the God of Isaac, and the God of Jacob"? He is not the God of the dead but of the living' (*Matt.* 22:31–32). This affirmation of life beyond death is born out of an awareness of what the covenant of grace promises.

When these Old Testament foreshadowings are taken together, it seems impossible to avoid the conclusion that the Old Testament believer anticipated life beyond the grave in communion with the Lord of the covenant. Nor does it seem possible to resist the conclusion that the Old Testament teaches the rudiments of a doctrine of punishment for the wicked and blessedness for the righteous after death. Nevertheless, these remain foreshadowings. Only in the light of the fuller disclosure of new covenant revelation do we find these rudiments confirmed and clarified.[1]

---

[1] For a sketch of the divergent views on the intermediate state in intertestamental Judaism, see Herman Bavinck, *The Last Things:*

THE PROMISE OF THE FUTURE

II. GENERAL NEW TESTAMENT AFFIRMATIONS

Several passages in the New Testament clearly reveal that believers and unbelievers alike upon death continue to experience a conscious form of existence.[1] However, this form of existence differs dramatically between believers and unbelievers: whereas believers enjoy a life of provisional blessedness in the presence of the Lord, unbelievers experience a provisional foretaste of eternal punishment under the judgement of God. Though our interest is primarily focused upon the experience of believers in this intermediate state, we cannot but mention as we proceed the corresponding state of unbelievers.

One of the most striking passages in this connection is the well-known parable of the rich man and Lazarus in Luke 16:19–31.[2] Jesus describes in this passage the contrasting states of the rich man and Lazarus, first before death, and then after death. Though the rich man enjoyed an existence of luxury and pleasure, subsequent to death he finds himself 'in Hades . . . in torment' (verse 23). The poor man by contrast, though he did not enjoy this world's goods during his life, finds himself after death in the bosom of Abraham,

---

Hope for This World and the Next, ed. John Bolt, trans. John Vriend (1928; repr. Grand Rapids: Baker, 1996), pp. 34–5.

[1] I use the language 'form of existence' to emphasize that only the believer enjoys 'life' in communion with God through Christ. Though unbelievers continue to 'exist', they do not 'live', at least not in the biblical sense of life that is life indeed.

[2] There is some debate as to whether this is a parable or a story based upon historical events. See Norval Geldenhuys, *Commentary on the Gospel of Luke* (NICNT; Grand Rapids: Eerdmans, 1951), p. 428, n. 3. Though I believe it is appropriately designated a 'parable', it is not explicitly identified as such in the text. Some appeal to the 'parabolic' character of this passage to suggest that it cannot be used to support any doctrine about the intermediate state. But this is a case of special pleading; the passage makes its point only if the descriptions offered refer to actual states of affairs. The biblical authors typically do not suffer a modern notion that you can affirm a truth though it has no basis in reality.

in a place of blessedness and honour. Furthermore, Jesus describes the relationship between these respective places and states as one in which a 'great chasm' is fixed between them, preventing any passage from one to the other. Without attempting to interpret fully all the details of this passage, it seems to affirm clearly that immediately upon death the righteous and the wicked enter upon two separate modes of existence. The righteous are found in a state of provisional blessedness in the presence of God; the wicked are found in a state of provisional and inescapable torment. 'Hades' and 'Abraham's bosom' do not describe two compartments of the same place (the realm of the dead), but distinct places, like two wholly divergent anterooms to the final state.

This striking affirmation of an intermediate state in Luke 16:19–31, however, does not stand alone in the New Testament. It is confirmed in several other passages as well. For instance, in Luke 23:43, Jesus, speaking to the criminal on the cross who had requested that Jesus remember him 'when You come in Your kingdom', answered, 'Truly I say to you, today you shall be with Me in Paradise.' Now it might be argued that 'today' in this answer should be read with the expression, 'Truly I say to you'. Thus, Jesus is simply underscoring the time of this pronouncement. Though this is grammatically possible, it is quite unlikely for at least two reasons. First, Jesus would have no contextual reason to stress the fact that he makes this affirmation 'today'. It would be redundant, for example, were I to add the word 'today' in order to underscore the time of my writing this sentence. Second, in other instances in which Jesus uses the formulaic expression, 'Truly I say to you', the word 'today' is not present. There seems, then, to be no legitimate reason to reject the straightforward reading of this text. Read in its context, Jesus is affirming the criminal's fellowship with him immediately upon death in 'paradise'.[1]

[1] The term 'paradise' is also used in the New Testament in 2 Corinthians 12:4 ('this man . . . was caught up to paradise') and Revelation 2:7 ('To him who overcomes, I will give the right to eat

Similarly, in Revelation 7:9–17 the Apostle John provides an account of the circumstance of the saints 'before the throne and before the Lamb' (verse 9) in heaven. In his vision he sees a great multitude which no one could count 'clothed in white robes, and palm branches were in their hands'. When, in the course of the vision's recounting, the question is asked, 'Who are they, and from where have they come'? (verse 13), the answer is given, 'These are the ones who come out of the great tribulation, and they have washed their robes and made them white in the blood of the Lamb' (verse 14). The description of these saints clearly expresses conscious communion with and worship of God, though they are not yet experiencing the final state described in Revelation 21 and 22, since they worship 'day and night in his temple'.[1] This description parallels that of Revelation 6:9–10 where the 'souls of those who had been slain because of the Word of God' are depicted crying out 'with a loud voice, saying, "How long, O Lord, holy and true, wilt Thou refrain from judging and avenging our blood on those who dwell on the earth?"'. It also corresponds to the frequent descriptions in Revelation of departed saints who live in the presence of God and reign with Christ in heaven (cf. *Rev.* 3:12, 21; 4:4; 19:14; 20:4).

In addition to these passages that affirm the believer's conscious fellowship with the Lord in the state intermediate between death and the final state of resurrection glory, other passages speak of the unbelieving and wicked experiencing a state of provisional torment upon death. Echoing the language of Luke 16, with its description of the rich man in

---

from the tree of life, which is in the paradise of God'). It refers to the place of restored fellowship and communion with God, to what we would commonly term 'heaven'.

[1] In Revelation 21 and 22, the new heavens and the new earth do not have a temple (the whole earth has become the temple, the dwelling place of God with his people through the Lamb) and there is no longer any 'night' there.

torment, Christ rebukes the unbelieving in Capernaum in Matthew 11:23, declaring that they 'will go down to Hades' rather than to heaven. In this passage Hades is a place of punishment, reserved for the unbelieving and wicked upon death, a place that anticipates the final punishment of the wicked in hell. This language also corresponds to the language of 2 Peter 2:4 which describes the judgement of God upon disobedient angels who are 'kept for judgement' after being 'cast' into hell by God.

Admittedly, these New Testament affirmations do not warrant any unnecessary speculation about the intermediate state, nor do they provide us a great deal of detail or description of the respective circumstances of believers and unbelievers after death. But they do warrant the general conclusion that believers experience after death a circumstance of provisional blessedness in fellowship with the Lord, and that unbelievers experience after death a circumstance of provisional punishment under the wrath of God. The declaration of the final judgement is anticipated for believers and unbelievers alike, when some will be welcomed into glory and others cast into hell

III. TWO IMPORTANT TEXTS

However, two further New Testament texts demand our attention. These texts explicitly affirm an intermediate state, in which believers will enjoy an intensified communion with the Lord prior to his coming again and the resurrection at the last day. With these texts, the Christian confidence of being ushered immediately into the presence of the Lord is confirmed.

2 CORINTHIANS 5:1–10

The first of these texts is 2 Corinthians 5:1–10, a passage that follows immediately upon the heels of the Apostle Paul's acknowledgement of death before the return of Christ (4:16–18). Though acknowledging this prospect of death and the dissolution of the 'earthly tent' of the body which death inevitably brings, the apostle declares his hope in the provision of a 'building from God, a house not made with hands, eternal in the heavens' (5:1). He also declares his confidence that though death brings a diminishment of the believer's creaturely existence in bodily form, it will not separate the believer from fellowship with the Lord. Indeed, death will bring the believer a fellowship with the Lord that is, in some largely unexplained sense, even greater than that presently enjoyed in the body.

One of the difficulties of this passage is the bold affirmation of verse 1, which seems clearly to refer to the ultimate clothing of the believer with an imperishable body, the resurrection body. What troubles some interpreters is the use of the present tense in this verse ('we have a building from God') which suggests the immediate reception of the resurrection body upon death. But this would not fit with the general biblical teaching that the resurrection body is only given in conjunction with the future resurrection of all believers. Some have suggested, therefore, that the Apostle Paul is describing a provisional body, given to believers in the intermediate state.[1] But neither does this find support elsewhere in Scripture.

Perhaps the best understanding of this verse is to take the use of the present tense as a way of describing a future that is absolutely certain.[2] When the apostle says, 'We have a building from God', he uses this language to describe what is for the believer an 'assured possession', namely, the resurrection body that will be given at the resurrection of the last day.[3]

[1] For example, J. Murray Harris, *Raised Immortal: Resurrection and Immortality in the New Testament* (Grand Rapids: Eerdmans, 1985), pp. 98–101, 138–42.

[2] Herman Ridderbos, *Paul: An Outline of his Theology*, p. 501, n. 35, cites Plummer's observation (*Commentary on Second Corinthians*, p. 144) that 'the present tense is often used as a future, which is absolutely certain'.

[3] John Calvin, in his *Commentary on the Second Epistle of Paul to the Corinthians*, ed. by D. W. Torrance and T. F. Torrance (*Calvin's*

However we take verse 1, for our purposes verses 6–9 more directly address the matter of the intermediate state. After acknowledging in verses 2–5 the diminishment that death brings (the Apostle Paul compares death in these verses to 'being unclothed'), we read:

> Therefore, being always of good courage, and knowing that while we are at home in the body we are absent from the Lord – for we walk by faith, not by sight – we are of good courage, I say, and prefer rather to be absent from the body and to be at home with the Lord. Therefore also we have as our ambition, whether at home or absent, to be pleasing to Him.

The contrast in these verses between 'being at home in the body' and 'being away from the body', and between 'being away from the Lord' and 'being with the Lord', corresponds to the contrast between our present bodily existence and our subsequent bodiless existence after death. This contrast characterizes the respective states of believers before and after death. Thus, these verses affirm that death (being away from the body) means for the believer that he or she will be at home with the Lord. Subsequent to death and prior to the

---

New Testament Commentaries; Grand Rapids: Eerdmans, 1964), p. 67, makes a helpful comment on this verse: 'With this Paul contrasts a building that will last for ever, although it is not clear whether he means by this the state of blessed immortality that awaits believers after death or the incorruptible and glorious body as it will be after the resurrection. Either meaning is quite suitable, but I prefer to take it that the blessed state of the soul after death is the beginning of this building, but its completion is the glory of the final resurrection. This explanation is better supported by the context.' Cf. E. Earle Ellis, *Paul and his Recent Interpreters* (Grand Rapids: Eerdmans, 1961), pp. 37–43, who argues that the apostle is not speaking in this text about the future of the individual believer in the intermediate state. Ellis maintains that the 'house' of which Paul speaks is the corporate and end-time solidarity of all believers with Christ as members of his body; it says nothing directly about the future of the individual believer. See Herman Ridderbos, *Paul: An Outline of his Theology*, pp. 500–505, for a refutation of Ellis' position.

resurrection of the body, believers will enjoy an intensified communion with the Lord.

Though these verses do not provide an opening for all kinds of curious questions about the nature of this being-at-home-with-the-Lord, they do warrant the confession of an intermediate state. The comfort for the believer who walks by faith and not by sight is that he or she will not experience, even in death, a breaking of the communion with Christ which he or she now enjoys by faith. Rather, death will bring a new and more intimate fellowship with Christ than that which is presently known in the body.

PHILIPPIANS 1:21–23

A second important text that affirms an intermediate state is Philippians 1:21–23. Here we find the Apostle Paul making a bold and initially startling declaration about the relative desirability of life and death:

> For to me, to live is Christ, and to die is gain. But if I am to live on in the flesh, this will mean fruitful labor for me; and I do not know which to choose. But I am hard-pressed from both directions, having the desire to depart and be with Christ, for that is very much better.

According to the Apostle Paul, he finds himself torn between two desires. On the one hand, recognising that 'to live is Christ', he finds himself pulled in the direction of continued life in the flesh in which he can fruitfully labour for the churches of Jesus Christ. But on the other hand, recognizing that 'to die is gain', he finds himself pulled in the direction of wanting to depart in order to be with Christ. This latter desire, unlike the faithless desire of the prophet Elijah, for example, who wanted to abandon his calling and die (1 Kings 19:4), is a genuine one, born of the awareness of what death will bring him (and all believers).

The contrast in these verses, like that in 2 Corinthians 5:1–10, is drawn between life in the body and life (after death) apart from the body. Life in the body does not permit the more intensified communion and fellowship with Christ that only death, putting off the body, will bring. Again, though the expression to be 'with Christ' is not explained in any detail, it conveys the idea of a more intimate communion than that presently known or enjoyed. Thus, this text, like those already discussed, contributes to our understanding of the intermediate state as one of an intensified communion with Christ.

What about Purgatory?

Students of the Protestant Reformation are acquainted with the story of Johann Tetzel, the German monk and seller of indulgences who provoked Luther's ire and decision to affix his ninety-five theses to the door of the Castle church in Wittenberg, Germany. They may even recall the infamous slogan by which Tetzel advertised his indulgences: 'The moment the money tinkles in the collection box, a soul flies out of purgatory.'

Though it is not my interest here to trace the career of Tetzel or his practice of selling indulgences, I cite this incident to illustrate the importance of the doctrine of purgatory in the classic Roman Catholic understanding of the intermediate state. However crass and exaggerated Tetzel's practice may have been, even by the standard of medieval Roman Catholic teaching, he represented well the conviction that the souls of those who die in a state of grace ordinarily must endure a period of punishment and purification in purgatory before entering heaven and enjoying the vision of God. At the Council of Trent, called by the Roman Catholic Church to answer the Protestant Reformation, the doctrine of purgatory was defined as a 'dogma' of the church as follows: 'There is a Purgatory, and . . . souls there detained are helped by the suffrages of the faithful, but principally by the acceptable sacrifice of the altar'.[1] Those who opposed

[1] Twenty-Fifth Session, *Canons and Decrees of the Council of Trent*, in *The Creeds of Christendom. Vol. II: The Greek and Latin Creeds*, ed. Philip Schaff (1931; repr. Grand Rapids: Baker Book House, 1985), p. 198.

this dogma were anathematized by the same Council, and all bishops were commanded 'diligently [to] endeavour that the sound doctrine concerning Purgatory, transmitted by the holy Fathers and sacred Councils, be believed, maintained, taught, and everywhere proclaimed by the faithful of Christ'.[1]

Thus, before moving on to the subject of general eschatology, the biblical teaching concerning the future return of Christ and its accompaniments, we are obliged to take one last look at the subject of the intermediate state, particularly as it is represented by the Roman Catholic doctrine of purgatory. Because this doctrine represents a peculiar view of the intermediate state, albeit one which departs from the standard of biblical teaching, it merits our attention before we turn to the great event on the horizon of biblical expectation, the coming again of Jesus Christ.

I. THE DOGMA OF PURGATORY

It is important to realize when treating the doctrine of purgatory that it is a dogma of the Roman Catholic Church. This is not a doctrine or teaching that may or may not be believed by the faithful; it is a doctrine based upon tradition and biblical teaching, that has been infallibly defined and proposed to the faithful as an essential truth. One cannot be a faithful member of the Roman Catholic Church, and certainly not a faithful member of the ordained clergy, and yet deny this teaching. It was first officially defined by the Council of Trent in the period of the Reformation and has been reaffirmed ever since.[2]

---

[1] Twenty-Fifth Session, *Canons and Decrees of the Council of Trent*, in Schaff, *The Greek and Latin Creeds*, p. 198.

[2] Cf. *Catechism of the Catholic Church* (Liguori, Missouri: United States Catholic Conference, Inc. – Libreria Editrice Vaticana, 1994), par. 1032: 'From the beginning the Church has honored the memory of the dead and offered prayers in suffrage for them, above all the Eucharistic sacrifice, so that, thus purified, they may attain the beatific vision of God. The Church also commends almsgiving, indulgences, and works of penance undertaken on behalf of the dead.'

What, then, are the contours of this dogma? What exactly does the Roman Catholic Church's dogma regarding purgatory teach? This dogma teaches that the majority of believers who die in a state of grace go to purgatory, a place of anguish and suffering. Though some believers, the 'saints' who have lived righteous lives and fully satisfied for the temporal penalties of their sins, go directly to heaven, most believers must spend a period of time in purgatory, during which they suffer punishment for their sins and endure a period of cleansing or purification to fit them for heaven. Whereas formerly the emphasis in Catholic writings fell upon suffering punishment for sin's penalties in purgatory, more recently the emphasis has fallen upon purgatory as a place of cleansing or purification.[1]

The importance of purgatory in traditional Roman Catholic teaching rests upon a particular understanding of the role of good works in meriting the reward of eternal life. Some baptized members of the church who fall into mortal sin and thereby from a state of grace, because they have not been restored through the sacrament of penance before death, go immediately to hell. Most believers, however, with the exception of the saints who go immediately to heaven, fail to make full or plenary satisfaction in this life for the temporal penalty of their sins.[2] Purgatory is the place where all

---

[1] *Catechism of the Catholic Church*, par. 1030: 'All who die in God's grace and friendship, but still imperfectly purified, are indeed assured of their eternal salvation; but after death they undergo purification, so as to achieve the holiness necessary to enter the joy of heaven.' The accent in this new Catechism of the Roman Catholic Church falls upon the theme of purification rather than punishment. For a similar emphasis in a recent defence of purgatory, see Zachary J. Hayes, 'The Purgatorial View', in *Four Views on Hell*, ed. William Crockett (Grand Rapids: Zondervan, 1996), pp. 91–118.

[2] It is important to recognize that in traditional Catholic teaching the priest is authorized to remit in Christ's name the eternal penalty for sin in the sacrament of penance. Nevertheless, the priest thereupon stipulates 'satisfactions' that must still be made for the temporal penalty of sin. Purgatory satisfies this temporal judgement and its unmet obligations, not the eternal judgement against sin.

remaining satisfaction for venial sins committed in this life must be paid. Even though all good works and satisfactions are themselves produced by the co-operation of the believer with God's grace, these good works and satisfactions are the necessary prerequisites for entrance into eternal life. Purgatory, in this respect, represents eloquently the Roman Catholic insistence upon the indispensable role of meritorious good works to salvation.

The length of the believer's stay in purgatory, as well as the severity of the punishment suffered, varies. Some endure a longer and more severe suffering than others. The length and severity of the believer's stay in purgatory depends, as we have just noted, on the kind of life the believer lived before death. But it also depends to some extent upon the assistance granted believers in purgatory by their friends on earth. Prayers offered on their behalf, indulgences purchased in their name, and masses spoken for them (for which payment is often made),[1] all contribute to lessening the severity and duration of the believer's suffering in purgatory. When Tetzel sold indulgences in the early sixteenth century, provoking the ire of Luther and the Reformers, he was justifiably promising the friends of departed believers that these indulgences would lessen their stay in purgatory. Though he may have been guilty of a crassly commercial presentation of this practice, even exaggerating the benefits that would accrue to those on whose behalf the indulgence was purchased, he was

---

[1] The Council of Trent for this reason also emphasized the legitimacy of masses offered on behalf of the dead, or masses offered though none of the living faithful are present to receive the body and blood of the Lord. See Twenty-Fifth Session, *Canons and Decrees of the Council of Trent*, in Schaff, *The Greek and Latin Creeds*, pp. 199–206. The whole conception of the mass as an unbloody sacrifice, a propitiatory rite that merits grace, is closely linked to this understanding of purgatory. For a popular study of the dogma of purgatory, written from a Roman Catholic viewpoint, see J. P. Arendzen, *Purgatory and Heaven* (from *What Becomes of the Dead?;* New York: Sheed and Ward, 1951).

nonetheless acting consistently with a teaching that remains an essential part of Catholic dogma to this day.

It should also be added that the pope plays a key role in the administration of purgatory and the determination of the severity and length of the believer's suffering the temporal penalty of sin. It is the pope's prerogative to grant indulgences that not only lighten the severity of the punishment but also terminate it altogether.

These are the main lines of the traditional Roman Catholic dogma of purgatory.[1] There are considerable debates within Catholicism over such matters as the location of purgatory, the nature and quality of the pains suffered, the duration of the purifying process, and the method by which the work of the living benefits those in purgatory. But none of these has been given a dogmatic answer. The essential elements of Catholic teaching are the insistence that most believers need, subsequent to death, to undergo a further period of making satisfaction for the temporal penalty of sin and cleansing before they enjoy the blessed vision of God, and that the duration and severity of this satisfaction are

---

[1] To complete this summary of the Roman Catholic teaching regarding the intermediate state and purgatory, it is necessary to mention the traditional understanding of what are termed the *Limbus patrum* ('the place of the fathers') and the *Limbus infantum* ('the place of infants'). The first of these, the *Limbus patrum*, is the place reserved for the souls of Old Testament saints as they await the coming of Christ and his 'descent into hell', at which he announced to them his victory and secured their release into paradise. The second of these, the *Limbus infantum*, is the place reserved for infants who die still in the guilt and corruption of original sin, without opportunity having been given them through baptism to come to salvation. This *Limbus infantum* is not an intermediate state, but a permanent department of hell, a place of lesser punishment, to which such infants are consigned. Though the teaching regarding the *Limbus patrum* is a settled part of Catholic teaching, there continues to be considerable debate regarding the status and nature of the *Limbus infantum*. See Louis Berkhof, *Systematic Theology*, 4th ed. (Grand Rapids: Eerdmans, 1941, and London: Banner of Truth, 1958), pp. 687–8.

lessened by the assistance of the living who do good works on their behalf.[1]

II. THE BASIS FOR THIS DOGMA

If these are the main lines of the Roman Catholic dogma of purgatory, the question that cannot be bypassed is, On what is it based? What constitutes the ground underneath this dogma that permits the Roman Catholic Church to teach it as dogma to the faithful?

Before evaluating the Scriptural evidence cited in support of this dogma, it is important to recognise the history to its development. In the second century, Justin and Tertullian, two of the church fathers, taught that the dead are waiting in the grave for the consummation. Only in the third century do we find Origen teaching the idea of a particular purification for individuals prior to their ultimate salvation. Origen, however, developed this teaching, which became a germ for the development of a full-fledged doctrine of purgatory, as part of his teaching of the universal salvation of all men (called 'apocatastasis'). It was not until the thirteenth century at the Second Council of Lyons (1274), and the fifteenth century at the Council of Florence (1439), that Roman Catholic teaching on purgatory took full shape. At these Councils, purgatory is clearly understood to be a place of penal and expiatory suffering immediately after death and before entrance into God's presence.

I briefly cite this history because it illustrates one aspect of the weakness of the basis for the dogma of purgatory.

---

[1] The Greek Orthodox church has a doctrine of purgatory, though it is not an essential element of the dogma of the church. This doctrine explicitly rejects the medieval Catholic teaching that the believer suffers a 'material' fire in purgatory. However, it is taught that the prayers of the living and the oblation of the bloodless sacrifice of the body and blood of Christ in the sacrament do aid the dead in their attainment of a blessed resurrection. See the *Longer Catechism of the Eastern Church*, in Schaff, *The Greek and Latin Creeds*, p. 504.

In the famous saying of Vincent of Lérins, a fifth-century theologian, the dogma of the church is defined as that 'which is believed everywhere, always, and by all'. This saying has served historically as a kind of 'rule of thumb' to determine what belongs to the official dogma or teaching of the Roman Catholic Church. The problem is that this rule of thumb is much too stringent to permit purgatory to qualify as a dogma of the church. It simply cannot be shown that it has been everywhere and always and by all believed to be an essential teaching.

But what of the Scriptural evidence for this dogma? Three passages have traditionally been cited in support of this teaching: 2 Maccabees 12:43–45; Matthew 12:32; and 1 Corinthians 3:12–15. Other passages have been cited as well (for example, *Isa.* 4:4, *Mic.* 7:8, *Zech.* 9:11, *Mal.* 3:2, 3, *Matt.* 5:22, 25–26, *Rev.* 21:27); but only the first three approximate to a proof for this dogma.

The first of these passages, 2 Maccabees 12:43–45, is found in one of the apocryphal books of the Old Testament, which are not recognized as canonical or authoritative by the Protestant churches. The two books of Maccabees treat the Jewish struggle for religious and political freedom against the Seleucid kings and are full of apparent exaggerations and moralisms. 2 Maccabees 12:43–45 describes a certain valiant Judas who makes provision for offerings to be taken and an 'expiatory sacrifice' to be made on behalf of 'the dead, so that they might be released from their sin'.[1] Though this passage seems to lend some support for the idea of actions performed on behalf of the dead which release them from

---

[1] *The New Jerusalem Bible, Reader's Edition* (Garden City, New York: Doubleday & Company, Inc., 1968) translates this passage as follows: 'For had he [Judas] not expected the fallen to rise again, it would have been superfluous and foolish to pray for the dead, whereas if he had in view the splendid recompense reserved for those who make a pious end, the thought was holy and devout. Hence, he had this expiatory sacrifice offered for the dead, so that they might be released from sin.'

punishment, it does not come close to proving the dogma of purgatory. For example, the dead on whose behalf sacrifice and prayer are offered include soldiers who have committed the mortal sin of idolatry, a sin which cannot be atoned for in purgatory or by others who act on behalf of the person who dies in such mortal sin. Thus, even this apocryphal text does not support the dogma of purgatory, since it speaks of satisfaction made in purgatory for mortal sin.

The second of these passages, Matthew 12:32, speaks of the sin against the Holy Spirit: 'And whoever shall speak a word against the Son of Man, it shall be forgiven him; but whoever shall speak against the Holy Spirit, it shall not be forgiven him, either in this age, or in the age to come.' Though this text clearly means only to teach that such sin will never be forgiven, it is taken by Roman Catholic exegetes to imply that some sins may be forgiven, not only in this age, but also in the age to come. However, even were this a plausible reading of the text (which it is not), it would still not answer to the need. For since the 'age to come' clearly refers to the age subsequent to Christ's return, this refers to a period that follows purgatory and therefore cannot coincide with it. Purgatory will have ceased to exist, according to Catholic teaching, after the return of Christ and the establishment of the 'age to come'.

The third of these passages, 1 Corinthians 3:12–15, describes a fire of judgement that will reveal and test the works of the righteous. In verses 13–15, we read: 'each man's work will become evident; for the day will show it, because it is to be revealed with fire; and the fire itself will test the quality of each man's work. If any man's work which he has built upon it remains, he shall receive a reward. If any man's work is burned up, he shall suffer loss; but he himself shall be saved, yet so as through fire.' Roman Catholic exegesis of this text argues that this is a description of a literal fire through which 'the souls' of the departed will be cleansed. This fiery cleansing coincides with the state of purgatory.

Here again, a close examination of the text proves the error of this exegesis. This passage describes not the cleansing of the souls of the departed, but the revealing and testing of the works of believers. Furthermore, this passage speaks of the believer being saved 'as through' fire, not 'through' fire in the sense of a literal punishment. Lastly, this passage describes what will occur on 'the day', that is, on the day of judgement when purgatory will be a thing of the past. Really nothing, then, lends itself in this passage to the interpretation traditionally found among Roman Catholic defenders of the dogma of purgatory.

Not only do these most important passages fail to prove the dogma of purgatory, but also the passages cited in addition to them give no support whatever to this dogma. A reading of these passages could only support the dogma of purgatory, were that dogma already presumed and brought to the reading of them. There is, accordingly, no adequate basis for the dogma of purgatory, either in the tradition of the church or in the text of Scripture.

III. THE UNCHRISTIAN CHARACTER OF THIS DOGMA

It is not only the lack of biblical support for this dogma, however, that is so disturbing. It is also the substantially unchristian character of this teaching that must be recognized. Significant aspects of the gospel of salvation through the perfect work of Jesus Christ, our Mediator, are imperilled by this teaching.

First, this dogma shifts the emphasis in our understanding of salvation from God to the believer. The focus of the dogma of purgatory falls upon the believer's activity, co-operating with God's grace to be sure, in performing satisfactions to remit the temporal penalty of sin. Not only must such satisfactions be made in this life – through the sacrament of penance and other good works – but they also extend into the intermediate state in purgatory. Furthermore, only those who escape purgatory are said to be 'the saints', believers who are said to have done 'works of supererogation', that is, works that surpass what is required and accrue to the benefit of others. Likewise, living believers can perform a diversity of good works on behalf of their beneficiaries in purgatory which 'merit' a shortening of their stay in purgatory or the severity of their punishment. All of this smacks of a view of salvation in which the sovereign grace of God is diminished and the meritorious acts of believers are exalted. But this plainly contradicts the Scripture's teaching that sinners are incapable of doing any saving good (cf. *Rom.* 3:21–27; 7:14–25; 8:3) and that God alone is able to save his people to the uttermost (cf. *Psa.* 32:1–2, *Rom.* 7:24–25, *Eph.* 2:8–10, *Titus* 3:4–7, *1 Pet.* 1:19).

Second, the dogma of purgatory, in keeping with this shifting of emphasis from the work of God to the work of man, steals from the glory and perfection of the work of our Saviour. To echo the language of John Calvin, we should do away with all talk of any 'miserable satisfactions' performed by us, even if only done to satisfy the temporal penalty of our sins. Such satisfactions, including the unbloody sacrifices of the mass, are rendered altogether superfluous by the all-sufficient sacrifice and work of atonement Christ has accomplished on behalf of his own (cf. *Heb.* 9:12, 26; 10:14). As the Scripture teaches, 'The blood of Jesus Christ his Son cleanses us from all sin' (*1 John* 1:7; cf. *Heb.* 5:9, *Rev.* 1:5). The inevitable and unhappy fruit of the dogma of purgatory is that it diminishes the gospel of the triumph of God's grace in Christ. Rather than rejoicing in God's grace and mercy, richly lavished upon us in Christ Jesus, believers are taught to divert their eyes to their own and others' works on their behalf.

Third, the concern of the dogma of purgatory, to stress the need for purification and cleansing so as to fit the believer for God's presence, cannot be met by the human satisfactions and good works which this dogma encourages. The believer's cleansing occurs through free justification and inward sanctification by the Holy Spirit (*Rom.* 5:1, *2 Thess.* 2:13). Salvation by grace alone does not militate against the need for cleansing and purification; it only ascribes this cleansing and purification to the powerful working of the Holy Spirit, Who alone is able to cleanse the believer through and through. Christ is given to his people for righteousness and sanctification (*1 Cor.* 1:30). This means that the purification of the believer comes not through purgatory or works of satisfaction, but through the work of the Spirit who writes the law of God upon the heart (*Heb.* 10:16).

Fourth, there is in the Roman Catholic dogma of purgatory the frightening spectre of a church whose authority exceeds the boundaries of what is lawful. The authority of the church in the administration of the gospel is always a ministering authority, an administration of the free grace of God in Jesus Christ. The church has no authority to bind the consciences of believers beyond the Word of God or to impose satisfactions, upon pain of punishment, not required in that Word. Nor does the church (or pope) have the authority to release believers from purgatory. The fact cannot be escaped that the dogma of purgatory grants to the church an unbiblical and cruel tyranny over believers, a tyranny that is at odds with the gospel overtures of grace and mercy. It is impossible to square this dogma with an overture like that found in Isaiah 55:1: 'Ho! Every one who thirsts, come to the waters; and you who have no money come, buy and eat. Come, buy wine and milk without money and without cost.'

More could be said about any one of these problems with the dogma of purgatory. But this should be enough to illustrate how it robs the believer of that comfort which is rightfully his in Jesus Christ. It also conflicts with the blessed hope of an immediate and intensified communion with the Lord upon death in the intermediate state. Against this dogma, it is enough to confess as believers that our only comfort in life and in death is that we belong to our faithful Saviour, who has fully satisfied for all our sins. The preaching of this gospel comfort in our Lord Jesus Christ must over-shadow and displace the unbiblical dogma of purgatory.

Conclusion

When considering the biblical teaching about the intermed-iate state, we should remember the Apostle Paul's citations from the prophecy of Isaiah in 1 Corinthians 2:9: 'Things which eye has not seen and ear has not heard, and which have not entered the heart of man, all that God has prepared for those who love him.' The danger here is that we go beyond what the Bible authorises and begin to speculate in ways that are not helpful to the people of God. There is so much that God has not been pleased to reveal to us about the inter-mediate state.

However, this should not prevent us from receiving with gratitude what God has been pleased to reveal to us in his Word. If we remember what was emphasized in a previous chapter – that the great hope of the believer remains fixed upon the glory of Christ's work in the resurrection at the last day, when the first-fruits of the harvest issue in the full in-gathering – we need not shrink back from confessing that not even death can separate us from the love of God in Christ Jesus. We need not shrink back from the comfort of knowing that believers who 'die in the Lord' are promised an immedi-ate, unbroken, and intensified communion 'with the Lord' in the state intermediate between death and resurrection.

Though death may still be recognized as the believer's 'last enemy', and though at the graveside of believers we may confess together 'the resurrection of the body', believers have every biblical reason to comfort one another with the knowledge that those whose bodies are dissolved and laid in the grave have gone to be with the Lord, which is far better.

This comfort is not a futile shaking of the fist in the face of the inescapable reality of death. It is not the last vestige of Greek thinking that remains like an intruder within the orbit of Christian truth. Rather, it is the confident hope of every believer who can say with the Apostle Paul, 'For me to live is Christ, and to die is gain. . . I am hard-pressed from both directions, having the desire to depart and be with Christ, for that is very much better.'

As the hymn writer well expressed it,

> *I fear no foe, with Thee at hand to bless;*
> *Ills have no weight, and tears no bitterness:*
> *Where is death's sting? Where, grave, thy victory?*
> *I triumph still, if Thou abide with me.*

Henry F. Lyte

PART THREE

The Future of Christ

4

The Second Coming of Christ

IN THE PRECEDING CHAPTER on the intermediate state, we
noted that it has been customary to distinguish between
'individual' and 'general' eschatology. The former addresses
the kind of topics treated thus far, such as physical death,
immortality, and the state of the believer between death and
the resurrection of the body. The latter addresses more
directly the Bible's teaching about the 'end times' or the
future of all things. Within the orbit of general eschatology
are found such topics as the expectation of Christ's return or
second advent, the 'signs of the times', the millennium, the
resurrection of the body, the final judgement and the final
state.

The Centrepiece of Biblical Expectation

To introduce the subject of general eschatology, we begin by
focusing upon the biblical teaching regarding the return of
Christ. This is the great centrepiece of biblical hope and
expectation for the future. All of the other subjects that will
demand our attention are like so many points on the circum-
ference of a circle, each related in its own way to what lies at
the centre. Whether the topic is the nature or timing of the
millennium, the 'signs of the times', the resurrection of the

body, the final judgement, or the final state, each finds its focus and meaning in relation to this great and impending event which consummates the present epoch in the history of redemption. It is only fitting, then, that we orient ourselves to the broad subject of 'general eschatology' by beginning with a survey of the Bible's teaching regarding Christ's return.

I. THREE COMMON TERMS

One way to grasp what is basic to the biblical understanding of Christ's return is to note that three common terms are employed in the New Testament to describe its nature. Though some have attempted to make too much of the difference between these terms, even arguing that they refer to different stages in the return of Christ, it is evident that they all refer to the same event.[1] These terms are 'revelation' (*apokalupsis*), 'appearance' (*epiphaneia*), and 'coming' (*parousia*). Though it is impossible to cite all the instances in the New Testament in which these terms are employed to describe Christ's coming again, the pervasiveness of the theme of Christ's return should be readily evident from the following sampling.

The term 'revelation', which literally means the 'removal of a veil', disclosing an object otherwise concealed from view,

[1] In Chapters 8 and 10, we will consider the dispensationalist view of Christ's return. Dispensationalism commonly distinguishes between Christ's 'parousia', which occurs at the time of the 'rapture' of believers and prior to the period of tribulation, and Christ's 'revelation' or 'appearing', which occurs after the tribulation and before the establishment of the millennial kingdom. Though this view is not our primary interest here, it rests in part upon the unwarranted idea, often expressed in earlier dispensational literature, that these terms describe different events, or at least different stages of one event. For a summary of the dispensational view of a two-staged second coming of Christ, see Paul D. Feinberg, 'The Case for the Pretribulational Rapture Position', in *The Rapture: Pre-, Mid-, or Post-Tribulational*, by Gleason L. Archer Jr., *et al.* (Grand Rapids: Zondervan, 1984), pp. 45–86; and Herman A. Hoyt, 'Dispensational Premillennialism', in *The Meaning of the Millennium: Four Views*, ed. Robert G. Clouse (Downers Grove, IL: Intervarsity, 1977), p. 91.

is often used in the New Testament to describe Christ's return. In 1 Corinthians 1:7–8, the Apostle Paul writes, 'Therefore you do not lack any spiritual gift as you eagerly wait for our Lord Jesus Christ to be revealed. He will keep you strong to the end, so that you will be blameless on the day of our Lord Jesus Christ' (NIV) .Here the apostle parallels the revelation of Jesus Christ with what he terms the 'end' or the 'day of our Lord Jesus Christ'. In a vivid passage in 2 Thessalonians 1:7 we read that the suffering and militant church will be granted 'rest . . . when the Lord Jesus is revealed from heaven in blazing fire with His powerful angels' (NIV). This language of Christ's return as a revelation of the glory and majesty of his person is also found in similar passages in which the people of God are encouraged to continue steadfast in the faith in the hope of the day of Christ's coming (cf. *1 Pet.* 1:5, 13; 4:13; 5:1, *2 Thess.* 2:3, 6 ,8).

In language which belongs to the same arena of discourse as that of 'revelation', the coming again of Christ is also termed an 'appearing' (the word used is one from which we get the word 'epiphany'). Christ's coming will mean that he will be visibly seen by all whom he comes to judge in righteousness and truth. Christ himself, in Matthew 24:30, speaks of how 'the sign of the Son of Man will appear in the sky, and the nations of the earth will mourn. They will see the Son of Man coming on the clouds of the sky, with power and great glory.' When the Apostle Paul encourages Timothy in the way of obedience, he does so by reminding him of the 'appearing of our Lord Jesus Christ' (*1 Tim.* 6:14). In 2 Thessalonians 2:8 the description of the 'man of lawlessness' concludes with the confident declaration that the Lord Jesus will destroy him 'by the appearance of his coming'. Frequently, references to the 'appearing' of the Lord Jesus are used to encourage believers to remain faithful to the end (cf. *2 Tim.* 4:8, *Titus* 2:13, *1 Pet.* 5:4, *Col.* 3:4, *1 John* 2:28; 3:2), or to warn of the judgement that awaits the unbelieving when he comes (*2 Tim.* 4:1).

The third term, 'coming', or parousia, is the most technical of the three terms. Used in pre-Christian literature to describe the formal visitation of an emperor, king, or person of prominence, it is often used in the New Testament to designate the great event anticipated by believers, when Christ the King returns to judge the living and the dead and complete his work of bringing all things into subjection to the Father.

This language is used several times in Matthew 24, in Christ's discourse given in response to the disciple's question, 'and what will be the sign of your coming and of the end of the age?' (verse 3; also verses 27, 37, 39). It is also frequently found in the epistles of the Apostle Paul. In 1 Corinthians 15, the 'coming' of Christ coincides with the believer's participation in the resurrection harvest, of which Christ's resurrection was the 'first-fruits' (verse 23). The coming of Christ serves to heighten the exhortation to faithfulness and blamelessness on the part of his people, who are encouraged to be prepared for his coming (cf. *1 Thess.* 2:19; 5:23, *James* 5:7, 8, *1 John* 2:28). Like the earlier references to Christ's 'revelation' or 'appearing', the language of his 'coming' is also used to warn those who will be liable to judgement and condemnation (*2 Thess.* 2:8, *2 Pet.* 3:12). Other passages employ this language in a highly technical and generalized sense, as a short-hand designation of the great event of Christ's return (cf. *1 Thess.* 4:15, *2 Thess.* 2:1, *2 Pet.* 1:16; 3:4).

In addition to these and other passages that speak of the 'revelation', 'appearing', or 'coming' of the Lord Jesus Christ, others employ less common, though alternative, designations of the same event. It is sometimes simply called 'the end' (for example, *Matt.* 24:6, 14, *1 Cor.* 1:8; 15:24; *2 Cor.* 1:13–14). Elsewhere it is described as 'the end of the ages' (*Matt.* 13:39, 40, 49; 24:3; 28:20). In several passages, 'the day' is used as a technical phrase with various modifiers, such as 'the day of judgement' (*1 Cor.* 3:13, *2 Pet.* 2:9), 'the day of the Lord' (*1 Cor.* 5:5), 'the day of God' (*2 Pet.* 3:12), and 'that day' (*Luke* 10:12).

Even though these verses represent only a sample of the biblical passages which speak of Christ's return, they provide a basis for drawing some preliminary conclusions about the nature and character of this event. Each of these conclusions is encapsulated in 2 Thessalonians 1:6–10, a passage which can serve as a specimen of biblical teaching regarding Christ's return:

> For after all it is only just for God to repay with affliction those who afflict you, and to give relief to you who are afflicted and to us as well when the Lord Jesus shall be revealed from heaven with His mighty angels in flaming fire, dealing out retribution to those who do not know God and to those who do not obey the gospel of our Lord Jesus. And these will pay the penalty of eternal destruction, away from the presence of the Lord and from the glory of His power, when He comes to be glorified in His saints on that day, and to be marveled at among all who have believed – for our testimony to you was believed.

First, the return of Christ will be an event, at the close of the present age, in which the present splendour, honour and authority that belong to the risen and ascended Lord will be visibly, personally and publicly displayed in his being revealed from heaven. The return of Christ is not first of all an event that promises relief and comfort to the beleaguered people of God in this world. It means first of all the revelation of the triumph and consummation of the reign of the mediatorial king, the Lord Jesus Christ, who is already by his Spirit and Word bringing all things into subjection to himself (*1 Cor.* 15:25–28).

The outstanding and unifying thread in the biblical terms commonly employed to describe this event is this idea of the revelation and disclosure of who Jesus is and what he has done, in all the glory and power conferred upon him at his ascension to the Father's right hand. What is presently only known to believers by faith will then be an object of sight: that God has given Christ a name which is above every name, crowning him with glory and honour at his right hand, and entrusting to him the authority to govern all history in the interest of his church-gathering work. At Christ's return his present mediatorial reign will be concluded and a public demonstration will be given of his glory and dominion. What is presently concealed (and known only to faith on the basis of the Word of God) will then be revealed. Both those who love the Lord and long for his appearing and those who are his enemies, indeed even those who pierced him, will see him in all of his splendour and authority in that day (cf. *Acts* 1:11; *Rev*. 1:1).

For this reason, it is a profound deviation from biblical teaching to detract in any way from the truth that Christ's return will be personal and visible, a real occurrence marking the end of the present epoch of history. Thus, the so-called 'fundamentalists' were right in the early decades of the twentieth century, when they insisted that the bodily and literal return of Christ from heaven was a fundamental doctrine of the Christian faith. They correctly discerned, for example, when a large number of liberal Presbyterian ministers signed the 'Auburn Affirmation' in 1923, declaring that the visible, bodily return of Christ is only a 'theory' and not an essential component of biblical expectation, that one of the cardinal doctrines of the Christian faith was imperilled.[1]

---

[1] For a sketch of the history of the Auburn Affirmation, written from a perspective partly sympathetic to its signatories, see Lefferts A. Loetscher, *The Broadening Church* (Philadelphia: University of Pennsylvania, 1954), pp. 117–120. This 'Auburn Affirmation', which takes its name from Auburn, New York, the place of its origin, was a response to the action of the 1923 General Assembly of the (northern) Presbyterian Church, declaring five doctrines to be essential doctrines of the Christian faith. These doctrines were: the infallibility of the Bible, the virgin birth of Jesus Christ, Christ's substitutionary atonement on the cross, Christ's bodily resurrection and his mighty miracles. The Auburn Affirmationists declared the insistence upon the 'literal truth' of these doctrines to be a fundamentalist attempt to impose upon others their particular 'theories' regarding them. With

Second, to use an expression from Titus 2:13, the return of Christ is the blessed hope of the church of Jesus Christ and every true child of God. The children of God are people who can be defined as those who are 'looking for the blessed hope and the appearing of the glory of our great God and Saviour, Christ Jesus'.

It is interesting to notice how the revelation of Christ is described in 2 Thessalonians 1:7 as a revelation from heaven. This reminds us that the hope of every Christian ultimately lies not in some political programme or party, not in some new strategy for world evangelisation, not in some denominational structure or institution, not in some economic system, not in some 'war to end all wars', not in some educational programme or psychology, not in the power of modern technology, but only in the Lord who will come bringing full redemption from heaven to earth. That is why the *Heidelberg Catechism*, when it describes the comfort of Christ's return to 'judge the living and the dead', speaks of the believer as one who 'with uplifted head' looks for the coming of his Saviour from heaven.

Perhaps this is the reason for so little talk about or expectation of the return of Christ in many contemporary churches. Many churches betray by their teaching and practice a triumphalism that says 'we will bring in the kingdom of God in history by dint of our own efforts'. Or a horizontalism is often present which says 'we will build and expand the kingdom through feeding and clothing the poor, advocating social justice, and fighting oppression'. Often a humble awareness is absent of the church's powerlessness to bring about the kingdom of God on earth, an awareness

the so-called 'fundamentalists', however, we must insist that the Bible teaches as reality, or 'fact', the bodily and glorious return of Christ at the end of the age. This does not mean, of course, that the sum of the Christian faith can be reduced to several fundamentals, as has sometimes been true of those who claim to be fundamentalists.

which compels believers to look for their King to come from heaven to destroy his and his people's enemies and to take 'all his chosen ones to himself into heavenly joy and glory'. Admittedly, the expectation of Christ's return from heaven could give birth to an other-worldly piety and passivity in the face of this world's ills. Nevertheless, from a biblical perspective the return of Christ must always be the great and ultimate focus of the believer's hope for the full establishment of the kingdom of God.

Third, the biblical descriptions of Christ's return often undergird urgent exhortations to constant wakefulness and eager expectation. Believers who might be tempted to despair under the weight of persecution are encouraged by the prospect of Christ's return, when he will grant them relief from their present distress and victory over their enemies, who are also his. Other believers who might be tempted to apostatize or lag in their zeal for the cause of the gospel are also warned to live a life worthy of their calling, recognizing that Christ will come to judge the living and the dead and to deal with all according to what they have done in the body (2 Cor. 5:10). These frequent exhortations, buttressed by the certain prospect of Christ's return, strike a fine balance between words of encouragement in the midst of present distress and words of warning in the context of the temptation to lose hope or fall away. They stress the truth that the Christian life is always framed by the ascension of Christ on the one hand, and his coming again on the other (*Acts* 1:11).

Fourth, the promise of Christ's return, which brings such encouragement to the believing child of God, is invariably understood to be a fearful prospect for the wicked. When the Apostle Paul writes to encourage the church in Thessalonica with the promise of Christ's revelation from heaven, he describes the returning Christ as coming with 'His mighty angels in flaming fire, dealing out retribution to those who do not know God and to those who do not obey the gospel of our Lord Jesus'.[1] The return of Christ is awe-inspiring and terrible in its consequences for the impenitent and unbelieving. As the Apostle John describes it in Revelation 1:7, 'Behold, he is coming with the clouds, and every eye will see him, even those who pierced him; and all the tribes of the earth will mourn over him.' The consequences of the Lord's return for the wicked are such as to lend great urgency to the preaching of the gospel and the call to faith and repentance.

Admittedly, any one of these features of the biblical understanding of Christ's return and its implications could be further elaborated. These, however, are the main emphases found in the biblical texts. Many of them will surface more directly as we travel through the biblical terrain relating to Christ's return and the subject of general eschatology. They provide us at least an initial glimpse of the great future of Christ, when he comes again to judge the living and the dead.

A Consummating Event

The event of Christ's return is, then, the great centrepiece of biblical expectation for the future. All lines of history converge in the event of Christ's triumphant return from heaven to conclude his mediatorial reign (*1 Cor.* 15:28) and demonstrate his kingly rule over all things for the sake of the church.

Unfortunately, though few Christian believers would dispute this claim, little unanimity exists among them regarding the circumstances that will precede, accompany, or follow Christ's return. Perhaps no area of biblical teaching is as disputed as that which pertains to the future and the return

---

[1] Reflection upon this text suggests that those who have difficulty with the 'imprecatory' Psalms, that is, the Psalms in which the believer prays for God's judgement to fall upon his and the Lord's enemies (for example *Psa.* 137), cannot escape the difficulty by running to the New Testament. The biblical descriptions of Christ's return and its consequences for the wicked indicate that any believer who longs for Christ's appearing, also thereby longs for the overthrow and condemnation of the unbelieving and wicked.

of Christ at the end of the age. To anticipate a topic that we will consider in more detail later, there are diverse views of the so-called millennium, or thousand-year reign of Christ, mentioned in Revelation 20. These views often represent profoundly different perspectives on the return of Christ, the meaning of the present period in the history of redemption, and the course of future events.

Two areas of dispute that we cannot avoid, even at the outset of our treatment of the Bible's teaching about the future, relate directly to the expectation of Christ's return. The first of these has to do with the question whether Christ's return is a consummating event, an event that marks the close of the present age, concluding Christ's work of redemption and inaugurating the state of God's eternal kingdom. Will Christ's return be accompanied by the resurrection of the dead, the just and the unjust, and the judgement of all people (cf. *John* 5:28–29)? Or will it be an event that only inaugurates a new phase in the history of redemption, possibly a millennial period of one thousand years in which Christ will reign on earth?

The second of these areas of dispute has to do with the time of Christ's return. If the return of Christ is an event that is at the centre of biblical expectation for the future, can we know anything of its imminence, even to the point of knowing perhaps when it will occur? Throughout the history of the Christian church, there have been repeated attempts to date the precise time of Christ's return. The question is whether such attempts are misguided and illegitimate, or are warranted by the teaching of Scripture.

In this section, we will take up the first of these questions, whether the event of Christ's return is an event that draws history to a close. In the next section, we will take up the second, whether we may attempt to determine the time of Christ's return. After these introductory matters regarding Christ's return have been considered, we will turn in the following chapters to the subject of the 'signs of the times'.

I. A COMMENT ON THE ALTERNATIVE

Before presenting the biblical case for the return of Christ as an event that closes the present age, I would like to elaborate a little on the alternative to this view. Why do some Christians maintain that the return of Christ is not a consummating event at the end of the age? Since many features of the Bible's teaching about the future, including the subject of the 'signs of the times', make sense only on the assumption that Christ's return is the event that will conclude the present age, it will be helpful to address this question at the beginning of our consideration of general eschatology.

Now admittedly, for many this question may not be pressing. Those who are familiar with the Apostles' Creed know that it speaks of Jesus Christ being presently seated at the right hand of the Father, 'whence he shall come to judge the living and the dead'. The simple, straightforward understanding of this article regarding Christ's return is that it will occur at the end of the age and mark the close of the history of redemption. When Christ comes, he will immediately judge the living and the dead, and the eternal state of God's kingdom will commence. Christ's return is, accordingly, commonly taken to be a consummating event, an event that closes the present age.

However, this is strongly disputed by those who favour what are commonly known as premillennialist and dispensationalist views of the history of redemption. These views share the conviction that Christ's return will occur in history, sometime in the near or more distant future, but it will not conclude present history. Rather, it will only inaugurate the period of the millennial kingdom, only after which will the present age be closed. Both of these views are pre-millennialist in the specific sense that they regard Christ's return as an event that will precede a historical millennium on earth. Only at the end of the millennium, one thousand years after Christ's return, will the consummation of history occur, the judgement of all human beings take place, and the final state commence.

THE PROMISE OF THE FUTURE

In Dispensationalism, this premillennial conception of Christ's return has often included the view that Christ will first come secretly for believers at his coming 'for the saints', and only after the period of tribulation will Christ be publicly revealed at his coming 'with the saints'. In this view Christ's return will be a distinctly two-phased event, and even at the second phase of Christ's return, present history will not be concluded but commence a new and millennial phase. Though there are other aspects of these views – including the insistence within Dispensationalism that the millennium will mark a period in history in which God's special purpose for the Jews will resume and be fulfilled – this common feature, the notion that Christ's return will not be to judge the living and the dead at the end of history, is what we are concerned to address.[1]

II. BIBLICAL EVIDENCE

Both of these views are at odds with the teaching of the Bible. The conviction that the return of Christ marks the close of

[1] As noted above, in the older literature of Dispensationalism a sharp distinction was drawn between Christ's parousia, his 'coming for his saints', and Christ's revelation or appearing, his 'coming with his saints'. The first of these comings was identified with the 'secret rapture' allegedly taught in 1 Thessalonians 4; the second of them was regarded as a public event, inaugurating the millennium. Though it was formerly argued that the different terms used for Christ's second coming reflected clearly these two phases, it is generally acknowledged today, even by many dispensationalists, that no sharp distinction can be drawn between the terms 'parousia', 'appearing' and 'revelation'. It should also be noted that historic Dispensationalism was predominantly 'pre-tribulational', viewing the first coming of Christ as occurring before a seven-year period of tribulation. However, some within Dispensationalism teach a 'mid-tribulational' rapture and a 'post-tribulational' rapture (hence the short-hand references to 'pre-tribs', 'mid-tribs' and 'post-tribs'). For a refutation of the view that Christ's return will occur in two phases, see George E. Ladd, *The Blessed Hope* (Grand Rapids: Eerdmans, 1956); and Robert H. Gundry, *The Church and the Tribulation* (Grand Rapids: Zondervan, 1973).

the present age, not only enjoys favour among many Christians but also remains the best understanding of what the Bible teaches about Christ's return.

What biblical evidence supports the view that Christ's return will be a consummating event? Several strands of biblical evidence, when woven together, constitute a compelling case for viewing this as an end-time event in the strict sense.

First, in the New Testament Gospels, Christ's coming again or revelation is viewed as an open, public event, at which time the future kingdom of God and the salvation of the people of God will be realized.

When Christ instructs his disciples about the subject of his return in Matthew 24:27 and Luke 17:24, he warns them against deceivers who will come proclaiming to be Christ or declaring that he is 'here or there'. The disciples should not be deceived when this occurs because, as Christ teaches them, his coming will be as public and visible as the lightning striking across the sky from one end to the other. Furthermore, the Gospels use the terms of Christ's 'coming' and his 'revelation' as synonyms for the same event (*Matt.* 24:37–40, *Luke* 17:30). There is no hint that these terms might describe different aspects of Christ's return, aspects that are distinguishable in time so as to allow for an intervening period of tribulation or even a literal, earthly reign of Christ for a period of one thousand years. It is also instructive to notice how Christ's teaching about his return in the Gospels includes the promise that it will signal the inauguration of God's eternal kingdom and the full redemption of all his people (*Matt.* 24:33, *Luke* 21:27–28, 31).

Second, at the coming of Christ, there will be an immediate and simultaneous judgement of both the just and the unjust.

In 2 Thessalonians 1:6–10, we find one of the more vivid accounts in Scripture of the return or 'revelation' of Christ and its consequences for believer and unbeliever alike. In these verses the Apostle Paul promises the beleaguered believers of Thessalonica that they will be granted 'rest' at the revelation of Christ from heaven. However, for the unbeliever Christ's revelation with the 'angels of his power in blazing fire' promises only a fearful prospect of punishment. When Christ is revealed, he will 'deal out retribution to those who do not know God and to those who do not obey the gospel of our Lord Jesus'. At Christ's return the unbelieving will 'pay the penalty of eternal destruction, away from the presence of the Lord and from the glory of His power, when He comes to be glorified in His saints on that day, and to be marveled at among all who have believed. . .' The different consequences of Christ's revelation for the believing and unbelieving make it quite evident that the event of Christ's return will close the present age and introduce the final state.[1]

Third, the return of Christ is described in the New Testament as the termination or ultimate end point of the believer's hope for the future.

Frequently, when the final hope of Christian believers is described in the New Testament, the event referred to is the event of Christ's return. There is no suggestion that, when Christ returns, this will only mark the commencement of a somewhat different phase in the course of redemptive history, at the end of which still lies another consummating event. In 1 Corinthians 1:7–8, for example, the Apostle Paul holds out as the object of the believer's hope for the future, the certainty of Christ's revelation. He describes the believers in Corinth as those who are 'awaiting eagerly the revelation of our Lord Jesus Christ, who shall also confirm you to the end, blameless in the day of our Lord Jesus Christ'.

In several other passages that use a diversity of expressions to refer to Christ's return, the believer's reward and anticipated salvation are directly linked to the return of Christ. Whether it be called 'the day of Christ Jesus' (*Phil.* 1:6,10), the 'coming' of Christ (*1 John* 2:28), 'that day' (*2 Tim.* 4:8),

---

[1] The same coincidence of the judgement and final state of the just and the unjust is taught in John 5:28–29, a text cited earlier.

or 'His appearing and kingdom' (*2 Tim*. 4:1), no other future event is in the believer's line of vision than that of Christ's return. To suggest that Christ's return only initiates a new phase of his ongoing work in history would be to belie all that these passages promise about the coming again of Christ.

Fourth, at the coming of Christ, there will be a 'rapture' of the living and the dead leading to the resurrection transformation of all believers.

In one of the more controversial passages relating to the return of Christ, 1 Thessalonians 4:13–18, which speaks of a 'rapture' or of believers being 'caught up' with Christ in the air at his coming from heaven, the return of Christ brings for all believers an everlasting communion with the Lord. Though this passage is one that we will consider again in connection with an evaluation of Dispensationalism, here it is only necessary to note that Christ's return is described as the final, consummating event so far as the future of all believers is concerned. When Christ comes from heaven, he will come with those saints who died or 'fell asleep' before his coming. These departed saints who will come with Christ, together with all saints who are alive at his coming, 'will meet the Lord in the air'. 'Thus', says the Apostle Paul by way of conclusion, 'we shall always be with the Lord.' The natural reading of this text confirms that Christ's return from heaven will consummate the present course of history, inaugurating the final state for all believers, those who have fallen asleep before Christ's coming as well as those who are still alive.

And fifth, the return of Christ will bring a number of accompaniments, not the least of which is God's creation of a new heavens and earth.

In addition to the preceding lines of biblical evidence, it is noteworthy that several biblical descriptions of Christ's coming indicate that it will introduce the final state of the new heavens and new earth. In 2 Peter 3:3–13, a familiar passage which speaks of God's patience in delaying the return of Christ so as to provide occasion for many to repent and come to a knowledge of the truth, the coming of Christ is directly linked with a fiery purification of the earth, a judgement that will befall all people, and the consequent creation of a new heavens and a new earth. According to this passage, the Lord's coming will be sudden and unexpected – like the arrival of a thief in the night for the wicked. This coming will bring about the passing away of the present heavens and the production of a 'new earth wherein righteousness dwells'.

Likewise, in Romans 8:17–25, the Apostle Paul describes believers (and even the creation itself) as awaiting the time when there will be a full deliverance from sin and its effects. Believers are described in this passage as those who are awaiting 'the freedom of the glory of the children of God' (verse 21), when the curse is lifted from the creation and all the miseries and frustrations arising from the presence of sin will be removed. The fulfilment of this expectation is joined directly with expressions like: the believer's being 'glorified with Christ' (verse 17), the 'glory about to be revealed unto them' (verse 18), 'the revelation of the sons of God' (verse 19), 'the freedom of the glory of the children of God' (verse 21), and 'the adoption, the redemption of the body' (verse 23). All of these expressions show that the fulfilment of the believer's hope – and that of the whole creation's – will occur simultaneously, at the time of that great event that concludes the history of redemption, the return of Christ.[1]

---

[1] Another text that might be mentioned here is 1 Corinthians 15:22–28. This text speaks of the 'end' that will come after Christ's 'coming' (verses 23–24), indicating that the return of Christ will conclude his present mediatorial reign. However, many premillennialists interpret this text differently, maintaining that there is a period of time – the millennium – between Christ's coming and the end. See Cyrus I. Scofield, ed., *The New Scofield Reference Bible*, editorial committee E. Schuyler English et al. (New York: Oxford University Press, 1967), note on 1 Corinthians 15:24. The *New Scofield Reference Bible* represents a revised or modified version of the classic Dispensationalism

Believers have every biblical reason, therefore, to continue to hold to the simplest understanding of the article in the Apostles' Creed, 'whence he shall come to judge the living and the dead'. This article links Christ's coming with the judgement of all human beings at the close of the present age. In doing so it echoes the biblical teaching we have been considering.

When believers today expectantly look to the future, anticipating the return of Christ, they should do so as those who are convinced this will mark the end of the present period of history and inaugurate the final state. All that believers hope for in respect to the future finds its focus in this consummating event, an event that will fulfil all the promises of God that have their 'yes' and 'amen' in Christ.

Whose Time No One Knows

A strong impulse exists among students of the Bible's teaching about the future to date the return of Christ. This is one of the questions that must be addressed at the outset of any consideration of general eschatology, the Bible's teaching about the future of all things. May we legitimately attempt to determine whether Christ's return will take place in the near or distant future? And may we even go so far as to set a time for Christ's coming and allow that time to shape our conduct in the period before it?

That this is not simply an academic question has been illustrated recently through the publication of two books by Harold Camping, president of Family Radio and a well-known commentator and Bible teacher. These books, bearing the revealing titles, *1994?* and *Are You Ready?*,[1] openly defend the thesis that we may, even must, determine the date of Christ's

---

represented by the original *Scofield Reference Bible*, ed. C. I. Scofield (New York: Oxford University Press, 1909). This interpretation will be treated in more detail later, when we address the subject of Premillennialism in Chapters 8, 10, and 11.

[1] New York: Vantage Press, 1992 and 1993, respectively.

return. The date of Christ's return in Camping's reckoning was to be the month of September, 1994. Though it is not my purpose to review Camping's argument here, the fact that he would attempt to date the return of Christ illustrates how the temptation to do so continues to overcome many believers.[1]

I mention this in order to show how important this question is. We cannot avoid dealing with the question whether the Bible gives us information about or any clues concerning the 'when' of Christ's return. What constitutes a biblical position on this question? Despite the curiosity about this on the part of many people, we may not excuse their attempts to predict a date for it, if the Bible warns us against this practice.

I. THE 'DELAY' OF CHRIST'S COMING?

Before dealing with the biblical passages which speak about the impropriety of dating Christ's return, we need to consider whether the Bible gives any evidence for a delay of Christ's coming.

Many radical interpreters of the Bible have argued, for example, that the New Testament itself contains evidence for such a delay. Indeed, these interpreters sometimes argue that there are contradictions within the New Testament. Some passages, they allege, teach that Christ's return would occur within the lifetime of the first generation of believers, and other passages teach that it has been postponed. Jesus himself taught – so it is claimed – that he would return within the lifetime of his disciples, only to be proven wrong by the subsequent course of events. The Apostle Paul similarly is said to have changed his view on the time of Christ's return. Though Paul's earlier epistles taught Christ's return within

[1] See my review of the first of these books, *1994?*, in *The Outlook* ('1994?: Another Misguided Attempt to Date the Return of Our Lord', vol. 43/8 [1993], pp. 14–17). Popular defenders of Dispensationalism like Pat Robertson and Hal Lindsey maintain, for example, that the establishment of Israel as a nation in 1948 is a sign of the imminence of Christ's return in the present generation.

his lifetime, some of his later epistles express a different point of view.[1]

To see whether this suggestion is valid, we need to consider several passages in the Gospels and in the epistles of the Apostle Paul that speak of the time of Christ's return. In this way, the claim of contradiction within the writings of the New Testament can be tested.

In the Gospels roughly three types of passages speak of the time of Christ's return. Some passages speak of it as an event that is imminent or very soon, possibly within the lifetime of those to whom Christ originally spoke. Other passages speak of it as an event that will only occur at some future time, after certain events that must precede it have occurred. Still other passages speak of it at an unknown or unknowable time in the future.

II. Christ's coming is imminent

Among passages of the first type, three are especially important. They are Mark 9:1 (parallels in Luke 9:27 and Matt. 16:28), Matthew 24:34 (parallel in Mark 13:30), and Matthew 10:23.

In the first of these passages, Mark 9:1, we read that Jesus said to his disciples, 'Truly, I say to you, there are some standing here who will not taste death before they see the kingdom of God come with power.' Similar and parallel statements are found in Luke 9:27, where Jesus is reported to have said that some would not taste death 'before they see the kingdom of God', and in Matthew 16:28, where Jesus speaks of 'the Son of Man coming in his kingdom'.

---

[1] For a representation of this critical view of a 'delay' of the *parousia*, see Oscar Cullmann, *Salvation in History*, trans. S. G. Sowers (New York: Harper and Row, 1967), pp. 214–5; and Werner Kümmel, *Promise and Fulfilment*, trans. Dorothea M. Barton (London: SCM, 1957), pp. 59–61. See G. C. Berkouwer, *The Return of Christ*, trans. James Van Oosterom (Grand Rapids: Eerdmans, 1972), chap. 3, 'Crisis of Delay', pp. 65–95, for an extensive discussion of this view in the context of modern discussions of biblical eschatology.

Those who speak of a 'delay' of Christ's coming typically argue that in this text and its parallels Christ is teaching that he will return within the lifetime of many to whom he first spoke these words. They claim that when Christ speaks of his 'coming with power', he is speaking of the great event of his return at the end of the age. Since Christ did not return within the lifetime of those to whom he first spoke these words, he was mistaken about the imminence of his coming.

Though this understanding of the text has a superficial attractiveness, it would be better to understand this text and its parallels as a reference to the events of Christ's resurrection, ascension and outpouring of his Spirit at Pentecost. In each of these events, there was a dramatic demonstration of the power of Christ and his kingdom, and in each of them Christ's powerful and living presence with his people was realized. Since these passages speak particularly of the coming of the kingdom of God within the lifetime of those to whom Jesus' words were spoken, it is best to understand them as references to these events in which the power of Christ was disclosed (cf. *Rom.* 1:4).

Of course, this does not exclude the possibility that the 'coming' of God's kingdom referred to in this text also includes the great event of Christ's second coming when the kingdom of God will be fully realised. After all, the events of Christ's resurrection, ascension and Pentecost, all of which occurred within the lifetime of those to whom this promise was first made, are events which form one complex with the great event of Christ's return at the end of the age. The resurrection is, for example, in the strictest sense an 'end-time' event; it represents the 'first-fruits' of the resurrection harvest which is yet to come (*1 Cor.* 15).[1]

The second passage where the imminence or 'soon-ness' of

[1] This has led some interpreters of these texts to speak of a 'prophetic foreshortening'. Christ speaks of one event, his 'coming', which actually has a twofold fulfilment in its initial ('first-fruits') and final phases ('harvest'). So intimately linked are these phases that the first can do 'double duty', including within itself a reference to the

Christ's return seems to be taught in the Gospels is Matthew 24:34: 'Truly, I say to you, this generation will not pass away until all these things take place' (parallel in Mark 13:30). This kind of passage is said to show clearly that Jesus believed that his coming again would occur within the lifetime of the generation to whom he first spoke these words.

In answer to the higher critics reading of this passage, some Reformed interpreters have pointed to two important features of Christ's words in their context. First, the language, 'this generation', might be translated as 'this kind of generation'. Because Jesus elsewhere qualifies 'this generation' as an 'evil' (*Matt.* 12:45, *Luke* 11:29) or 'adulterous' (*Matt.* 12:39; 16:4) generation, he may have been saying that his coming would not take place until the evil generation of his day as well as ours had passed away and all things been fulfilled. The reference to 'this generation' may include all generations which share the quality of being 'evil' or 'adulterous', including the generation living today. Second, when Jesus speaks of 'all of these things' taking place, he seems to be referring to all the events that must occur before the event of his second coming. Because 'all of these things' include such things as the preaching of the gospel to all the nations, it does not seem likely that Jesus would have meant his words to be restricted to the generation alive when these words were first spoken.[1] On this understanding of the text, Jesus was

---

second. Thus, the 'coming' of the kingdom of God in the resurrection of Jesus Christ is inseparably joined with the return of Christ in glory. You might say that the resurrection is a 'preview' of the last day; they are not so much two distinct events, as they are aspects of one great event – the coming of the kingdom. Cf. Herman Ridderbos, *The Coming of the Kingdom*, pp. 498–510.

[1] For example, Anthony Hoekema, *The Bible and the Future*, p. 117: 'By "this generation", then, Jesus means the rebellious, apostate, unbelieving Jewish people, as they have revealed themselves in the past, are revealing themselves in the present, and will continue to reveal themselves in the future. This unbelieving and evil generation, though they reject Christ now, will continue to exist until the day of his return, and will then receive the judgement which is their due.'

not teaching his disciples that his coming would necessarily occur within their lifetime.

The difficulty with this resolution of the problem, however, is that 'this generation' most likely refers to the generation living at the time Jesus first spoke these words. At least three reasons commend this reading. First, though it may be true that the language of 'evil' or 'adulterous' generation is used in other passages, this language is not used in Matthew 24 or Mark 13. Second, if the reference were to a kind of generation of people who live throughout history, then the term to be used would have been *genos*, meaning 'kind' or 'race', rather than *gennea*, meaning 'generation'.[1] And third, in most of the instances of the expression 'this generation' in the New Testament, the reference is clearly to the then-existing generation.[2] For these reasons, it does not seem possible to escape the clear implication that Jesus was speaking of 'all these things', including his coming, and that he believed they would occur during the life of the generation to whom he was speaking.

Some interpreters of this passage, therefore, have offered a different answer to the critics' charge that Jesus was mistaken about the time of his coming. According to these interpreters, Jesus was teaching his disciples that his coming would occur during their lifetime, during which 'all of these things' – that is, all the signs and events described in the Olivet Discourse of Matthew 24 or Mark 13 – would transpire. According to their reading of this text, the things referred to, including the coming of Christ, took place in the past during the first century. Sometimes termed a preterist reading of this passage, this interpretation takes the coming of Christ to be a reference to the events that occurred in conjunction with the destruction of Jerusalem in AD 70. Though these were not

---

[1] This term is used elsewhere in the New Testament, e.g., *Mark* 7:26 and *Acts* 4:36.

[2] See, e.g., *Mark* 13:30; *Luke* 1:48; 21:32; *Matt.* 1:17; 23:36; *Acts* 13:36; 14:16; 15:21; *Eph.* 3:5; *Col.* 1:26.

the event of Christ's final coming at the end of the age, Jesus was correctly predicting a coming in judgement upon Jerusalem that did occur in the first century.[1] Thus, the critics are wrong to charge Jesus with error; his teaching that he would come at the destruction of Jerusalem was fulfilled even as he promised.

Though this second interpretation and answer to the radical claim that Jesus was mistaken about the time of his coming has much to commend it, another understanding is more plausible. It acknowledges, along with the preterist reading, that 'this generation' most likely refers to those to whom Jesus originally spoke. But because his Olivet Discourse answers a twofold question of his disciples – when will the temple in Jerusalem be destroyed? and, What will be the sign of his coming and the 'end of the age?' – this interpretation maintains that the 'all things' of Matthew 24:34 refers to those things in the immediate context that coincided with the destruction of Jerusalem in AD 70. It does not refer to or include, however, other things mentioned in the broader

---

[1] For a summary and defence of this preterist reading, see J. Marcellus Kik, *An Eschatology of Victory* (Phillipsburg, NJ: Presbyterian and Reformed, 1971), pp. 53–173; Gary DeMar, *Last Days Madness* (Atlanta: American Vision, 1994), pp. 25–45, 297–302; R. C. Sproul, *The Last Days According to Jesus* (Grand Rapids: Baker, 1998), pp. 27–68. These authors represent what is sometimes termed a 'partial' preterism. Though they maintain that many of the references, including that in Matthew 24 and Mark 13, to Christ's coming in the New Testament, designate a past event, the destruction of Jerusalem in AD 70, they nonetheless maintain the doctrine of a final coming of Christ in the future. Sproul's argument is almost entirely shaped by his concern to answer the critical claim that Jesus was wrong in his prediction of the time of his coming. See J. Stuart Russell, *The Parousia. A Study of the New Testament Doctrine of Our Lord's Second Coming* (1887; repr. Grand Rapids: Baker Book House, 1983), for a comprehensive defence of what is sometimes termed 'full' preterism, the view that all of the New Testament references to Christ's coming are now in the past. Full preterism denies one of the cardinal doctrines of the historic Christian church, namely, the future second coming of Christ.

context of the discourse that refer to Christ's coming at the end of the age, such as the 'signs of the times' described in Matthew 24:1–14, or the event of Christ's coming at the end of the age whose 'day and hour' no one knows (verses 29–31, 36). Because Christ's discourse answers to both of the disciples' questions, two parts are woven together, one answering to the first, another to the second. John Murray, representing this reading of the passage, notes that 'it is reasonable to suppose that in Matthew 24:34 (cf. Mark 13:30, Luke 21:32) Jesus is answering the first part of the disciples' question, that pertaining to the destruction of the temple'.[1] Because the 'all things' of verse 34 refers to the events surrounding the destruction of Jerusalem rather than the specific time of Jesus' coming at the end of the age, the critics' claim that he was mistaken is without basis.

Admittedly, the interpretation of this passage is notoriously difficult. But our survey of three responses to the radical claim that Jesus was mistaken, two of which are highly plausible, shows that the higher critics' position is itself open to the charge of prejudice.[2]

---

[1] 'The Interadventual Period and the Advent: Matt. 24 and 25', in his *Collected Writings*, vol. 2 (Edinburgh: Banner of Truth, 1977), p. 394. Murray adds: 'Our Lord is making a sharp distinction, in regard to eventuation, between the destruction of the temple and his advent, that is to say, between the two elements of the question asked by the disciples. This is the force of the contrast in verses 34 and 36. We must not fail to appreciate the sequence and the antithesis . . . "this generation shall not pass until all these things be accomplished . . . but of that day and hour no one knows . . . but the Father only." Of particular significance is the contrast between what he knew and fore-told (verses 34, 35) and what he did not know (verse 36) . . . This would have made clear to the disciples the distinction between the destruction of Jerusalem and correlative events on the more proximate horizon, on the one hand, and the day of his advent, on the other.'

[2] In Chapter 6 I will return to the subject of Jesus' Olivet Discourse. Though my treatment here of the preterist reading of the discourse has been rather abbreviated, this reading will be evaluated more thoroughly at that time.

The third text in which the imminence of Christ's return seems to be taught is Matthew 10:23. In this passage, which describes Christ's commission of the twelve disciples to preach the gospel of the kingdom to the lost sheep of the house of Israel, Christ promises them, 'Truly, I say to you, you will not have gone through all the towns of Israel, before the Son of Man comes.' Here again, those who propose an unanticipated delay in the return of Christ insist that Christ is teaching that he would return within the timespan of the disciples' preaching throughout all the towns in Israel, that is, soon after his resurrection and ascension to heaven. This passage confirms, therefore, that Jesus believed he would return soon after his resurrection and ascension to heaven.

However, in the context of Jesus' instruction to his disciples in Matthew 10, some sayings clearly refer to future activities that will take place after Christ's ascension into heaven (compare verses 16–22). Some of these activities include circumstances that would be appropriate to the Christian church throughout history (compare verses 24–25, 26–39). Furthermore, the reference in this passage to the coming of Christ need no more be limited to the second coming of Christ than in the first text, Mark 9:1, already discussed. It is conceivable that in this passage Jesus links together circumstances that would precede his coming in power at his resurrection and his final coming at his return from heaven at the end of the age. Whether the coming of the Son of Man refers to Christ's resurrection or second coming, it is clear that his disciples will not have 'gone through all the towns of Israel' before this event occurs.

III. CHRIST'S COMING ONLY AFTER CERTAIN EVENTS OCCUR

In addition to these passages that seem to speak of the imminence of Christ's return, others speak of a delay or extension of the period of time before Christ's return. They indicate that some events must occur before Christ's coming, events whose fulfilment cannot take place without a considerable period of time elapsing. For example, in Matthew 24:14 (a text in a passage to which appeal is also made for the idea that Christ's coming will be soon), Christ teaches that 'this gospel of the kingdom will be preached throughout the whole world, as a testimony to the nations; and then the end will come'. The preaching of the gospel to the nations is called in this passage one of the 'signs of the times', one of those signals of Christ's present work in the world pointing to his coming again. This sign has to be fulfilled, accordingly, before Christ comes again, a fulfilment that strongly suggests something of an extension of the time needed for it to occur.

A similar passage is found in Mark 14:9 in which Jesus, describing the woman who anointed him with costly perfume, declared that 'wherever the gospel is preached in the whole world, what she has done will be told in memory of her'. In this passage the presumption is that the gospel will be preached in the whole world, not only among the villages of Israel, before Christ returns.

Many of Jesus' parables of the kingdom indicate a period of time elapsing before the end will come. These parables speak of the growth of the kingdom being one that requires an intervening period of maturing and ripening. The parable of the pounds in Luke 19:11, for example, speaks of those 'who supposed that the kingdom of God was to appear immediately', but whose belief Jesus corrected in part by means of the parable. In the well-known parable of the talents, Jesus uses language, 'after a long time', that assumes a considerable period of time has gone by before the day of judgement arrives (*Matt.* 25:19). The same suggestion of a period of delay or maturation is found in the parables of the ten virgins (*Matt.* 25:5, 'as the bridegroom was delayed'), the servants (*Luke* 12:41–8, 'my master is delayed in coming'), the tares, mustard seed, and the leaven (*Matt.* 13).

A balanced and complete reading of the Gospels, therefore, reveals a double emphasis. Some passages emphasize the 'soon-ness' or imminence of Christ's coming; others suggest something of a delay or a considerable period of time intervening. The best understanding of them, therefore, is one that acknowledges the certainty and 'soon-ness' of Christ's return (it is 'soon' in the perspective of the history of redemption, since it is the only event remaining on the horizon that marks the conclusion of God's saving work), but does not draw the improper conclusion that little or no time remains before it will occur. Within the framework of a clear and lively expectation of Christ's coming again, the believer learns that a great deal is being accomplished, indeed must be accomplished, before all things are fulfilled and the great day of Christ's return arrives.

A similar conclusion can be drawn from the writings of the Apostle Paul. Though it is true that in some passages the apostle emphasises the 'soon-ness' of Christ's return, other passages emphasise the events which must precede his coming. Something of the same twofold emphasis found in the Gospels is also found in these epistles. Some passages speak of Christ's return as though it were immediately 'at hand': in Romans 13:11–12 we read that 'the night is far gone; the day is at hand'; in 1 Corinthians 7:29 the apostle declares that 'the appointed time has grown very short'; and in Philippians 4:5, it is said that 'the Lord is at hand'. In two passages the Apostle Paul speaks of 'we' in a way that suggests he might still be alive at the time of Christ's coming (*1 Thess.* 4:15, *1 Cor.* 15:51–52). However, none of these passages actually teaches that Christ's return will occur within the apostle's lifetime. At most, this possibility is suggested. Other passages in the epistles clearly indicate something of a delay and period intervening before Christ comes again (cf. *1 Thess.* 5:9–10; *2 Thess.* 2:1–12).

The New Testament contains no evidence, then, for the existence of any real contradictions on the subject of a delay of Christ's return. Some passages emphasise its imminence. Other passages emphasise the events which will precede and delay its occurrence. Each kind of passage is understandable within the perspective of the history of redemption. Because Christ has already come, his coming in glory at the end of the age is 'at hand'. Because Christ has already come, the gospel must be preached to all the nations and all things be made ready for his triumphant return.

IV. NO ONE KNOWS THE DAY OR HOUR

The more obvious and familiar form of the question concerning the when of Christ's return is the question of its precise timing or date. If the return of Christ has the significance and meaning that we have suggested, it is not surprising that many have found the temptation all but irresistible to determine how near or far we are from this event's occurrence. Even in the record of Christ's teaching in the New Testament, it is apparent that Jesus' disciples were anxious to know the 'day' and the 'hour' of Christ's coming again.

The biblical answer to this question can be found already expressed in the sixteenth- and seventeenth-century confessions of the Reformed churches. In the *Belgic Confession*, Article 37, for example, when the certain event of Christ's return and the final judgement is described, it is almost noted in passing that 'the time appointed by the Lord . . . is unknown to all creatures'. Similarly, the *Westminster Confession of Faith*, Chapter 33.3, speaks of the day of Christ's return and the final judgement as one which Christ himself will have 'unknown' to all men. The biblical wisdom and truth of these two confessions becomes readily evident from the following considerations.

In several instances in the New Testament, we are told that no one knows the day or the hour of Christ's return. When Jesus instructs his disciples in Mark 13 concerning the signs that would precede and alert them to his return, he clearly declares that 'of that day or hour no one knows, not even the angels in heaven, nor the Son, but only the Father' (verse 32).

This remarkable saying has often raised questions among believers who wonder how it is possible that even the Son of God does not know the time of his coming again. For our purpose, we do not need to pursue this difficult question. We need only note that Jesus could not make the unknowability of the time of his return more clear or emphatic – no one knows, not even the Son himself, the day or the hour!

Nor is this an isolated passage. Similar words are found in Matthew 25:13, where Jesus, warning his disciples, says, 'Watch, therefore, for you know neither the day nor the hour.' In Luke 12:39–40, we read that 'the Son of Man is coming at an hour you do not expect'. And, if these texts were not enough, we find in Acts 1:7 that Jesus answered his disciples' question whether he was about to restore the kingdom to Israel by saying, 'It is not for you to know times or epochs which the Father has fixed by his own authority.'

The clear implication of these texts cannot be escaped. Harold Camping, in his attempt to date the return of Christ in his book *1994?* seeks a way of escape by arguing that Jesus only forbade the knowing of the day and hour of his return, not the month and the year. He also suggests that what was deliberately withheld from the early church is now being revealed to believers through hidden truths long concealed within the biblical texts. But these claims contradict the obvious meaning of these texts. If Camping's (or anyone else's) attempt to escape the simple meaning of these texts is permissible, then the confession that the Bible's meaning is ordinarily clear and accessible has been abandoned. In the approach of Camping and others like him who attempt to date the time of Christ's return, only those who read the biblical texts with the key to unlock their secrets can profit from them.

However, in addition to these texts which explicitly speak of the unknowability of the time of Christ's return, several also speak of it as an event that will come unexpectedly (*Luke* 12:39–49), even like the coming of a 'thief' in the night.

Though these passages must be carefully considered and their differences acknowledged, they commonly teach that the return of Christ is essentially unpredictable.

For example, in Matthew 24:43–44, Jesus compares the head of a household's need to be alert because of the possible coming of a thief in the night with his disciples need to be alert in the face of his own certain, but unknown, time of coming. In Revelation 16:15, Christ announces his coming with the solemn words, 'Behold, I am coming like a thief. Blessed is the one who stays awake and keeps his garments, lest he walk about naked and men see his shame.' In this passage, not only is Christ's coming like that of a thief in terms of its unknowability, it is also like that of a thief in that it will mean judgement for the unwashed and unclothed.

This is a feature of another text that speaks of Christ's coming as being like that of a thief. In 1 Thessalonians 5:2 the Apostle Paul, speaking of 'the day of the Lord', notes that the believers in Thessalonica 'know full well that the day of the Lord will come just like a thief in the night'. The day of the Lord will be like the coming of a thief to the unbelieving and wicked, because it will bring destruction when they least expect it. However, the Apostle Paul goes on to contrast this with the circumstance of believers who, as he describes them, 'are not in darkness, that the day should overtake you like a thief'. Here the point is not that believers will know the exact time of Christ's coming, but that this coming will not overtake them as those who are unprepared or who need fear the prospect of Christ's return.[1]

---

[1] Camping, 1994?, pp. 56–61, tries to argue that this passage only denies the knowledge of the time of Christ's return to unbelievers, for whom it will be like the coming of a thief in the night. Because Christ's coming will not be like the coming of a thief for believers, it remains possible for believers to know the time of his return. The problem with this reading of the text is that it plays too much upon the imagery of the 'thief'. Though believers do not need fear Christ's coming, like the unbeliever fears the coming of a thief, they nonetheless know no more about the time of Christ's coming than does anyone who is

Conclusion

It should be apparent, then, from all of these biblical considerations that no one knows or may legitimately seek to know the exact time of Christ's return. Some passages remind us of the certainty, even the 'soon-ness' within the perspective of the timeline of the history of redemption, of Christ's coming. But others remind us of those events that must take place before Christ's return, which permit us to speak of God's 'patience' in this present period in calling the nations to repentance (2 *Pet.* 3:3–4). Furthermore, several passages clearly forbid any attempt to know the day or the hour of Christ's second coming.

In the light of these biblical considerations, Christian believers are duty-bound to be cautious and circumspect about the time of Christ's return. We must live expectantly, knowing the time is short and Christ's return is certain. But we must also live responsibly, carrying on with the work demanded of us in the interim period between Christ's ascension and coming again. Such responsible living demands that we resist the temptation to predict the time of Christ's return. Those who attempt to set a timetable for the return of Christ disobey the teaching of God's Word. They also risk bringing the gospel of our Lord Jesus Christ into disrepute, should their allegedly 'biblical' predictions fail to come to pass.

Our duty is the same as that given by the Apostle Paul to the church in Thessalonica. When considering the 'day of the Lord', he gave them this charge: 'But since we are of the day, let us be sober, having put on the breastplate of faith and love, and as a helmet, the hope of salvation. For God has not destined us for wrath, but for obtaining salvation through our Lord Jesus Christ' (1 *Thess.* 5:8–9).

---

approached by a thief. Even for believers there will be one feature of Christ's coming like that of a thief – it will not be announced in advance or trumpeted from a distance.

PART FOUR

---

*The Future Marked
by the 'Signs of
the Times'*

5

Signs of
God's Grace

S O FAR OUR TREATMENT of general eschatology has been
somewhat introductory in character. We have seen that
the return of Christ is the great event on the horizon of the history
of redemption; that it will bring this present age to a close;
but that the time of its occurrence is unknown to us. Everything in the biblical picture concerning the future course of
events focuses upon Jesus Christ, the exalted Lord, who is
seated at the Father's right hand 'whence he shall come to
judge the living and the dead' (*The Apostles' Creed*).

We are now in a position to consider what are commonly
termed 'the signs of the times'. A number of events in the
present period of history, between Christ's first and second
comings, are like reminders or signposts that the end is
coming and the day of the Lord is at hand.

Introducing the Signs of the Times

Despite the rather common use of the expression 'the signs of
the times', it is found in only one place in the New Testament, and there it does not refer to future events.

In Matthew 16:1 the Pharisees and Sadducees came to
Jesus asking him to show them 'a sign from heaven'. To this

question and test Jesus responded by saying, 'Do you know how to discern the appearance of the sky, but cannot discern the signs of the times?' Jesus is referring to those works of God which disclose his will and purpose, like those deeds listed in Matthew 11:5, which confirmed that Jesus was the promised Christ: 'The blind receive their sight and the lame walk, lepers are cleansed and the deaf hear, and the dead are raised up, and the poor have good news preached to them.'

Though we do not find the Scriptures speaking of 'the signs of the times' to refer to those historical occurrences that signify the nearness or certainty of Christ's return, it is not difficult to understand how the expression has come to be commonly used in that way. Just as signs in the history of redemption in the Old and New Testament eras served to disclose and confirm God's purpose, so signs in this present age point to Christ's coming again.

'The signs of the times' are, therefore, all those events or portents revealed in the Word of God which confirm that the present course of history is moving towards the day of the Lord. To the people of God, who walk by faith and not by sight, they are indicators that Christ will come as he promised, and reminders that he is seated at the Father's right hand, ruling all things for the sake of his church and bringing history to its appointed end.

1. Mistaken views of these signs
Even within this framework of understanding, however, we need to guard carefully against some mistaken views about 'the signs of the times'. Partly because of the popularity of the phrase, several unbiblical notions are common about what will characterize history before Christ's return.

One such mistaken notion is the idea that the signs in question refer exclusively to those events which will occur immediately prior to Christ's return. On the timeline of history, they are understood to be a cluster of events that will take place in a short period just before the end.

The problem with this approach should be obvious. By 'the signs of the times' the Bible refers to a variety of signs, many of which span the whole period between Christ's ascension into heaven and his coming again. Furthermore, some of these are clearly events that took place at the time of the destruction of Jerusalem in AD 70. They are mentioned in Matthew 24, Mark 13, and Luke 21, in a passage sometimes termed the Olivet Discourse or the Little Apocalypse. This rich diversity of signs just cannot be accommodated by the idea that they all must occur in the period shortly before the second coming of Christ.

Another mistaken notion, closely linked with this, maintains that 'the signs of the times' enable us to date the exact time of Christ's return. The tendency is to think of these signs as indicating that Christ's return is imminent. As soon as believers detect one or more of these signs, whether it be in the form of wars or rumours of wars or in the form of earthquakes and other portents, the conclusion is swiftly drawn that we must be living in 'the last days' and that the return of Christ is drawing rapidly near.

This temptation involves a misreading of biblical prophecies having to do with the end times. Too often these passages are read as though they were newspaper reports on events in the future, written as though they were already in the past.[1] The manner in which the New Testament speaks of the fulfilment of the prophecies of the Old Testament should alert us to the danger of this approach. The signs of the times are not intended to afford us an exact timetable for Christ's return or to predict all kinds of developments in advance of their occurrence.

[1] G. C. Berkouwer, *The Return of Christ*, p. 244 n, warns against what he calls a reportorial view of these signs that allows us to predict the exact time and circumstances immediately prior to Christ's return. It is evident that the various eschatological passages in the New Testament are not reportorial, not mere narrative accounts, especially not narrative accounts of events to take place in a localized end time disassociated from our time or that of the disciples which has not yet begun.

One other notion that often plagues our understanding of 'the signs' is the idea that they are always abnormal, catastrophic and spectacular. [1] When they are being considered, the tendency is often to think of unusual circumstances that will characterize the period of history before Christ's return. Wars, rumours of wars, earthquakes, the Antichrist, Armageddon – this is the stuff of which 'the signs of the times' are made.

However, it should be noted that the Bible expressly warns us against this kind of identification. In Luke 17:20–21 Christ is recorded as saying, 'The kingdom of God is not coming with signs to be observed; nor will they say, Lo, here it is! or There! for behold, the kingdom of God is in the midst of you.' It should also not be forgotten that the Scriptures warn the believer that 'the man of lawlessness' will deceive many with 'pretended signs and wonders' (2 Thess. 2:9, Rev. 13:13–14). Many of the signs refer to ordinary events that belong to this period of history, precisely as that period which prepares for and issues in the coming again of Christ.

Because these mistaken ideas are so influential, it is especially important that we be cautious in seeking to understand what the Bible has to say on this subject. We must not expect to discover some grand scheme of spectacular occurrences which will permit us to determine the exact course of events and the timing of Christ's return.

II. GENERAL CHARACTERISTICS OF THESE SIGNS

Given the widespread nature of these misunderstandings, it is important to correct them. We do this by noting that the Bible highlights certain characteristics of 'the signs' in its teaching about them.

---

[1] For example, Abraham Kuyper, in his *Dictaten Dogmatiek*, vol.5, 2nd ed. (Grand Rapids: J. B. Hulst, n.d.), *Locus de Consummatione Saeculi*, pp. 136 ff., maintains that what distinguishes these signs is their extraordinary quality or abnormality.

First, while these signs are often thought of as pointers to the future, many of them, ironically, refer as much to the history of God's dealings with his people in the past and have their antecedents in the Old Testament. This is true, for example, of such events as wars and rumours of wars, earthquakes, the battle of Armageddon, and false prophets. Many such occurrences marked the way of God's dealings with his people in the Old Testament; many of them have already occurred in the past or are presently occurring. All of them call the people of God to constant vigilance, to a hope-filled anticipation of the future under the plan and purpose of God, who has entrusted the administration of all things to his Son.

Even so, it is nonetheless appropriate that these signs should be associated in our minds with the future, especially with the event of Christ's return. Whenever New Testament passages speak of various events that will take place during the course of history, they speak of them as indicators that the end is drawing near. They remind the believer that history is moving forward, toward an appointed goal, namely, the revelation of Christ from heaven at the end of the age.

Second, another feature often present in the Bible's delineation of 'the signs of the times' is the stress upon the antithesis in history between the kingdom of God and the powers of evil. As history moves forward under the lordship of Jesus Christ, the opposition between the kingdom of Christ and the kingdom of the Antichrist becomes increasingly evident, and the certain triumph of Christ's cause is foreshadowed.[1]

---

[1] Though not normally included among the signs of the times, the resurrection and ascension of Christ, as well as the outpouring of the Spirit at Pentecost, are all end-time events, signs of the fulfilment of God's promises and the certain prospect of the consummation of his saving work. That is why at Pentecost, the Apostle Peter can speak of Jesus Christ as 'a man attested to you by God with miracles and wonders and signs' (*Acts* 2:22, *Heb.* 2:4).

'The signs of the times' are, accordingly, like indicators of the realization of God's redemptive purposes in history, purposes which include the gathering of the church and the proclamation of the gospel of the kingdom to the ends of the earth. Far from being frightening portents of the triumph of the Antichrist and his forces, these signs testify to the triumph of Christ's cause and the subjection of all things under his feet. Just as in Revelation 12, the casting down of Satan from heaven to the earth issues in an intensified conflict between the church and the world, so these signs attest the intensification of the antithesis between the kingdom of darkness and the kingdom of light. In doing so, they none-theless promise the certain triumph of Christ and his kingdom at his coming. Therefore, rather than being alarm-ing signs of the uncertain prospect of Christ's cause, the signs of the times certify the inexorable march of the history of redemption toward its consummation at Christ's triumphant revelation from heaven.

Finally, 'the signs of the times' remind believer and unbeliever alike that today is the day of salvation, and not tomorrow when it will be too late, God's patience having run its course. They call believers especially to a stance of constant watchfulness and expectation of the coming day of the Lord. In the context of an extended discourse on the signs of the times, Christ said to his disciples, 'Watch, therefore, for you do not know on what day your Lord is coming' (*Matt.* 24:42). Like the announcement of an impending mar-riage ceremony, these signs are a call to be prepared for the coming of the heavenly bridegroom, Jesus Christ, who will receive his bride unto himself and cast his enemies into ever-lasting destruction (*2 Thess.* 1:6–10).

III. IDENTIFYING THESE SIGNS

In order to chart a course for our study, it is helpful to con-sider the various signs according to specific categories. Anthony Hoekema, in his book *The Bible and the Future* has distinguished three kinds of signs: first, signs that reveal the present working and eventual triumph of the preaching of the gospel in this present age, signs evidencing the grace of God; second, signs that reveal the intensifying conflict between the kingdom of Christ and the kingdom of the Antichrist, a conflict that will issue in the ultimate triumph of Christ and subjection of all things under his feet; and third, signs that reveal God's judgement and anticipate the great crisis that will occur at Christ's return.[1]

We will follow this order and the signs that we will consider are:

i. SIGNS OF THE PRESENT WORKING AND TRIUMPH OF GOD'S GRACE:
   a. The preaching of the gospel
   b. The salvation of 'all Israel'

ii. SIGNS OF THE CONFLICT BETWEEN CHRIST AND ANTICHRIST:
   a. Tribulation
   b. The Great Tribulation
   c. Apostasy
   d. The Antichrist

iii. SIGNS OF GOD'S JUDGEMENT ANTICIPATING THE GREAT JUDGEMENT:
   a. Wars and rumours of wars
   b. Famine and earthquakes
   c. The battle of Armageddon

This list demonstrates how much attention is given in the Bible to this particular subject and therefore how important it is, even though many difficulties and questions arise in the attempt to understand their meaning. It shows that nothing in the present course of history may be divorced from the great purpose of all things being brought into subjection to Christ, inaugurating and eventually consummating his glorious kingdom.

We consider now the two signs of God's grace at work in the world. The first is the preaching of the gospel to all the nations. The second is the preaching of the gospel to and the salvation of all Israel.

[1] *The Bible and the Future*, p. 137.

Preaching to All the Nations

One indication that many Christian believers have an unbiblical view of the 'signs of the times' is the common failure to note that the preaching of the gospel of Christ to the nations is a sign of the period between Christ's first and second coming. So much literature about 'the signs of the times' focuses upon the unusual and catastrophic events that will mark the period of redemptive history as it draws closer to the great day of Christ's return.

However, this reflects an unbiblical and distorted view which fails to do justice to the note of triumph that rings throughout the New Testament, a note that also characterizes its understanding of the signs of the times. Christ is king and has been granted all authority in heaven and on earth (*Matt.* 28:18–20). Nothing can stand in the way of the forward march of the gospel and the gathering and preservation of Christ's church. Not even the gates of hell can prevail against the church (*Matt.* 16:18). Christ will come again to judge the living and the dead, and so the consummation of God's kingdom will bring present history to a close.

Therefore, in the biblical view of history and the future of Christ's work, it should not surprise us that one of the great signs of the times is the preaching of the gospel to the nations. This sign confirms the gospel promise that Christ has been exalted to the Father's right hand and has been given a name which is above every name (*Phil.* 2:9, *Eph.* 1:21).

I. THE OLD TESTAMENT PROMISE

To appreciate the importance of preaching as a sign of the times, it is critical that we go back to the Old Testament promise concerning the coming of the Messiah. This promise included as one of its features the anticipation of an age when the gospel would go forth to all the nations.[1]

---

[1] See Johannes Blauw. *The Missionary Nature of the Church: A Survey of the Biblical Theology of Mission* (1962; repr. Grand Rapids: Eerdmans, 1974), pp. 15–54, for a comprehensive survey of the Old Testament's promise of the mission of God to all the nations.

At the beginning of the Lord's dealings with his own covenant people, his promise of salvation included blessings for all the families and nations of the earth. The Lord declared to Abraham, the father of all believers, that he would be given an heir through whom blessing would be extended to every family and nation (*Gen.* 12:3). This passage is commonly regarded as describing the formal establishment of the covenant of grace and harks back to the Lord's original promise to Eve that her seed would crush the head of the serpent (*Gen.* 3:15). Later, Abraham was promised a great reward (*Gen.* 15:1), an heir through whom the Lord's grace would extend to all peoples. When Abraham was ninety-nine years old, the Lord appeared to him and promised: 'I will establish My covenant between Me and you, and I will multiply you exceedingly. . . And you shall be the father of a multitude of nations. No longer shall your name be Abram, but your name shall be Abraham; for I will make you the father of a multitude of nations' (*Gen.* 17:2–5).

This great promise constitutes a starting point[1] for understanding the Old Testament anticipation of the day when the salvation of the Lord would extend through Israel to all the nations. The Lord's gracious dealings with Israel set the stage in the history of redemption for the eventual extension of gospel blessings to all families of the earth. However much this broad and comprehensive scope of God's saving purpose may have been sinfully suppressed among the Old Testament people of God, it is basic to an understanding of redemptive history leading up to the sending of the Messiah, or Saviour, in the fullness of time.[2]

---

[1] I say a starting point, since the account in Genesis 1–3 of the Lord God's creation of the heavens and the earth, and of Adam and Eve as his image-bearers, already announces that the Lord of the covenant is king over all creation and peoples. The particularism of the Lord's dealings with Israel is set within the awareness that he is the universal sovereign, the king over all his creation-kingdom.

[2] The song of Simeon quoted earlier, sung on the occasion of Christ's presentation at the temple, indicates that the lively expectation of the

Not only is the promise of salvation for all the peoples through Abraham's seed repeated subsequently in the book of Genesis (see *Gen.* 18:18; 22:18; 26:4; 28:14) but it is also illustrated throughout the Old Testament epoch by the inclusion of non-Israelites into the number of the people of God (for example, Rahab, Ruth, household servants and aliens).

It is remarkable in this connection to see how the inclusion of the nations within the saving purpose of God is celebrated throughout the Psalter, the songbook for the worship of the Old and the New Testament people of God. In the Psalter, the universal presence and rule of the Lord over all the nations is frequently announced (for example, *Psa.* 8; 19:1–4; 67:4; 103:19). Psalm 24:1 declares that 'the earth is the Lord's, and all it contains, the world, and those who dwell in it'. The rule of the promised king in the line of David will, accordingly, be a rule over all the earth (see 72:19). The worship of the Lord included frequent rejoicing in his certain triumph over all his enemies (47:2; 77:13; 136:2), the call to make him known among the nations (9:11; 108:3) and the invitation to the nations to join in the worship of the Lord (50:4; 87; 98:4; 113:3; 117). Among these invitations, none is more powerful than Psalm 96:7: 'Ascribe to the Lord, O families of the peoples, ascribe to the Lord glory and strength.' The language of the Psalter echoes and re-echoes the promise that the Lord, who is the creator of heaven and earth and all the nations, intends to make himself known among all the nations and extend the blessings of his covenant favour to every people.

In the prophetic writings of the Old Testament, the announcement of the coming of the Lord in salvation and judgement also clearly surfaces.[1] It will be the occasion for

---

fulfilment of this Old Testament promise had not been extinguished among the faithful people of God.

[1] See George Van Groningen, *Messianic Revelation in the Old Testament* (Grand Rapids: Baker, 1990), chapter 14, 'The Prophets Messianic Message for the Nations', pp. 441–63, for a survey of the prophets' preaching of a future conversion of the nations.

the blessings of salvation to be extended far beyond the borders of Israel. Though there are many different facets to this announcement, central to them all is the conviction that the Lord himself will come to judge the nations in righteousness and grant salvation to all peoples (*Psa.* 59:5; 82:1, 8; 96:13). The day of the Lord, though variously described and understood, promises the outpouring of the Spirit of the Lord upon all flesh (*Joel* 2:28). Isaiah eloquently announces that 'in the last days, the mountain of the house of the Lord will be established as the chief of the mountains . . . and all the nations will stream to it. And many peoples will come . . .' (see *Isa.* 2:1–4; 44:8; 66:19). Zechariah does the same (*Zech.* 8:18–23). A new day is promised in which all the nations will see the glory of the Lord and enter into the enjoyment of full salvation.

Though these kinds of Old Testament themes and motifs could be expanded upon, this should be sufficient to illustrate the pervasiveness of the Old Testament promise of a future age of salvation and blessing for all the nations. The Lord's purposes do not terminate with Israel but extend this saving power and kingdom through Israel to the ends of the earth. The mother-promise will be fulfilled. The seed of the woman, the son of Abraham, will come; and in him the blessings of the covenant will be imparted to every family and people.

II. THE NEW TESTAMENT FULFILMENT

Only within this Old Testament setting is it possible to appreciate the significance of the New Testament fulfilment. The preaching of the gospel to the nations, mandated by Christ himself (*Matt.* 28:18–20), is an end-time fulfilment of what the Lord had earlier promised.

Though this is not often adequately appreciated, perhaps because it has become such an ordinary part of the ministry of the church of Christ, it is really a striking development in the history of redemption. The preaching of the gospel that is 'the power of God for salvation to everyone who believes, to the Jew first, and also to the Greek' (*Rom.* 1:16), is one of the clearest signs that we live in the last days of redemptive history, days in which God's promises of old are being fulfilled and the triumph of his covenant grace in Christ is being manifested.

This is explicitly taught in the New Testament Gospels. In Matthew 24, perhaps the most important New Testament passage concerning the signs of the times, we are told that the disciples came to Jesus and asked the question, 'Tell us, when will these things be [the destruction and rebuilding of the temple], and what will be the sign of Your coming, and of the end of the age?' (verse 3). In response to this question, Jesus mentioned a number of signs, among them wars and rumours of wars (verse 6), famines and earthquakes (verse 7), and tribulation and apostasy (verses 9–10). Especially prominent among these signs, however, is the preaching of the gospel: 'And this gospel of the kingdom', Christ announces, 'shall be preached in the whole world for a witness to the nations, and then the end shall come' (verse 14; see also Mark 13:10). In this passage, Jesus clearly affirms that the preaching of the gospel is a sign of the times that must precede the end of the age and the coming again of the Son of Man.

Also important is the way in which the New Testament preaching of the gospel of the kingdom is linked with the Old Testament promises of blessing for all nations in the end times. It is not difficult, for example, to notice how the Great Commission of Matthew 28 breathes the spirit of the Lord's original covenant promise and purpose with Abraham. When Christ, within the context of his being granted all authority in heaven and on earth, tells the disciples to go and make disciples of all the nations, this is certainly to be seen as a fulfilment of the promise to Abraham. These last words of Matthew form a fitting conclusion to the Gospel which begins with the genealogy of Jesus Christ, the son of David, the son of Abraham (Matt. 1:1). The same emphasis upon the preaching of the gospel to all the nations is seen in parallel passages in the Gospels of Mark (16:15–16) and Luke (24:46–49).

That the preaching of the gospel as a testimony to the nations marks off this period as the last days is also evident in the book of Acts, which records Christ's ministry through the apostles in the establishment of the New Testament church. At Pentecost, the promised outpouring of the Holy Spirit upon all flesh occurs, this outpouring expressed especially in the triumphant and powerful preaching of the gospel of Christ (*Acts* 2). The book of Acts as a whole traces the marvellous way in which the gospel advances, in the power and presence of the Spirit, beginning at Jerusalem but extending to the uttermost parts of the earth (*Acts* 1:8). 'For the promise is for you', says Peter at Pentecost, 'and your children, and for all who are far off, as many as the Lord our God shall call to Himself' (*Acts* 2:39).

Similarly in the New Testament Epistles, it is evident that the apostles understood their preaching in this way (see *1 Pet.* 2:6–10). Frequently, the preaching of the gospel, though to the world a thing of foolishness and weakness, is regarded as a demonstration of the Spirit and of power (*1 Cor.* 1:18–31; 2:4–5). Consequently, the apostles in their preaching exhibited not a spirit of fear and timidity but a Spirit of power (*1 Cor.* 4:20, *1 Thess.* 1:5, *2 Cor.* 4:7). The mystery of the gospel of our Lord Jesus Christ, hidden through the centuries but now revealed in the fullness of time, includes God's invincible purpose to save an elect people from every tribe and tongue and people and nation (*Eph.* 1:3–14). This purpose will be fulfilled through the ministry of the gospel of reconciliation in Christ.

A great deal more could be said to illustrate this theme. However, these aspects of the witness of the New Testament, understood within the context of their Old Testament background and promise, should be enough to show that the preaching of the gospel is perhaps the single most important sign of the times. It is the evidence of the triumph of God's gracious purposes in history, preparing the way for the coming again of the Lord of glory, much as John the Baptist did for his first coming.

III. AN IMPLICATION FOR THE CHURCH

We may observe among many churches today a decline of respect for and emphasis upon the preaching of the gospel. This is sometimes evidenced in declining enrolments at seminaries which prepare students for the ministry of the Word. It is evidenced in the trend to disparage the place and importance of preaching in Christian worship. It is also exhibited in the argument sometimes heard that the preaching of the gospel is only one among a variety of legitimate 'kingdom callings' and so ought not to be given any special emphasis. Sometimes it is reflected in Christian parents' unwillingness to encourage their children to consider the gospel ministry as a high and holy calling.

Though there may be several different explanations for this decline in esteem for the office and calling of preaching the gospel, it certainly reflects a loss of biblical insight and conviction about preaching. Many believers have lost the biblical view of the central place of preaching in this period of redemptive history – the one which exists for the preaching of the gospel to the nations.[1]

This loss of understanding has been accompanied by a corresponding loss of confidence in the power of the Word preached to bring salvation and advance the interests of Christ's kingdom. Various means of spreading the gospel are regarded as equal to or more useful than preaching. And sometimes it is even thought that the kingdom of Christ can better be advanced through political means and strategies.

---

[1] For a defence of this biblical view of the centrality of preaching in the history of redemption, see *Mid-America Journal of Theology. Theme Issue: Preaching,* 10 (Dyer, Indiana: Mid-America Reformed Seminary, 1999).

However, those who have a biblical view of the power of preaching as a sign of the triumph of Christ's grace and cause in this present age should not fall prey to any spirit that diminishes it. It is by means of preaching that Christ's kingdom advances, his name is proclaimed, and his people are discipled. Nothing should restore the confidence of God's people in preaching more than the realization that it is a sign that we live in the last days, days of opportunity and salvation. Soon the end will come, and the gospel will no longer be preached.

In the period between his ascension and coming again, Jesus Christ, the Lord of history, gives this great commission to his church:

> All authority has been given to Me in heaven and on earth. Go therefore and make disciples of all the nations, baptizing them in the name of the Father and the Son and the Holy Spirit, teaching them to observe all that I commanded you; and lo, I am with you always, even to the end of the age (*Matt.* 28:18–20).

The Salvation of All Israel

One further aspect of the preaching of the gospel still needs to be considered. It concerns what might be termed the salvation of the 'fullness' of Israel. What does the Bible teach about God's purpose with respect to his peculiar people, Israel? In the preaching of the gospel to the nations, is this people forgotten or left behind?

This subject raises a host of questions regarding the future, and it cannot be completely disassociated from divergent views of the so-called millennium. Premillennialists and dispensationalists have an answer to this question that conforms to their general conception of the future, particularly the realisation of God's purpose for Israel and the church. Since we will be considering these and other views of the millennium in several future chapters, we will refrain as much as possible from discussing them at this point. But the specific question of God's saving purpose regarding Israel cannot be avoided or postponed, because it relates directly to the preaching of the gospel to the nations in this present period and its implications for the salvation of Israel.

To address this question, we need to begin with a brief review of some Old Testament promises regarding the restoration and salvation of Israel. They will provide a context in which Romans 9–11, the most important New Testament passage about God's purposes regarding Israel, can be studied. Our main concern will be to consider what this passage teaches about God's saving purpose for Israel.

I. THE OLD TESTAMENT BACKGROUND

The Old Testament background relevant to this question extends the promise of salvation to all the peoples of the earth. However, it is important to note that this promise always included the continuance and fulfilment of God's saving purpose for Israel. The promise was not that God would forsake his people Israel, substituting the other nations as the object of his saving love, but that he would include all the nations under the canopy of his saving mercy. The Lord's promise to Israel was that through her, not apart from her, the promise would be extended to all peoples. This promise was confirmed throughout the history of the Lord's dealings with his old covenant people, whenever non-Israelites or aliens were gathered into and numbered among the people of God. However particular and limited the Lord's dealings may have been with a special nation, Israel, his purpose was never limited to this nation.

It should not surprise us, therefore, that the Lord's promise regarding a future gathering of the Gentile nations was joined to his promise of the salvation of Israel. His people Israel remained at the centre of the future realization of his purposes of salvation. When, for example, Psalm 22 speaks of the future day in which 'all the ends of the earth will remember and turn to the Lord, and all the families of the nations will worship before Thee' (verse 27), this will be in the company of 'all [the] descendants of Jacob . . . [and] the children of Israel' (verse 23). The blessing that falls upon Israel will be the means whereby the Lord's salvation will be made known among all the nations (*Psa.* 67). The announcement of salvation to Zion will take place in the sight of all the nations, that all the ends of the earth may see the salvation of our God (*Isa.* 52:7, 10). In the future day of the Lord's coming to save his people, the nations are described as coming to the light of Zion, and kings are said to come to 'the brightness of [her] dawn' (*Isa.* 60:1–3).

The story told in the book of Acts, which traces the gospel's testimony as it is preached first in Jerusalem and then to the remotest part of the earth (*Acts* 1:8), was therefore already promised in the Old Testament. The Apostle Paul's well-known declaration, 'I am not ashamed of the gospel, for it is the power of God for salvation to everyone who believes, to the Jew first and also the Greek' (*Rom.* 1:16), corresponds perfectly to the promise of the Lord that salvation for the Gentile peoples would be effected through Israel and not apart from her.

But in addition to these promises of the salvation of the nations, many promises are made of Israel's future restoration. These promises, which often received earlier and initial fulfilment in the restoration(s) of Israel in the Old Testament, also point forward to a great restoration yet to come.[1] Frequently the Lord spoke of how he would restore his people Israel to favour and salvation after a period of judgement and disfavour, provided they turned to him in repentance and faith (see *Deut.* 10:10, *1 Kings* 8:46–52, *Jer.* 18:5–10; 31:31–34; 29:12–14, *Ezek.* 36:33, *Hos.* 11:10).

---

[1] For example, when the children of Israel returned from their exile in Babylon, their restoration was an initial fulfilment of promises like those recorded in Jeremiah 31 and Ezekiel 36. However, it is evident from subsequent history that this initial restoration was itself but a type of an even more glorious one in the future (see *Heb.* 8:10–12).

THE PROMISE OF THE FUTURE

Therefore, the future held for Israel the prospect not only of the gathering of the nations and peoples to Zion but also of her restoration to renewed fellowship and favour with the Lord.

II. 'AND SO ALL ISRAEL SHALL BE SAVED'

All these Old Testament promises regarding the future of Israel bring us to Romans 9–11 and to Paul's great question: 'God has not rejected His people, has He?' (11:1). Since Romans 9–11 is the primary passage on this subject, we will proceed by taking a careful look at it.

THE PROBLEM

To understand the argument of these chapters, at least the part addressed to God's redemptive purpose for Israel, it is necessary to have a clear understanding of the problem posed in Romans 9:1–6. Put briefly, the problem is whether the Word and promise of God regarding Israel have failed.

This problem arises within the setting of the Apostle Paul's resounding conclusion and confident affirmation in Romans 8. Having set forth the mercy and grace of God in the salvation of his people in Christ through faith, the apostle exults that nothing will be able to separate those who have been called according to God's purpose and electing grace (*Rom.* 8:28–39) from his love in Christ Jesus. This song of confidence in God's grace and redemptive purpose seems almost to be the conclusion to which the entire argument in Romans 1–8 has been leading. Though all people are by nature sinners, deserving of the wrath and judgement of God, a way of salvation is provided for all who believe in Jesus Christ. Though the wrath of God is being revealed from heaven against all the ungodliness and unrighteousness of men who suppress the truth in unrighteousness (*Rom.* 1:18–32), and though 'there is none righteous, no not one' (*Rom.* 3:10), the grace and mercy of God in the free justification and salvation of sinners is the hope of all believers.

The conclusion of Romans 8 is a climactic affirmation of the victory of God's grace in Christ for all who believe.

However, this raises an inescapable problem for the Apostle Paul. How can he exult in the triumph of God's grace in Christ through faith, when this grace seems to be of no effect among the people of Israel in his day? If God's purposes and promises regarding Israel have terminated in failure and unbelief, how can he say that the gospel is the power of God unto salvation to the Jew first and also to the Greek? Indeed, if God's Word has failed with Israel, can he (and we) have confidence that God's promises will not likewise fail in regard to the Gentiles? This is the kind of problem that presses in upon the apostle at the outset of Romans 9–11, as the opening words of chapter 9 eloquently attest:

> I am telling the truth in Christ, I am not lying, my conscience bearing me witness in the Holy Spirit, that I have great sorrow and unceasing grief in my heart. For I could wish that I myself were accursed, separated from Christ for the sake of my brethren, my kinsmen according to the flesh, who are Israelites, to whom belongs the adoption as sons and the glory and the covenants and the giving of the Law and the temple service and the promises, whose are the fathers, and from whom is the Christ according to the flesh, who is over all, God blessed forever. Amen (*Rom.* 9:1–5).

The question, then, to which the entire argument of Romans 9–11 is addressed, is whether the Word and promise of God have failed due to the apparent unbelief of many of the children of Israel.

THE GENERAL RESOLUTION

To this troublesome question, the general answer of the Apostle Paul is a resounding 'No'. This is developed at some length in 9:6–11:12. The Word of God has in no wise failed. Rather, just as had been the case in the previous history of redemption, God's purpose according to election has been and is being realized (9:11). Just as that purpose of election discriminated between some who were children of Israel only according to the flesh, and others who were true children according to the promise and purpose of God, so that purpose of election continues to be realized in the salvation of some and not others.

Thus, the Apostle Paul answers generally the question regarding the supposed failure of God's Word and promise by arguing that throughout the whole history of the Lord's dealings with his people Israel, some were brought to salvation and others were hardened in their unbelief according to God's purpose of election. At no time in this history did God's purpose ever fail or fall short of being realized in any way.

Though, for our purposes, it is not necessary to trace out all of the steps in the apostle's argument, it is evident that he wants to address the question of Israel's apparent unbelief and apostasy from the standpoint of God's electing grace and purpose. Consequently, he cites in Chapter 11 the history associated with the prophet Elijah. Though many among the children of Israel disbelieved and fell away during his days, this in no respect meant that God had rejected his people. Even during this relatively low point, there remained a remnant according to God's gracious choice (11:5).

Despite this rather abbreviated statement of the general resolution to the question presented in this passage, it is not difficult to capture the gist of the apostle's answer to it. In the whole course of the history of redemption, God has been working out his electing purpose. This purpose is the only basis for the salvation of some from the entire number of the children of Israel in the past. It is also the only basis for the salvation of any, whether Jew or Gentile, in the present and the future. We can be certain of one thing: the apostle is insisting that God's purpose of election has not failed in the past, is not failing in the present, and will certainly not fail in the future. All those whom God has chosen to save in Christ will unfailingly be saved.

THE SPECIFIC RESOLUTION

However, that is only the general resolution to the question that the Apostle Paul offers in this passage. His specific resolution of it, which deals with the particular circumstance of the apparent unbelief and apostasy of many of the children of Israel at the preaching of the gospel, remains to be stated. This resolution takes the form of the Apostle Paul's inspired understanding of the depth of the riches of both the wisdom and knowledge of God (11:33) in his respective purposes for Israel and the Gentiles.

The main lines of the argument are as follows: In God's redemptive purpose, the unbelief and apostasy of many (though not all) of the children of Israel has been the occasion for the preaching of the gospel to the Gentiles. As many of the children of Israel disbelieved and took offence at the preaching of the gospel, the message has been extended to the Gentiles who, in the purpose of God, are being brought unto salvation. The Apostle Paul describes this as the cutting off of the natural branches of an olive tree, that is the children of Israel, and the ingrafting of Gentiles who believe (11:17–24). In the purpose of God, the unbelief of Israel has been the occasion for the gathering of the Gentiles and the realization of God's electing purpose. The poverty of Israel has thereby in God's wisdom been the occasion for the riches of the Gentiles (11:12).

But this is not the end of the story. By no means! According to the Apostle Paul's further argument, the riches of the Gentiles, their response by God's electing purpose to the preaching of the gospel, will be the further occasion by which Israel will be provoked to jealousy and her 'fullness' be saved. This is the climactic conclusion of the argument in Romans 11:25–26:

> For I do not want you, brethren, to be uninformed of this mystery, lest you be wise in your own estimation, that a partial hardening has happened to Israel until the fulness of

the Gentiles has come in; and thus all Israel will be saved; just as it is written, The Deliverer will come from Zion, He will remove ungodliness from Jacob.

The specific answer, therefore, to the question whether the Word of God had failed with respect to Israel is that in God's electing purpose, as it is being worked out in the history of redemption, the salvation of the Gentiles will serve to provoke Israel to jealousy and so the fullness of Israel will be saved. The gifts and calling of God are irrevocable (11:29), the apostle concludes, and therefore the unbelief of Israel will not be permanent and universal. The time is coming when the preaching of the gospel to the Gentiles will occasion the turning of Israel in faith to Christ.

THREE VIEWS

If this is the specific answer to the question regarding the place of Israel in God's saving purpose – that 'all Israel' will eventually be saved – then the one issue that still needs to be considered is the precise meaning of this phrase. How are we to understand 'all Israel'? There have been primarily three views on this in the history of the church.

The first view takes this phrase to refer to the people of Israel as a totality (though not necessarily every individual Jew) who will be converted at some time after the fullness of the Gentiles has been gathered. Among those who take this view, three distinct forms of it are often defended: first, dispensational interpreters link this conversion of Israel as a totality with God's special programme for the Jews in the future millennium;[1] second, premillennial interpreters who

---

[1] For a presentation and defence of the dispensational form of this view, see John F. Walvoord, *The Millennial Kingdom* (Findlay, Ohio: Dunham, 1959), pp. 167–92; J. Dwight Pentecost, *Things to Come*, (Findlay, Ohio: Dunham, 1958), pp. 504–7; and Michael G. Vanlaningham, 'Romans 11:25–27 and the Future of Israel in Paul's Thought', *The Masters Seminary Journal*, 3/3 (Fall 1992), pp. 141–74.

are not dispensationalists understand it to refer to a future conversion of the Jewish nation;[1] and three, some interpreters who are neither dispensationalists nor premillennialists take it to refer to a future conversion of the people of Israel, not as a separate nation or people, but as a large company of those among the Jewish people. In all of the various forms of this view, it is maintained that the fullness of Israel must refer to the special people of God who will be converted at some time in the future, as they are provoked to jealousy by the salvation of the Gentiles.[2]

The second view takes this phrase to be a reference to the salvation of all the elect, Jew and Gentile alike, gathered through the preaching of the gospel in the whole course of the history of redemption. John Calvin, for example, took this position and argued that Israel here refers, not to a distinct people among the peoples of the earth, but to the people of God in the general and comprehensive sense, embracing Jew and Gentile alike.[3]

---

[1] For a presentation and defence of the premillennialist form of this view, see George E. Ladd, *A Theology of the New Testament* (Grand Rapids: Eerdmans, 1974), pp. 561–3; Oscar Cullmann, *Christ and Time*, trans. Floyd V. Filson (Philadelphia: Westminster, 1960), p. 78.

[2] For a presentation and defence of this third form of the first view, see Charles Hodge, *A Commentary on the Epistle to the Romans* (Philadelphia: Alfred Martien, 1873), *ad loc.*; John Murray, *The Epistle to the Romans*, vol. I (NICNT; 1959; reprint, Grand Rapids: Eerdmans, 1975), pp. 91–103; G. Vos, *The Pauline Eschatology*, p. 89; Douglas J. Moo, *The Epistle to the Romans* (NICNT; Grand Rapids: Eerdmans, 1996), *ad loc.*; Keith A. Mathison, *Postmillennialism: An Eschatology of Hope* (Phillipsburg, NJ: Presbyterian and Reformed, 1999), pp. 121–30. Though many defenders of this position are postmillennialists, this position is not as such a sufficient condition for taking a postmillennialist view for the kingdom. Postmillennialism will be considered in subsequent chapters.

[3] *The Epistles of Paul the Apostle to the Romans and the Thessalonians*, trans. Ross Mackenzie, ed. David W. Torrance and Thomas F. Torrance (*Calvin's New Testament Commentaries*, 1960; reprint, Grand Rapids: Eerdmans, 1973), p. 255.

The third view takes this phrase to be a reference to the total number of the elect from among the people of Israel. According to this view, the fullness of Israel refers to the sum total of all elect Jews who constitute the remnant of believers gathered throughout the history of the church until the time of Christ's second coming.[1]

Though these views and the arguments for them are quite diverse and at times complicated, we would like to summarize briefly the reasons that lead us to adopt the first view as the best understanding of the phrase 'all Israel'.

'Israel' in this phrase must refer to the special people of God, not all the elect, whether Jew or Gentile, gathered throughout the entirety of redemptive history. This is because the term is used no less than eleven times in Romans 9–11, and in every instance it refers to the people of Israel. It is hard to see why Romans 11:26 should be an exception.

To take 'all Israel' as a reference to the total number of the elect among the people of Israel throughout all of the history of redemption would be anti-climactic and largely irrelevant to the Apostle Paul's interest in Romans 9–11. In these chapters, as we have seen, the apostle is dealing with the mystery of God's will for the salvation of the people of Israel, a people who have mostly disbelieved the gospel but whom God has not forsaken nor cast off irrevocably. Were the reference only to all the elect of Israel, the entirety of the remnant according to God's purpose of election, it would not answer

---

[1] Cf. Anthony Hoekema, *The Bible and the Future*, pp. 139–47, who provides an able defence of this view. Others who take this view include: Herman Bavinck, *The Last Things*, pp. 104–7; L. Berkhof, *Systematic Theology*, pp. 698–700; William Hendriksen, *Israel in Prophecy* (Grand Rapids: Baker, 1974), pp. 39–52; H. Ridderbos, *Paul*, pp. 354–61; O. Palmer Robertson, 'Is There a Distinctive Future for Ethnic Israel in Romans 11?' in *Perspectives on Evangelical Theology*, ed. K. S. Kantzer and S. N. Gundry (Grand Rapids: Baker, 1979), pp. 209–27; Robert B. Strimple, 'Amillennialism', in *Three Views of the Millennium and Beyond*, ed. Darrell L. Bock (Grand Rapids: Zondervan, 1999), pp. 112–18.

to the argument that the Apostle Paul specifically develops in this passage.

The argument of this passage is that the hardening of the people of Israel will eventually come to an end, and this will occur after the people of Israel have been provoked to jealousy by the conversion and riches of the fullness of the Gentiles. Through their being provoked to jealousy, the fullness of Israel (11:12) will come to salvation. This fullness is the equivalent in Romans 11 of what is variously described as the acceptance of Israel (11:15), the grafting in of Israel (11:23–24), or the 'all Israel' of this phrase (11:26).

Though the expression 'and so' that is used in Romans 11:26 refers primarily to the manner in which all Israel will be saved – that is, as Israel is provoked to jealousy by the conversion of the Gentiles – its temporal aspect cannot be suppressed. In Romans 9–11 the Apostle Paul is describing an obvious sequence of events in the history of redemption: the unbelief of the people of Israel leads to the preaching of the gospel to the Gentiles; the faith and conversion of the Gentiles thereupon leads to the jealousy and subsequent conversion of the fullness of Israel. Within this sequence of events, the phrase 'and so all Israel shall be saved' most naturally seems to mean that after the fullness of the Gentiles is ingrafted, the time will come when the people of Israel, provoked to jealousy, will be converted and God's purposes of redemption be accomplished in them.[1]

---

[1] Strimple, *Postmillennialism*, p. 116, appeals to the three instances of the adverb 'now' in verses 30–31 to argue that the apostles' concern in chapter 11 is not to predict the future but to explain the motive and purpose of his present ministry. However, the 'now' to which the apostle refers in these verses includes the entire present period of redemptive history. It does not exclude the possibility of a coming or future reversal in which the fullness of the Gentiles will be reciprocated by a corresponding fullness of Israel. Cf. Kenneth L. Gentry, Jr., 'A Postmillennial Response to Robert B. Strimple', in *Three Views of the Millennium and Beyond,* p. 134. Gentry's response to Strimple includes a good summary of the arguments for the view that all Israel in Romans 11:26 refers to a future conversion of Israel.

Finally, the main point of Romans 11:25 seems to be that the hardening of Israel will come to an end and thereupon Israel will be restored. This point would actually be undermined, were we to understand the 'all Israel' of Romans 11:26 to be a reference only to the total number of the elect people of Israel, who make up only a remnant throughout the history of redemption.

Though these considerations could be elaborated upon and various objections answered further, this should be enough to show that the most likely reading of this passage is one that takes it to teach the future ingathering and conversion of the totality of the people of Israel. This does not mean necessarily that every individual member of the people of Israel will ultimately be saved, or that all members of this people will be converted at some future time. The fullness of Israel need not mean the salvation of every member of this people any more than the fullness of the Gentiles means the salvation of every Gentile. However, it does suggest that the Apostle Paul taught that through the preaching of the gospel to the nations the time will come in which a fullness of Israel will be converted, an ingrafting again of Israel as a people, a restoration of this special people of God to gospel favour and blessing.

Conclusion

If this understanding of the future salvation of the fullness of Israel through the preaching of the gospel is correct, then two corollaries deserve to be mentioned in conclusion.

The first is that there is but one way of salvation for Jew and Gentile alike, and that is the way of faith in response to the preaching of the gospel (*Rom.* 10: 1–17). The burden of the argument of the Apostle Paul in Romans 9–11 is that all are saved only as they are grafted into the one olive tree, in fellowship through faith with the one and only Saviour whose righteousness answers to the need of Jew and Gentile. Nowhere in the Word of God do we have a clearer repudiation of any teaching that suggests different pathways to salvation for Jews and Gentiles. Today this idea is often taught in the form of a 'two-covenant theology', the one covenant unique to the people of Israel, the other unique to the Gentile nations. Though Romans 9–11 suggests that God's purposes of redemption include a purpose uniquely addressed and suited to the special people of Israel, it stands opposed to any such two-covenant position.[1] All who will be saved will be saved through faith in response to the same gospel and within the fellowship of the one people of God (*Eph.* 2:11–22).

The second corollary is that believers should have a keen interest in the preaching of the gospel to the people of Israel. Rather than concluding that God's purposes have ended for them, we should preach and evangelize in expectation that, because the gifts and calling of God are irrevocable, his calling of Israel will not terminate in her wholesale unbelief but rather in her fullness being saved. This should stimulate and encourage the church, then, to preach the gospel to the Gentiles as well as to the Jews. Any presumption that God has wholly abandoned Israel to her unbelief is just that: a presumption without biblical warrant.

And so let the gospel be preached to the Jew first and also to the Gentile, for God's purposes of salvation will not fail.

---

[1] A fine treatment of the general question of Israel and the church, including the issue of one covenant or two, is provided by David E. Holwerda, in his *Jesus and Israel: One Covenant or Two?* (Grand Rapids: Eerdmans, 1995). Holwerda also addresses the question of 'all Israel' in Romans 11:26 (pp. 168–75) and provides what might be called a 'soft' version of the view that 'all Israel' refers to a future 'eschatological fullness' (his expression) of Israel.

6

Signs of Opposition
and Judgement – I

IN OUR INTRODUCTION to the biblical teaching regarding 'the
signs of the times', we noted that they often stress the
antithesis in history between the kingdom of God and the
powers of evil. The coming of the Lord Jesus Christ in the
fullness of time and the preaching of the gospel of the kingdom to all the nations, provoke the opposition and hostility
of the world, to the extent that it remains under the tyranny
of the evil one. As history moves toward the time of Christ's
return or revelation from heaven, the conflict in history intensifies between the truth and the lie, the kingdom of God and
the kingdom of this world. This intensification, far from
witnessing to uncertainty regarding Christ's triumph, only
confirms that all things are being ripened for judgement and
the consummation of history at Christ's coming again.

Several signs of the times, therefore, reflect this intensified
conflict as the time of the end draws near. These are:
tribulation, the Great Tribulation, apostasy, and the coming
of Antichrist(s). In this chapter we will consider the first of
these: the tribulation experienced by the faithful people of
God during the present age. The Bible teaches that one of the
marks of the progress of history under the dominion of

Christ is the world's opposition to believers whose fellowship with Christ includes a participation in his suffering. Believers may expect their devotion to Christ and his cause inevitably to provoke the world's hatred, just as the world opposed Christ himself when he came proclaiming the gospel of the kingdom.

General References

A number of general references in the New Testament clearly teach that troubles will attend the way of the Christian believer in the present age. Though these passages may seem strange to our ears because the tendency today is to paint a very different picture of the Christian life and pilgrimage, they make clear that struggle and difficulty are the common circumstance of believers in the present period of history. Such tribulation is not limited to a specific period of time either in the past or the distant future; it spans the whole period between Christ's first and second coming. Nor will it cease before Christ's revelation at the end of the age (2 *Thess.* 1:6–8).

In the Sermon on the Mount, for example, Jesus taught his disciples that they should expect suffering and distress as a consequence of their discipleship. The words of Matthew 5:10–12 are well known: 'Blessed are those who have been persecuted for the sake of righteousness, for theirs is the kingdom of heaven. Blessed are you when men cast insults at you, and persecute you, and say all kinds of evil against you falsely, on account of Me. Rejoice, and be glad, for your reward in heaven is great, for so they persecuted the prophets who were before you'.[1] One of the so-called Beatitudes, this statement provides a general description of the experience of the believing disciple of Jesus Christ in the face of the world's persecution and insults. It suggests that such persecution will

[1] In a parallel passage in Luke 6:22, we read: 'Blessed are you when men hate you, and ostracize you, and cast insults at you, and spurn your name as evil, for the sake of the Son of Man.'

be the normal consequence of seeking to be faithful to Jesus Christ.

Other New Testament passages contain similar warnings. When Christ was teaching his disciples in the Upper Room prior to his crucifixion, he declared, 'Remember the word that I said to you, A slave is not greater than his master. If they persecuted Me, they will also persecute you' (*John* 15:20). Here Christ appeals to a principle consistent with the relationship of master and servant: if the master suffered at the hands of the world, surely the disciple can expect the same. The Lord issues a comparable warning in John 16:33, 'These things I have spoken to you that in Me you may have peace. In the world you have tribulation, but take courage; I have overcome the world.' In 2 Timothy 3:12, the Apostle Paul, immediately after describing the persecutions he had suffered in various places, notes that this will also be the experience of all believers: 'And indeed, all who desire to live godly in Christ Jesus will be persecuted' (cf. *Acts* 14:22).

Tribulation in the Olivet Discourse

One of the most important and comprehensive passages in the New Testament for an understanding of 'the signs of the times' is the so-called Olivet Discourse recorded in Matthew 24, with parallels in Mark 13:1–37 and Luke 21:5–36. As we have already seen in connection with the issue of the 'delay' of Christ's coming, the meaning of this passage is much disputed. Some interpreters argue that the signs of the times of which the Lord speaks in this passage are exclusively restricted to the period immediately prior to the destruction of Jerusalem in AD 70.[1] Undoubtedly, the primary reference of many of the signs in this passage is to this period, but they

---

[1] See, e.g., Gary DeMar, *Last Days Madness*, esp. pp. 47–146; and Keith A. Mathison, *Postmillennialism*, pp. 111–115. As noted earlier, these authors and others are preterists, who restrict the reference of this discourse to events now past.

may also describe the period of history extending to the time of Christ's coming at the end of the age.

This passage is known as the Olivet Discourse because it records the words of Jesus Christ spoken to his disciples while he was sitting on the Mount of Olives (*Matt.* 24:3). The disciples had pointed out the temple buildings to Christ, and he had responded by declaring, 'Do you not see all these things? Truly I say to you, not one stone here shall be left upon another, which will not be torn down' (verse 2). This response provoked a twofold question from the disciples: 'Tell us, when will these things [the destruction of the temple] be, and what will be the sign of Your coming, and of the end of the age?' In this question the disciples desire to know not only how Jesus' words regarding the tearing down of the temple will be fulfilled, but also what signs will characterize the period prior to his coming and the end of the age.

Christ responds by mentioning a number of signs that will characterize the present age before the end comes (verses 4–14). These signs will include such things as the hearing of 'wars and rumours of wars', 'famines', 'earthquakes', 'false prophets', 'lawlessness', and the preaching of the gospel 'in the whole world for a witness to all the nations'. Among these signs will also be the experience of tribulation: 'Then they will deliver you to tribulation, and will kill you, and you will be hated by all nations on account of My name' (verse 9). These verses seem to speak generally of signs that will characterize the age between the time of Christ's first and second comings.[1]

---

[1] John Murray, 'The Interadventual Period and the Advent: Matt. 24 and 25', (*Collected Writings of John Murray*, vol 2 (Edinburgh: Banner of Truth, 1977), pp. 387–8: 'In verses 4–14 Jesus deals with certain outstanding features of the interadventual period. We are reminded at verse 6 that the end is not immediately, that the activity of deceivers, and reports of wars and rumours of wars, are not to be regarded as portents of an imminent consummation (cf. Luke 19:11); and at verses

However, in what follows, especially verses 15–28, the focus of Christ's words seems clearly to be upon the events that will precede or accompany the destruction of the temple in Jerusalem. They speak of events in the period of time contemporary with those to whom Jesus first spoke. In fact, in verse 34 Jesus speaks of all these things taking place before the passing away of 'this generation', a phrase that seems likely to refer to the generation alive at the time. As noted earlier, a number of able and Reformed interpreters have argued that this discourse, together with all the signs described in it, refers to events that were fulfilled specifically in the year AD 70, when the temple was destroyed in Jerusalem.[1] Sometimes termed a 'preterist' or past-time reading of Matthew 24, this interpretation takes the tribulation mentioned in this passage, including the great tribulation referred to in verse 21, as a sign that has already been fulfilled and which therefore bears no relevance to present history before Christ's second coming.[2] This passage would not,

---

7, 8 that wars, famines, and earthquakes are but the beginning of sorrows. . . This section of the discourse brings us to what is surely of the same purport as the consummation of the age in the question of the disciples (verse 3), namely, "the end" – then shall the end come. So we are compelled to construe verses 4–14 as, in brief outline, a forecast of interadventual history.'

[1] In addition to the authors mentioned in the footnote on p. 142, see J. Marcellus Kik, *An Eschatology of Victory* (Phillipsburg, NJ: Presbyterian & Reformed, 1971), pp. 53–173, who argues extensively that Matthew 24:1–35 refers to events that took place before and during AD 70. Kik believes the chapter is divided at verse 36, which introduces for the first time the subject of the end of the age in the strict sense of Christ's second coming. Cf. Ed Stevens, *What Happened in 70 AD* (Ashtabula, Ohio: Northeast Ohio Bible Institute, 1981); and James Stuart Russell, *The Parousia*, pp. 66–114, for a defence of a radical preterist reading of Matthew 24, in which the entire discourse refers to the events of Jerusalem's destruction in AD 70.

[2] It should be added here, however, that, even were this reading correct, it would not mean that tribulation is not a present reality or

therefore, have anything to teach us about whether tribulation is a sign of the times during the entire period between Christ's first and second comings.

It may be true that many of the signs of the times in Matthew 24 refer primarily and immediately to the destruction of the temple in Jerusalem in AD 70, but for several good reasons we may conclude that they have a secondary and more remote reference to events that will characterize the present age until Christ's second coming:

i. To say that all the events described in Matthew 24 took place before or during AD 70 does not do full justice to the disciples' question and the expression 'the end of the age'. This, and the language about the coming (*parousia*) of Christ, used elsewhere in this passage (verses 27, 30, 42–44), commonly refer in the New Testament to the second coming of Christ (e.g., *Matt.* 28:20). In no other instance does the expression 'the end of the age' refer to an event prior to Christ's second coming.

ii. As we saw in a previous chapter on the sign of the preaching of the gospel to all the nations, this sign can only with difficulty be said to have been fulfilled prior to AD 70. This sign, and the language Christ employs, (verse 6) suggest that some time will elapse before all will have been fulfilled (see *Luke* 19:11, where the disciples are said to have misunderstood Jesus' words to mean that the kingdom of God was going to appear immediately).

iii. In verses 29–31, Jesus seems to be speaking of his second coming, an event that can hardly to be said to have already occurred in AD 70. He speaks of a visible advent in

sign of the times. The general references mentioned in our previous section are clearly not limited to any specific time period prior to Christ's return, but describe the circumstance of the believer during this present period of history. Consequently, the teaching that tribulation is a sign characteristic of the present age does not finally depend upon whether Matthew 24 or the Olivet Discourse refers to past events only.

verse 30b that parallels other New Testament descriptions (*Matt* 16:27, *Mark* 8:38, *Luke* 9:26, *Acts* 1:9–11, *1 Thess.* 4:17, *2 Thess.* 1:7 and *Rev.* 1:7). The reference to the sign of his coming echoes the language used by the disciples in the second part of their question, and the language of the great trumpet and the angels in verse 31 is characteristically used of Christ's return at the end of the age (*1 Cor.* 15:52, *1 Thess.* 4:16, *2 Thess.* 1:7).

iv. The teaching in verses 36–44 that no one knows the day or the hour can best be understood of Christ's second coming, not the destruction of Jerusalem in AD 70. This language also has New Testament parallels which uniformly refer to the second coming of Christ (*Matt.* 25:13, *Mark* 13:32, *Luke* 12:39–40, *Acts* 1:6–7, *1 Thess.* 5:2, *Rev.* 16:15).

v. Finally, it should be noted that Chapters 24 and 25 belong together. They are joined by the series of parables that illustrate the nature of Christ's coming and the need for preparedness in the light of its certainty, namely, the parable of the household (24:43–44), the parable of the wise and wicked servants (24:45–51), and the parable of the ten virgins (25:1–13). The language of Matthew 25:14–46, in its description of the final judgement of all, suggests that the Lord is still speaking of those events which will precede or accompany his coming at the end of the age.

Accordingly, since Matthew 24 seems to describe signs of the times that are characteristic of the whole period leading up to the coming of Christ at the end of the age, it confirms the testimony of those general references already mentioned that speaks of tribulation as the experience of the believer in this present age. No believer should be surprised by the world's hostility or opposition. Christ himself predicted that this would be a sign of the end of the age.

Some Observations about Tribulation

Assuming that tribulation will mark the life of the believing community during this present age, some observations about its nature and occasion may help to explain further what is meant by this sign.

First, the most common New Testament term for tribulation, *thlipsis* in Greek, describes the trouble or distress that results from the believer's commitment to Christ, his Word, and his kingdom. The term itself is very broad in its meaning, referring to whatever disruption or trouble attends the life of the believer because of his or her devotion to Christ. Interestingly, in 2 Thessalonians 1:6−8, the tribulation presently suffered by the believer is contrasted with the rest or peace that will result from Christ's coming at the end of the age. The contrast in this passage between the present and future circumstance of believers indicates that the tribulations of the present life are those which make the Christian's present pilgrimage difficult and which fall short of the peace that will attend the life to come. These troubles confirm the words of the Lord in Matthew 10:34, when he warned the disciples, 'Do not think that I came to bring peace on the earth; I did not come to bring peace, but a sword'.

It is crucial to notice that this tribulation results from believers' commitment to Christ. The tribulation that serves as a sign of the times is not just any circumstance of trouble or distress, but that which results specifically from their aim to be his faithful disciples. Consequently, in many references to the persecution and trouble that will attend the Christian life in the present age, we find language used that joins the experience of tribulation closely with the believer's relationship with Christ. Nowhere is this language bolder than in Colossians 1:24, where the Apostle Paul speaks of his joy in suffering and sharing in filling up that which is lacking in Christ's afflictions. This passage should not be understood to teach that there was any lack in Christ's atoning work, but it does speak clearly of a participation on the part of the church in the afflictions of Christ.[1] One important way in which the

---

[1] Cf. F. F. Bruce, *Commentary on Ephesians and Colossians* (NICNT; Grand Rapids: Eerdmans, 1956), p. 216: 'The sense in which

church has fellowship with Christ is suffering affliction for his name's sake. This is the reason Christ could confront Saul before his conversion on the way to Damascus, asking him, 'Saul, Saul, why are you persecuting Me?' (*Acts* 9:4) So intimate is the communion of the believer with Christ that the affliction or persecution of the believer is a communion or participation in Christ's affliction.

Second, tribulation in the life of the believer can take many forms. Often it takes the form of open persecution, in which the believer is exposed to the reproach and hostility of those who reject the gospel of Jesus Christ (*1 Thess.* 1:6, *2 Thess.* 1, *2 Tim.* 3:12–13, *Acts* 14:22, *Rev.* 1:9). It can mean imprisonment, something which the apostles and many believers ever since have experienced (*Acts* 20:23). Sometimes it means ridicule (*Heb.* 10:33), poverty (*2 Cor.* 2:4), illness (*Rev.* 2:22), or inner distress and sorrow (*Phil.* 1:17, *2 Cor.* 2:4). Whether a believer lives in a country or society friendly or hostile to the gospel, one or another of these forms of tribulation cannot be escaped. Each of them attests the genuineness of the believer's fellowship with Christ, as well as commitment and devotion to him and his gospel.

Third, this sign of tribulation, like the other signs, testifies not to the uncertainty of Christ's cause, but to its certain victory. One of the more dramatic confirmations of this is given to us in Revelation 12:7–12. In this passage we are given a vision of a great battle in heaven between Michael and his angels on the one hand and the dragon and his angels on the other. This battle ends in victory for Michael and the casting down of Satan to the earth – a victory which is said to have

---

the suffering and death of Christ have won justification and reconciliation for men is unique, unrepeatable. When Paul is so concerned as he is here to assert the sole sufficiency of Christ as Saviour and Mediator, it would be absurd to suppose that he means that he himself, by the hardships he endures, is in some way supplementing the saving work of Christ. . . But in the sense which Paul intends here, Christ continues to suffer in his members, and not least in Paul himself.'

been accomplished because of 'the blood of the Lamb and because of the word of their [the believers'] testimony' (verse 11). What is striking about this passage is how the defeat of Satan and his host results in his intensified pursuit and persecution of the church on earth, knowing that his time is short and his defeat certain. The suffering and affliction of the church witnesses, accordingly, to the victory of Christ's cross in the purposes of God. Far from its being a fearful prospect of doom and gloom for the faithful people of God, it reminds the believer that God's kingdom will prevail.

Fourth, the circumstance of tribulation in the life of the believer can be, and often is, an occasion for growth and maturity in discipleship. Nowhere so much as in affliction does the believer come to realize the depth and the extent of his fellowship with Christ. In suffering affliction believers reflect something of that same pattern evident in the life of Christ himself, who entered into his glory only after the shame and suffering of the cross.

Indeed, the prominent place of tribulation in the life of believers and the church serves as a constant reminder of the centrality of the cross of Christ, not only as the means of atonement, but also as a call to self-denying patience under circumstances of suffering (*1 Pet.* 2:21–25). Through the experience of affliction and trouble, the believer grows in perseverance and hope. As the Apostle Paul declares: 'We also exult in our tribulations, knowing that tribulation brings about perseverance; and perseverance, proven character, and proven character, hope; and hope does not disappoint, because the love of God has been poured out within our hearts through the Holy Spirit who was given to us' (*Rom.* 5:3–5).

For this reason, believers should count their trials 'all joy' and 'the testing of the faith' an occasion for growth in the Christian life, growth that produces maturity and completeness (*James* 1:2–4). In the midst of the trials and troubles of this life, the Christian is like a child disciplined by his or her father (*Heb.* 12:6), like gold which is refined through fire (*1 Pet.* 1:7), or like the vine pruned by the gardener (*John* 15:1– 8).[1]

The tribulation of the present age, like all of the Bible's other teaching about the future, serves to nurture the believer's hope. It reminds him of the triumphant words of the Apostle Paul at the end of Romans 8:

> But in all these things [tribulation, distress, persecution, famine, nakedness, peril, the sword] we overwhelmingly conquer through Him who loved us. For I am convinced that neither death nor life, nor angels, nor principalities, nor things present, nor things to come, nor powers, nor height, nor depth, nor any other created thing, shall be able to separate us from the love of God, which is in Christ Jesus our Lord' (*Rom.* 8:37–39).

The Great Tribulation

Having considered the sign of tribulation generally, we now look at what is often called the great tribulation. The question to be faced is: does the Bible teach that the tribulation of the present age will issue in a circumstance of intensified tribulation, a *great* tribulation, prior to the return of Christ? Should believers expect anything more than a general and intermittent distress or trouble during the entire period prior to Christ's coming?

The subject of the great tribulation has been especially prominent among Christian believers who are dispensational premillennialists. As we noted earlier, Dispensationalism teaches that the return of Christ will occur in two stages, the first often called the 'parousia', and the second often called the 'revelation' of Christ. According to this view, Christ will

---

[1] See John R. W. Stott, *The Cross of Christ* (Downers Grove, Illinois: InterVarsity, 1986), pp. 311–37, for a good survey of the ways the Christian life involves suffering in communion with Christ. Calvin, for this reason, made cross-bearing a distinctive feature of the Christian life.

first come for his saints at the time of the secret rapture, and only subsequently with his saints to reign upon the earth for a period of one thousand years, the millennium. Since in Dispensationalism the rapture of believers will precede the period of great tribulation (usually thought to be for a period of seven years), this position is often known as Pre-tribulationalism.[1] However, a distinct minority among dispensationalists have taught that the rapture would occur in the middle of the period of great tribulation. This position is known as Mid-tribulational Premillennialism. Non-dispensational premillennialists teach that Christ will return only after this period of great tribulation. Hence, this position is known as Post-tribulational Premillennialism.[2]

These various views within Premillennialism are only mentioned at this point because they illustrate the bearing which the issue of the great tribulation has upon the various millennial views that we shall consider. They cannot be wholly ignored at this point, since any position that concludes that believers will experience the great tribulation

[1] Though this is not the place to consider the biblical basis offered for Dispensationalism, the two passages most prominent in the argument for a pre-tribulational rapture of believers occurring before a seven year period of tribulation are 1 Thessalonians 4:13–18 and Daniel 9:20–27. The first of these passages is said to teach a secret rapture of believers who return with Christ to heaven during the seven-year period of tribulation. The second of these passages is said to describe 70 weeks during which the Lord's purposes with ethnic Israel will be realised, the seventieth week being the seven-year period of tribulation during which the Lord will resume his dealings with Israel (the period between the sixty-ninth and seventieth weeks being that interim period of the church in which the Lord deals with the Gentile nations through the gospel). See *The New Scofield Study Bible*, notes on Daniel 9:20–27 and 1 Thessalonians 4:13–18.

[2] For a discussion of the pre-, mid- and post-tribulational views, see Millard J. Erickson, *A Basic Guide to Eschatology: Making Sense of the* Millennium, rev. ed. (orig. *Contemporary Options in Eschatology*, 1977; Grand Rapids: Baker, 1998), pp. 109–81; and Gleason L. Archer, Jr., *The Rapture: Pre-, Mid-, or Post-Tribulational?* (Grand Rapids: Zondervan, 1984).

is incompatible with the traditional view of Dispensation-alism.[1] The position that we will defend could be compatible with some forms of Premillennialism, but not with classic Dispensationalism.[2]

1. THE GREAT TRIBULATION IN MATTHEW 24

The most important passage that speaks of a great tribulation is Matthew 24, a passage we have already considered more than once. In this passage, Jesus, as part of his answer to the disciples' questions about the destruction of the temple in Jerusalem and the sign of his coming and the end of the age, speaks of a coming period of great tribulation.

Because of the importance of this passage and its specific description of this great tribulation, it will be useful to quote it at some length:

> Therefore when you see the ABOMINATION OF DESOLATION which was spoken of through Daniel the prophet, standing in the holy place (let the reader understand), then let those who are in Judea flee to the mountains; let him who is on the housetop not go down to get the things out that are in his house; and let him who is in the field not turn back to get his cloak. But woe to those who are with child and to those who nurse babes in those days! But pray that your flight may not be in winter, or on a Sabbath; for then there will be a great tribulation, such as has not occurred since the beginning of the world until now,

[1] It should be noted, however, that the classic premillennial view of the future taught that the church and all believers would suffer this period of great tribulation before Christ returned to establish the millennial kingdom. The preponderance of Christian interpreters throughout history, accordingly, whether premillennialists, amillennialists or postmillennialists, have taught that Christ will return only after the great tribulation, not before.

[2] For a presentation of the post-tribulational view by a non-dispensational pre-millennialist, see Robert H. Gundry, *The Church and the Tribulation* (Grand Rapids: Zondervan, 1973), 49.

nor ever shall. And unless those days had been cut short, no life would have been saved; but for the sake of the elect those days shall be cut short (verses 15–22).

Here Christ clearly teaches that one of the signs that will precede the destruction of the temple is a period, not only of general but of intensified tribulation. He also associates this period of great tribulation with the fulfilment of Daniel's prophecy regarding the destruction of the temple which occurred in the year AD 70.

As we have noted before, the primary and immediate reference in these verses is to those events that took place in the period of the generation to whom Jesus first spoke these words. The question remains, however, whether they might not also have reference to further great tribulation that will occur prior to the end of the age.

Here it is not necessary for us to repeat our reasons for applying the signs of the times in Matthew 24 to the entire period between Christ's first and second comings. It is difficult, if not impossible, to restrict the application of these verses to the events around AD 70 because this passage, like many other biblical prophecies, displays the characteristics of prophetic foreshortening and biblical typology. Though the prophecy was clearly fulfilled in AD 70, that was an initial fulfilment which typifies circumstances that will subsequently recur and anticipates the return of Christ at the end of the age.

Admittedly, this understanding of the passage has some difficulties, but they are not as insurmountable as the understanding which insists that the reference is exclusively to events that occurred in the past (from our present vantage point) and has no bearing upon events in the present or future that will precede Christ's return.[1] Just as the

---

[1] For example, Jesus speaks of the elect in Matthew 24:22, a group that can only with difficulty be limited to those delivered at the time of the destruction of the temple in Jerusalem in AD 70.

prophecy of Daniel regarding the desecration of the temple had an earlier and initial fulfilment in the time of Antiochus Epiphanes (before the first coming of Christ), and then a subsequent and further fulfilment at the time of the destruction of the temple in Jerusalem, so we may understand our Lord's prophecy in Matthew 24 to include a further and final fulfilment at the end of the age.[1] According to this understanding, the tribulation that characterizes the circumstance of the faithful church in the interim period will reach its most intensified expression in the period preceding his second coming.

II. ADDITIONAL BIBLICAL REFERENCES

Any interpretation of Matthew's reference to a great tribulation that restricts it to an event in the past seems to conflict with several additional biblical references which suggest a period of intensified tribulation prior to Christ's coming at the end of the age.

In Revelation 2:22, in the letter to the angel of the church in Thyatira, Christ warns that he will 'cast her [the woman Jezebel] upon a bed of sickness, and those who commit adultery with her into great tribulation, unless they repent of their deeds'. Though some interpreters have sought to restrict this warning to the church in the first century, it would seem more appropriate to regard it as including a solemn warning to the church during the entire age prior to Christ's return.[2] However direct and specific this warning

---

[1] Antiochus Epiphanes was one of the kings of the Seleucid dynasty (founded in Syria by Seleucus, one of the generals of Alexander), which ruled Syria in whole or in part from about 321 to 65 BC. It is generally acknowledged that his destruction and desecration of the temple in Jerusalem in the second century BC was a fulfilment of the prophecy in Daniel 9:24–27.

[2] This is true, for example, of interpreters who read the book of Revelation in a strictly preterist manner. Often such interpreters are postmillennialists who minimise the presence of tribulation in the period between Christ's first and second comings. The preterist and postmillennialist reading of Revelation depends upon dating the book

may have been to the church of Thyatira in the first century, it remains one of Christ's warnings to the seven churches which typify the entirety of the church prior to the end of the age. Similarly, in Revelation 7:9–17 the Apostle John describes his vision of that 'great multitude, which no one could count . . . clothed with white robes' (verse 9) which is composed of those 'who are coming out of the great tribulation' (verse 14). This passage, like that in Revelation 2:22, would seem to use the language of 'great tribulation' to describe an ongoing experience of the saints in this present age. If such language can be employed to describe what is common to the period between Christ's first and second comings, it seems appropriate that it should also be applicable to the period just prior to his return.

Furthermore, though the term 'great tribulation' is not used in Revelation 20, it is instructive to observe that this passage also speaks of Satan's little season at the end of the millennium, the period of one thousand years during which Satan is bound so as not to be able to deceive the nations. It seems most likely that this little season corresponds to that period of intensified opposition to the gospel and the cause of Christ that will characterize the close of the age prior to Christ's return.

Another similar and important passage is 2 Thessalonians 2:1–15, which describes the coming of 'the man of

---

prior to the fall of Jerusalem in AD 70. For an able defence of this position, see Kenneth L. Gentry, Jr., *Before Jerusalem Fell: Dating the Book of Revelation* (Tyler, Texas: Institute for Christian Economics, 1989). For a recent defence of the traditional view that the book of Revelation was written later, at the end of the first century, see G.K. Beale, *The Book of Revelation: A Commentary on the Greek Text* (NIGTC: Grand Rapids: Eerdmans, 1999), pp. 4–27. I find the argument of Beale to be, on balance, more persuasive. It should be noted that the preterist and postmillennialist position must date the book of Revelation earlier in order for its construction of New Testament eschatology to work.

lawlessness' prior to the coming of Christ. In this passage, which follows one in which Christ's revelation from heaven will bring rest to the beleaguered and persecuted believers (2 *Thess.* 1), it is evident that the coming of 'the man of lawlessness' will be accompanied by persecution of and apostasy within the church. Interestingly, this passage bears a striking resemblance to the references in Daniel 9 and Matthew 24 to 'the abomination of desolation'. One of the features of this 'man of lawlessness' will be his effort to exalt himself above every so-called god or object of worship, so that he takes his seat in the temple of God, displaying himself as being god (verse 4).

Though we will consider such additional signs of the times as apostasy or the coming of the Antichrist in the next chapter, it appears likely that in these and other passages a constellation of signs – the Great Tribulation, the Great Apostasy, the Antichrist – mark out the period of history immediately prior to the close of the age. These passages suggest a pattern in which those signs of the times which bespeak opposition to Christ come to a culminating and intensified expression as the end draws near.

Concluding Observations

When we introduced this study of the Bible's teaching about the future, we emphasised the need for caution and circumspection in drawing hard-and-fast conclusions about some aspects of its teaching. This need is especially evident when we consider the Bible's teaching about the signs of the times, and so it is with a measure of tentativeness that the following concluding observations about the great tribulation are proposed.

First, the great tribulation that is likely to characterize history shortly before the close of the present age is but an intensified and culminating expression of that tribulation that marks the whole period between Christ's first and second comings. For this reason, it is even possible, as we have seen, to speak of a great tribulation that is an ongoing experience of the saints in this present age. However, as history draws to its close under the reign and rule of Christ, it appears that Satan's opposition to Christ will come to acute and final expression in a short season of more severe tribulation.

Second, the period of great tribulation is not one from which the church will be preserved through any pre-tribulational rapture, as has commonly been taught in Dispensationalism. In none of the passages we have considered is it taught that believers will be snatched away prior to the great tribulation. Rather, the consistent emphasis seems to be the call to patient endurance in the expectation of Christ's certain return and triumph. That return and triumph will bring rest to the beleaguered church at the end of the age (see *2 Thess.* 1).[1]

Third, the Bible's teaching about the prospect of a great tribulation shortly before the return of Christ ought not to be understood so as to allow any prediction of the time of Christ's return. For example, some might conclude from what we have said about this great tribulation that it is presently impossible that Christ should return. They might argue that since the church is not experiencing universally (in every place and situation) this acute trial or distress, we must not be living in a period that is proximate to the second coming of Christ. Similarly, they might argue that when such

---

[1] Though opinions differ among postmillennialists, most would restrict the reference in Matthew 24 and elsewhere concerning a 'great tribulation' to the events relating to the destruction of Jerusalem in AD 70. This view tends to reject the idea that the faithful church will experience an intensified tribulation as the return of Christ approaches. However, even those postmillennialists must reckon with the teaching of Revelation 20 that the millennium before Christ's return will conclude with Satan's 'little season', in which he will presumably be permitted to deceive the nations and turn them against Christ.

a circumstance of tribulation becomes manifest, it will then be possible to say with a certainty, 'Now is the time of Christ's coming.' Against this temptation to predict and to pinpoint when Christ is coming again, we need to recall what we said earlier about no one knowing the day or the hour, the time of his return. No one should be so confident of his understanding of the Bible's teaching about the great tribulation that he concludes that Christ could not return in the near future. Such a conclusion would be tantamount to claiming to know something about the day or hour of Christ's coming, namely, that the present cannot be the time.

And fourth, the Bible's teaching about the church's tribulation in this present age and in the period shortly before Christ's return is insufficiently clear to permit us any confident conclusions about the precise nature and course of a great tribulation that might be yet to come. We simply do not know whether this tribulation will suddenly befall the faithful church or whether it will gradually intensify as the end of the age draws near. Neither do we know whether such a great tribulation will come upon the whole church in every place at the same time or in the same way. Much remains unclear and uncertain in these respects. Consequently, no one may be too sure or dogmatic about these things.

Only one thing is absolutely certain: whatever the present trial and distress, whatever the future intensity of opposition to Christ's gospel and cause, Christ must reign until he has put all his enemies under his feet (1 Cor. 15:25). Tribulation, even great tribulation, cannot and will not separate us from the love of Christ (Rom. 8:35–39).

7

Signs of Opposition and Judgement – II

T HE OLD TESTAMENT contains a remarkable account of Jeremiah prophesying God's judgement upon the city of Jerusalem and the court of the Lord's house. This prophecy is striking, in that it was spoken within the sanctuary and it pronounced the Lord's curse upon the church of Jeremiah's day, and not the enemies of the Lord and his people.

We should not be surprised, therefore, to read that the response of the people was one of shock and anger. How could the prophet speak judgement against the house of the Lord? How dare he speak of the Lord's intention to make desolate the apple of his eye and the object of his unfailing favour? This was spiritual treachery on Jeremiah's part and, consequently, many called for his death. The priests and the prophets spoke to the officials and to all the people, saying, 'A death sentence for this man! For he has prophesied against this city as you have heard in your hearing' (*Jer.* 26:11).

Reading this account raises the question as to how the church of Jesus Christ today would respond to the prophecy of Jeremiah? It is easy to read the record and hold the whole matter at arm's length, as though it did not speak in any direct fashion to the circumstance of the church in our time. Indeed, many people who occupy positions of leadership in churches today might react similarly, were a prophet to stand in their midst and decry the church's unfaithfulness, even pronouncing God's judgement against it. Such behaviour would probably be regarded as troublesome and obnoxious, even impolite and unseemly. It is one thing to decry the sins of a secular and decaying culture; but it is quite another to decry the sins of the church, especially when it is done in the powerful language of the prophet Jeremiah.

But this account reminds us of one aspect of the Bible's teaching about 'the signs of the times' that we are apt to forget: that among those signs which express opposition to the gospel of Christ is the sign of apostasy and unfaithfulness among the people of God. Though it may be tempting to ignore it, the Bible does teach that God's judgement begins with the house of God (1 Pet. 4:17) and that apostasy has always been a feature of the church's life throughout the history of redemption. The prophecy of Jeremiah, like many such prophecies in the Word of God, should alert the church today to the continuing threat of apostasy; and it makes clear why, in our Lord's teaching about the signs of the times, the sign of apostasy plays such a significant role.

Apostasy

In the New Testament's teaching regarding the signs of the times, apostasy among the people of God often figures prominently. In addition to its being mentioned expressly, it is also implicit whenever the church is warned against unfaithfulness, in appeals often buttressed by the example of the apostasy of the Old Testament people of God.

In the Olivet Discourse, among the first signs of the times mentioned by the Lord is this sign of apostasy or falling away. In this passage, Christ prophesies that 'many will fall away, and betray one another, and hate one another. And many false prophets will arise and lead many astray. And because wickedness is multiplied, most men's love will grow cold' (*Matt.* 24:10–12; cf. *Luke* 8:13, *1 Tim.* 4:1). Christ adds that 'false Christs and false prophets will arise and show great signs and wonders, so as to mislead, if possible, even the elect' (*Matt.* 24:24). These verses present a sobering, even terrifying, picture of the church being assaulted, not simply by external enemies, but also by enemies within. Those who claim to speak for Christ within the church will actually be 'anti'-Christ. And those who are numbered among the visible people of God will, in truth, be opposed to the gospel of the kingdom of our Lord Jesus Christ. This, together with such signs as tribulation and the preaching of the gospel to all the world, will mark the period prior to the end of the age.

Other passages as well speak of apostasy as a characteristic sign of the times. The Apostle Paul, for example, in his first letter to Timothy, warns his spiritual son that the Spirit explicitly says that in later times some will fall away from the faith (*1 Tim.* 4:1). This departure may well be occasioned by the pressure of the world's hostility to the gospel, for, as the apostle adds in his second letter to Timothy, 'in the last days difficult times will come' (*2 Tim.* 3:1).

Furthermore, many of the words of exhortation, warning and encouragement in the New Testament indicate that apostasy will plague the people of God in this present age. In 2 Peter believers are exhorted to be on guard so as not to be carried away by the error of lawless men' (3:17). The book of Hebrews is pervaded by the theme of the temptation to fall away from the full truth of the new covenant, a falling away that would make it impossible for believers to be restored again to repentance (*Heb.* 3:12; 6:6).

This possibility of apostasy also underlies the promise that God will preserve and keep his people from falling. Thus, Jude 24, that well-known doxology with which the epistle concludes, praises God as the one 'who is able to keep [his people] from falling and to make them stand in the presence of His glory, blameless with great joy'. It also lends urgency to the Apostle Peter's exhortation: 'Therefore, my brothers, be all the more diligent to make certain about His calling and choosing you; for as long as you practice these things you will never stumble' (2 Pet. 1:10). The danger of apostasy leads the Apostle Paul to remind the Corinthians that God caused a record of the unfaithfulness of the old covenant people of God to be written in order that they might not become complacent (1 Cor. 10:1–6).

It becomes evident in these passages that the people of God in this present age will be severely tested and tried in their allegiance to Christ and the truth of God's Word. This testing will prove the faith of some, while exposing the unbelief of others. They will fall away or depart from the way of truth, the gospel of the kingdom, and this will occur even among leaders and office bearers of the church. Apostasy is a sign that directly involves and affects the people of God. It is a sign of internal opposition to Christ, not of external opposition by those who make no boast of being God's people. No one should be surprised by this. It has always been a feature of the church's existence in the world short of the end of the age. And it will most certainly be a feature of the church's existence during this present period between Christ's first and second advent.

I. A GREAT APOSTASY?

Does the Bible teach that, just as tribulation will issue in a period of great tribulation before Christ's return, so apostasy will issue in a period of great apostasy before the end comes? Do we find a similar pattern here, that this sign of the times intensifies as the end draws near and the return of Christ grows more imminent?

This seems to be the case, though here again we do well not to become too dogmatic or assured of our conclusions. But some passages suggest this. We have already referred to two of these passages in the foregoing. In 2 Timothy 3:1, we read of how in the last days difficult times will come. This passage is paralleled in 1 Timothy 4:1, which warns that 'the Spirit explicitly says that in later times some will fall away from the faith, paying attention to deceitful spirits and doctrines of demons'. The language employed in both of these passages seems to indicate that as the end approaches, apostasy will become ever more evident among the people of God.

However, the clearest example of this emphasis is found in 2 Thessalonians 2, a passage to which we will return again in our treatment of the subject of the Antichrist. Here the Apostle Paul is seeking to allay the anxiety of some believers in Thessalonica who have been shaken by the report of some that the day of the Lord has come (verse 2). In order to alleviate their anxiety, the apostle spells out some of the things that must take place before the day of the Lord.[1]

It is most important for us to notice that the apostle warns the church in Thessalonica that the day of the Lord will not come until 'the apostasy[2] comes first, and the man of

[1] For a representative statement of a preterist and postmillennialist reading of this passage see Mathison, *Postmillennialism*, pp. 228–33. At least two considerations argue against this reading. First, the language used to describe the coming of Christ, when compared with other New Testament passages (e.g., *1 Cor.* 1:8, *1 Thess.* 4:13–18; 5:2, *2 Pet.* 3:10), seems clearly to refer to *the* (not *a*) return of Christ at the end of the age. Second, this reading must assume a preterist reading of Matthew 24 and is constrained by the requirements of a postmillennialist construction. Were this passage to refer (as I believe it does) to the coming of Christ at the end of the age, it would not fit the postmillennialist claim that apostasy and rebellion will be relatively absent during the period prior to Christ's return. If this passage may be read as a description of an event already fulfilled in the first century, then most, if not all, the New Testament references to the coming of the Lord could equally well be referred to a past event, as J. Stuart Russell (*The Parousia*) and other radical preterists maintain.

[2] Many manuscripts use the language here of 'the rebellion' rather than 'the apostasy'. This textual difference, however, does not materially affect the teaching of this passage. In either instance the Apostle Paul teaches that the day of the Lord will be preceded by a period of extraordinary unfaithfulness, rebellion and apostasy among the people of God.

lawlessness is revealed, the son of destruction' (verse 3). The language used in this text, coupled with the description offered of 'the man of lawlessness' – he will evidently be someone of influence and significance within the church, for he 'takes his seat in the temple of God' (verse 4) – intimates that there will be a period of substantial turning or falling away within the church before the coming of Christ. One signal that the end is approaching will be this great and unparalleled unfaithfulness, at least from the standpoint of preceding history, among the community of those who profess to be believers.[1] And so the apostle warns the believers in Thessalonica against any premature conclusion that the day of the Lord has come; this day will not come until the apostasy occurs and the man of lawlessness is revealed.

The most likely conclusion to be drawn from this passage and the others cited above is that the sign of apostasy will reach an intensified and acute expression in the period prior to the return of Christ. Just as we saw previously that the sign of tribulation will issue in great tribulation, a period of more acute distress for the people of God, so we see now that the sign of apostasy will also issue in a period of great apostasy.

II. A WARNING TO THE CHURCH

If apostasy within the church is a sign of the times, and if the threat of it may become more pressing as the time of Christ's return approaches, then there are some inescapable consequences for the people of God and the church of Jesus Christ.

First, this sign reminds us that the church's greatest enemy arises not from the world without, or even from the wily devices of the devil himself, but from within her own ranks.

---

[1] It is interesting to observe that in Revelation 20:1–6, reference is made to a 'little season' in which Satan will be permitted once more to 'deceive the nations' just prior to the end of the millennium. Without yielding to the temptation to look at this passage here – we will have to do so at some length in Chapter 11 – this teaching of Satan's 'little season' corroborates the teaching of 2 Thessalonians 2, of a period of severe testing and apostasy before Christ's second coming.

This is an aspect of the Bible's teaching which cannot be emphasized too much. For some people in the church naively believe that the church is immune today from the danger of real apostasy, actual falling away from the truth of the gospel and the Word of God. Such people might be willing to concede that the church is not perfect and the like, but they never reckon with apostasy as a genuine threat to her well-being and witness. They are unwilling to believe that those who claim to speak in the name of Christ, even leaders and office bearers among the people of God, may be deceived and in serious error.

Such naiveté is clearly exposed in the Word of God as foolish. Anyone who reads the record of Israel's repeated apostasies or listens carefully to the New Testament warnings against unfaithfulness has to realize that the danger of falling away is ever present. Indeed, such apostasy functions as a sign of the times, as a signal within the unfolding purpose of God that the time is growing short and the day of the Lord is at hand.

Second, no one who takes seriously the biblical teaching about this sign of apostasy can afford the luxury of being 'at ease in Zion', blithely confident that the church is a safe haven of rest in the midst of the storm and fury of history. Strange as it may seem, the antithesis sometimes cuts across lines within the church as much as it separates the church from the world.

For this reason, one of the deadliest temptations facing the church of Jesus Christ is institutionalism or denominationalism. Both of these 'isms' express a blind and unyielding loyalty to organizations and agencies that takes precedence over loyalty to Christ and his Word. Whether rooted in nostalgia, sentiment or wishful thinking, such blind loyalty has no place in the life of a believer and yet it is frequently found within the church. The sign of apostasy serves as an antidote to such blind loyalty, warning every believer and church to beware the sin of inordinate love for any denomination or institution. Christians are not to place their trust in princes, least of all ecclesiastical princes, nor in institutions. Their trust is in the Lord who alone will preserve his church by the working of his Spirit and Word. They recognize that the Lord of the church stands ready to remove the candlestick from any church that falls away from the faith (see *Psa.* 118:8–9, *Rev.* 2:5).

And third, only that church which remains resolute and vigilant in the preservation of the faith has the right to claim the promise that the gates of hell will not prevail against her. The sign of apostasy serves as a clarion call to the church to be on guard against the temptation to fall away, to let go her rich inheritance in the Word of God and the gospel.

The corridors of history are littered with the dead corpses of once strong and vibrant churches. Many churches that once offered sturdy and uncompromising testimony to the truth of the gospel are today no more than social halls or clubs for people with particular political views. Such churches offer compelling testimony to the truth of the Lord's words regarding apostasy within the church.

Thus, this sign of the times ought to be a sufficient deterrent to any complacency. There is no room in a true church of Jesus Christ for smugness or self-satisfaction. The presumption that we 'have arrived' or that we are immune from falling is just that, a presumption without any basis in the Word of God. No particular church has the biblical right to claim the Lord's promise that it will be preserved unless it is able with integrity to sing, 'Onward Christian Soldiers, Marching as to War'.[1] When the Apostle Paul speaks of the coming apostasy that will precede the day of the Lord, he

---

[1] I use the term 'particular' church in order to distinguish it from the church catholic, the church as it is being gathered and established by Christ himself in the earth (*Matt.* 16:18). Some manifestations of the church may fall away, but the one holy catholic and apostolic church will not. The *Belgic Confession*, for example, says that the catholic church 'has been from the beginning of the world, and will be to the end thereof; which is evident from this that Christ is an eternal

hastens to encourage the church to stand firm and hold to the traditions which they were taught (2 *Thess.* 2:15). Unless the church remains vigilant and careful to hold fast to the apostolic Word inscripturated in the New Testament, it risks becoming apostate and falling away from the truth.

Thus, with many of the signs of the times, the sign of apostasy speaks a word of warning and a word of encouragement. It warns the church against complacency, alerting it to the dangers faced within and without. But it also reminds the church that Christ will preserve a faithful people. It is interesting to notice that when Christ speaks of apostasy in Matthew 24, he speaks of those who show great signs and wonders, so as to mislead, if possible, even the elect (verse 24). This language, though it sounds a note of warning, carries with it also the assurance of steadfastness on the part of the elect church. Those who make their calling and election sure need not be afraid, for Christ will keep them in his care.

The Antichrist

Of all 'the signs of the times' mentioned in the Scriptures, none is better known nor more commonly the subject of speculation than the sign of the coming Antichrist. The temptation to go beyond the clear teaching of Scripture and to fall prey to an unbiblical curiosity about the signs of the times and the unfolding of God's purposes in history is nowhere more acute than in respect to this particular sign.[1]

King, which without subjects he cannot be. And this holy Church is preserved or supported by God against the rage of the whole world; though it sometimes for a while appears very small, and in the eyes of men to be reduced to nothing; as during the perilous reign of Ahab the Lord reserved unto him seven thousand men who had not bowed their knees to Baal' (*Article 27*).

[1] For general surveys of the biblical teaching and historical views of Antichrist, see G. C. Berkouwer, *The Return of Christ*, chapter 9, The Antichrist, pp. 260–90; Arthur W. Pink, *The Antichrist* (Grand Rapids: Kregel, 1988); and M. J. Van Der Westhuizen, *De Antichrist in het Nieuwe Testament* (Amsterdam: H. A. Van Bottenburg, 1916).

THE PROMISE OF THE FUTURE

Though a recent writer on the subject of the Antichrist has spoken of an 'evangelical fascination' with the game of 'pin the tail' on the Antichrist, this fascination is not new in Christian history.[1] The early church Fathers showed a great deal of interest in the identification of the Antichrist, and during the period of the Reformation the issue of the Antichrist was quite prominent.[2] There have been many attempts in history to identify a particular person and/or historical movement with the biblical references to the Antichrist. Of all the signs of the times, this one seems the most concrete and capable of being identified with precision.

Those who are anxious to identify the Antichrist with a particular historical figure, or who hope to determine a precise timetable for the future based upon the emergence of the Antichrist, will likely be disappointed with our treatment of this sign. Just as we have issued similar words of caution before on the signs of the times, so we wish to do so here.

I. THE GENERAL BIBLICAL TEACHING ABOUT ANTICHRIST(S)

It is remarkable to notice that in those biblical texts that speak expressly of an Antichrist, none of them fix our attention exclusively upon one figure or person. Nor do they speak of the Antichrist so much as of a figure of political power and influence. Rather, they speak of various antichrists whose outstanding and defining characteristic will be their anti-Christian teaching. In only four places in the Epistles of the Apostle John are the terms 'antichrist' or 'antichrists'

[1] Kim Riddlebarger, The Antichrist, Modern Reformation, May/June 1994, p. 4.

[2] Because this figure arises within the orbit of the temple or church, many of the Reformers, including Calvin, identified the man of lawlessness or the Antichrist with the institution of the papacy. The Westminster Confession of Faith (1647), for example, originally spoke of the pope as the Antichrist (xxv:6). This is not, however, the confessional position of the Reformed churches. Most Presbyterian denominations that subscribe to the Westminster standards have removed the reference to the pope as the Antichrist from these standards.

used. In the now familiar passage on the signs of the times in the Gospel of Matthew, the language used is that of 'false' or 'pseudo' Christs who are associated with 'false' or 'pseudo' prophets.

Within the extensive discourse in Matthew 24, we read: 'Then if anyone says to you, Behold, here is the Christ, or There He is, do not believe him. For false Christs and false prophets will arise and will show great signs and wonders, so as to mislead, if possible, even the elect. Behold, I have told you in advance' (verses 23–25; cf. *Mark* 13:21–23). These words are a solemn warning to the disciples that the coming of Christ will be preceded by the emergence of false Christs, figures who will claim to be or to speak for Christ, even performing signs and wonders but, in truth, enemies of Christ and the gospel. They constitute a warning to the disciples, and the church of all ages, to beware the claims of those who are not genuinely Christian, even though they bear Christ's name and represent themselves to others as though they were of Christ.

Only within the Epistles of the Apostle John do we find the term antichrist used, and that in four different places. In 1 John 4:2–3, we find perhaps the most extensive of these references: 'By this you know the Spirit of God: every spirit that confesses that Jesus Christ has come in the flesh is from God; and every spirit that does not confess Jesus is not from God; and this is the spirit of the antichrist, of which you have heard that it is coming, and now it is already in the world.' This passage speaks of false teaching, the spirit of the Antichrist, which denies the coming of Christ in the flesh. According to the Apostle John, this anti-Christian denial of Christ's incarnation was already present in the early history of the church.

A similar thought is conveyed in 1 John 2:22: 'Who is the liar but the one who denies that Jesus is the Christ? This is the antichrist, the one who denies the Father and the Son'; and in 2 John 7: 'For many deceivers have gone out into the world, those who do not acknowledge Jesus Christ as coming in the flesh. This is the deceiver and the antichrist.'

None of these three passages speaks of a specific Antichrist. However, in 1 John 2:18 we also read: 'Children, it is the last hour; and just as you heard that antichrist is coming, even now many antichrists have arisen; from this we know that it is the last hour.' Though this passage echoes earlier passages – that there are many antichrists, some of whom were manifest already in the period of the early church, whose anti-Christian character was evident in their denial of Christ's coming in the flesh[1] – it adds the further thought of a specific person in whom the spirit of this anti-Christian denial would be embodied. It supplements the teaching of the other passages by speaking of a future personal Antichrist in whom the spirit of these antichrists would take striking expression.

If these general passages speaking of 'Antichrist' and 'antichrists' are considered together, then at least three preliminary conclusions may be drawn concerning this biblical teaching.

First, as with the signs of the times considered previously, this sign may not be relegated to some brief and unusual period just prior to the end of the age. The references to the antichrists we have considered thus far all refer to figures contemporary with the writing of the New Testament. They are figures of the past time, so far as the church of today is concerned, though of course they continue to be typical of new figures who arise throughout history to deny the gospel of Jesus Christ. These passages clearly teach that we live in that period of history known as the 'last hour', characterized

---

[1] Many commentators on these passages surmise that the Apostle John may have had in mind an early form of what later became known as Gnosticism, a movement defined by its unwillingness to confess the incarnation, the coming into the world and the assumption of human flesh by the Son of God. See, for example, Alexander Ross, *Commentary on the Epistles of James and John* (NICNT; Grand Rapids: Eerdmans, 1954), pp. 114–17.

by opposition to the gospel and the emergence of figures hostile to the gospel, even at times from within the fellowship of the church itself. Thus, any teaching about the Antichrist that misses this emphasis cannot be said to be faithful to the teaching of the Scriptures.

Second, there are several, even many, who are antichrists. It is frequently taught today that the Antichrist is to be understood only as a single figure and as one who could not have been known to the writers of the New Testament. However, much of the New Testament's emphasis regarding the Antichrist or antichrists aims to arouse the people of God from their stupor and complacency. The teaching is not intended to provide an occasion for armchair reflections or the writing of many books, most of whose content is unbiblically speculative. This teaching aims to warn the church not to be deceived. Not all those who bear Christ's name are truly his servants. Some are wolves in the garments of sheep. Some may even be antichrist, that is, opposed to the truth regarding the person and work of Christ.

And third, the telltale evidence of the presence of antichrist is the presence of anti-Christian teaching, not the presence or exercise of governmental or political power. This needs to be noted, especially in the context of so much emphasis upon the alleged political power of the Antichrist. Though this emphasis is fuelled by descriptions of the beast or the mark of the beast in the book of Revelation, descriptions which are thought to parallel those pertaining to the Antichrist, the predominant emphasis in the New Testament is upon the false doctrine associated with the person/s of Antichrist.[1]

[1] The language employed in the book of Revelation to describe the beast out of the sea suggests a figure who personifies and exercises dominion over Babylon and all those forces in history arrayed against Christ and his people (cf. *Rev.* 13; 17:8; 19:20; 20:4). This figure exercises political and economic power, though his aim is, in the narrower sense, religious: he opposes the cause of Christ on the earth. In Revelation 13:17–18, reference is made to the 'number of the beast'. That number is 'the number of a man, and his number is six hundred

THE PROMISE OF THE FUTURE

Those who deny the incarnation of Christ, who call into question the deity of Christ and the doctrine of the Trinity, are as likely to fit the biblical picture of the Antichrist as figures who wield political power in opposition to the cause of the Christian gospel.[1]

II. WHAT ABOUT 'THE' ANTICHRIST?

When the Apostle John speaks in 1 John 2:18 of the antichrist that is coming, the question which begs to be asked is: 'Does the Bible also teach that one particular person is coming who will be *the* Antichrist, in distinction from the many antichrists that have been present throughout the history of the church in the present dispensation?' It is commonly believed by many Christians that this is what the Bible teaches, but where is this taught, and what is the nature of the Bible's teaching regarding this figure?

----

and sixty-six'. This number has sparked considerable speculation as to the identity of this figure. See Kenneth L. Gentry, Jr., *The Beast of Revelation* (Tyler, Texas: Institute for Christian Economics, 1989), for a vigorous defence of the identification of this figure with Nero. Gentry's position corresponds to his claim that the book of Revelation was written prior to the fall of Jerusalem in AD 70 and that the appearance of this figure is an event of the past. For compact treatments of the various interpretations of this number, see G. K. Beale, *The Book of Revelation*, pp. 718–30; and Robert H. Mounce, *The Book of Revelation* (NICNT: Grand Rapids: Eerdmans, 1977), pp. 261–5. Beale cites several problems with the identification of this figure as Nero and argues that in its literary context, the number is used metaphorically and figuratively to refer to incompleteness and imperfection (p. 722). The beast and his people, by contrast to the perfection and completeness of Christ and the 144,000 saints, are unable to win the decisive victory. The beast is destined for defeat. In my judgement, Beale has the stronger and more convincing case, one that is based upon a more secure hermeneutical footing in the interpretation of the book of Revelation.

[1] By this standard, a noted liberal theologian with great influence might more plausibly be regarded as antichrist than a political figure like Hitler, whom many Christians earlier in this century regarded as the Antichrist.

We have seen already in 1 John 2:18, that reference can be made in the New Testament to a particular figure who is, in some unique sense, *the* Antichrist. Moreover, in another important passage usually taken to refer to the Antichrist, 2 Thessalonians 2, the Apostle Paul speaks of the coming of 'a man of lawlessness'.

This passage has antecedents in the Old Testament and calls to mind some of the description in Matthew 24 regarding the 'abomination of desolation' that will be set up in the temple in Jerusalem. Though this passage does not speak in so many words of 'the Antichrist', it is commonly and appropriately taken as a further description of the coming of an Antichrist, a particular figure or person in history who will appear prior to the return of Christ. To appreciate the teaching of this passage, it will be helpful to begin with some comments regarding the Old Testament antecedents as well as the reference in Matthew 24 to the 'abomination of desolation'.

In the Old Testament book of Daniel, two passages speak of an 'abomination that makes desolate' or 'causes desolation'. The first passage speaks prophetically of the coming of those who will 'desecrate the sanctuary fortress and do away with the regular sacrifice. And they will set up the abomination of desolation' (11:31). The second passage speaks similarly of how 'from the time that the regular sacrifice is abolished, and the abomination of desolation is set up, there will be 1,290 days' (12:11). Many interpreters of the book of Daniel take these two passages to be a reference to the profaning of the temple in Jerusalem by Antiochus Epiphanes.[1]

---

[1] Antiochus Epiphanes has been mentioned earlier, especially in connection with the language used in Matthew 24. Descriptions of these events are found in the apocryphal books (cf. 1 Maccabees 1:45–46, 54, 2 Maccabees 6:2). In the first of these passages, the term 'abomination of desolation' is derived from the Greek expression used in the Septuagint in Daniel 11 and 12.

However, in Matthew 24 Christ speaks of the destruction of the temple in Jerusalem as a fulfilment of Daniel's prophecy regarding 'the abomination of desolation'. Certainly in this passage Christ is speaking about the events that occurred in AD 70, at the time of the destruction of the temple in Jerusalem by the Roman emperor Titus and his conquering legions.

Interestingly, these earlier fulfilments of prophecy, both at the time of the destruction of the temple in Jerusalem by Antiochus Epiphanes and later by the emperor Titus, may themselves be types or prefigurements of a coming event in which the temple of the Lord, the church, will be invaded by another figure and the house of the Lord will once more be profaned. This seems to be the teaching of 2 Thessalonians 2, in which the Apostle Paul employs language reminiscent of Daniel 11 and 12 and Matthew 24 to describe the coming of another 'man of lawlessness'.[1]

The importance of the description of this 'man of lawlessness' in 2 Thessalonians warrants quoting the passage at some length:

> Now we request you, brethren, with regard to the coming of our Lord Jesus Christ, and our gathering together to Him, that you may not be quickly shaken from your composure or be disturbed either by a spirit or a message or a letter as if from us, to the effect that the day of the Lord has come. Let no one in any way deceive you, for it will not come unless the apostasy comes first, and the man of lawlessness is revealed, the son of destruction, who opposes and exalts himself above every so-called god or object of worship, so that he takes his seat in the temple of God, displaying himself as being God. Do you not remember that while I was still with you, I was telling you these things?

---

[1] Many manuscripts of the New Testament read man of 'sin' rather than 'lawlessness'. Whatever the reading, the same thought is being suggested: this man will be characterized by active rebellion and disobedience to the law and will of God.

And you know what restrains him now, so that in his time he may be revealed. For the mystery of lawlessness is already at work; only he who now restrains will do so until he is taken out of the way. And then that lawless one will be revealed whom the Lord will slay with the breath of His mouth and bring to an end by the appearance of His coming; that is, the one whose coming is in accord with the activity of Satan, with all power and signs and false wonders, and with all the deception of wickedness for those who perish, because they did not receive the love of the truth so as to be saved. (2 *Thess.* 2:1–10)

Several general observations may be made regarding this passage which have a direct bearing upon the question of the identity and nature of the Antichrist.

First, the coming of this 'man of lawlessness' is associated with the period of great apostasy and disobedience that will plague the church and people of God in the period immediately before the return of Christ. This sign of the Antichrist, accordingly, confirms some of the themes that we have emphasized in our treatment of the signs of the times. It not only belongs to those signs which bespeak opposition to Christ and his cause, but it also expresses the intensification of these signs as the end approaches. As with tribulation and the great tribulation, so with this sign: there will be many antichrists, and toward the end of the age *an* Antichrist.[1]

Second, the language of this passage suggests that the Antichrist will be a particular person in history. Though some have sought to argue that 'the man of lawlessness' may only be a figure of speech, using personification to lend urgency to the appearance of a principle of lawlessness and disobedience, it seems that the Apostle Paul is describing a

---

[1] The emergence of a figure like the Antichrist fits with the biblical picture of a relatively brief period of heightened apostasy and opposition to Christ in the period before the end of the age. The Antichrist is the kind of figure who fits the character of the 'little season' of Satan's rebellion at the end of age (*Rev.* 20:3) and the description of the beast in Revelation 17.

person in these verses.[1] He is called 'the' man of lawlessness, 'the' son of perdition, and 'the' one who opposes God and exalts himself against every so-called god or object of worship. This language implies the emergence of a single person in whom the spirit of Antichrist will be pre-eminently displayed.

Third, one of the striking features of this man of lawlessness will be his claim to divine status and worship. Just as with the earlier fulfilments of the prophecy of Daniel, in which the temple of the Lord was profaned and an 'abomination of desolation' set up, so the coming of this man of lawlessness will be evident in his profanation of the true temple of the Lord, the church of Jesus Christ. Like those before him, this Antichrist will be a deceiver and an impostor, one who pretends to be a friend of Christ though in reality he will be Christ's deadliest enemy. Furthermore, his appearing and work will be aimed at the people of God themselves, from among whom he will arise and whom he will seek to lead astray.

Fourth, the man of lawlessness will test the church's loyalty to Christ and his Word. As with the other signs of the times, the opposition to the gospel and person of Jesus Christ, the sign of the Antichrist will be an occasion for the church to

---

[1] Cf. G. C. Berkouwer, *The Return of Christ*, p. 271: 'There is no reason to posit with certainty on the basis of the New Testament that the antichrist as portrayed there is a person of the end of history.' Herman Ridderbos, *Paul*, pp. 508–21, maintains, against Berkouwer, that the Apostle Paul's language in 2 Thessalonians 2, particularly his reference to the restrainer, suggests that the man of lawlessness will be a particular figure or person. Though I am inclined to agree with those who maintain that this language refers to a particular figure or person, Berkouwer issues a proper caution with his language, 'posit with certainty'. A measure of tentativeness in the identification of this figure is undoubtedly necessary, particularly in view of the many false roads travelled on this subject throughout Christian history. It is certainly possible, within the framework of the biblical language for the end times, that this figure may be a personification of forces already at work at this juncture in the history of redemption.

stand its ground, to resist temptation and to persevere in faithfulness. What will make this testing peculiarly poignant is that the Antichrist, like the false Christs of Matthew 24, will perform many powerful signs and wonders. These signs and wonders will tempt the people of God to be deceived. As Christ says in Matthew 24, the false Christs would deceive even the elect, were this possible. And for this reason the Apostle Paul in 2 Thessalonians stresses the church's obligation, in the face of the temptations of this Antichrist, to hold fast the [apostolic] traditions she has received.

And fifth, despite much unsatisfactory debate and speculation about the identity of that which restrains or he who restrains the coming of the man of lawlessness, the eventual defeat of this enemy of Christ is certain.[1] Like the other signs of opposition to the cause of Christ, the sign of the Antichrist is a sign not of defeat but of sure and certain victory for Christ and his people. Not for one moment should the church fear that Antichrist will be able to frustrate the fruition of God's purposes in Christ.

---

[1] The language of these verses suggests that the restrainer may be a person and/or a historical power; both impersonal ('what restrains', verse 6) and personal ('he who restrains', verse 7) language is used. The restrainer has been taken to be: the preaching of the gospel (for example by Calvin), the institution of government (for example by Hendriksen), or the Person of the Holy Spirit (for example by dispensationalists). For representative treatments of this issue, see: John Calvin, *The Epistles of Paul to the Romans and Thessalonians*, trans. R. Mackenzie, ed. D. W. Torrance and T. F. Torrance (1960; repr. Grand Rapids: Eerdmans, 1979), p. 403; William Hendriksen, *I and II Thessalonians* (NTC: Grand Rapids: Baker, 1955), pp. 179–83; *The New Scofield Reference Bible*, notes on 2 Thess. 2:6–7; Hoekema, *The Bible and the Future*, pp. 160–2; and Ridderbos, *Paul*, pp. 521–26. It is notoriously difficult to choose among these alternatives. However, it seems unlikely (*contra* Dispensationalism) that God would remove himself, in the Person of the Holy Spirit, prior to the day of the Lord. For our purposes, it is most important to see that God through Christ holds providential dominion over the rising and falling of this Antichrist.

An Initial Conclusion

The temptation to speculate about the identity and nature of the Antichrist is difficult to escape. Many different attempts have been made at various points in church history to determine the exact identity of this mysterious figure. However, we want to draw our consideration of the Bible's teaching about this figure to a close by reaching an initial position.

We conclude that the Bible does teach that the Antichrist will appear prior to Christ's return at the close of this present age. This Antichrist will likely be a person in whom the growing opposition to the gospel and truth of God's Word will be concentrated. Whereas during this 'last hour' there will be many antichrists – figures who falsely claim to represent Christ but deny the truth concerning his person and work – toward the end of this age one person will emerge in whom these antichrists will find their antitype.

Furthermore, in a pattern we have observed before, the Scriptural teaching regarding the Antichrist calls the church not only to vigilance but also to renewed hope. However difficult may be the circumstance of Christ's church, however close to home – even from among her own ranks! – may be the opposition to Christ's person and work, Christ will not fail to return in power to consummate his saving work. The true people of God do not tremble at the prospect of the Antichrist. They do not become anxious whenever someone reports that he may have come. Rather, they remember the encouraging words of the Apostle Paul, written to comfort the church and steady her hand, that when the man of lawlessness is revealed, Christ will return and 'slay him with the breath of His mouth and bring [him] to an end by the appearance of His coming' (2 *Thess.* 2:8).

Signs of God's Judgement

In our introduction to the biblical teaching about 'the signs of the times', we suggested, following the lead of Anthony

Hoekema, that they can be divided into three groups. The first group of signs bespeaks the present working and triumph of God's grace in Christ. Here we considered the signs of the preaching of the gospel to all the nations and the salvation of all Israel. The second group refers to those signs that disclose the conflict between Christ and the Antichrist, between the kingdom of God and the kingdom of the world. Here we considered the signs of tribulation (including the great tribulation), apostasy and the Antichrist. Now that we have considered these first two groups and their individual signs, only the third group remains, those signs which deal with God's judgement in anticipation of the great judgement to come.

These signs of God's judgement are reminders that God's work of redemption in Christ has not been concluded, but that it soon will be. Furthermore, they remind us that God's kingdom will triumph over all of his enemies and that, in the day of judgement to come, all the unrighteousness and wickedness of the sinful creature will be exposed to and come under the judgement of God. Like those signs which have already been considered, they indicate the tension of this period, between the time of Christ's first and second advents. They not only speak of the conflict in history that continues between the work of Christ and his enemies, but they also promise and point forward to the consummation of the ages, the great Day of Christ's coming in glory to judge the nations and peoples in righteousness.

I. IDENTIFYING THESE SIGNS OF JUDGEMENT

As with many other signs of the times, these signs of God's judgement are most prominently mentioned in the Olivet Discourse in Matthew 24. In this discourse, Christ declares: 'And you will be hearing of wars and rumours of wars; see that you are not frightened, for those things must take place, but that is not yet the end. For nation will rise against nation, and kingdom against kingdom, and in various places there will be famines and earthquakes. But all these things are merely the beginning of birth pangs' (verses 6–8). In the parallel passage in the Gospel of Luke (21:11), there are two slight differences in language. The earthquakes mentioned are said to be great and, in addition to the sign of famine, the sign of plagues or pestilence is mentioned. The language of the parallel passage in Mark 13:7–8 is virtually identical to that of Matthew 24.

Since these signs – wars and rumours of wars, earthquakes, pestilence and famines – are so familiar and vivid in the minds of many believers, it will be useful to make a number of interpretative comments about them. These comments are especially necessary, given the amount of misunderstanding that exists.

It is interesting to observe, for example, that all of these signs have antecedents in the Old Testament. This feature is especially evident when we contemplate these signs of God's judgement. Indeed, when the Lord Jesus Christ speaks of nation rising up against nation and kingdom against kingdom, he is using the language of Isaiah 19:2 and 2 Chronicles 15:6. Moreover, earthquakes frequently occur in the Old Testament as a signal of God's direct working in history (*Judg.* 5:4–5, *Psa.* 18:7; 68:8, *Isa.* 24:19; 29:6; 64:1). The signs of plagues and famines are also evident in the preceding history of the Lord's dealings with the nations in general and Israel in particular (*Exod.* 7–11 [the plagues upon Egypt], *Deut.* 28:15ff., *Jer.* 15:2, *Ezek.* 5:16–17; 14:13). None of these signs, therefore, is new. They continue what might almost be termed a pattern of the Lord's dealings with the nations.

This pattern indicates the presence of the Lord in history in judging the sinful rebellion and disobedience of the nations and his own people. These judgements do not imply that all who suffer on their account are personally guilty and the special objects of God's wrath (*Luke* 13:1–5). They illustrate the fact that the world still lies under the curse of God (*Gen.* 3:17) and remind us that the wrath of God continues to be revealed from heaven against all the ungodliness and wickedness of men (*Rom.* 1:18). As signs of God's just displeasure with the sinfulness of the nations, they prefigure and anticipate the great day of judgement to come, when the justice of God will be manifested in the judgement exercised by Christ (*Acts* 17:31). As such they are a continual reminder that the judge is at the door (*James* 5:9).

Another interesting feature of this group of signs is that they do not promise, in the strictest sense, that the end of the age has come. In Matthew 24:6, Christ adds to his words about these signs, 'But that is not yet the end.' Then, in a phrase that characterises all of these signs, he remarks that all these are 'the beginning of birth pangs' (verse 8). Thus, like the other signs of the times we have considered, these are not to be relegated to a brief period just prior to the end of the age. Nor should they be cited as clear evidence that the return of Christ is imminent, as is so often done. The common opinion that, because we hear of wars and rumours of wars, we must be living in the time just prior to Christ's coming again, is not supported by biblical teaching.

Rather, these signs designate features of the Lord's dealings with the nations that will characterise the entire period between Christ's first and second advents. Even the mention of birth pangs reminds us that the travail and distress of this present period in redemptive history will be extensive and prolonged. This language is reminiscent of similar language in Romans 8:22, where the Apostle Paul speaks of 'the whole creation . . . groaning as in the pains of childbirth right up to the present moment'. So long as Christ remains seated at the Father's right hand, his dominion over the nations will take the form not only of the gathering of his people but also of the exercise of judgements which prefigure and anticipate the great day of judgement to come.

Accordingly, these signs of judgement are an indication of the present rule and certain triumph of Christ's kingship in all the earth and over all the nations. By no biblical measure are these signs to be contemplated as evidence of failure or uncertainty respecting the coming of God's kingdom. They are, rather, one clear body of evidence for its presence and eventual triumph.

II. THE BATTLE OF ARMAGEDDON

When addressing the wars or battles associated with the end times, the battle of Armageddon cannot be ignored, if for no other reason than that it has been the object of so much dispute and often useless speculation in the history of the church. More positively, it cannot be ignored because it is one of those signs mentioned in the Bible that will portend the consummation of the present age.

It may surprise many, especially in view of the popular interest in the subject of Armageddon, that this battle is only explicitly mentioned as an end-time event in Revelation 16:16. There we read: 'Then they gathered the kings together to the place that in Hebrew is called Armageddon.' In this context, the battle of Armageddon occurs after the sixth angel has poured out the sixth bowl of wrath on the Euphrates (verse 12). The kings who come together at this place are gathered under the leading of demonic spirits in opposition to God and his people (verses 13–14). We are also told that they gather for the war of the great day of God, the Almighty (verse 14), prior to the pouring out of the seventh and last bowl of God's wrath in anticipation of the final victory of the Lamb of God over all his enemies (*Rev.* 17). Remarkably, this great battle occurs in the midst of a series of events in which God's just wrath is being poured out upon the nations, accompanied by such signs as famines, pestilence, earthquakes and the like. The setting and meaning of this sign, therefore, fits well with what we have already noted regarding this group of signs. It relates to God's judgement in the period prior to the end of the age.

Though this is the only instance in the New Testament where the battle of Armageddon is expressly mentioned, a number of passages in the book of Revelation speak of *the* war or *the* battle that will take place prior to the final victory of Christ and his people over their enemies (*Rev.* 17:14; 19:19; 20:8).[1] This language is apocalyptic, describing end-time events in language drawn from earlier Scriptural prophecies, and therefore ought not to be pressed too literally. But the language nonetheless underscores the present reality and future intensification of opposition to the Lord and his church, opposition whose futility and certain defeat is symbolised in the great victory to be won in this final battle/ upheaval at the close of the age. The battle of Armageddon fits well with the general biblical teaching that with the approaching of Christ's second advent, opposition to his rule will intensify but be definitively overcome in the day of the Lord's appearing.

Furthermore, it should not be overlooked that this theme of a great and final conflict echoes several prophetic passages in the Old Testament. For example, in Joel 3:2 we are told that when Jerusalem, the city of God, is restored, all the nations will be gathered together against it in the valley of Jehoshaphat. In Zechariah 14:2, the Lord declares that in the future he will gather all the nations to Jerusalem to fight against it.[2] Similarly, Ezekiel 38 and 39 contain references to

[1] In Chapter 11, we will indicate why we conclude that the references in these passages parallel the reference to the battle of Armageddon in Revelation 16. Dispensationalism typically teaches that this battle will conclude the seven-year period of tribulation between Christ's coming for his saints (the rapture) and his coming with his saints prior to the millennium. See the *New Scofield Reference Bible*, note on Revelation 16:16.

[2] See Meredith Kline, 'Har Magedon: The End of the Millennium', *Journal of the Evangelical Theological Society* 39/2 (June 1996), pp. 207–22; and R. H. Charles, *A Critical and Exegetical Commentary on The Revelation of St. John* (ICC; New York: Scribners, 1920), II: pp. 50–51. Kline and Charles cite these kinds of texts to argue that Jerusalem is the likely location of this battle, though neither believes that the location should be taken literally. Kline also argues that

a great battle on the mountains of Israel in which Gog, chief prince of Meshech, will be defeated (passages to which allusion is made in Revelation 19:19 and 20:8, both of which speak of a final war between the Lord and his enemies). These passages intimate, as a prophetic theme or motif, that the conclusion of God's redemptive working in history will be signalled by a great warfare between himself and his enemies, the end of which will be the latter's utter destruction.

Perhaps this helps to provide a context for the specific reference to this final war or battle as the battle of *Armageddon*. The Apostle John identifies this term as being derived from the Hebrew. This may be a reference to Mount Megiddo, a site on the great plain of Esdraelon in Issachar, near the valley of Jezreel (see *Judg.* 5:19).[1] Thus, the battle of

---

the etymological derivation of Armageddon supports the translation 'Mount of Gathering', a translation that fits with the reference to Jerusalem.

[1] This is the position of most interpreters of the book of Revelation. See Beale, *The Book of Revelation*; pp. 838–41; and Mounce, *The Book of Revelation*; pp. 301–2. Also, for a survey of the problem of identifying this term, see J. Jeremias, 'Har Magedon (Apc. 16:16)', *Zeitschrift für die neutestamentliche Wissenschaft* 1 (1932), pp. 73–77; and idem, s.v. 'Har Magedon', in the *Theological Dictionary of the New Testament*, trans. G. W. Bromiley, ed. Gerhard Kittel and G. Friedrich (Grand Rapids: Eerdmans, 1964), I: p. 468. Against the identification of this place as Mount Megiddo, it is sometimes argued that it was actually only a small hill or tell, not a mountain. This argument seems too pedantic and insensitive to the symbolism so often characteristic of the book of Revelation. As Beale observes, 'That "Armageddon" is not literal is evident from the observation that OT prophecies of the final battle of history place it, without exception, in the immediate vicinity of the city of Jerusalem and Mount Zion or its surrounding mountains . . . But the plain of Megiddo is about a two days' walk north of Jerusalem. Furthermore, John himself places the battle directly outside Jerusalem in 14:20 and 20:8–9, though he typologically universalizes the OT references and speaks in spiritual instead of literal geographical terms.'

Armageddon may hark back to the great battle recorded in Judges 4 and 5, a battle in which the Lord led his people to victory over her enemies. Mount Megiddo was a strategic military stronghold at which many important battles and wars were fought in Israel's history (cf. *Judg.* 6:33, *1 Sam.* 31, *2 Sam.* 4:4, *2 Kings* 23:29–30; 9:27). In the account in Judges 4 and 5, we are told that Israel, the people of God, were oppressed by the Canaanite King, Jabin, and his general, Sisera. In this circumstance of oppression, Israel was, humanly speaking, in an impossible position. How could she stand against her enemy's nine hundred chariots of iron, when she did not even have a spear or a shield (*Judg.* 5:8)? And yet the Lord himself, through the judges Deborah and Barak, led his people in a great and marvellous victory over their enemies. To appreciate the significance of this victory, one must read the account and the celebration in song of the Lord's triumph composed by Deborah and Barak (*Judg.* 5).[1]

If we take these Old Testament antecedents into account, the meaning of the language of the battle of Armageddon in Revelation 17 becomes somewhat clear. This meaning confirms what we have already seen regarding this group of signs of God's judgement, a group of which the battle of Armageddon is but one specimen.

The battle of Armageddon is a sign and reminder that as the end approaches and the return of Christ becomes ever more imminent, opposition to the gospel and the kingdom of Christ will intensify. This opposition will issue in a final battle, signifying the Lord's judgement upon the nations and the certain triumph of his cause in the earth. Even as things

---

[1] Interestingly, this song refers to an earthquake that accompanied the Lord's victory (verse 5). In Revelation 16:18 earthquakes are also associated with events which follow the battle of Armageddon. All of this suggests that the battle of Armageddon signifies the day of the Lord's presence in judgement and victory over his enemies, a day which is foreshadowed and typified by this earlier day of victory in the time of the Judges.

appear most hopeless for the people of the Lord, suddenly and dramatically Christ will come to his people in victory and triumph to crush both his and their enemies under his feet.

Accordingly, it is fitting that we conclude our treatment of all the signs of the times, including this group signalling God's judgement in history upon his enemies, with the sign of the battle of Armageddon. For this sign confirms the one grand theme we have found interwoven throughout the Scriptural teaching regarding the signs of the times: as the present age draws to a close, and as the antithesis between the kingdom of God and of this world intensifies, the certainty of the accomplishment of God's redemptive purposes in Christ and for his people becomes all the more clear. Nothing, not even the combined opposition of the kings and leaders of the nations against the Lord's anointed and his people, will be able to prevent Christ's dominion from reaching its appointed end, the subjection of all things to him and the defeat of all his enemies, including the last enemy, death (1 Cor. 15).

PART FIVE

The Future of the Kingdom

8

Premillennial
Views

THE TITLE OF A RECENT BOOK, *The Millennial Maze: Sorting
Out Evangelical Options*,[1] nicely captures the difficulty
of sorting out the differing views found among Christian
believers on the subject of the millennium. The person who
attempts to make sense of these views faces a challenge not
unlike that of traversing a bewildering and confusing maze.
One is often found going down a blind alley or even coming
to an abrupt stop, but seldom does there appear to be a clear
way through to the exit. To find a clear and direct way
through is a daunting challenge.

Perhaps some have had this experience already, as we have
been considering various aspects of the Bible's teaching about
the future. But if the saying is true, to be forewarned is to be
forearmed, it is likely that the subject of the Bible's teaching
about the millennium will prove more challenging than those

[1] Stanley Grenz, *The Millennial Maze* (Downers Grove, Illinois:
InterVarsity, 1992). This book provides a good introduction to the
major millennial views. Two other introductions to these views have
previously been noted: Robert G. Clouse, ed., *The Meaning of the
Millennium: Four Views* (Downers Grove, Illinois: InterVarsity, 1977);
and Millard J. Erickson, *A Basic Guide to Eschatology* (Grand Rapids:
Baker, 1998).

subjects considered thus far. Here we need more than ever to remember something that has been repeatedly emphasized, namely, the importance of staying within the boundaries of the Scriptures, saying as much as they clearly permit us to say but no more. This is the only safe procedure to follow.

Introducing the Millennial Views

In order to introduce this subject, it will be helpful to consider briefly the meaning of the term 'millennium', and then take a brief retrospect and prospect of our study of the Bible's teaching regarding the future. It will also be useful to recognize that among the maze of differing viewpoints respecting this subject, there are ultimately only two major types of millennial views. The four major millennial views normally considered are but variations on one or the other of these types.

I. THE TERM 'MILLENNIUM'

'Millennium' is a Latin word. It is the equivalent of two Greek words which are used six times in Revelation 20:1–7 and mean 'a thousand years'. In discussing the Last Things, the term 'chiliasm' is sometimes used, which transliterates the Greek word for a 'thousand' used in this chapter of Revelation. 'Millennialism' and 'chiliasm' are synonyms and refer to the teaching about the thousand-year reign of Christ referred to in Revelation 20.[1]

Though this is not the place to consider the difficult question of the meaning of the thousand years in Revelation 20,[2] it clearly denotes a period in which Christ reigns subsequent to the binding of Satan. This period closes with a 'little season' of Satanic rebellion prior to Christ's ultimate victory over his enemies at the end of the age. When we speak

[1] Chiliasm, however, tends to be used more narrowly, that is, to refer to those views that regard the millennium as a distinct period in history, not the entire period between Christ's first and second advents. I will be using it in this way in what follows.

[2] See Chapter 11 below for an extended treatment of this passage.

of various millennial views, therefore, we are referring to differing interpretations of this thousand-year period. Does it describe a future period in which Christ will reign upon the earth in a way that is significantly different from his present reign at the Father's right hand in heaven? Or does it describe a circumstance that is presently realised or about to be realized, one which characterizes the period between Christ's first and second advent? Furthermore, what is the nature of this millennial reign of Christ? Will it be a period, literally, of one thousand years' duration, not one year more, not one year less? Or are we to understand the millennium as a protracted period in history of peace and prosperity, when the reign and rule of Christ will be almost universally acknowledged by the nations and peoples of the earth?

It would not be difficult to multiply these questions here. However, for our present purpose we need only note that they illustrate the complexity and range of opinion held as to the meaning and significance of this millennial reign of Christ. A further complicating factor, as we shall see, is that Revelation 20 is the only passage in all of Scripture that speaks of a thousand-year period of Christ's reign. The meaning of this perplexing passage will depend upon the extent to which it is either interpreted in the light of other Scripture passages, or is allowed to stand on its own, teaching something that is not clearly taught in any other passage.

II. A RETROSPECT

To illustrate the importance of the subject of the millennium in the Bible's teaching about the future, we need to recall the subjects that we have considered thus far.

We have treated the general biblical teaching about the future; the intermediate state or the state of believers in the period between death and the day of resurrection; the central focus of biblical teaching about the future upon the first coming of Christ and his return at the end of the age; and the biblical teaching regarding the 'signs of the times'.

THE PROMISE OF THE FUTURE

A number of prominent themes in our treatment of these subjects have a bearing upon and intersect with many of the questions raised by the subject of the millennium. For example, we have seen that the coming of Christ in the fullness of time was an end-time event, a fulfilment of the promises of the Lord made to his old covenant people. The complex of redemptive events which coincided with Christ's first advent – his death, resurrection, ascension and the outpouring of the Holy Spirit at Pentecost – mark off this present period of history, between the times of Christ's first coming and his return, as the final epoch in redemptive history prior to the consummation of all things. Consequently, as we argued in our chapter on the return of Christ, the second advent of Christ is, from the perspective of a biblical view of the future, the concluding event in redemptive history. It is a consummating event at the end of the age, one which does not leave room for any further expectation of additional events subsequent to it.[1]

Furthermore, in the preceding chapters dealing with the signs of the times, we have seen that these signs characterize the present age as the end times. Coincident with the Bible's teaching that Christ's return at the end of the age will consummate the course of redemptive history, these signs distinguish the entire present period of history as one defined by the first and future comings of Christ. Each of these signs, in differing ways, discloses the triumph of Christ's gospel as well as the futility of all opposition to the proclamation of his Word in the power of the Spirit. They signal the present lordship of Jesus Christ and the eventual triumph of his cause in all the earth, whether they do so as signs of grace, signs of opposition, or signs of divine judgement.

---

[1] By arguing earlier that the return of Christ is such a consummating event, I have anticipated one feature of the critical evaluation of Premillennialism: if the return of Christ consummates God's redemptive purposes in history, then it cannot be an event that takes place 'before' (or pre-) the millennium.

These themes are mentioned again because they bear directly upon questions that will recur in our consideration of the millennium. No view of the millennium could be termed fully biblical if it fails to do justice to any of these themes. For example, any view of the millennium that relegates Christ's reign to some future point in history could hardly comport with what we have seen already of Christ's present rule in history and his coming triumph. Or a view of the millennium that treated the return of Christ as though it brought nothing new or promised nothing beyond what is already the case, would be equally suspect. A biblically responsible understanding of the millennium will have to be one that can be interwoven with the various threads of biblical teaching that we have sought to distinguish thus far.

III. A PROSPECT

Only within the context of these biblical themes can we properly take up the subject of the millennium. To direct us in this enterprise, we turn to a brief look at what lies ahead.

In this chapter and the next, we will provide a summary of those representative millennial views that require consideration. This chapter will treat the two most common premillennial views; the next chapter will treat the two most common post-millennial views. In treating each of the four major millennial views, we will sketch their respective histories, adherents and distinctive features. Only then will we evaluate these views in the light of Scriptural teaching. In evaluating these millennial views, some features of particular views will require special attention, such as the subject of the rapture, the relation of Israel and the church, and the dispensational insistence upon a literal hermeneutic. Due to the importance of Revelation 20 to the entire dispute respecting the millennium, we will devote a chapter to an extended treatment of this passage.

IV. TWO MAJOR VIEWS, FOUR VERSIONS

One matter remains to be clarified before we take up the subject of these millennial views, and that is the identification of the chief and representative views that we will be describing. The simplest way of identifying and classifying these views is in relation to Christ's return. All the millennial views place the millennium either before or after the second coming of Christ. Consequently, there are two major types of millennial positions: those that are *postmillennial* – 'post', because Christ comes after, or post-millennium – or *premillennial* – 'pre', because Christ comes before, or pre-millennium. It is important to keep this basic distinction in mind, because this is the point of greatest divergence among them. Recognizing that all views fall into one of two major types will preserve some clarity in the debate regarding other, subordinate issues.

Moreover, each of these major types has two prominent varieties. Among postmillennial views, the two primary versions are Amillennialism and Postmillennialism.[1] Among premillennial views, the two primary versions are Historic Premillennialism and Dispensational Premillennialism. In this chapter and the next, we will treat these four millennial views in the following sequence: Historic Premillennialism; Dispensational Premillennialism; Postmillennialism; and Amillennialism. Only after having sketched these four views will we subject them to critical scrutiny and evaluation.

Historic Premillennialism

Though it is common today simply to identify Pre-millennialism with Dispensationalism, Premillennialism has two predominant expressions: an *historic,* and a more recent

---

[1] One of the varieties of what I am calling the first major type, Postmillennialism, has a name that sounds like it has no millennial view at all ('a'-millennialism literally means 'no millennialism' or 'no millennium'). The other variety has the same name as the one that I have given to the first major type, of which it is a variety. This is confusing, to say the least! However, this is the terminology that has become 'common coin' in discussions about the millennium. Though it would be helpful were this terminology to be improved, such an improvement is not likely to occur.

form known as *dispensational,* Premillennialism. In this section we consider the first of these.[1]

I. A BRIEF HISTORICAL OVERVIEW

Before noting some of the main features of this viewpoint, it is important to recognize that it has had its adherents throughout the history of the Christian church. Some defenders of Premillennialism will even go so far as to argue that it has been the predominant view of the Christian church throughout the centuries, and that the other views are, in contrast, minority viewpoints. Though this is an overstatement of the matter, there is reason to speak of a classic or historic form of Premillennialism.

In the early history of the church, a number of the church Fathers advocated a form of premillennial teaching. Among the second-century apologists or defenders of the faith, Justin Martyr taught that the return of Christ would inaugurate a one-thousand-year period of peace and righteousness upon the earth, with the Old Testament prophecies regarding Israel's restoration and future blessing literally fulfilled. This view was shared by many other influential teachers, among them Ireneaus, Hippolytus, and Lactantius. Support for this understanding was often derived from the *Epistle of Barnabas* and the teaching that the time of creation, subsequent to the first creation week, spanned a period of six days, each of one thousand years'

[1] The sketch of Historic Premillennialism that follows is based upon the following sources: George Eldon Ladd, *Crucial Questions About the Kingdom of God* (Grand Rapids: Eerdmans, 1952); idem, *The Blessed Hope* (Grand Rapids: Eerdmans, 1956); idem, *The Gospel of the Kingdom* (Grand Rapids: Eerdmans, 1959); idem, *Commentary on the Revelation of John* (Grand Rapids: Eerdmans, 1972); idem, 'Historic Premillennialism', in *The Meaning of the Millennium,* ed. Robert G. Clouse, 17–40; Stanley J. Grenz, *The Millennial Maze,* pp. 127–47; Millard J. Erickson, *A Basic Guide to Eschatology,* pp. 91–106; and D. H. Kromminga, *The Millennium in the Church* (Grand Rapids: Eerdmans, 1945).

duration.[1] In this understanding, the millennium would occur six thousand years after creation and represents the seventh day, or the last period in history of one thousand years.

Due to a variety of factors, most prominently the influence of Augustine's view of the millennium, this early form of Premillennialism largely disappeared during the Middle Ages. It revived in new forms in the period of the sixteenth-century Reformation and again in more recent times. One factor that led to its demise was the excessive literalism and even materialism that characterized the views of early premillennialists. By contrast, many theologians during this period began to spiritualize and even allegorize the biblical texts, treating many of the promises of the Scriptures as referring primarily to spiritual rather than material blessings. Furthermore, the excesses of some defenders of Premillennialism, particularly the teachings of the Montanists, who embraced a form of premillennialist teaching, contributed to the decline of premillennial views.[2] Premillennialism

[1] The *Epistle of Barnabas* is one of the earliest Christian writings (possibly early second century) that we have, and it exercised a considerable influence among many of the early church Fathers. Though this letter clearly teaches the idea of history comprising 'days' of one thousand years'duration, it is not so clear that it actually teaches Premillennialism, as many assume. Two useful surveys of the early history of Premillennialism are: D. H. Kromminga, *The Millennium in the Church*; and Charles Hill, *Regnum Caelorum: Patterns of Future Hope in Early Christianity* (Oxford: Clarendon, 1992). The study of Hill is especially interesting, as he convincingly challenges a common claim that the preponderance of early church teachers espoused a premillennialist view.

[2] The Montanists were a prophetic sect that began in the late second century and eventually broke with the Catholic Church, proclaiming a new prophecy regarding the imminent return of Christ and granting great prominence to two prophetesses, Prisca and Maximilla. Among the most prominent of Montanists was the church father Tertullian, who joined this sect later in his life. See 'Montanus, Montanism', in *The New Schaff-Herzog Encyclopedia of Religious Knowledge*, ed. S. M. Jackson, et al. (reprint, Grand Rapids: Baker, 1950), VII:pp. 485–7.

was discredited among many segments of the church as a Jewish heresy, one which failed to see the unity of the people of God and placed too much emphasis upon the earthly prosperity of the future millennium. When the influential church father Augustine adopted a view of the millennium coinciding with the present age of the church and the proclamation of the gospel, the influence of Premillennialism began to wane.

But there was a resurgence of interest in and commitment to a premillennialist view at two important junctures. During the Protestant Reformation, though most of the Reformers followed Augustine and rejected Premillennialism, some among the Anabaptists advanced their own forms of premillennial teaching. However, due to the extreme forms which their views often took, most of the churches of the Reformation rejected Premillennialism. Only in the nineteenth and twentieth centuries has Premillennialism enjoyed a renewed popularity, although often in the form of Dispensational Premillennialism, a form not present in earlier church history.

Even the Reformed tradition, which has not been confessionally or explicitly premillennialist throughout its history, has had notable examples of premillennialist teaching. The Christian Reformed Church, for example, saw a controversy over this view in the early part of the last century. Known as the Maranatha controversy, it revolved about the person and teaching of the Rev. Bultema, author of the book *Maranatha*, who was deposed for espousing premillennial views, including a denial of Christ's present kingship over all the nations.[1] In a sequel to this controversy, Dr D. H. Kromminga, church historian at Calvin Seminary, advocated a premillennial eschatology and appealed to the synod of the Christian Reformed Church to determine whether this view

[1] For a brief account of this controversy, see John H. Kromminga, *The Christian Reformed Church: A Study in Orthodoxy* (Grand Rapids: Baker, 1949), 72–75. This controversy gave birth to the Berean churches.

was consistent with the Reformed confessions, asking particularly for a change in the *Belgic Confession*, Article 37, which teaches that the number of the elect is completed before Christ's return.[1]

Though it is evident from this brief historical overview that Premillennialism has not been the predominant view of the church throughout its history, nor the view of the Reformed churches, Premillennialism, when its dispensational expression is included, has become the prevalent viewpoint among conservative Protestants today.[2]

II. THE MAIN FEATURES OF HISTORIC PREMILLENNIALISM

So far we have identified only the major feature of Historic Premillennialism, namely, its insistence that the millennium will take place after Christ's return at the end of the age. It remains for us to consider its other features, and we will do this by means of a general outline, overlooking the finer points of difference among historic premillennialists.

[1] For more on this subject and Kromminga's appeal, see John H. Kromminga, *The Christian Reformed Church*, p. 79; D. H. Kromminga, *The Millennium* (Grand Rapids: Eerdmans, 1948); and the *Acts of Synod* of the Christian Reformed Church, 1946 and 1947. Since Dr Kromminga died before his appeal could be handled by a Christian Reformed synod, no official answer was ever given to the questions he raised regarding the permissibility of holding a premillennialist view and subscribing to the Reformed confessions (Heidelberg Catechism, Belgic Confession, Canons of Dort). Conservative confessional Presbyterians have shown a willingness to permit the holding and advocating of Historic Premillennialism as compatible with the Reformed faith. Kromminga was correct, however, to note that Premillennialism does not seem compatible with Article 37 of the Belgic Confession.

[2] R. C. Sproul, *The Last Days According to Jesus*, lists only J. Barton Payne, George Eldon Ladd, R. A. Torrey and Theodor Zahn as more recent advocates of Historic Premillennialism. Hoekema, *The Bible and the Future*, p. 183, includes the names of Henry Alford, H. Grattan Guinness, Robert H. Gundry, S. H. Kellogg, D. H. Kromminga, Alexander Reese, and Nathaniel West. The preponderance of premillennialists in North America are dispensationalists.

The first feature of Premillennialism is its insistence that the return of Christ will introduce a millennial period during which Christ, having returned to the earth at his second coming, will reign upon the earth for an extended period of time. Not all premillennialists insist that this period will be of exactly one thousand years' duration, although this is the most common position. However, Christ will be bodily present upon the earth, reigning over the nations from the earthly seat of his kingdom in Jerusalem. This millennial reign, in sharp contrast to those signs of the times that characterize this present age prior to Christ's return, will be a period of universal peace and prosperity between and among the nations of the earth. Though sin and its consequences will not be utterly extinguished, the millennium will be a golden age in which the earth and its inhabitants will enjoy an unprecedented blessedness.

During the millennium, Christ will exercise a complete and uncontested sovereignty, having utterly defeated the Antichrist and all his enemies at his coming. The promise of Philippians 2:10–11, that every knee shall bow and every tongue confess that he is Lord, will be fulfilled. Christ's rule will introduce a period of righteousness in which the characteristics of the kingdom of God, as these are set forth, for example, in the Sermon on the Mount, will be generally honoured. In fulfilment of the prophecy of Isaiah, the nations will beat their swords into ploughshares and their spears into pruning hooks (*Isa.* 2:4; cf. *Mic.* 4:3). The creation itself will in some sense experience the liberation of the children of God (*Rom.* 8:22–23; cf. *Isa.* 11:8–9; 65:25). And the saints will be given the special privilege of reigning together with Christ on the earth.

Another feature that stands out in Historic Premillennialism is its insistence that the return of Christ will come suddenly and cataclysmically, after a period of intensified opposition to and trouble for the people of God. There will not be a gradual improvement during the period prior to the millennium. Rather, the various signs of the times which express opposition to Christ and his people will intensify. Tribulation, apostasy among the people of God, the coming of the Antichrist – these events will immediately precede Christ's return, the triumph over his enemies and the inauguration of his kingdom on earth. For this reason, Historic Premillennialism is often referred to as *post-tribulationalism*, in distinction from the *pre-tribulationalism* that is commonly a feature of Dispensational Premillennialism. It is given this designation because it teaches that the return of Christ will occur only after a period of tribulation which the believing people of God will suffer before Christ's return.[1] As we approach the end and the return of Christ, Historic Premillennialism anticipates a period of great trial for the people of God that will be cut off only at the time of Christ's return.

Although Historic Premillennialism teaches that there is ultimately only one people of God, the church, comprising Jewish and Gentile believers alike, it reserves a special place in God's purpose and kingdom for the Jewish nation and people. Many promises of the Old Testament have been fulfilled in the gospel of Jesus Christ. However, among these promises, and especially in the teaching of the Apostle Paul in Romans 9–11, remains the expectation that God's purposes with national Israel have not come to an end. When Christ returns and the millennium commences, national Israel will experience a corporate conversion and receive a place of special prominence in the millennial kingdom. Though historic premillennialists reject many of the tenets of Dispensationalism regarding the millennium – for example, that the sacrificial system will in some sense be reintroduced in Israel for the Jews – they do maintain that the majority of the Jewish people (though not every individual) will be

[1] When we consider the teaching of Dispensational Premillennialism in the following, we will have occasion to critique its argument that Christ's second coming will occur in two stages, the first of which, the rapture, will occur before a seven-year period of great tribulation.

converted and find many of the special promises of God's Word for them fulfilled in this period of the millennium.

One further feature of Historic Premillennialism is its insistence on two separate bodily resurrections, one occurring at the beginning of the millennium and the other at the end. Premillennialists appeal to Revelation 20 in defence of the view that believers will enjoy the first resurrection before the millennium, to reign with Christ upon the earth for the thousand years of the millennium, and unbelievers will be raised only in the second resurrection at the end of it, to be judged and subsequently receive their just punishment in hell, which is the second death.

III. Two important biblical passages

In order to complete this brief sketch of Historic Premillennialism, we need to consider two biblical passages which form the basis for its distinctive aspects. George Eldon Ladd, perhaps the most able recent defender of this view, has conceded that these passages constitute the primary biblical basis for this position.

The first and most important of these passages is Revelation 20:1–6, the only biblical passage which speaks explicitly of the millennium or thousand-year reign of Christ.

> And I saw an angel coming down from heaven, having the key of the abyss and a great chain in the hand. And he laid hold of the dragon, the serpent of old, who is the devil and Satan, and bound him for a thousand years, and threw him into the abyss, and shut it and sealed it over him, so that he should not deceive the nations any longer, until the thousand years were completed; after these things he must be released for a short time. And I saw thrones, and they sat upon them, and judgment was given to them. And I saw the souls of those who had been beheaded because of the testimony of Jesus and because of the word of God, and those who had not worshiped the beast or his image, and had not received the mark upon their forehead and upon their hand; and they came to life and reigned with Christ

for a thousand years. The rest of the dead did not come to life until the thousand years were completed. This is the first resurrection. Blessed and holy is the one who has a part in the first resurrection; over these the second death has no power, but they will be priests of God and of Christ and will reign with Him for a thousand years.

Historic premillennialists argue that this passage lends compelling support to their position because of its teaching of two bodily resurrections separated in time: the first, of believing saints at the time of Christ's return and the beginning of the millennium, the second, of unbelieving sinners at its end. By way of extra support it is pointed out that the same expression is used to describe the two resurrections, namely, 'they came to life', and this language must refer, as is ordinarily the case in the Scriptures, to a bodily resurrection (*Rev.* 2:8; 13:14; *Ezek.* 37:10).[1] Furthermore, those who come to life in the first resurrection are believing saints who reign with Christ for a period of one thousand years. Those who participate in the second resurrection are 'the rest', presumably those who have no part in the first resurrection and are subject, unlike believers, to the second death. The picture that emerges from this passage, then, is in full agreement with the premillennialist view of the future: when Christ returns, Satan will be bound, believers will be raised to reign with him for a thousand years on the earth, and only at the end of this millennial period will the unbelieving come to life in order to be subjected to judgement.

Premillennialists also appeal to the literal implications of this passage's description of the millennium.[2] In the vision

---

[1] See Henry Alford, *The Greek Testament* (Boston: Lee and Shepard, 1872), IV: p. 732, for a classic statement of this claim. We will have to see whether this is so when we consider Revelation 20 in more depth in Chapter 11 below.

[2] Historic Premillennialism shares with its cousin, Dispensational Premillennialism, a preference for a literal reading of the biblical texts, even texts like those in the book of Revelation that employ rich

of the Apostle John in Revelation 20, he sees Satan bound and thrown into the abyss 'so that he should not deceive the nations any longer, until the thousand years were completed'. This language describes a millennial period during which Christ will reign with his saints over the nations in a manner that supersedes anything known in this present period of history. Unlike the present period in which the nations and peoples continue to exhibit a great deal of hostility and rebellion against the rule of Christ, the millennium will be a period in which the kingdom of Christ will be openly manifest and triumphant upon the earth. A straightforward reading of this text, it is claimed, leaves no other interpretation open than this view of the millennial reign of Christ, and it also fits well with the understanding that in the future the people of Israel will be restored to God's favour and many of the Jews will be converted. For premillennialists this, too, is a facet of the millennium that is to come.

The other passage worthy of notice here is 1 Corinthians 15:20–26:

> But now Christ has been raised from the dead, the first fruits of those who are asleep. For since by man came death,

---

symbolism and apocalyptic language. However, it also concedes that many Old Testament prophecies regarding the future do not have a literal fulfilment in the New Testament. See G. E. Ladd, 'Historic Premillennialism', in *The Meaning of the Millennium*, ed. R. G. Clouse, pp. 17–29. Unlike the older Premillennialism of the early church, which was preterist in its reading of the book of Revelation, contemporary premillennialists tend to be preterist and futurist in their reading of the book. As noted earlier, a preterist reading is one that regards the events described and prophesied in the book of Revelation to be events in the past, events which coincided with the time of the early church to whom the book was first addressed. A futurist reading is one that regards the events described and prophesied to be events in the future, at the end of history just prior to and including the return of Christ, etc. For summaries of the major interpretative approaches to Revelation, see G. K. Beale, *The Book of Revelation*, pp. 44–9; and C. Marvin Pate, ed., *Four Views on the Book of Revelation* (Grand Rapids: Zondervan, 1998).

by a man also came the resurrection of the dead. For as in Adam all die, so also in Christ all shall be made alive. But each in his own order: Christ the first fruits, after that those who are Christ's at His coming, then comes the end, when He delivers up the kingdom to the God and Father, when He has abolished all rule and all authority and power. For He must reign until He has put all His enemies under His feet. The last enemy that will be abolished is death.

In this passage, Ladd and other premillennialists argue, we are taught that history has three distinguishable stages. The first of these stages is the age of the Christian church, during which Christ's reign is largely hidden. The second of these stages is the age of the millennium, during which Christ's reign is manifest for all to see. And the third of these stages is the age of the eternal kingdom when the kingdom reverts to God the Father.

Though premillennialists admit that the temporal sequence of these stages is not explicitly revealed in this passage, they claim that it is implicit. When, for example, we read in 1 Corinthians that the resurrection victory of Christ will occur in a particular order, we find the sequence of events taught in Revelation 20 confirmed. Christ's resurrection is the first fruits, introducing the age of the church and the proclamation of the gospel. Then, when Christ returns, those who are Christ's at his coming will be given a share in his victory; this is the first resurrection of Revelation 20, marking the beginning of the age of the millennium. Then again, when the age of the millennium is concluded, the end will come and Christ will deliver up the kingdom 'to the God and Father, when he has abolished all rule and all authority and power'. The sequence of events in this passage – Christ's resurrection, at his coming the resurrection of believers, at the end the turning over of all things to the Father – corresponds to the sequence of events in Revelation 20. Thus, this passage confirms the premillennialist reading of that controversial passage.

Though we will have occasion to evaluate Historic Pre-millennialism in a subsequent chapter, the main lines of this understanding of the millennium ought to be clear. Historic Premillennialism, a view of the millennium that has had its advocates throughout Christian history, teaches that, as the return of Christ approaches, the signs of opposition to Christ's gospel and church will intensify. The age of the church will be closed with the coming of the Antichrist and great tribulation for the people of God. However, Christ will suddenly come from heaven and utterly vanquish Satan and his host, binding him for a period of one thousand years. During this period Christ will reign upon the earth together with all his saints. Especially prominent among them will be many of the Jewish people who will be converted in the last days. These saints will be believers who were alive at Christ's coming or deceased saints who have a part in the first resurrection. This millennial period will be one of tremendous blessing, righteousness and prosperity on the earth. Many of the promises regarding a future age of divine favour and blessing will be fulfilled. The millennium, however, will close with a 'little season' of Satanic rebellion which will be put down by Christ. Then the rest of the dead, the unbelieving, will be raised in the second resurrection to be judged and condemned to eternal punishment in hell. Then the end will come, the inauguration of the eternal form of the kingdom of God in which God becomes all in all.

Dispensational Premillennialism

Few Christians in North America, at least among those who follow developments in the churches, are unfamiliar with the writings of Hal Lindsey (*The Late Great Planet Earth*), the Scofield Reference Bible or an institution like Moody Bible Institute. Probably more of them are familiar with the subject of the rapture than any group of Christians previously in the history of the church. Many are keenly interested in the historical developments of the twentieth century, most

notably the restoration of many Jews to their ancient homeland in Palestine, and regard these developments as portents
of the close of the present age and the return of Christ. With
the return of the Jews to Palestine, one of the most important
conditions for the coming millennium has been met – at
least, so many Christians believe.

I. A BRIEF HISTORICAL OVERVIEW

Unlike the former view, Dispensational Premillennialism is a
relative newcomer to the debate regarding the millennium.
Though the terms 'dispensations' or 'economies' in the
history of redemption have been used throughout the history
of the church, only more recently have they become common.
This is due to the growing influence of this millennial
position.

The story of modern Dispensationalism begins around
1825 and is associated with an Irishman by the name of John
Nelson Darby. He was a clergyman in the Church of England
and originated a meeting in Plymouth, England, giving rise
to the name Plymouth Brethren. Darby established himself as
an influential Bible teacher, and through his many writings
and lecture circuits he introduced many of the features of
what would come to be known as Dispensationalism.

Though a number of influential ministers and Bible teachers followed Darby's interpretation of the Bible, the single
most important figure in the subsequent growth and spread
of Dispensationalism was Cyrus I. Scofield. Scofield was a
Congregationalist minister in the United States who had
heard Darby lecture and embraced many of his views.
Although Scofield's training was in law and not in theology,
he prepared his own study Bible with extensive notes placed
throughout the Scriptures. This Bible, known popularly as
the Scofield Reference Bible, was first published in 1909 and
became the single most important means in the spread of
dispensationalist teaching. Many who have used this Bible
and its second, revised edition tend to read the Scriptures in

terms of the notes and interpretative comments found throughout its pages.[1]

Next to the influence of Darby and Scofield, nothing contributed more to the spread of Dispensationalism, especially in North America, than the emergence of a number of fundamentalist Bible institutes and colleges in the early decades of the twentieth century. Many of these Bible institutes and colleges were established by conservative or fundamentalist Christians who opposed the liberalism and modernism of many mainline church institutions, and whose commitment to a dispensational and literal reading of the Bible was often fortified by the conviction that alternative views were merely the fruits of an unbelieving approach to the Scriptures. To this day much of the influence and spread of dispensationalist teaching is due to the work of these institutions. Among those institutions that remain dispensationalist or predominantly dispensationalist, the following deserve mention: the Philadelphia College of the Bible (founded by Scofield), Moody Bible Institute, Dallas Theological Seminary (the largest dispensationalist Seminary), the Master's Theological Seminary, the Bible Institute of Los Angeles (BIOLA) and Talbot Theological Seminary, Grace Theological Seminary and Western Conservative Baptist Seminary. Of those influential or well-known ministers and theologians who hold a dispensationalist view today, the following are only a sampling: John F. Walvoord, Dwight Pentecost, Charles Ryrie, John MacArthur, and Charles Swindoll.[2]

---

[1] The revised or *New Scofield Reference Bible* was issued in 1967 and is the product of a nine-member committee of leading dispensationalist theologians. This revision represents the predominant dispensationalist view, one in which some of the more extreme positions of the original Dispensationalism have been muted. The revisions are not as radical, however, as those being promoted by present-day progressive dispensationalists. I will consider this more radical revision briefly in what follows.

[2] R.C. Sproul, *The Last Days According to Jesus*, p. 198, also lists Gleason L. Archer, Donald G. Barnhouse, M. R. De Haan, Charles L.

THE PROMISE OF THE FUTURE

Despite the recent development of Dispensational Premillennialism, and despite some evidence of a waning of its influence and popularity, this understanding of the millennium remains the majority opinion among many conservative Christians, especially in North America. Indeed, in many places it is still regarded as a litmus test of commitment to the truthfulness of the Scriptures. Those, for example, who do not embrace Dispensationalism are often regarded with suspicion by dispensationalists, since their view of Scripture is suspected as being something less than it should be.[1]

II. THE MAIN FEATURES OF DISPENSATIONALISM

To attempt to summarize the main features of Dispensationalism is an act of folly. There are so many varieties that it has become impossible to keep track of them all. Moreover, the old Dispensationalism has been increasingly modified and in some cases even overturned. Despite these difficulties, however, some primary features of Dispensationalism continue to distinguish it as a particular view, even amidst its many variations.[2]

III. THE IDEA AND TERMINOLOGY OF DISPENSATIONS

Perhaps the simplest place to begin is with the name itself. What is meant by 'Dispensationalism' or 'dispensation'?

Feinberg, Norman L. Geisler, Harry A. Ironside, Walter C. Kaiser, and Hal Lindsey.

[1] If I may be permitted a brief autobiographical note, I can attest to this general suspicion often found among dispensationalists against those who do not hold this view. As a high school student, I attended a Baptist academy whose teachers were dispensationalists and whose students, if they carried a Bible with them, always carried the Scofield Bible (was there any other?). It was always a difficult assignment for me to convince teachers and classmates that my opposition to Dispensationalism was not the product of a liberal or unbelieving view of the Bible.

[2] Despite the diversity of viewpoints among dispensationalists, the existence of a standard source like the *New Scofield Reference Bible* makes it possible to speak of a normative Dispensationalism.

This term derives from a biblical term from which we get the English word 'economy' (see *Eph.* 1:10; 3:2, *Col.* 1:25).[1] It refers originally to the arrangement or manner in which a household is administered. In Dispensationalism, however, this term is used to describe the various ways in the history of redemption by which God regulates man's relationship with himself. In the old Scofield Reference Bible, a dispensation is defined as 'a period of time during which man is tested in respect to some specific revelation of the will of God'.[2] A more recent publication of dispensational authors defines a dispensation as 'a particular arrangement by which God regulates the way human beings relate to him'.[3] In the course of God's administration of history, spanning the period from the creation of humankind before the Fall to the ultimate consummation of history at the end of the millennium, God has employed a diversity of arrangements or stewardships in regulating his dealings with his image-bearers.

Though dispensationalists debate the precise number and significance of these different dispensations, the most common position distinguishes seven such dispensations or economies: the dispensation of innocence from creation until humankind's expulsion from the garden of Eden; the dispensation of human conscience from humankind's expulsion until the great flood; the dispensation of human government from the time of the flood until the calling of Abraham; the dispensation of promise from the call of Abraham until the giving of the law at Sinai; the dispensation of the law from the time of Sinai until the crucifixion of Christ; the dispensation of the church from the cross of Christ until his coming for his saints; and the dispensation of the kingdom or the millennium when Christ reigns over

---

[1] English translations will often render this word as 'administration' or 'stewardship'.

[2] (1909), note on Genesis 1:27.

[3] Craig A. Blaising and Darrell L. Bock, *Progressive Dispensationalism: An Up-to-date Handbook of Contemporary Dispensational Thought* (Wheaton, Illinois: Victor Books, 1993), p. 14.

restored Israel on David's throne in Jerusalem for one thousand years.

Within this dispensational conception of the history of redemption, each successive dispensation is introduced to further God's purposes in a distinct manner and with respect to a particular people. The most important of these dispensations are the last three, the dispensations of law, of the gospel, and of the kingdom.

One especially difficult question that arises in connection with the distinguishing of these various dispensations is whether there is one way of salvation, indeed one Saviour, during these different periods. Though the implication of the original definition of a dispensation – and the popular form in which Dispensationalism is often taught and believed – seems to be that there are several ways of salvation, official statements today of Dispensationalism typically deny this conclusion. For example, in the doctrinal statement of faith of Dallas Theological Seminary, Article v, dealing with 'The Dispensations', declares that 'according to the "eternal purpose" of God (*Eph.* 3:11) salvation in the divine reckoning is always "by grace through faith", and rests upon the basis of the shed blood of Christ'. This doctrinal affirmation actually represents a tendency in more recent expositions of Dispensationalism to modify or minimize an earlier sharper division of the economy of redemption into distinct administrations.

IV. THE UNIQUENESS OF THE CHURCH

Within the broad framework of this dispensational view of history, Dispensationalism insists upon the uniqueness of the church, especially its distinction from Israel and God's dealings with Israel before and after the dispensation of the church.[1]

---

[1] Charles C. Ryrie, *The Basis of the Premillennial Faith* (New York: Loizeaux, 1953), p. 126: 'In brief, premillennialism with a dispensational view recognizes the Church as a distinct entity, distinct from Israel in her beginning, in her relation to this age, and in her promises.'

In its earliest expression, this view argued that Christ began his ministry upon earth after his first coming by preaching the gospel of the kingdom, offering to restore the fortunes of national Israel and assume the throne of David in Jerusalem. However, when the Jewish people of his day rejected him, the establishment of the kingdom of heaven was postponed and God commenced the dispensation of the church. The dispensation of the kingdom of heaven, because it has to do with God's purposes for earthly Israel in a literal, Messianic kingdom, has now been put on hold, as it were, so that God's purposes for the church might be realised.[1] This accounts for the description of the church dispensation as a parenthesis or intercalation in the course of the history of redemption, a dispensation during which God's peculiar dealings and purposes for Israel have been delayed or put off until they can resume again in the future.

With the suspension of God's dealings with his earthly people, Israel, there is revealed, after the crucifixion and resurrection of Christ, what is often termed the mystery phase of the kingdom of God. This mystery phase unveils the peculiar purposes of God to gather in this present dispensation a predominantly Gentile people, the church, through the proclamation of the gospel to the nations and the call to faith and repentance. This is the mystery of the gospel

[1] I use the phrase 'kingdom of heaven' here purposefully. Many dispensationalists have argued that this term in the Gospel of Matthew is to be distinguished sharply from the term 'kingdom of God', since it concerns God's earthly programme for Israel, not his purpose for the church. What this means for the present relevance of the Gospel of Matthew, including the Sermon on the Mount, should be evident. Those portions of the Scriptures that are directly related to the dispensation of the kingdom of heaven are not directly binding upon us in the present dispensation. However, there is no real difference in meaning between the expressions 'kingdom of heaven' and 'kingdom of God'. The former phrase, found in the Gospel of Matthew, only confirms the Jewishness of Matthew's first audience. It was customary among the Jews to use this term, in part to avoid the too frequent and casual use of the name 'God'.

taught, for example, in a passage like Colossians 1:25–27. Though hidden from his people throughout all preceding dispensations in the economy of redemption, God has now made it known through the gospel that he has, alongside his earthly people, Israel, a heavenly people, the church. This period or mystery phase of the kingdom of God coincides, according to Dispensationalism, with the period between the sixty-ninth and seventieth weeks of Daniel 9:24–27, the period from Pentecost, the birth of the New Testament Gentile church, and the rapture of the saints at Christ's coming.[1]

V. OLD TESTAMENT PROPHECIES AND THE CHURCH

At this point one of the most significant features of Dispensationalism comes into full view, namely, the sharp separation it makes between God's earthly people, Israel, and his heavenly people. This separation informs an all-embracing method of reading and understanding the Bible.

According to Dispensationalism, the prophecies and promises of the Old Testament regarding Israel do not find their fulfilment in the dispensation of the church but in the dispensation of the kingdom or millennium yet to come. These prophecies and promises, which have to do with earthly blessings (a new Jerusalem, a restored Davidic kingdom and throne, universal peace among the nations,

---

[1] If someone objects that the passage in Daniel makes no mention of this period between the sixty-ninth and seventieth weeks (after the cutting off of the Messiah), the response is predictable: no mention is made of it because it was previous to the revelation of the New Testament, a mystery kept hidden from God's people. For treatments of this difficult text that argue that it refers to the fulfilment of redemption in the work of Christ, see E. J. Young, *The Prophecy of Daniel* (Grand Rapids: Eerdmans, 1949), pp. 191–221; Meredith Kline, 'Covenant of the Seventieth Week', in *The Law and the Prophets: Old Testament Studies in Honor of Oswald T. Allis*, ed. John H. Skilton (Presbyterian and Reformed, 1974), ; and Kenneth L. Gentry, Jr., *He Shall Have Dominion* (Tyler, Texas: Institute for Christian Economics, 1992), pp. 310–24.

economic and material blessing, the restoration of Israel to the land of promise), have to be interpreted literally, and not spiritually or allegorically. And since they have not been and cannot be literally fulfilled in the present dispensation of the church, they must await their fulfilment when God's purposes for Israel recommence. Because the earthly, national and political aspects of God's promises to Israel were not fulfilled at Christ's first coming – when his own people rejected him – they await their fulfilment during the dispensation of the millennium.

This is one of the most distinctive features of Dispensationalism and its approach to the interpretation of the Scriptures: its insistence upon a literal hermeneutic or manner of reading the Bible's promises in the Old Testament. If the Old Testament promises a rebuilt temple (Ezekiel), the temple in Jerusalem must be rebuilt. If the Old Testament promises that David's Son will sit upon his throne (2 Samuel), this throne must be located in a literal Jerusalem still to come. If the Old Testament speaks of a renewed creation in which prosperity and peace will be enjoyed (Isaiah), then this must be fulfilled during a literal, earthly period of Christ's reign upon this earth. It is simply inadequate to interpret these promises as having been or being fulfilled in the present age. Were that the case, so Dispensationalism argues, the language of Scripture would no longer be reliable or literally true.[1]

The only solution available is to treat the Old Testament prophecies and promises as directed to a future age in which God's purposes for his earthly people will be realised in history, the dispensation of the millennium. Furthermore, the fact that God's dealings with the church do not fulfil Old Testament expectation only confirms that they are part of

[1] One prominent application of this principle is the insistence that when the Bible uses the word 'Israel', it must refer to the national people of God, the Jewish community, not the church community (which comprises predominantly Gentiles). See *New Scofield Reference Bible*, notes on Genesis 12:3 and Romans 11:1, 26.

that hidden or mystery phase of the kingdom which God had purposefully kept concealed from his Old Testament people, Israel.

VI. THE PRE-TRIBULATIONAL RAPTURE OF THE CHURCH

If God's dealings with the church are a parenthesis or interruption of his dealings with Israel, the obvious question for dispensationalists is: How is it anticipated that God will resume his dealings with Israel in the future?

At this point the dispensationalist argues that the church dispensation will be concluded at the time of the rapture, or Christ's coming for his saints. As previously noted, a distinction is often made between this rapture, or parousia, in which Christ will come 'for' his saints, and a return seven years later, in which Christ will come 'with' his saints. Some early dispensationalists even argued that the first phase, or rapture, is termed in the New Testament Christ's 'coming' (parousia) or 'appearing', and that, similarly, his return is termed his 'revelation'. More recent dispensational writers acknowledge that this sharp distinction in the use of terms for Christ's return cannot be maintained.

Furthermore, most dispensationalists believe that the rapture referred to in 1 Thessalonians 4:17 will occur before the period of great tribulation. Their view is known as pre-tribulational rapturism.[1] At the rapture, the blessed hope of every Christian, resurrected believers and transformed believers will be caught up with Christ in the clouds to meet him in the air. Thereupon the body of believers, the raptured church, will go with Christ to heaven to celebrate with him the seven years of the marriage feast of the lamb. Meanwhile, the seventieth week of Daniel 9 will commence on the earth. This period will be a period of tribulation on the earth, the latter half being the period of great tribulation during the reign of the Antichrist (the beast out of the sea). This period of great tribulation will witness the conversion of the elect

---

[1] As noted before, a few dispensationalists advocate a mid-tribulational and even fewer a post-tribulational rapture. See Millard J. Erickson, *Basic Eschatology* (Grand Rapids: Baker, 1998), pp. 125–81.

Jews and conclude with Christ's final triumph at the Battle of Armageddon over Satan and his host.

VII. THE MILLENNIAL KINGDOM

Thus, during this seven-year period, God's programme and purpose for Israel will resume in earnest and issue in the one-thousand-year, or millennial, dispensation. At the return of Christ, the second phase of his coming after the seven-year period of tribulation, the Jews, many of them gathered to their ancient homeland, Palestine, will for the most part believe in him and be saved, fulfilling Old and New Testament prophecy (cf. *Rom.* 11:26). The devil will be literally bound and cast into the abyss for a literal period of one thousand years.

Dispensationalism believes that the millennium will begin with the first of at least two resurrections, the resurrection of saints who died during the seven-year period of tribulation and the remaining Old Testament saints. These saints, together with the raptured church, will live and reign in heaven, while the Jewish saints on earth will begin to reign with Christ from Jerusalem for a period of one thousand years.[1] Two judgements will also occur at this time: the judgement of the Gentiles who persecuted the people of God during the seven-year period of tribulation (cf. *Matt.* 25:31–46) and the judgement upon Israel (cf. *Ezek.* 20:33–38).[2]

The millennium that ensues at the return of Christ will be,

[1] The literalistic understanding of Dispensationalism is particularly evident in its insistence that even the temple sacrifices in the temple will be revived during the millennium – though they will not be expiatory or detract from the one sacrifice of Christ. Classic Dispensationalism so separated these two peoples of God that, during the millennium and even in the final state, there will be a spiritual people of God in heaven and an earthly people upon the earth. This has been modified in the revised Dispensationalism represented by the *New Scofield Reference Bible*, and abandoned altogether by progressive Dispensationalism.

[2] Some dispensationalists distinguish no less than seven different judgements and seven different resurrections, depending upon the

according to the dispensationalist, a literal fulfilment of the Old Testament prophecies of a future golden age on earth. Universal peace and economic prosperity will prevail. Christ will reign with his saints, Israel, upon the earth. However, the experiences of life and death, marriage and family will still exist. At the end of the millennium, nominal believers and others will join Satan in his 'little season' of rebellion, only to be crushed under foot by Christ. The millennium will end with the resurrections of those saints who died during this period and the second resurrection of all the unbelieving. The unbelieving will be subject to the Great White Throne judgement and be cast with Satan into hell. All believers, the church and Israel, will then enter into the final state, when the heavenly Jerusalem descends to the earth.

VIII. PROGRESSIVE DISPENSATIONALISM

In order to complete this admittedly brief sketch of Dispensational Premillennialism, mention must be made of a contemporary movement within Dispensationalism known as 'progressive Dispensationalism'. This movement has introduced some considerable modifications into the older, more classical form of Dispensationalism.[1] Among the newer emphases of this progressive Dispensationalism, the following are most important.

First, Progressive Dispensationalism, while retaining the distinction between the various successive dispensations,

---

time and persons involved. These judgements are to be distinguished from the Great White Throne judgement, which will occur at the end of the millennium, in which those who join Satan in his final rebellion will be condemned to eternal punishment.

[1] In addition to the book of Blaising and Bock cited earlier (p. 209), the following sources provide a good summary of this view: Craig A. Blaising and Darrell L. Bock, eds., *Dispensationalism, Israel and the Church: The Search for Definition* (Grand Rapids: Zondervan, 1992); Craig A. Blaising, 'Premillennialism', in *Three Views on the Millennium and Beyond*, ed. Darrell L. Bock (Grand Rapids: Zondervan, 1999); and Robert L. Saucy, *The Case for Progressive Dispensationalism* (Grand Rapids: Zondervan, 1993).

argues that ultimately God's redemptive purposes bestow the same redemptive blessings upon the whole people of God, Gentile as well as Jew. Without rejecting the distinction between the dispensation of the church and the earthly kingdom or millennium, Progressive Dispensationalism denies that the dispensation of the church is an interruption or intrusion into the course of redemptive history. In fact, the spiritual blessings of salvation granted to the church will be the portion of the entire people of God in the final state. There will not be, in the final state, a separation between an elite class of Jews whose salvation is upon the earth, and a secondary class of Jews and Gentiles whose salvation is in heaven. All the purposes and blessings of salvation, spiritual and material, will terminate upon one people of God.

Second, Progressive Dispensationalism, as its name suggests, endeavours to emphasize more adequately the continuity and progress of the history of redemption. Rather than emphasising the differences between the dispensations in the redemptive economy, the progressive dispensationalist wants to emphasise the progress from one dispensation to the next, noting where appropriate the manner in which each successive dispensation fulfils and continues what was promised and begun in a previous dispensation. Consequently, though progressive dispensationalists still distinguish the various economies, they also acknowledge that these economies represent the historical realization of one kingdom programme and purpose. Moreover, the differences between the various covenants do not mitigate a genuine covenantal unity throughout the Scriptures.

Third, because of its willingness to acknowledge the progress from one dispensation to another, Progressive Dispensationalism has modified the older Dispensationalism's view of the Old Testament promises and their fulfilment. Rather than insisting upon the literal and exclusive fulfilment of these promises during the millennium, Progressive Dispensationalism allows the fulfilment of these promises to occur in progressive stages. Many promises, for example, of the Old Testament are fulfilled not only at one level during the dispensation of the church but find a further and related fulfilment in the dispensation of the millennial kingdom.

Fourth, and perhaps most decisively, Progressive Dispensationalism rejects the radical separation between two peoples and two purposes of God in the history of redemption. Ultimately, God has but one people, comprising Jew and Gentile alike, and one programme of salvation. However multiform or diverse may be the progressive and successive working out of his redemptive purpose in the dispensations of redemptive history, the purpose of God is to save one people in Christ.

A careful study of Progressive Dispensationalism suggests that in many ways it represents a departure from the classic form of Dispensationalism and a return to Historic Premillennialism. Those features of Dispensational Premillenialism that distinguish it from Historic Premillennialism – the strict separation of Israel and the church, the insistence that Old Testament prophecy has no fulfilment in the dispensation of the church, the understanding that the church is a parenthesis in history – have all been largely abandoned by the progressive dispensationalists. It is hard to find any substantial difference between this modification of Dispensationalism and its older and more historic cousin, classical Premillennialism. This does not mean, however, that the older Dispensationalism has been abandoned or no longer has any viability. The advocacy of Progressive Dispensationalism has been, until now, largely an academic pursuit among scholars who retain their place within the broader orbit of Dispensationalism. The older Dispensationalism, only slightly modified, remains alive and vital for many believers and their churches. However, the fact that such a substantial revision of Dispensationalism is underway from within the ranks of dispensationalists themselves may not bode well for the future vitality of the older Dispensationalism.

9

Postmillennial
Views

Having summarized the views of historic Premillennialism and Dispensationalism, it might seem appropriate to proceed with an evaluation of them. To do so, however, would be premature because the biblical case against both views presumes an acquaintance with the views of Postmillennialism and Amillennialism. We will therefore postpone our critique to the next chapter and first take up these other forms of millennial teaching.

A Comment about Terminology

In our introduction to the subject of the millennium, we noted that the primary difference in millennial positions lies between a premillennial and a postmillennial conception of the return of Christ. Both of the views we have considered thus far teach that the return of Christ will precede the establishment of the millennial kingdom. The two remaining views share the conviction that the return of Christ will occur after the millennium – hence 'Post'-millennialism.

We also mentioned earlier the difficulty connected with the terms 'Postmillennialism' and 'Amillennialism'. Whatever differences exist between the two views, they have in common an identical framework. That is, they share one feature that distinguishes them from all premillennial views: the conviction that the return of Christ will occur after the period of the millennium, and that his coming will conclude this present epoch of redemptive history and immediately introduce the state of consummation.

It should be observed that the terms 'Postmillennialism' and 'Amillennialism', which are commonly used today, are of rather recent vintage. Though we will have more to say about the term 'Amillennialism' in the next section, the term 'Postmillennialism' has until recently been used to describe all forms of the view that Christ's coming will follow the millennium, including those views which today are distinguished as postmillennialist and amillennialist. Though the differences between postmillennial and amillennial views have long existed in the history of the church, they were not until recently explicitly described with these terms.

As recently as the first half of the twentieth century, the term 'Postmillennialism' was still being used in a general way. B. B. Warfield, for example, noted that the terms 'premillennial' and 'postmillennial' were 'unfortunate', but apparently regarded them to be the only options available.[1] Geerhardus Vos, in his *The Pauline Eschatology*, published in 1930, distinguished his view from some forms of Postmillennialism but considered himself to be, in a more basic sense, postmillennialist in distinction from premillennialist.[2] His discussion of Premillennialism gives every impression that he regarded the primary difference in eschatological views to be between pre- and post-millennialism. Perhaps even more compelling is the fact that the *International Standard Bible Encyclopedia*, first published in 1915 and then published in revised form in 1929–30, has no entry for

[1] *Selected Shorter Writings*, vol. 1 (Nutley, New Jersey: Presbyterian and Reformed, 1970), p. 349.
[2] See *The Pauline Eschatology*, pp. 226–60, where Vos treats the question of 'chiliasm' in the eschatology of the Apostle Paul.

Amillennialism but has one for Postmillennialism. At this point in history, whatever the differences, all those who rejected a premillennialist view were categorized as post-millennialists.[1]

A Brief Historical Overview

The problem of definition and terminology also plagues the way in which the history of Postmillennialism is often told. Some postmillennial authors maintain that this has been the predominant eschatological position of the Christian church.[2] Others are more cautious and maintain only that it has been a continuing and significant position of many in the Reformed tradition.[3] Since this debate can finally be settled only upon the basis of a consensus regarding the meaning of Postmillennialism, our survey of the history of Post-millennialism will be rather brief and modest in its claims.

---

[1] Perhaps an analogy might help to explain this terminological difficulty. Prior to the American Civil War, differences already existed between the two sides of this brewing conflict, but all citizens of the United States were first and foremost Americans. Only after the war broke out did the terms 'northerner' or 'southerner' come to have the sharpened meaning of 'antagonist'. Similarly, before the terminology of 'Amillennialism' was coined to distinguish one form of Post-millennialism from another, all representatives of the view that Christ's coming would follow the millennium were known as postmillennialists. Only more recently has the difference between these two kinds of Postmillennialism become a matter of clear distinction, even in the terms used to describe these views.

[2] For example, Kenneth L. Gentry, Jr., *He Shall Have Dominion*, pp. 77–91.

[3] For example, John Jefferson Davis, *Christ's Victorious Kingdom* (Grand Rapids: Baker, 1986), pp. 16–22. In addition to the studies of Gentry and Davis, the sketch of Postmillennialism in this section is based as well upon the following sources: Loraine Boettner, *The Millennium* (Philadelphia: Presbyterian and Reformed, 1957); J. Marcellus Kik, *An Eschatology of Victory*; Kenneth L. Gentry, Jr., 'Postmillennialism', in *Three Views on the Millennium and Beyond*, ed. Darrell L. Bock, pp. 11–57; and Keith Mathison, *Postmillennialism*.

Without resolving the dispute whether Postmillennialism has been the predominant position of the Reformed tradition, it is undoubtedly true that the Reformed tradition has witnessed the most significant expressions of post-millennialist thought. Though many postmillennialist authors insist that John Calvin was a postmillennialist, it is probably more accurate to say that Calvin gave expression to some ideas that received greater emphasis in later Presbyterian and Puritan writers who were more evidently postmillennialist in outlook.

Frequently, the beginnings of modern forms of Post-millennialism are associated with the name of Daniel Whitby, an Anglican, who published his *Paraphrase and Commentary on the New Testament* in 1703. However, at the same time and even before the publication of this treatise, a number of Puritan writers, such as Thomas Brightman, John Cotton and John Owen, were advocating a postmillennialist point of view. In 1651, Owen preached a sermon before the English House of Commons, 'The Kingdom of Christ', in which he expressed the conviction that the multitudes and the nations would be converted and come under the lordship of Jesus Christ. It is also generally agreed that the *Savoy Declaration* of 1658, which modified the *Westminster Confession of Faith* for the congregational churches, gave expression to a postmillennialist outlook.[1]

Perhaps the greatest flourishing of Postmillennialism occurred in North America, first in the writing and preaching of Jonathan Edwards and then in the nineteenth and early

---

[1] This Declaration includes the statement: 'We expect that in the latter days, Antichrist being destroyed, the Jews called, and the adversaries of the kingdom of his dear Son broken, the churches of Christ being enlarged and edified through a free and plentiful communication of light and grace, shall enjoy in this world a more quiet, peaceable, and glorious condition than they have enjoyed' (Chapter XXVI:5; quoted from Philip Schaff, *The Creeds of Christendom*, vol. 3: *The Evangelical Protestant Creeds* [1931; repr. Grand Rapids: Baker Book House, 1985], p. 723).

twentieth centuries. Edwards articulated his postmillennialist position in his *The History of Redemption,* a work which taught the triumph of Christ's kingdom in the not-too-distant future and the utter destruction and desolation of the kingdom of the evil one. Postmillennialism was a dominant viewpoint in the influential Princeton tradition, represented by Archibald Alexander, J. A. Alexander, A. A. Hodge, Charles Hodge and B. B. Warfield. Though especially prominent among many conservative Presbyterian theologians during this period, including Robert Lewis Dabney, W. G. T. Shedd, and James Henley Thornwell, other influential writers held a basically postmillennialist view as well. Among these writers were the Baptist theologian Augustus Strong and the Scotsman Patrick Fairbairn.

The twentieth century has seen a substantial decline in the influence of Postmillennialism. Some postmillennialist authors, such as J. Marcellus Kik, John Jefferson Davis, and Iain Murray,[1] have continued to articulate a more traditional form of Postmillennialism. More recently, however, many advocates of Postmillennialism have been 'reconstructionists' or 'theonomists'. Among these reconstructionist post-millennialists, the primary authors are Rousas J. Rushdoony, Greg Bahnsen, Gary North, David Chilton, and Ken Gentry. Perhaps due to the rather controversial nature of the reconstructionist movement, Postmillennialism is today frequently regarded to be a fringe position, despite its having enjoyed considerable support among able and conservative Reformed writers for many centuries.

The Main Features of Postmillennialism
Since the dispute regarding the predominance of Post-millennialism in the Christian tradition depends so much upon the definition of Postmillennialism that is being used, it

[1] *The Puritan Hope: Revival and the Interpretation of Prophecy* (London: Banner of Truth, 1971).

is vitally important to come to a clear understanding of this position and its main features. Though self-professed postmillennialist writers offer different summaries of this position, most postmillennialist thought shows some readily identifiable features.

I. THE TRIUMPH OF THE GOSPEL

The most obvious feature of all postmillennialist positions is the insistence that in the period of history prior to the return of Christ at the end of the age, the preaching of the gospel will triumph on the earth and bring about the conversion of the nations and the preponderance of the human race. Loraine Boettner, a well-known exponent of the post-millennialist view, gives clear expression to this in the following definition:

Postmillennialism is that view of the last things which holds that the kingdom of God is now being extended in the world through the preaching of the gospel and the saving work of the Holy Spirit in the hearts of individuals, that the world eventually is to be Christianized and that the return of Christ is to occur at the close of a long period of right-eousness and peace commonly called the millennium.[1]

According to Postmillennialism, the Great Commission of Matthew 28 is not a charter for a missionary enterprise that holds no prospect of certain success. Rather, it is a charter that outlines the way in which Christ, through the preaching and teaching of the gospel, will receive the nations as his rightful inheritance.

In the writings of many postmillennialists, care is taken to distinguish this triumph of the gospel from the optimism of the old 'social gospel' teaching of liberalism in the nineteenth and early twentieth centuries, as well as the theory of histor-ical progress often associated with evolutionism. The growth

---

[1] 'Postmillennialism', in *The Meaning of the Millennium: Four Views*, ed. Robert G. Clouse, p. 117. See Gentry, 'Postmillennialism', pp. 13–14, for a similar definition.

of the church will be realized by spiritual means, the preaching of the gospel in the power of the Spirit of Pentecost, and not by worldly strategies or methods.

II. A GOLDEN AGE

With the triumphant spread of the gospel and the conversion of the nations, a golden age will emerge in history prior to the return of Christ. This golden age, the period of the millennium, will be a significant period of time during which the standards and precepts of the gospel and the Word of God will prevail on the earth and among the nations. Though it will not be a period of absolute perfection and righteousness – sin will still be present in human life – it will be a period marked by moral righteousness, universal peace among the nations and peoples of the earth, and unprecedented economic prosperity. The blessing of God will rest upon the nations, and a glorious epoch of the kingdom of Christ will be realized upon the earth.

Among postmillennialists, differences in respect to this golden age exist. Some interpret 'one thousand years' more literally than others, though most take it in a symbolic sense to refer to a period of long duration within the purpose and will of God. Some anticipate that this golden age will emerge almost imperceptibly as the gospel progresses and the church grows among the nations. Others, however, believe that the introduction of this golden age will occur suddenly. Furthermore, though Postmillennialism historically regarded this golden age as a period in the future, subsequent not only to Pentecost but also to the early centuries of the Christian era, more recently some postmillennialists have suggested that it is coterminous with the period of time which began with the destruction of Jerusalem in AD 70. and the rebuilding of the temple (the church).[1]

[1] Many reconstructionist postmillennialists, for example, seem to view the millennium as covering either the entire inter-advental period (between Christ's first and second comings) or at least the period since the destruction of the temple in Jerusalem in AD 70. The older, more

III. THE SEQUENCE OF END-TIME EVENTS

The sequence of events in the outlook of Postmillennialism is similar to that of Amillennialism, a viewpoint that we have yet to consider. Allowing for some divergence among advocates of Postmillennialism, the general sequence of events is as follows: As the gospel progressively advances and the nations are converted, the millennium commences; at the close of this millennial age, Satan is released for a 'little season' of rebellion, only to be defeated decisively by Christ at his second coming; the second coming of Christ will coincide with the general resurrection of the righteous and the unrighteous and the final judgement; and, with the conclusion of the final judgement, the final state will commence, in which the wicked will be consigned to hell and the righteous will enter everlasting life in the new heavens and earth.

Though this sequence bears considerable resemblance to that of Amillennialism, the chief difference is the relegation of many of the signs of the times – tribulation, wars and rumours of wars, apostasy – to the period before the millennium. However, even here differences of viewpoint exist among postmillennialists, some of whom would acknowledge the presence of these signs re-emerging in the period of Satan's little season after the millennial age.

IV. THE CONVERSION OF THE JEWS

One less obvious feature of Postmillennialism relates to the conversion of the Jews prior to or during the period of the millennium. The reason this feature is less obvious than the two considered thus far is that though most post-millennialists expect the large-scale conversion of the Jewish

---

historic, form of Postmillennialism was more explicitly chiliast in its expectation of a future period in history that would be the period of the millennium of Revelation 20. See Gentry, *He Shall Have Dominion*, p. 71, where he speaks of 'a time in earth history (continuous with the present) in which the very gospel already operative in the world will have won the victory throughout the earth in fulfillment of the Great Commission'.

people, some who affirm this expectation do not advocate a postmillennialist eschatology. Consequently, though the teaching of the conversion of the preponderance of the Jews prior to the return of Christ may be a telltale evidence of Postmillennialism, it is not a sufficient condition for identifying someone as a postmillennialist.[1]

Historic representatives of Postmillennialism have taken the position that the Bible teaches (especially in Romans 11:11–32) that the great preponderance of the Jewish people, in their racial and national existence, will be converted through the preaching of the gospel. This does not mean that every individual Jew will be converted. But it does mean that the greater number will be brought to salvation through the gospel at some point prior to Christ's return. This conversion will be a distinctive feature of the millennial age, though it is not believed that it will occur in the same way as has been understood in premillennialist views, especially of the dispensationalist kind. Postmillennialism teaches that all are saved, Jew and Gentile alike, by way of faith in Jesus Christ and through incorporation into the one people of God, the Christian church. It rejects the sharp lines of distinction drawn between Jew and Gentile in most forms of Premillennialism.[2]

---

[1] Sometimes postmillennialists will include John Murray among their number, in part because Murray in his commentary on the Epistle to the Romans holds the view that 'all Israel' in chapter 11 refers to the Jews corporately being converted at some future time before the return of Christ. However, as noted earlier, this is not a sufficient basis for regarding someone to be a postmillennialist. Cf. Gentry, *He Shall Have Dominion*, p. 36; idem, 'Postmillennialism', p. 19. Gentry's list of postmillennialists tends to be too inclusive and therefore unreliable.

[2] Sometimes it is claimed that the *Westminster Confession of Faith* is postmillennialist, because in the *Westminster Larger Catechism*, Q. & A. 191, the Christian's prayer, 'Thy kingdom come', is said to refer, among other things, to the calling of the Jews. Though many of the authors of the *Westminster Confession* and *Catechisms* were postmillennialists, this answer is an insufficient basis for concluding that these confessions are postmillennialist. They certainly do not teach Postmillennialism as an essential part of the biblical system of doctrine to which adherents of these standards must subscribe.

v. The Dominion of Christ

In presenting and defending Postmillennialism, its advocates often insist that the triumph of the gospel and the emergence of the millennium at some point in history prior to Christ's return are an expression and necessary implication of Christ's universal dominion as King. With his instalment as King at his Father's right hand, Christ has commenced his mediatorial reign and exercise of authority in heaven and on earth. Thus, those who would argue that we should not anticipate the victory of the gospel or the prevalence of Christ's kingdom in this present age prior to his return are guilty of an unbiblical pessimism. Christ's reign at the Father's right hand must come to concrete and visible expression on the earth prior to his return. Since the other millennial views do not view with confidence the prospects for the gospel and the church in this present age, they really amount to a denial of Christ's present dominion.

Notice should be taken of a recent form of Postmillennialism that has given a peculiar expression to this view of Christ's dominion. Within the Reformed, especially conservative Presbyterian, tradition, a movement has developed which is called variously Christian reconstructionism, dominion theology, or theonomy. Though not all present-day postmillennialists are reconstructionists, all of those who adhere in some way to this movement are postmillennialists.

According to the chief representatives of this movement, the dominion of Christ will come to expression in history by way of the reconstruction of society according to biblical norms and laws. Christ's millennial reign in history requires that Christian believers seek to bring all aspects of life – not only ecclesiastical, but also familial, economic, social, political, etc. – under the lordship of Jesus Christ. In the public square as much as in the private, the explicit principles and teachings of the Word of God must and will direct the affairs of the nations. The terminology of 'theonomy' is used to insist that the biblical laws, including the Old Testament case laws and their prescribed capital punishments for various offences (adultery, homosexuality, idolatry, disobedience to parents) be honoured and applied in exhaustive detail by governments today.[1] The same laws, including the judicial laws, that were set forth for the governance of Israel, the Old Testament people of God in the days of the theocracy, should also be held out today as the standard for governments and their judicial instruments.

The Biblical Case for Postmillennialism

Most who defend Postmillennialism are ready to agree that the case for it must be a biblical one. Even though some appeal to extra-Scriptural considerations to support their case,[2] the decisive evidence for or against Postmillennialism must be biblical. For this reason, postmillennialists often bristle at the criticisms of those who appeal to non-biblical evidences that seem to belie the optimism of postmillennialist thought. When critics of Postmillennialism, for example, point out how the church is declining in numbers and influence in many western countries, or at the increasing secularism of modern culture, postmillennialists are frequently unimpressed. They rightly argue that the debate regarding the millennium is a debate fundamentally about the teaching of the Word of God.

---

[1] For a standard presentation of the theonomist position, see Greg L. Bahnsen, *Theonomy in Christian Ethics*, 2nd ed. (1977; Phillipsburg, New Jersey: Presbyterian and Reformed, 1984). The language of the abiding validity of the law in 'exhaustive detail' is Bahnsen's. Discussions among critics and advocates of theonomy suggest that this language is somewhat misleading, since not all of the law's sanctions are applied directly and exhaustively to modern circumstances. For a survey of these discussions, see Greg L. Bahnsen, *No Other Standard: Theonomy and Its Critics* (Tyler, Texas: Institute for Biblical Economics, 1991); and William S. Barker and W. Robert Godfrey, eds., *Theonomy: A Reformed Critique* (Grand Rapids: Zondervan, 1990).

[2] Loraine Boettner does this to some extent in his contribution to the volume, *The Meaning of the Millennium* (pp. 125 ff.).

THE PROMISE OF THE FUTURE

If this is the case, what biblical reasons are most often cited in support of Postmillennialism? Obviously, it is not possible to give the case for Postmillennialism in any completeness here. But it is important that some of the main lines of the biblical argument be noted.

I. THE PROMISES OF UNIVERSAL COVENANT BLESSING

One of the most common points of departure in arguments for Postmillennialism is the biblical promise of universal covenant blessing. Postmillennialists are fond of referring to the many passages in the Old and New Testaments that describe the way in which the Lord's salvation will extend to all the families and nations of the earth.

It is noted, for example, that, when the Lord covenanted with Abraham, the father of all believers, he promised that in him all families will be blessed. The number of Abraham's descendants was promised to be as innumerable as the dust of the earth (*Gen.* 13:16; cf. *Gen.* 15:5; 17:6; 22:17–18, *Num.* 23:10). When Christ gave the Great Commission to his disciples, he mandated that they make disciples of all the nations (*Matt.* 28:18–20). Christ himself, when asked whether few would be saved, confidently asserted that 'they will come from north, south, east and west' (*Luke* 13:29). Reading these and other passages, especially those which speak of the surprising growth of the kingdom (*Matt.* 13:31–33), postmillennialists insist that the biblical picture, on balance, is one of a vast multitude who will be saved. Rather than suggesting the prospect of a meagre, insignificant response to the gospel, these passages encourage an expectation of assured and amazing results.

II. THE PRESENT AUTHORITY AND DOMINION OF CHRIST

These promises of a great ingathering of the nations and peoples into the kingdom of God are correlated, in the view of many postmillennialists, with the biblical understanding of the present authority and dominion of Jesus Christ. In the Messianic Psalms of the Old Testament (for example, *Psa.* 2;

22; 45; 67; 72; 110), the prophecies of Isaiah (e.g., *Isa.* 2:2–4; 9:6–7; 11:6, 9–10; 40:4–5; 49:6), and the New Testament descriptions of Christ's authority, we are presented with a picture of Christ the King who reigns in the midst of history, overcoming his enemies and subjecting all things under his feet (*1 Cor.* 15:25).

According to many postmillennialist authors, alternative views only pay lip-service to these kinds of biblical passages. Only within the framework of Postmillennialism are the biblical descriptions of Christ's present lordship adequately appreciated. If Christ is the reigning Lord, if he has been given all authority in heaven and on earth, if the nations are his by right of inheritance, if the power and works of the devil have been broken and defeated by his cross, resurrection and ascension – then the only view which answers to these biblical themes is one that anticipates the success of Christ's church-gathering and kingdom-building work in history. The problem with alternative views, according to the post-millennialist reading of these biblical passages, is that they spiritualize the concreteness of the biblical understanding of Christ's kingdom or relegate to the final state what is already to be expected in the period of history prior to Christ's return.

III. A PRETERIST VIEW OF THE SIGNS OF THE TIMES

One of the key elements in the argument for Postmillen-nialism is the insistence that many of the signs of the times, particularly those signs which evidence opposition to Christ and the gospel, will be fulfilled prior to the establishment of the millennial kingdom in the present age. Though views differ regarding whether these signs of the times have already been fulfilled either in part or in whole, postmillennialists generally regard these signs to be virtually absent during the period of the millennium. In Matthew 24, for example, the passage that most comprehensively describes the signs of the times, postmillennialists typically find a description of those signs that were present in the period before the destruction of Jerusalem in AD 70. The great tribulation and the other signs of opposition to Christ's kingdom are events that will precede Christ's coming in power and glory to establish his millennial kingdom. This understanding is often termed a preterist interpretation of this chapter and other biblical references to the signs of the times.[1]

IV. THE MILLENNIUM OF REVELATION 20

Postmillennialism shares many of the emphases of Amillennialism's interpretation of Revelation 20. But it has several distinctive features of its own as well. The most common postmillennial reading of this passage takes the events described in it, particularly the binding of Satan, as occurring at some point in history subsequent to the events described in Revelation 19:11–21; a chronological sequence between the end of Revelation 19 and the beginning of Revelation 20 is posited. Revelation 19 describes the manner in which Christ will progressively defeat in history all the forces that are arrayed against him. After Christ has defeated all of those opposed to him, Satan will be bound for a period of one thousand years.

Though postmillennialists do not necessarily regard this as a literal period of one thousand years, most take the binding of Satan to be a description of what will occur in history, in the near or distant future, when Christ will bring about a 'complete cessation of Satan's earthly influence'.[2] As one postmillennialist describes this event, 'This binding refers to a particular spiritual event in the heavenly realm, subsequent to the earthly ministry of Jesus, and yet future from the

---

[1] J. Marcellus Kik, in his *An Eschatology of Victory*, pp. 30–40, 59–173, argues that the discourse in Matthew 24:1–35 refers to the events related to the destruction of the temple in Jerusalem in AD 70 and that only in verse 36 and following do we find a reference to the second coming of Christ at the end of the present age.

[2] Davis, *Christ's Victorious Kingdom*, p. 93.

perspective of the church, which will place a complete quarantine on Satan's activities.'[1] According to Postmillennialism, the binding of Satan can only mean the complete defeat of Satan and the introduction of a period in which his activity is not merely curtailed, but completely terminated.

These brief comments about the features and purported biblical basis for Postmillennialism, though inadequate in some respects, will have to suffice for our summary at this point. However, the main lines of Postmillennialism should be clear. Postmillennialism teaches that the millennium will occur before the return of Christ, at that point in history when the cause of Christ and the gospel will prevail on the earth. A great period of time, whether a literal period of a thousand years or an indefinite period of many centuries, will see unparalleled righteousness, peace and prosperity. Warfare between and among the nations will cease. The nations will be populated by Christian believers who acknowledge and live out of the awareness of Christ's lordship. Governments will govern and maintain justice in accord with the standards of the Word of God in Scripture.

Though it has become more common among contemporary defenders of this postmillennialist position to maintain that the millennium roughly coincides with the entire Christian era, at least the period subsequent to the destruction of Jerusalem in AD 70, the historic 'chiliasm' of the postmillennialist vision regards the millennium as a future period in which these glorious circumstances will be realized.

Amillennialism

In the preceding treatment of the major millennial views, we have stressed that they fall into two kinds according to whether they regard the coming of Christ as preceding or following the millennium. Classical and Dispensational Premillennialism take the former view, and Postmillennialism

[1] *Ibid.*, p. 94.

and Amillennialism, the latter. Despite this fundamental similarity, however, Postmillennialism and Amillennialism can be distinguished in a number of respects. To complete our survey of millennial views, therefore, we need to consider the view commonly known as Amillennialism. Following the pattern previously used, we will begin with a comment on terminology and then consider briefly its history and a number of its characteristic features.

I. YET ANOTHER COMMENT ABOUT TERMINOLOGY

Perhaps the most obvious and immediate problem with the term 'amillennial' is that literally it means 'no millennium'. At first glance, therefore, it would appear that Amillennialism is a position that rejects the idea of a millennium altogether and that it is not a millennial view at all but a rejection of all forms of millennialism. However, this is not the case, as we shall see.

The term 'amillennial' has been coined because this view rejects the chiliasm of the other major millennial views. Unlike both Premillennialism and Postmillennialism, it does not look for a golden-age millennium either after the return of Christ or just before it. Amillennialism regards the entire period of history between Christ's first and second coming as the period of the millennium. Because it rejects the idea of a distinguishable millennium or golden age that commences at some point after the early history of the Christian church, this view has been given the name Amillennialism.[1]

In order to prevent misunderstanding of this view, some have suggested alternative terminology. Jay Adams, for example, in his study of the book of Revelation, *The Time is*

---

[1] Some postmillennialists are fond of calling this view 'pessi-millennialism' because it does not teach that the cause of Christ's kingdom will necessarily triumph and prevail throughout the earth for a lengthy period of many centuries. This term is an example of partisan labelling that does not promote understanding or communication among those who hold differing views, particularly among postmillennialists and amillennialists.

At Hand, has proposed the term 'realized millennialism'.[1] This reflects the real emphasis of Amillennialism that the millennium is a present reality, having commenced with the events of Christ's ascension and the outpouring of the Holy Spirit at Pentecost. Another proposal has been made by Gordon Spykman who, in his *Reformational Theology*, offers the term 'pro-millennialism' as more appropriate and positive language for this eschatological view;[2] it is not a negative view which denies the reality of the millennium, but a positive view which affirms the presence of the millennium here and now before the return of Christ. Of these two proposals, Spykman's is the more attractive in that it retains a parallelism with the other millennial views, each of which is denominated by a prefixed form of the term 'millennialism'. Terms have a life of their own, however, and it is highly unlikely that either these or any other candidates will displace the traditional term 'Amillennialism'.[3]

II. A BRIEF HISTORY OF AMILLENNIALISM

The view which today is known as Amillennialism has a long history of advocacy going back to the beginning of the Christian era. Since the fourth and fifth centuries, it has been the predominant position within the Christian church. Though Premillennialism has had its advocates throughout the

[1] Rev. ed. (1966; Philadelphia: Presbyterian and Reformed, 1976), pp. 7–11.

[2] Grand Rapids: Eerdmans, 1992, pp. 540–43. It is not difficult to anticipate the objection to this terminology from advocates of the other views: what right does Amillennialism have to the proud title of 'pro-'millennial?

[3] If I were able to choose a label for this position, I would prefer to term it *now*millennialism. This term retains the parallelism with the other terms and expresses well the main difference between this form of Postmillennialism and golden-age Postmillennialism, namely, that the kingdom of Christ spans the period between his first and second coming. I doubt, however, that this suggestion will catch on with many.

history of the Christian church and has enjoyed a resurgence recently among conservative evangelicals in North America, it is safe to say that Amillennialism has been the consensus position of the largest portion of the Christian church. Louis Berkhof is correct when he remarks as follows regarding Amillennialism:

> Some Premillenarians have spoken of *Amillennialism* as a new view and as one of the most recent novelties, but this is certainly not in accord with the testimony of history. The name is new indeed, but the view to which it is applied is as old as Christianity. It had at least as many advocates as Chiliasm among the Church Fathers of the second and third centuries, supposed to have been the heyday of Chiliasm. It has ever since been the view most widely accepted, is the only view that is either expressed or implied in the great historical Confessions of the Church, and has always been the prevalent view in Reformed circles.[1]

Though Berkhof does not mention the claim of many present-day postmillennialists that Amillennialism, not Postmillennialism, is the relative newcomer, his observations are applicable to this claim.

It is generally agreed that though the view known today as Amillennialism was already present in the earliest period of the Christian church, the great church father, Augustine, was instrumental in establishing this view as the predominant one. By treating the millennium of Revelation 20 as a symbolical description of the church's growth in the present

---

[1] *Systematic Theology*, p. 708. The following sources offer representative presentations of the amillennial view: A. Hoekema, *The Bible and the Future*; idem, 'Amillennialism', in *The Meaning of the Millennium*, ed. Robert G. Clouse, pp. 155–88; G. Vos, *The Pauline Eschatology*; G. C. Berkouwer, *The Return of Christ*; William E. Cox, *Amillennialism Today* (Philadelphia: Presbyterian and Reformed, 1972); William Hendriksen, *More Than Conquerors* (Grand Rapids: Baker, 1939); and Robert B. Strimple, 'Amillennialism', in *Three Views on the Millennium and Beyond*, ed. Darrell L. Bock, pp. 81–129.

age, Augustine gave impetus to the amillennialist contention that the millennium does not follow chronologically the early history of the New Testament church. With the exception of some exponents of Premillennialism, the tenets of amillennialist teaching prevailed throughout the Middle Ages and during the Reformation. The Reformers were aligned with this broad tradition, though soon after the Reformation advocates of Postmillennialism arose especially within the Reformed tradition.

However strong the influence of Postmillennialism may have been within the Reformed churches, especially in North America during the eighteenth and nineteenth centuries, the predominant view today is that of Amillennialism. Though advocates of Postmillennialism are found among the Reformed churches, and though the majority of conservative evangelicals in North America are premillennialists, the prevailing view among the Reformed churches and the Christian church, broadly conceived, remains that of Amillennialism.[1] Where the historic creeds and confessions address themselves to the subject of the future, they are more congenial to an amillennialist view than to the other major millennial views. This is true of the Reformed confessions, though they do not explicitly address some of the differences between Amillennialism and Postmillennialism.[2]

---

[1] Though the Roman Catholic and Eastern Orthodox churches do not have a dogmatic position on the millennium, their traditions have commonly identified the kingdom of Christ with the church during the present age. If the term applies, therefore, they are amillennial in outlook.

[2] The one exception to this pattern may be the *Second Helvetic Confession* of 1566. This confession was first written by Heinrich Bullinger, Zwingli's successor and an influential Reformer in his own right, and later adopted by the Swiss Reformed churches as a confession of their faith. Next to the *Heidelberg Catechism*, it has been the most popular Reformed confession among the international family of Reformed churches. This confession seems to condemn Postmillennialism when it declares: 'Moreover we condemn the Jewish dreams

III. THE MAIN FEATURES OF AMILLENNIALISM

Because of the significant areas of agreement between Postmillennialism and Amillennialism, our summary of the main features of Amillennialism will often focus upon those things that distinguish these two views. Just as with the other millennial views, this summary will be very general, recognizing that among amillennialists there are many differences in emphasis and on particular issues.

IV. THE MILLENNIUM IS NOW

Perhaps the most important way to distinguish Amillennialism from the other millennial views is to note that it teaches the present reality of the millennial kingdom. Amillennialism regards the millennium of Revelation 20 to be a symbolical representation of the present reign of Christ with his saints. During the period of time between Christ's first advent and his return at the end of the age, Satan has been bound in such a way as no longer to be able to deceive the nations. The millennium, therefore, is not a literal period of one thousand years. The period of one thousand years (ten times ten times ten) represents the complete period within God's sovereign disposition of history during which he has granted to Christ the authority to receive the nations as his inheritance (see *Psa. 2*, *Matt.* 28:16–20).

Amillennialism is, accordingly, opposed to all forms of 'chiliasm', that is, the teaching that the millennium is a distinguishable period that concludes the period of history between Christ's first and second coming. This view rejects

---

that before the day of judgement there shall be a golden age in the earth, and that the godly shall possess the kingdoms of the world, their wicked enemies being trodden under foot; for the evangelical truth (Matt. 24 and 25, Luke 21), and the apostolic doctrine (in the Second Epistle to the Thessalonians 2, and in the Second Epistle to Timothy 3 and 4) are found to teach far otherwise' (Chap. 11; quoted from *The Creeds of Christendom,* ed. Philip Schaff [1931; reprint, Grand Rapids: Baker, 1985], III: p. 853).

the idea that at some (future) point in the history of the church the millennial kingdom will be established. Though opinions vary among amillennialists as to the nature of the millennium – some are more pessimistic and others more optimistic about the triumph of the gospel of Jesus Christ among the nations – amillennialists typically do not believe that Christ's kingdom will prevail upon the earth in the post-millennialist sense. Amillennialists ordinarily reject the postmillennialist conviction that the millennium will be a period marked by universal peace, the pervasive influence and dominion of biblical principles in all aspects of life, and the subjection of the vast majority of the nations and peoples to Christ's lordship. Amillennialists believe that the biblical descriptions of the inter-advental period suggest that the world's opposition to Christ and the gospel will endure, even becoming more intense as the present period of history draws to a close.

V. The Signs of the Times

Amillennialism commonly understands that the signs of the times, including in particular the signs of opposition to Christ's gospel and people (for example, tribulation, apostasy, the spirit of Antichrist), are present and future realities. The entire period between the ascension of Christ and his return at the end of the present age will see an ongoing conflict, sometimes more, sometimes less intense, between the church and the world, the kingdom of God and the kingdom of the evil one. Though there may be in different places or countries and at different times, periods of relative peace and prosperity for the church and people of God, there will never be a time, certainly not a millennial period, in which the cause of Christ will so triumph in the earth that suffering and distress will no longer be experienced by the church of Jesus Christ.

This view of the signs of the times regards them as characterizing the history of redemption in the entire period during which Christ is gathering his church by his Spirit and

Word. Postmillennialism, by contrast, regards many of these signs to have been (or to be) fulfilled at some point prior to the millennium. As we have noted, postmillennialists commonly regard the signs of the times enumerated in Matthew 24 as referring to the events prior to the destruction of Jerusalem in AD 70.[1] This means that, from the point of view of the millennium, signs of opposition to Christ, like tribulation and apostasy, will no longer characterize history, at least for the duration of the millennium until Satan's 'little season' just prior to Christ's return at the end of the age.

VI. REVELATION 20

Throughout the preceding discussion of millennial views, the teaching of Revelation 20 has always been close at hand. In the final analysis, the various millennial views can only be tested and justified on biblical grounds, and the key biblical text is, undoubtedly, Revelation 20. Consequently, we will devote a later chapter to this key passage. In this sketch of Amillennialism, however, it is necessary to summarize the standard view of Revelation 20 among amillennialists.

Most amillennialists read Revelation 20 as a passage which, in parallel with several sections of the book of Revelation, describes a vision sequence which covers the entire period from Christ's first to his second coming. Unlike many postmillennialists who read Revelation 19 and 20 in chronological succession – Revelation 19 describing the commencement of the millennial period in history, Revelation 20 describing the millennium itself – amillennialists view the vision of the millennium as a symbolic portrayal of the period of the church's mission in the world. The binding of Satan described in this vision is a picture of the restraint God has placed upon Satan, preventing him from deceiving the

---

[1] In my previous treatment of the signs of the times, I addressed this issue and took a position at odds with Postmillennialism. Though I did not say so at the time, my view of the signs of the times, if correct, supports an amillennialist and not a postmillennialist view. We will return to this issue in Chapter 12.

nations, and of the certain prospect of the church's success in discipling them.

Though opinions differ among amillennialists regarding the 'first resurrection' and the 'coming to life' of the saints who reign with Christ, most amillennialists understand the first resurrection to be a spiritual one in which all believers participate, particularly the martyred and deceased saints who reign with Christ in heaven. By virtue of this first resurrection, believers are no longer subject to the power of death and have a share in Christ's reign over all things. Only at the end of the period of Christ's gathering his church and the reign of his saints will he return, the dead be raised, and the resurrection of the body (the second resurrection) occur. The reign of Christ and his saints described in this vision is not a reign of the saints upon the earth, but a reign of the saints who are with Christ in heaven. Thus, Revelation 20 does not describe an earthly millennium, a golden age in the postmillennialist sense, but the history of the progress of Christ's kingdom upon the earth, as the gospel is preached to the nations, and believers, especially those who are deceased, even martyred for the faith, are given to reign with Christ in the expectation of his triumph at the end of the age.

VII. THE CHRISTIAN'S HOPE FOR THE FUTURE

Another distinctive feature of Amillennialism is its insistence that the great hope of the Christian and the believer for the future is the return of Christ at the end of the age. Though postmillennialists would regard Christ's return to be the final, consummating event at the end of this present age, they tend to view history in such a way as to deflect attention from this event to the expectation of a future millennial age. Amillennialists, on the other hand, anticipate that the victory of Christ, and the triumph of the kingdom of Christ, will occur only when Christ returns.

This is a somewhat elusive and difficult point to make. Often postmillennialists decry amillennialists for their pessimism about the prospects of Christ's kingdom in this present age. Amillennialists, conversely, criticize postmillennialists for being unjustifiably optimistic. Amillennialists are said to be too other-worldly in their expectations for the future; postmillennialists are said to be too this-worldly in their expectations.

Without attempting to resolve this dispute here, it certainly is true that these two views differ greatly on this score. Amillennialism always insists that in the biblical descriptions of the future, the great and final hope of every Christian focuses upon the event of Christ's return, his revelation from heaven when he will subdue all of his enemies and bring relief to his troubled church (2 *Thess.* 1). Unlike the expectation of Postmillennialism, which teaches a future millennium of one thousand years (or more) of Christ's reign upon the earth, an expectation which undoubtedly diminishes the urgency and eager anticipation of Christ's second coming, Amillennialism does not expect any substantial or qualitative change in the circumstance of the church prior to Christ's return. Indeed, one of the ways in which Postmillennialism and Amillennialism may be distinguished, is that Amillennialism has a clearer expectation of the imminence (the 'soon-ness') of Christ's return than does Postmillennialism. Postmillennialism regards the return of Christ to be a distant reality, one whose fulfilment can only follow upon the millennium or golden age to come.

Conclusion

If these main features of Amillennialism are brought together, it is evident that Amillennialism is really a form of postmillennialist teaching without the 'chiliasm' that characterizes classic Postmillennialism.[1] With Postmillennialism,

[1] Some readers might wonder why I have not included a certain view of the conversion of Israel as a feature of Amillennialism. Just as many postmillennialists teach the future conversion of the preponderance of the Jewish people, so many amillennialists reject this teaching

Amillennialism believes that the return of Christ will occur after the millennium. However, against Postmillennialism, Amillennialism rejects the notion that Christ's return will follow a distinct millennial period comprising only a segment of the period between his first and second comings. Amillennialism, as we have seen, regards the millennium as the entire period of history between Christ's resurrection and ascension and his coming again. Unlike the expectation of a golden age before the return of Christ, in which the kingdom of God will be realized upon the earth (though falling short of absolute perfection), the amillennialist expects a continuing history of growth as well as struggle, of advance as well as of temporary retrenchment, for the church of Jesus Christ in this present age. Only at the end of the age, with the return of Christ in glory and power, will every enemy be subdued and Christ's reign be openly acknowledged in all the earth.

This summary of the main features of Amillennialism concludes our survey of the four major views of the millennium. No doubt more could be said regarding any one of these views, and it would be possible to note various differences that exist among their advocates. Our aim thus far has been only to sketch the most important distinctives of each of the four major millennial views. To the evaluation of these views we now turn.

---

and take the reference to 'all Israel' in Romans 11:26 to be a reference to all the elect Jews (and perhaps even Gentiles) gathered into the church through the centuries. However, as I have noted previously, the advocacy or rejection of this view of the conversion of the Jews is not an adequate basis for being either a postmillennialist or amillennialist, respectively. Strimple, 'Amillennialism', p. 113: 'It should be emphasized . . . that the conclusion that Paul in Romans 11 predicts a future mass conversion of ethnic Israel prior to Christ's return does not, by itself, prove the correctness of any particular millennial position. After all, that interpretation has been presented not only by both premillennialists and postmillennialists, but by some leading amillennialists as well.'

IO

Evaluating Premillennialism

S O FAR WE HAVE SURVEYED in turn each of the four major millennial views. We must now evaluate them by the standard of the Scriptures. Indeed, this is the most important task that remains, namely, to determine which of these views enjoys the support of the Bible. Thus far we have avoided interacting with the arguments frequently presented for one view or the other. The luxury of avoiding these arguments, however, is now over.

To do this we will proceed in a way that roughly coincides with the order in which the four views were presented. We will begin with an evaluation of Premillennialism and argue that the general teaching of the Bible does not support the teaching that Christ's return will occur before the period of the millennium. In subsequent sections of this and the following chapter, some of the distinctive features of Dispensational Premillennialism will be subjected to special scrutiny. This will require that particular attention be given to the subject of the rapture and the teaching of the most important text relating to the millennium, Revelation 20:1–6. Only after dealing at some length with these will we turn to the differences between Postmillennialism and Amillennialism. Though Postmillennialism offers a necessary biblical correction to the pessimism that often characterizes amillennial views, it compromises several aspects of biblical teaching. We will advocate the amillennial view as the more consistently biblical of the two.

The Problem with Premillennialism

The common feature of all premillennial teaching is the claim that Christ's return at the end of the age will take place before the period known as the millennium. Whatever differences exist between Historic and Dispensational Premillennialism – and they are considerable – this teaching is common to them. Though a number of arguments are offered for a premillennial return of Christ, two biblical passages are often cited in support of it. These are 1 Corinthians 15:23–26 and Revelation 20:1–6. The latter is the more important passage because without its teaching some premillennialists acknowledge that 1 Corinthians 15:23–26 would not obviously suggest a return of Christ before the millennium.[1]

Since we will treat Revelation 20:1–6 in some detail in the next chapter, our evaluation will be restricted here to two matters. First, we will consider what might be termed the 'general analogy' of the Scripture on the return of Christ at the end of the age. Second, we will evaluate the appeal to 1 Corinthians 15:23–26. We will show that neither supports the premillennialist position.

[1] For example, George Eldon Ladd, 'Historic Premillennialism', in *The Meaning of the Millennium: Four Views*, ed. by Robert G. Clouse, p. 38. Unlike many dispensational premillennialists who find the doctrine of the millennium in many biblical passages, Ladd acknowledges that only Revelation 20:1–6 teaches a 'millennial' period. He admits that 1 Corinthians 15:23–26 confirms a premillennialist position only when this position has already been established from the clearer teaching of Revelation 20:1–6.

THE PROMISE OF THE FUTURE

I. THE GENERAL TEACHING OF SCRIPTURE

As we begin our evaluation, a question worth raising is whether anyone would argue for a premillennial return of Christ, were it not for the supposed teaching of the two passages just mentioned. Does the Bible anywhere else support this position? This question leads into the subject of the general analogy of Scripture with regard to the return of Christ. It is a commonly recognized rule of thumb for interpretation that the general analogy of Scripture has more weight in determining what the Bible may be said to teach than one or two passages that are somewhat more obscure or difficult to interpret. Louis Berkhof, for example, in his *Principles of Biblical Interpretation*, describes the general analogy of Scripture as any teaching that 'does not rest on the explicit statements of the Bible, but on the obvious scope and import of its teachings as a whole . . .'[1] Such a general analogy or teaching of Scripture is confirmed and strengthened when it is supported by a variety of texts throughout the Bible. Furthermore, when this general teaching of the Scriptures is apparently contradicted by a relatively more obscure Scriptural text, it is appropriate to interpret this more obscure passage in the light of the general analogy of Scripture.[2]

Now it is remarkable to notice that the usual presentation of the return of the Christ in the Scriptures, and in a number of different passages, is that it is a consummating event at the

[1] Grand Rapids: Baker, 1950.

[2] It is interesting to observe that Berkhof cites Revelation 20:1–4 as an instance of a relatively obscure passage that may not be used to contravene the clear teaching of Scripture throughout on the subject of the return of Christ (*Principles*, p. 166). Because most premillennialists believe the teaching of Revelation 20:1–6 to be plain and clear in its support of their position, they would insist that Berkhof has misapplied this rule of interpretation in this particular case. In their approach, the teaching of those passages that speak of Christ's return must be understood in the light of the clear premillennialist teaching of Revelation 20:1–6.

close of the age. A number of features of the Bible's teaching regarding the return of Christ confirm this general pattern of teaching:[1]

Christ's coming will be a visible, public event that will bring about the salvation of the people of God and the realization of the kingdom of God in fullness (*Matt.* 24:27, 33, *Luke* 17:24; 21:27–28, 31).

When Christ is revealed from heaven, he will bring rest immediately and simultaneously for his beleaguered church and eternal punishment upon the unbelieving and impenitent (*2 Thess.* 1:6–10).

In the New Testament descriptions of the believer's expectation for the future, the common thread is a focus upon the return of Christ as the event that brings the fullness of salvation, beyond which there is no further event that will surpass it in redemptive significance (cf. *1 Cor.* 1:7, 8, *Phil.* 1:6,10, *1 John* 2:28, *1 Tim.* 4:8, *2 Tim.* 4:1). The premillennial teaching that Christ's return will introduce a millennial period, whose conclusion will be marked by a new outbreak and manifestation of Satanic opposition to Christ and his people (Satan's 'little season' of Revelation 20:3), hardly seems to fit this focus and expectation.

When Christ returns, a rapture of the living and the dead leads to the resurrection transformation of all believers and their uninterrupted and undisturbed communion with the Lord from that day forward (*1 Thess.* 4:13–18). Though we will return to this passage and the subject of the rapture in the next section of this chapter, this communion with the Lord, as it is described in this passage, does not fit the conception of the millennium and Satan's 'little season' which characterizes the premillennial view.

Rather than teaching that the return of Christ will bring a provisional phase of God's kingdom, the millennium, which itself will be surpassed in the final state of God's eternal kingdom, the New Testament teaches that Christ's return

[1] See Chapter 4, 'The Second Coming of Christ'.

will introduce the final state of new heavens and a new earth
(*2 Pet.* 3:13, *Rom.* 8:17–25).

Finally the resurrections of the just and the unjust will
coincide (*Dan.* 12:2, *John* 5:28–29, *Acts* 24:14–15, *Rev.*20:11–
15). In the premillennialist conception of the return of Christ,
the resurrection of believing saints is commonly distinguished
and separated in time – by at least one thousand years! –
from the resurrection of the unbelieving. However, in New
Testament teaching the resurrection of believers is said to
occur at the 'last day' (*John* 6:40, *1 Thess.* 4:16, *Phil.* 3:20–21,
1 Cor. 15:23), the day that marks the close of this present age
and the introduction of the (final) age to come.

When considered together, the cumulative effect of these
features of biblical teaching is to confirm that when Christ
returns, his coming will conclude history as we now experience it and introduce the final state. The pervasive testimony
of the New Testament conforms to the natural reading of the
Apostles' Creed when it describes the return of Christ 'to
judge the living and dead'. This judgement presumably will
prepare the way for the 'resurrection of the body and the life
everlasting', commencing the final state. Unless clear and
compelling evidence from one or more biblical text supports
the premillennialist view, it would seem that we should
follow the rule that the general teaching of Scripture has
more weight than one text, especially when the teaching of
that text is not clear and undisputed.[1]

II. The teaching of 1 Corinthians 15:23–26

George Eldon Ladd, an able defender of the premillennialist
view, has argued that 1 Corinthians 15:20–28, and especially
verses 23–26, teaches three stages in the unfolding of redemptive history, which include an interim period that is the
equivalent of the millennium of Revelation 20:1–6. Though
this passage does not speak expressly of a millennium, it at

---

[1] However, as we shall see in the next chapter, there is probably no
more disputed text in all of the Bible than Revelation 20:1–6.

least corroborates, according to Ladd, the sequence of events clearly set forth in Revelation 20. He summarizes his position as follows:

> There is . . . one passage in Paul which may refer to an interim kingdom if not a millennium. In 1 Corinthians 15:23–26 Paul pictures the triumph of Christ's kingdom as being accomplished in several stages. The resurrection of Christ is the first stage (*tagma*). The second stage will occur at the parousia when those who are Christ's will share his resurrection. 'Then comes the end, when he delivers the kingdom to God the Father after destroying every rule and every authority and power. For he must reign until he has put all his enemies under his feet. The last enemy to be destroyed is death.' The adverbs translated 'then' are *epeita, eita,* which denote a sequence: 'after that'. There are three distinct stages: Jesus' resurrection; after that (*epeita*) the resurrection of believers at the resurrection; after that (*eita*) the end (*telos*). An unidentified interval falls between Christ's resurrection and his parousia, and a second undefined interval falls between the parousia and the *telos,* when Christ completes the subjugation of his enemies.[1]

Ladd's argument is that, though this passage may not explicitly speak of a millennial period, it allows for an intervening period between the time of Christ's coming and the resurrection of believing saints, and the time of Christ's subjection of all his enemies at the end of the age. This intervening period is the millennium of Revelation 20.

Though Ladd's argument can be defended on strictly grammatical grounds that the adverbs 'then . . . and then' used by the Apostle Paul can express a sequence in which a period of time could intervene, this requires an unnatural reading of this passage for several reasons.

First, in all the other New Testament instances where the words used in this passage ('*epeita . . . eita*') are found, they

---

[1] Ladd, 'Historic Premillennialism', in *The Meaning of the Millennium: Four Views,* ed. Robert G. Clouse, p. 39.

are used to express events in the closest temporal connection, without any protracted period of time intervening (*Luke* 8:12, *Mark* 4:17, *John* 20:27). In the immediate context of 1 Corinthians 15:23–26, we find the same adverbs used interchangeably, and there, too, they express a simple sequence of events (*1 Cor.* 15:5–7). Furthermore, the second of these two, 'and then', is used alone in 1 Thessalonians 4:17 to express an immediate sequence of events. If context and ordinary usage have a bearing upon the interpretation of a text, then it seems evident that these words ought to be read as expressing a simple sequence of events – when Christ comes, the dead in Christ will be raised and the end state will ensue with all things subject to him.

Second, the New Testament generally and the epistles of Paul particularly, show a close connection between the 'coming' (*parousia*) of Christ and the 'end' (*telos*). However, on Ladd's and the premillennialists' construction of this passage, these terms in 1 Corinthians 15:23–26 refer to distinct events, separated by a period of one thousand years. In 1 Corinthians 1:7–8, the Apostle Paul speaks of the 'revelation' and the 'day' of the Lord as the end to which believers look forward and until which they will be kept blameless. When Christ is revealed, the end will come and the believer's need to persevere in hope will conclude (cf. *2 Cor.* 1:13–14, *Matt.* 10:22; 24:6, 13–14, *Mark* 13:7,13, *Luke* 21:9, *Heb.* 3:6, 14; 6:11, *1 Pet.* 4:7). Thus, treating the 'coming' of Christ and the 'end' in 1 Corinthians 15:23–26 as events that are closely connected, or even conjoined, is in keeping with the ordinary pattern found in the New Testament. That pattern is broken by Ladd's view.

And third, the believer's victory over death is said in 1 Corinthians 15:54–55 to occur when believers receive resurrection bodies. This coincides with what is said in 1 Corinthians 15:23–26 to occur in conjunction with both the 'coming' of Christ and the 'end', when the believer's last enemy, death, will be overcome. The simplest and most obvious reading of these verses in their context is that when Christ comes and believers share in his resurrection, this event will coincide with or introduce the 'end', that circumstance in which death has been swallowed up in victory.

In short, though Ladd's reading of this passage is grammatically possible, there are good and powerful reasons to conclude that it is contextually and comparatively most improbable. When 1 Corinthians 15:23–26 is read in its immediate context and in the more remote context of New Testament teaching generally, it corroborates the pattern we earlier termed the general analogy of Scripture: when Christ comes at the end of the age, this will mark the closure of redemptive history and commence (with the resurrection of the just and the unjust, the judgement of the living and the dead, etc.) the final state. The Scriptures simply contain no clear evidence for a premillennialist understanding of the return of Christ, with the possible exception of Revelation 20:1–6.

Christ's Return and the Rapture

No evaluation of Dispensational Premillennialism may ignore its teaching of a two-phased return of Christ, the first phase of which is commonly known as the rapture. This feature is its most widely known aspect. Popularized by such best-selling books as Hal Lindsey's *The Late Great Planet Earth*, the film *The Return*, and bumper stickers warning others that in the event of the rapture the vehicle will be without driver and possibly passengers – Dispensationalism has enjoyed a large following among conservative Christians, especially in North America.

The view that has predominated in Dispensationalism is known as *pre-tribulational rapturism*. As noted previously, the older classical version of Dispensationalism held that the first phase of Christ's return, his 'coming' or 'parousia', would precede a seven-year period of tribulation, and that the second phase of Christ's return, his 'revelation' or 'appearing', would introduce the millennium or one-thousand-year reign of Christ on the earth. The first phase, Christ's coming, is the rapture[1] of 1 Thessalonians 4:17, an event that represents Christ's coming 'for' his saints in contrast to his subsequent return (the second phase) or coming 'with' the saints. Though this view has been somewhat modified in more recent Dispensationalism, it remains far and away the most popular view among dispensationalists to this day. The views known as mid-tribulationism and post-tribulationism, as the terminology suggests, differ as to the timing of the rapture, but have relatively few defenders.[2]

In the notes of the *New Scofield Reference Bible*, the rapture is viewed as an event that can occur at any moment.[3] There are no events in the biblical timetable for the future that must occur before the first phase of Christ's return can take place. Christ's return for his saints will be preceded by the resurrection of all believing saints. After the resurrection of deceased saints, all living believers will be immediately transformed. All of these saints, resurrected and transformed, will then be caught up (raptured) with Christ – whose return to earth will only be partial and for this purpose alone – and meet him in the air. Thus, the church of Jesus Christ will be raptured from the earth and taken to heaven for a period of seven years, the 'marriage feast of the Lamb', during which period great tribulation will befall the earth.

While the raptured church enjoys this period of the marriage feast, a number of events will occur upon the earth. A period of tribulation will begin, the latter half of which

[1] The term 'rapture' comes from the Latin Vulgate translation's use of *rapiemur* (*raptus*), to render the expression 'caught up'.

[2] See Millard J. Erickson, *Basic Eschatology* (Grand Rapids: Baker, 1998), pp. 125–181.

[3] *The New Scofield Reference Bible*, notes on Luke 21:27, 2 Thessalonians 2:3, Titus 2:11, Revelation 19:19. See Lewis Sperry Chafer, *Systematic Theology* (Dallas: Dallas Seminary Press, 1948), 4: pp. 367–8; and J. Dwight Pentecost, *Things to Come* (Findlay, Ohio: Dunham, 1958), pp. 202–4.

will be a period of 'great tribulation'. This fulfils the prophecy of Daniel 9:27. In this latter half of the period of tribulation, the Antichrist will arise, the beast out of the sea, who will impose great cruelties on the earth and pretend to be divine. During this period of great tribulation, the elect of the children of Israel and a great number of the Gentiles will be saved. The end of this period of great tribulation will witness a period of intensified opposition to the people of God. The kings of the earth, the armies of the beast and the false prophet will join forces against the people of God. However, Christ will return with his saints and destroy all of his enemies at the battle of Armageddon. Thereupon, the millennial kingdom, during which Christ will rule upon the earth, will commence.[1]

II. CHRIST'S RETURN NOT A TWO-PHASED EVENT

Though we have not included in this summary the many details and variations upon this view, these should be sufficient for our purpose. Two key questions must be addressed in respect to pre-tribulational rapturism. First, does the Bible teach that Christ's return will take place in two phases, separated by an intervening period of seven years' duration? Second, does the Bible teach that the first of these phases will be the rapture envisioned by Dispensationalism?

To some extent we have already treated the first question by noting that the return of Christ is a consummating event at the end of the present age, but some of the arguments offered for the idea of a two-phased return of Christ have not yet been directly addressed.

In the earlier period of Dispensational Premillennialism, it was suggested that the New Testament uses the three common terms for the return of Christ – *parousia* (presence, coming), *apokalupsis* (revelation) and *epiphaneia* (appearance) – to distinguish the two phases of Christ's return. The

[1] *The New Scofield Reference Bible*, notes on Daniel 9:24, Revelation 7:14, 11:2, 19:19.

first term was said to be the term for Christ's initial coming, his coming 'for' his saints at the rapture. The second and third terms were said to be used for Christ's coming at the end of the seven-year period of tribulation, his coming 'with' his saints.

This claim, however, cannot withstand scrutiny. The New Testament shows clearly that *parousia* and *apokalupsis* are used interchangeably, as are *apokalupsis* and *epiphaneia,* to refer to the one return of Christ at the end of the age. For example, in 1 Thessalonians 4:15, the Apostle Paul uses the first term, *parousia,* to describe the rapture. But in 1 Thessalonians 3:13, he uses the same term to describe the 'coming of our Lord Jesus with all his saints'. According to Dispensationalism, this latter event occurs only at the revelation of Christ, seven years after the rapture. Similarly, in 2 Thessalonians 2:8, the Apostle Paul uses the term *parousia* to refer to the event when Christ will destroy the 'man of lawlessness' or Antichrist, an event which in Dispensationalism is said not to occur until the revelation at the end of the seven-year period of tribulation. Most unsettling to the dispensationalist argument is the fact that this passage uses two of the three terms for Christ's return in close proximity, as synonyms, when it speaks of how Christ will 'bring to nought' the man of lawlessness 'by the appearance of his coming'.

Moreover, both the terms *apokalupsis* and *epiphaneia* are used in the epistles of the Apostle Paul for what dispensationalists would regard as the first and second phases of Christ's return. In 1 Corinthians 1:7, *apokalupsis* is used to describe what would be called the rapture, since the believers in Corinth are said to be 'waiting for the revelation of our Lord Jesus Christ'. However, in 2 Thessalonians 1:7,8, this term is used to describe what dispensationalists would regard as the 'revelation' or 'second' second coming of Christ. The same interchangeability is evident in 1 Timothy 6:14, where *epiphaneia* is used to describe the rapture, and in 2 Timothy 4:1, where it refers to Christ's coming as Judge of the living and the dead.[1] In its use of these terms, the New Testament offers no support for the idea that this return will occur in two distinct phases.

In arguing for a two-phased return, dispensationalists, in addition to the appeal to the use of terms, also insist that the church will not suffer the tribulation, including the great tribulation that will characterize the seven-year period between Christ's coming and his revelation. This insistence, however, cannot be sustained by appeal to the New Testament Scriptures.

In the Olivet Discourse recorded in Matthew 24, Jesus, in reply to the disciples' question, speaks of a great tribulation that will occur prior to his coming. This tribulation will be so severe that it will be shortened for the sake of the elect (verse 22). The reference in this passage to the elect indicates that believers will not be raptured before the tribulation of those days, but will experience it themselves. Dispensationalist teaching maintains that the elect in these verses can only refer to the Jews and not to the church, noting that the term 'church' is not used in this chapter. This is an argument from silence, and it is considerably weakened by the fact that the Gospels seldom use the term 'church'.[2] The most evident

---

[1] Some dispensationalists also argue that a sharp distinction is to be drawn between the 'parousia' and the 'day of the Lord', that is, the revelation of Christ after the seven-year period of tribulation. For a moderate expression of this distinction, see the *New Scofield Reference Bible*, notes on 2 Peter 3:10 and Revelation 19:19. However, in 2 Thessalonians 2:1, 2, these expressions are used to describe the same event – 'Now we request you, brethren, with regard to the coming of our Lord Jesus Christ, and our gathering together to Him, that you may not be quickly shaken from your composure or be disturbed either by a spirit or a message or a letter as if from us, to the effect that the day of the Lord has come.' For a more complete evaluation of Dispensationalism's teaching of a two-phased return of Christ, see George E. Ladd, *The Blessed Hope* (Grand Rapids: Eerdmans, 1956); and Robert H. Gundry, *The Church and the Tribulation* (Grand Rapids: Zondervan, 1973).

[2] In the Gospels of Matthew, Mark and Luke the word 'church' is used in only three places (once in Matthew 16:18, twice in 18:17). It

reading of this passage is to take it as a reference to tribulation that befalls the people of God, the elect (whether Jew or Gentile), before the return of Christ at the end of the age.

It is also important to observe that in this same passage dealing with the 'signs of the times', Christ describes the rapture in a way that indicates that it will not only follow the period of tribulation but also mark the close of the age. In Matthew 24:31, we read the following description of what will occur after the tribulation of those days: 'And He [the Son of Man] will send forth His angels with a great trumpet and they will gather together His elect from the four winds, from one end of the sky to the other.' This description is similar to the language used in 1 Thessalonians 4:16–17 to describe the events that will occur at the time of the rapture – the descent of the Lord, the sound of the trumpet, the gathering of the elect. It is difficult to see why these passages should be taken as descriptions of different events, as in Dispensationalism, which sees the description in Matthew 24 as the second phase of Christ's return and thus as an event distinct from the rapture. It is not difficult, however, to see why Dispensationalism is compelled to distinguish these passages: if Matthew 24:31 referred to the rapture, then that would place the rapture after the period of tribulation rather than before it.

The same kind of difficulty confronts the dispensationalist when it comes to the teaching of 2 Thessalonians 2, with its description of the man of lawlessness, who will come before the day of the Lord. According to Dispensationalism, the

---

should also be noted that the immediate reference of these verses in Matthew 24 is the tribulation experienced at the time of the destruction of the temple in Jerusalem in AD 70. Although I have previously argued that the secondary and more remote reference of these verses is to a period of tribulation preceding the return of Christ at the end of the age (of which this earlier tribulation is an antitype), the obvious reference to the destruction of Jerusalem in these verses strongly militates against the dispensationalist view.

events of this passage will occur during the period of tribulation, especially the great tribulation, between the time of the rapture and the time of Christ's revelation. However, this would undermine the point of the Apostle Paul's teaching in this passage. The point of this passage is to warn the believers in Thessalonica not to be deceived into thinking that the coming of the Lord has already occurred (verse 2), because the man of lawlessness and the great apostasy must occur first. This passage, which is written primarily to Gentile Christian believers – and not Jewish believers, as dispensationalists commonly teach[1] – speaks of a number of events that will precede the coming of Christ and the day of the Lord. These events include the period of tribulation and the Antichrist that Dispensationalism places after the rapture, but which in this passage will occur before the rapture or the coming of the Lord to grant relief to his people or church.

Though it would be possible to explore these passages further, it should be evident that the problem facing Dispensationalism at this point is the same problem confronted in our previous discussion of the return of Christ as a consummating event at the end of the age. Unless the Bible reader brings to many of these passages a pre-conceived doctrine of two distinct phases in the return of Christ, there is little prospect that such a teaching would be discovered or proven from them. The biblical teaching is that Christ will return after the period of tribulation to grant his church relief and his enemies eternal destruction (2 *Thess.* 1). These consequences of Christ's return coincide and therefore do not permit the teaching of two distinct phases in the return of Christ.[2]

[1] *New Scofield Reference Bible*, note on 2 Thessalonians 2:3.

[2] It is instructive to observe that two passages in the book of Revelation (2:22; 7:9–17) refer to 'great tribulation' in reference to circumstances that are, from the point of view of the present, in the past. These passages illustrate how the dispensationalist restriction of

THE PROMISE OF THE FUTURE

II. THE RAPTURE OF 1 THESSALONIANS 4:13–18

In order to complete this consideration of pre-tribulational rapturism, we have to give some attention to 1 Thessalonians 4:13–18, which is the one passage in Scripture that directly describes the rapture. A careful study of this passage will show, however, that it does not teach the pre-tribulational rapture advocated by Dispensationalism.

The first observation to be made about this passage is that it is addressed to a pressing question in the church at Thessalonica. Among these believers, some were fearful that those saints who had previously 'fallen asleep' in Jesus would not take part in the joy and blessedness accompanying the coming of Christ. For this reason, the Apostle Paul begins this passage by saying:

> But we do not want you to be uninformed, brethren, about those who are asleep, that you may not grieve, as do the rest who have no hope. For if we believe that Jesus died and rose again, even so God will bring with Him those who have fallen asleep in Jesus. For this we say to you by the Word of the Lord, that we who are alive, and remain until the coming of the Lord, shall not precede those who have fallen asleep.

These words indicate how strong their fears were and how much the apostle wanted to assure them by an answer from the Word of the Lord himself.

After acknowledging their concern that the departed saints might be left out of the joy of Christ's coming, the apostle goes on to answer it more directly with an account of the coming rapture, in which believers will be caught up together with Christ in the air:

> For the Lord Himself will descend from heaven with a shout, with the voice of the archangel, and with the trumpet of

---

tribulation, especially great tribulation, to the seven-year period between the first and second phases of Christ's return, does not fit the biblical pattern of teaching regarding the future.

God; and the dead in Christ shall rise first. Then we who are alive and remain shall be caught up together with them in the clouds to meet the Lord in the air, and thus we shall always be with the Lord. Therefore comfort one another with these words.

What do these words mean? According to Dispensationalism they teach that at the parousia, or first coming of Christ, the first resurrection will occur, which will be a resurrection of all believing saints, and of them alone. They, together with the glorified saints who are living at the time of the Lord's coming, will be raptured or 'caught up with' the Lord in the air in order to return with him to heaven whence he came. Resurrected and glorified, they will then be with Christ in heaven for the seven-year period of tribulation, at the end of which they will return with him to reign upon the earth for the one-thousand-year period of the kingdom on earth (the millennium).[1]

But is this what is taught in this passage? Four observations suggest that this interpretation is a classic example of finding something in a text that is not there but has been imported into it, and subsequently is extracted from it.

First, when in verse 16 we read that the dead in Christ will rise first, this refers to the fact that those saints who have fallen asleep in Jesus will be raised before the living saints are caught up with them and the Lord at his coming. They will, in other words, enjoy a privilege – being raised first – not granted to those who are alive at Christ's coming. The dispensationalist teaching that this is the first resurrection, the resurrection of believing saints at the time of the rapture, in distinction from the second resurrection, the resurrection of the unbelieving at the close of the millennium more than one thousand years later, is not found in the text, nor is it the point of the apostle's use of the term 'first'.

---

[1] *New Scofield Reference Bible*, notes on 1 Thessalonians 4:17 and Revelation 19:19.

Second, this passage speaks of all believers being caught up together to meet the Lord in the air. Dispensationalists maintain that this refers to a meeting in the air which leads to a return of Christ and all the saints with him to heaven whence he came. Returning to heaven, the Lord Jesus and his saints will remain there for seven years. But nothing of this is stated in the text. The text actually speaks of a being caught up together in the air 'unto a meeting' between the Lord and the resurrected saints and the remaining saints who were alive at his coming.[1] The word used in this text for 'meeting' typically means a meeting between a visiting dignitary and representatives of the city or village being visited. Such a meeting would occur outside of the city or village, and the visitor and welcoming party would return to the city.[2] This word is used twice elsewhere in the New Testament (*Acts* 28:15, *Matt.* 25:6), in both cases referring to a meeting which takes place before the parties return to the place being visited. The meaning and use of this term suggests that in the case of the rapture, the saints who meet the Lord in the air will thereupon return with him, not to heaven, but to the earth to which he comes at his parousia.

Third, the result of this rapture, or being caught up with the Lord in the air, is said to be the blessedness of being always with the Lord. This language best fits the circumstance of the final state in which believers, now resurrected and glorified, will dwell forever in the most intimate and unbroken fellowship with the Lord Jesus Christ. Being always with the Lord is not to be limited to a period of seven years in heaven or even one thousand years upon the earth. Rather, the simplest reading of this passage is to take it to be a description of the final state.

[1] The words expressed in most translations, 'to meet', actually translate two Greek words, *eis apanteesin*, literally, 'unto meeting'.

[2] See E. Peterson, *apanteesis*, *Theological Dictionary of the New Testament*, ed. Gerhard Kittel, trans. Geoffrey W. Bromiley (Grand Rapids: Eerdmans, 1964), I: pp. 380–81.

And fourth, several features of the description of this rapture do not fit well with the dispensationalist position. The coming of the Lord, as described in these verses, is a visible, public event, one which is signalled by the descent of Christ from heaven 'with a shout, with the voice of the archangel, and with the trumpet of God'. However, in Dispensationalism, the first return of Christ is said to be a secret rapture, in which believers will be suddenly snatched away without notice. This teaching is based partly upon an appeal to Matthew 24:40–41 which is seen to be a parallel description of the rapture, though we have already noted that that passage does not teach a pre-tribulational rapture. But the description in 1 Thessalonians 4:16–18 corresponds to the descriptions of Christ's revelation from heaven at the end of the age in other passages (cf. *1 Cor.* 15:23–24, *2 Thess.* 2:8). These passages speak of Christ's return as a public event that will bring the present period of history to a close.

Thus, the teaching of a pre-tribulational rapture as understood within the framework of Dispensationalism is not founded upon the teaching of any biblical passage. Nor is it a teaching that can withstand careful scrutiny, particularly when measured against the general teaching of the Scriptures regarding the return of Christ at the end of the age. The Bible teaches neither that believers will be exempted from present or future tribulation at the end of the present age, nor that the rapture will be the event described by Dispensationalism. The one passage that speaks of the event commonly known as the rapture scarcely supports the view that enjoys such popularity among dispensationalists.

Israel and the Church

We have frequently noted that one of the principal tenets of Dispensational Premillennialism is the strict separation between God's earthly people, Israel, and his heavenly people, the church. It could even be argued that this separation between Israel and the church is the root principle of classical – as distinguished from 'progressive' Dispensationalism. From this separation of an earthly and a spiritual people stems another basic feature of Dispensationalism, one which we will consider in a subsequent section of this chapter: its insistence on a literalistic reading of the Bible. This actually stems from the insistence of classical Dispensationalism that the promises of the Lord to his earthly people, Israel, must be interpreted in a strictly literal rather than a figurative or spiritual way. Furthermore, among the seven distinct dispensations, the most important from the point of view of the future are those that reflect this separation between Israel and the church. The earliest dispensations of human conscience and government, for example, are of only passing interest in the overall scheme of Dispensationalism.

I. The Distinction between Israel and the Church

Before subjecting the dispensational distinction between Israel and the church to biblical evaluation, a brief summary of the basic features of this separation is necessary. The following notes from the original *Scofield Reference Bible* clearly articulate these features:

> (1) 'I will make of thee a great nation.' Fulfilled in a threefold way: (a) In a natural posterity – 'as the dust of the *earth*' (Gen. 13:16, John 8:37), viz., the Hebrew people. (b) In a spiritual posterity – 'look now toward *heaven* . . . so shall thy seed be' (John 8:39, Rom. 4:16, 17; 9:7, 8, Gal. 3:6, 7, 29), viz. all men of faith, whether Jew or Gentile. (c) Fulfilled also through Ishmael (Gen. 17,18–20) [sic].[1]

> The Christian is of the heavenly seed of Abraham (Gen. 15:5, 6, Gal. 3:29), and partakes of the spiritual blessings of the Abrahamic Covenant (Gen. 15:18, *note*); but Israel as a nation always has its own place, and is yet to have its greatest exaltation as the earthly people of God.[2]

[1] *Scofield Reference Bible* (1909), note on Genesis 15:18.
[2] *Ibid.*, note on Romans 11:1. *The New Scofield Reference Bible* retains the second of these notes but revises the first. The revised

As these notes indicate, classical Dispensationalism regards God's purposes in history as twofold, corresponding to these two distinct peoples, the one earthly, the other heavenly. God's dispensational dealings with these two peoples have two quite distinct ends in view: the salvation of an earthly people that is consummated in an eternal kingdom upon the new earth, and the salvation of a heavenly people that is consummated in an eternal kingdom in the new heavens. Thus, just as God has two distinct peoples and programmes of salvation in history, so he has in mind two quite distinct eternal destinies. The line of separation that keeps Israel and the church apart in history will continue into the final state in which the earthly and heavenly natures of these peoples will correspond to salvation blessings that are distinctively earthly and heavenly.

This separation between Israel and the church corresponds to Dispensationalism's emphasis upon a literal understanding of Old Testament prophecies on the one hand, and the contrast between the present 'age of the church' and the coming 'age of the kingdom' or the millennium on the other. The prophecies of the Old Testament, insofar as they are directed to the earthly people of God, Israel, must be understood in their literal or earthly sense. A promise of the possession of the land, for example, must mean the earthly land of Canaan. A promise of a restored temple, must refer to the temple in Jerusalem.

The present age of the church, because it represents God's dealings with his heavenly people, must also be regarded as a 'parenthesis' period of history, a period between God's former dealings and his soon-to-be-resumed dealings with Israel in the millennial age to come. During the present age of God's dealings with the church, his dealings with Israel have

---

version, however, does not fundamentally alter the basic dispensationalist insistence that these two peoples are to be kept distinct.

been temporarily suspended, but when the time of fulfilment comes (preceded by the rapture), the prophetic promises will be fulfilled. Because these were directed to Israel, they are silent for the most part respecting God's dealings with the church, dealings comprised by the mystery which God had kept hidden until the gospel age.

Though this represents only a brief sketch of the classical dispensationalist separation between Israel and the church, it will serve as background for our consideration of the question, Who, according to the teaching of the Bible, is the 'Israel of God'? Does the Bible actually draw this line of separation between these two peoples of God, Israel and the church? To answer this question, we will have to consider several features of the Bible's teaching about the Israel of God.

II. THE CHURCH IS NO PARENTHESIS

The biblical understanding of the church, however, cannot be squared with this understanding of it as a parenthesis. In the New Testament, the church is commonly understood to be in direct continuity with the people of God in the Old Testament; the images used in the Old Testament to describe the people of the Lord are used in the New Testament to describe the church. The New Testament word for the church, *ekklesia*, is the equivalent of the common Old Testament word, *qahal*, meaning the 'assembly' or 'gathering' of the people of Israel.[1] The New Testament church is also called the 'temple' of God (*1 Cor.* 3:16–17, *Eph.* 2:21–22), evoking the imagery and symbolism of the Old Testament, in which the temple was regarded to be the special place of the Lord's dwelling in the midst of his people. Just as the temple was the place where fellowship between the Lord and his people was

---

[1] The Septuagint (LXX) rendering of this Hebrew term for the 'assembly' of Israel is commonly the word *ekklesia* (*Exod.* 12:6, *Num.* 14:5, *Deut.* 5:22, *Josh.* 8:35).

provided for (through the sacrificial rites and ordinances) and experienced, so the church is the place of the Lord's dwelling by his Holy Spirit. Accordingly, the church can also be identified with Jerusalem, the city of God, which is above and which comprises believers from every tribe and tongue and nation. In Hebrews 12:22–23, this is expressly stated: 'But you have come to Mount Zion and to the city of the living God, the heavenly Jerusalem, and to myriads of angels, to the general assembly and church of the first-born who are enrolled in heaven, and to God, the Judge of all, and to the spirits of righteous men made perfect.'

Rather than being regarded as an interruption in God's dealings with his people, Israel, the church of the new covenant is regarded as the fulfilment of the Lord's promises to the people of God of the old covenant. The great covenant promise made to Abraham was that in his seed all the families and peoples would be blessed (*Gen.* 12:3; 22:18). Throughout the Old Testament, the Lord's dealings with Israel are never isolated from his promises of redemption for all the nations and peoples of the earth. This theme of the salvation of the nations is interwoven throughout the fabric of the Old Testament, not only in the provisions in the law for the inclusion in the community of Israel of strangers and aliens,[1] but also in the explicit language of the Psalter, the song book of Israel's worship, and in the prophets.

The Psalms contain references throughout to the Lord's purpose to gather the nations into the fellowship of his people. Psalm 2 includes a record of the Lord's vow to grant the nations to his beloved Son. Psalm 22 speaks of how 'all the ends of the earth will remember and turn to the Lord, and all the families of the nations will worship before Thee

---

[1] Perhaps this is the place to note how Matthew, in writing his genealogy of Jesus Christ, seems deliberately to have included names of Gentiles whose incorporation into the family of David (and of God) serves as a reminder that God's saving purpose never fixed exclusively upon Israel as a racial or national entity (*Matt.* 1:1–17).

(verse 27). Psalm 67 calls all the nations to join Israel in singing God's praises. These are not isolated notes; they echo and re-echo throughout the Psalms. Furthermore, in the prophets, many promises speak of the day when the Gentile nations will be joined with the people of Israel in the service and praise of the Lord (for example, *Isa.* 45:22; 49:6, *Mal.* 1:1).

The simplest understanding of the Old and the New Testament people of the Lord recognizes the church to be his new covenant people, in direct communion with Israel, his old covenant people. Though salvation may historically be to the Jew first and, secondly, also to the Gentile (*Rom.* 1:16), the Lord is gathering to himself in history only one people, comprising Jew and Gentile alike. However, lest this appear to be a premature conclusion based upon an inadequate consideration of the biblical material, we turn now to other biblical considerations.

III. THE KINGDOM IS NOT POSTPONED

Closely linked to the idea that the church is a parenthesis in history is the dispensationalist claim that God's dealings with Israel have been postponed during the present time. It is taught that because the Jews did not receive him as their promised Messiah and King, Jesus deferred the establishment of the kingdom, the earthly manifestation of God's salvation to the Jews, until after the dispensation of the gospel to the Gentiles. This idea of the kingdom's postponement has several problems.

First, it suggests that the church is an afterthought in the plan and purposes of God. This view of history seems to teach that Christ was frustrated in his original purpose for the establishment of the Davidic kingdom for Israel and was obliged to adjust the divine programme of redemption accordingly. However, such a suggestion is consistent neither with the biblical presentation of God's sovereignty over history nor with the Bible's view of the church.

Christ's Great Commission to his disciples (*Matt.* 28:16–20), fulfils his earlier declaration regarding the church that he will build, against which the gates of Hades shall not prevail (*Matt.* 16:18–19). Far from being an afterthought or interim project, the church in these passages is described as the central accomplishment and interest of the Lord Jesus Christ in history. Indeed, this church which is being gathered from all the nations can be understood only as a fulfilment of the promises God made to the Son of David, to whom the nations would be given as his rightful inheritance (see *Psa.* 2: 8). Consequently, when the Apostle Paul describes the church of Jesus Christ, he can speak of it as the 'fullness of him who fills all and all' (*Eph.* 1:22–23), through which the manifold wisdom of God is being made known 'in accordance with the eternal purpose which He carried out in Christ Jesus our Lord' (*Eph.* 3:8–11). None of these descriptions of the church suggest that it is anything less than the central focus and instrument through which God's final purpose of redemption in history is being realized.

Second, the dispensationalist idea of a postponement of the kingdom is based upon a misreading of the Gospel accounts of Christ's preaching of the kingdom. Though it is true that many of the Jews in Jesus' day did reject him as the Messiah, it must not be forgotten that Jesus himself was born from among the Jewish people – and he is a member, indeed the foremost member, of the church! – and that many of the Jews did respond to him in faith and repentance, though his proclamation of the nature of this kingdom did not always accord with the expectations of many of the people.

It should not be overlooked, for example, that the twelve disciples, the nucleus of the New Testament church, were all from among the Jewish people. In the account in Acts of the growth of the early church, the pattern of 'to the Jew first, and then to the Gentile' is clearly in evidence. Though some among the Jewish Christian community resisted the inclusion of Gentile believers, it is clear that Christ's work through his apostles was directed to the salvation of Jew and Gentile alike. Christ and his apostles preached the gospel of the kingdom (for example, *Acts* 20:28), a kingdom that Christ proclaimed was 'among them' (*Matt.* 12:28) and that would be built through the preaching of the gospel (*Matt.* 16:19). The idea that Christ offered the kingdom to the Jews, only to have them reject it, is contradicted by these realities and Christ's own testimony that they had misunderstood his kingdom (see *John* 18:36). Were Christ to have offered the kingdom to the Jews, only to have them reject it, one would expect this to have been included among the charges brought against him at his trial. However, the Gospel accounts make no mention of any such charge brought against him, namely, that he had offered to establish the kingdom among them only to have this offer refused.

Third, the idea of a postponement of the kingdom implies that the suffering and crucifixion of Christ might have been delayed, even become unnecessary, were the Jews of his day to have received him as their earthly king. This means that Christ's own teaching, that he must first suffer and only then enter his glory, would have been invalidated (*Luke* 24:26). It also means that the uniform testimony of the New Testament Gospels and epistles, that Christ came in order to be obedient to his Father's will, including his death upon the cross, would be compromised. Though dispensationalists might attempt to argue that Christ's death would have nonetheless been necessary, even were his offer of the kingdom to have been accepted by his countrymen, it seems difficult to envision how it might have occurred. Surely the establishment of his earthly kingdom would have mitigated any need to endure suffering and death on behalf of his people.[1]

---

[1] For a dispensationalist's defence against this charge, see Charles Ryrie, *Dispensationalism Today* (Chicago: Moody, 1965), pp. 161–8. Ryrie appeals to statements of dispensational authors that affirm the necessity of Christ's crucifixion for the salvation of Jew and Gentile alike. He also notes that the language of postponement lends credence

The mere suggestion that Christ's death was the result of the Jewish people's unbelief contradicts a variety of New Testament teachings. In the Gospel accounts of Christ's suffering and death, the evangelists frequently note that all of this occurred to fulfil what was written in the Scriptures (for example, *Matt.* 16:23; 26:24, 45, 56). After his resurrection from the dead, Christ was compelled to rebuke the men on the way to Emmaus because they did not believe in 'all the prophets had spoken'. They did not understand that it 'was necessary for the Christ to suffer these things and to enter his glory' (*Luke* 24:25–26). The Gospel of John frequently testifies that Jesus Christ, the Word become flesh, came into the world for the express purpose of doing his Father's will, namely, to be the 'Lamb of God who takes away the sin of the world' (cf. 1:29; 2:4; 6:38; 7:6; 10:10–18; 12:27; 13:1–3; 17).

The same emphasis upon Christ's death as the purpose for his coming is found in the book of Acts and the epistles of the New Testament. In his sermon at Pentecost, the Apostle Peter notes that Jesus was 'delivered up by the predetermined plan and foreknowledge of God' (*Acts* 2:23). When the Apostle Paul summarizes his gospel, he speaks of how 'Christ died for our sins according to the Scriptures . . . and that he was raised on the third day according to the Scriptures'. The writer to the Hebrews describes at length the manner in which Christ's coming, priesthood and sacrifice are the fulfilment of the old covenant types and shadows. Christ came, he writes, in order 'that He might become a merciful and faithful priest in things pertaining to God, to make propitiation for the sins of the people' (2:17). In a striking passage, this writer also speaks of God bringing Jesus up from the dead

---

to this criticism of Dispensationalism. However, he does not provide an adequate account of how the necessity of the cross can be accounted for on dispensationalist assumptions about the radical distinction between Israel and the church, or between the kingdom and the church age.

'by the blood of the eternal covenant' (13:20). Nothing in this is congenial to the view that Christ's death was occasioned primarily by the Jewish people's refusal to acknowledge him as their earthly king.

And fourth, the idea that the kingdom has been postponed does not correspond to the New Testament's insistence that Christ is now king and Lord over all. In the New Testament accounts of Jesus' death, resurrection and ascension, it is evident that Christ has been installed as King at the Father's right hand.[1] He exercises as Mediator a rule over all things for the sake of the church. This kingly rule of Christ, moreover, fulfils the promises that had been made to his father, David, regarding his inheritance of the nations. At the angel Gabriel's announcement of Christ's birth, it was declared that 'the Lord God will give him [the child to be born to Mary] the throne of his father David' (*Luke* 1:32).

When Christ mandated that the disciples go and make disciples of all nations, he declared, 'all authority has been given to Me in heaven and on earth' (*Matt.* 28:18). Peter, in his sermon at Pentecost, claimed that with God's raising of Jesus from the dead, 'all Israel' was to acknowledge that 'God has made Him both Lord and Christ' (*Acts* 2:33–36). Christ is the Davidic King to whom the nations will be given as his rightful inheritance (see *Acts* 4:24–26). Or, as the Apostle Paul describes the Lord, he has been 'declared the Son of God with power by the resurrection from the dead' (*Rom.* 1:4). Christ has now been given all rule and authority and power and dominion (*Eph.* 1:20–23; cf. *Phil.* 2:9–11). Therefore, he must 'reign until He has put all His enemies under His feet' (*1 Cor.* 15:25).

In the light of these and other passages that describe the present kingship of Jesus Christ, the Son of David, it seems

---

[1] See the *New Scofield Reference Bible*, notes on 2 Samuel 7:16 and Revelation 3:21, for a representation of the dispensationalist denial that Christ is currently seated upon the throne of his father, David.

wrong to distinguish sharply between the present age of the church and the future age of the kingdom. Though the present form and administration of the kingdom of Christ may not be earthly or physical in the dispensationalist sense of these terms, there is no escaping the biblical teaching that Christ now reigns upon the earth through his Spirit and Word and manifests his kingly rule primarily through the gathering of his church from all the tribes and peoples of the earth. Serious injury is done to the biblical conception of Christ's kingship when Dispensationalism relegates it to some future period during which God's dealings are directed narrowly to the earthly people of God, Israel.

IV. GOD'S ONE PURPOSE OF SALVATION FOR HIS PEOPLE

The basic reason why Dispensationalism wrongly speaks of the church as a parenthesis in history and of the postpone-ment of the kingdom, is that it fails to see that God has one purpose of salvation for his people in the old and new covenants. Contrary to the dispensationalist view, the Israel of God of the old covenant is one people in direct continuity with the people of God, the church of Jesus Christ, of the new covenant. Israel and the church are different ways of referring to the one people of God. To put it as straight-forwardly as possible: Israel is the church, and the church is Israel. This can be illustrated in various ways from the New Testament.

In 1 Peter 2:9–10, the apostle gives a summary statement regarding the New Testament church. Writing to the scat-tered believers and churches throughout Asia Minor, Peter defines the new covenant church in terms drawn from the old covenant descriptions of the people of Israel:

> But you are a chosen race, a royal priesthood, a holy nation, a people for God's own possession, that you may proclaim the excellencies of Him who has called you out of darkness into His marvelous light; for you once were not a people,

but now you are the people of God; you had not received mercy, but now you have received mercy.[1]

What is so remarkable about this description of the church is that it identifies the church with the exact terminology used in the Old Testament to describe the people of Israel with whom the Lord covenanted. The best reading of this language takes it literally to mean that the new covenant church is altogether one with the old covenant church. The Lord does not have two peculiar peoples, two holy nations, two royal priesthoods, two chosen races – he has only one, the church of Jesus Christ.

Similarly, in Romans 9–11, the Apostle Paul discloses God's purposes of redemption in the salvation of the Gentiles and subsequently of all Israel (*Rom.* 11:25) in a way that makes it unmistakably clear that the people of God are one, not two.[2] Dispensationalists argue that the salvation of all Israel mentioned in Romans 11:25 refers to the future national conversion of Israel and her restoration to the land of Palestine. This salvation will occur in the context of God's resumed dealings with his earthly people, Israel.[3] The great problem with this reading of the Apostle Paul's argument in Romans 9–11 is that the argument depends upon the most intimate interrelationship between elect Israel and the elect Gentiles in God's purposes of redemption.

The main thrust of the argument in these chapters is that the unbelief of many of the people of Israel has been in the purpose of God the occasion for the conversion of the 'fullness of the Gentiles'. This conversion of the fullness of the Gentiles, however, will in turn under God's blessing provoke

[1] In these two verses alone, the apostle explicitly refers to the following Old Testament passages: Isaiah 43:21, Exodus 19:6, Hosea 1:10; 2:23.
[2] For a more complete treatment of this passage, see my earlier discussion of it in Chapter 5.
[3] See the *New Scofield Reference Bible*, notes on Romans 11:1 and 11:26.

Israel to jealousy and lead to the salvation of 'all Israel'. No mention is made regarding the restoration of the nation of Israel as a racial entity to the land of Palestine. Nor is anything said about the establishment of an earthly form of the Davidic kingdom. On the contrary, the salvation of all of God's people, Jew and Gentile alike, is described in terms of their belonging to the one olive tree, the church of Jesus Christ. All who are saved are saved through faith in Jesus Christ and are incorporated into the one fellowship of his church. This passage militates in the strongest possible terms against the idea of the existence of two separate olive trees or two separate purposes of salvation, a present one for the Gentiles, a future one for the Jews.

Thus, in the account of the growth of the church in the book of Acts, the earliest members of the church were drawn predominantly, though by no means exclusively, from among the Jewish people. Indeed, the incorporation of Gentile believers into the one fellowship of the church was initially resisted considerably. It is especially striking, then, to read the account of the Apostle Paul's preaching at the synagogue (note well!) in Antioch. In his preaching, the Apostle Paul announces that the 'holy and sure blessings of David' are being fulfilled through the proclamation of the gospel of the forgiveness of sins in Jesus Christ. In this sermon, the apostle declares that Jesus is the promised Davidic King and Saviour through whom the promised blessings to the fathers are now being realized in the community of those who believe. No clearer identification could be imagined of God's purposes with Israel through David and his Son, and his purposes with the church through Jesus Christ. The words of this sermon speak for themselves:

> And we preach to you the good news of the promise made to the fathers, that God has fulfilled this promise to our children in that He raised up Jesus, as it is also written in the second Psalm, 'Thou art My Son; today I have begotten Thee.' And as for the fact that He raised Him up from the

dead, no more to return to decay, He has spoken in this way: 'I will give you the holy and sure blessings of David' (Acts 13:32–34).[1]

In these respects, as well as in those previously mentioned, it is apparent that God's purpose of redemption in history is to gather one people, all of whom are the spiritual descendants of Abraham (*Gal.* 3:28–29), the father of all believers. The Lord has but one people, not two. Indeed, it is his purpose to join this people together in the most perfect unity (*Eph.* 2:14), not to leave them forever separated from each other into Israel and the church.

V. WHO BELONGS TO THE 'ISRAEL OF GOD' (*GAL.* 6:16)?

In addition to the cumulative force of the preceding points against the dispensationalist view of a separation between Israel and the church, one text by itself sufficiently refutes this position: it is Galatians 6:15–16. We will conclude this part of our evaluation of Dispensationalism with a consideration of this text.

These verses come towards the end of the Epistle to the Galatians, and they draw upon many of the emphases previously set out. The Apostle Paul makes this solemn and sweeping declaration: 'For neither is circumcision anything, nor uncircumcision, but a new creation. And those who will follow this rule, peace and mercy be upon them, and upon the Israel of God.' In Galatians, it is clear that the Apostle

[1] It is interesting to note how matter-of-factly the oneness of the people of God is expressed by our Lord in his answer to the question put to him, 'Are there a few who are being saved?' (*Luke* 13:23). Jesus concludes with the confident declaration that 'they will come from east and west, and from north and south, and will recline at the table in the kingdom of God'. This description of the growth of the kingdom uses the imagery of a banquet hall and table, in which a great throng gathers, of Jew ('Abraham and Isaac and Jacob and all the prophets in the kingdom of God', v. 28) and Gentile ('from east and west, and from north and south'), all of whom are reclining at the same table in the same kingdom.

Paul is emphatically rejecting the idea that what commends anyone to God is obedience to the law, particularly the law prescribing circumcision as a sign of the covenant. He is opposing the false gospel of the Judaizers who were teaching that in order for a person to be acceptable to God, to be justified or found innocent before him, they had to submit to the requirements of the law, specifically the stipulations regarding circumcision. Against this false gospel, the apostle places the gospel of salvation by grace through faith in Jesus Christ, a gospel that is equally valid for Jew and Gentile alike. He sums up his argument with the formulation, 'neither is circumcision anything, nor uncircumcision, but a new creation'.

Having stated this governing principle, however, the Apostle Paul goes on to pronounce a benediction upon 'those who will follow this rule': 'peace and mercy be upon them, and upon the Israel of God.' The language used in this benediction is striking. The blessing of God rests upon those and only those who follow this specific rule or canon.[1] Conversely, those who do not follow or acknowledge it may not expect to receive God's peace and mercy.

But what is even more striking, for our purpose, is the apostle's identification of the church, comprising Jew and Gentile alike, as the Israel of God. The Israel of God in this text refers to the church as it honours this rule or canon, making no distinction, so far as justification before God is concerned, upon the basis of circumcision or uncircumcision. The Apostle Paul here sets forth a rule for the whole people of God, the church consisting of Jews and Gentiles, that seems to conflict with any separation at all between Israel as an earthly people and the church as a heavenly people. Such a separation makes the matter of circumcision

---

[1] The word used here for 'rule' is the Greek word, *kanon* or 'canon'. It has the sense of a binding and absolutely authoritative rule or principle of faith and practice.

and uncircumcision a fundamental principle of distinction between those who are of Israel and those who are not.

Now, it is possible to argue that when the apostle speaks in this text of 'peace and mercy upon them, *and* upon the Israel of God', he is actually distinguishing the Gentile church ('them') from the Jewish believing community ('the Israel of God'). This has in fact been proposed by dispensationalist authors.[1] However, the problem with this suggestion should be clear: it excludes believing Jews from 'all who will follow this rule', an exclusion which would be contradictory and self-defeating. Were the word 'and' here to have this sense of 'and also', as dispensationalists maintain, the Apostle Paul would be pronouncing a benediction not only upon those who follow this rule, but also upon others, believing Jews, who may not follow it. The apostle would thus be denying the very rule or canon that he had asserted previously. Believing Jews would be exempt from this rule, thus rendering it null and void as a rule for faith and practice among all the people of God. Perhaps for this reason, the New International Version translates these verses as follows: 'Neither circumcision nor uncircumcision means anything; what counts is a new creation. Peace and mercy to all who follow this rule, even to the Israel of God.' Here the NIV is following a long tradition of interpreters, including Calvin, who understand the connector, 'and', as equivalent to 'even' or 'that is'.[2]

The sense of this text is that the apostle extends peace and mercy to those who follow this rule that in the church of

[1] For example, John F. Walvoord, *The Millennial Kingdom* (Findlay, Ohio: Dunham, 1958), p. 170.

[2] In this instance, the NASB, the version I have been using, may be liable to misunderstanding, since it simply translates the connector (Greek: *kai*) as 'and'. The context makes clear, however, that this connector has here the sense of 'even' or 'that is', one of its normal uses in the New Testament and in the Greek language. The NIV is not alone in making clear the sense of the connector here. This is also true, for example, in the Revised Standard Version, the Jerusalem Bible and the New English Bible.

Jesus Christ circumcision and uncircumcision count for nothing so far as our standing with God is concerned. He pronounces this benediction 'to all who follow this rule, even to the Israel of God'. Thus, he answers the question – who belongs to the 'Israel of God'? – by declaring emphatically that the Israel of God comprises all believers, Jews and Gentiles, who subscribe to and live by the principle that what alone counts before God is a new creation.

In short, no more emphatic word could be spoken that in the church illegitimate distinctions are no longer permitted between Jew and Gentile, circumcised or uncircumcised. This should not surprise us, coming as it does from the same apostle who reminded the church in Ephesus that Christ 'Himself is our peace, who made both [Jew and Gentile] one, and broke down the barrier of the dividing wall' (*Eph.* 2:14). By the standard of this apostolic teaching and rule, Dispensationalism seems to be in serious error in its distinction between Israel and the church.

The Hermeneutic of Literalism

One of the characteristic features of Dispensationalism is its insistence upon a 'literal' reading of the Bible. Throughout its history many of its advocates have alleged that alternative millennial views reflect a low view of the Scripture's authority because they do not follow this hermeneutic.[1] Especially when it comes to the prophecies of the Bible that relate to the earthly people of God, Israel, dispensationalists insist that these be read literally. It is often argued that alternative readings of these prophecies undermine the authority of the Bible by illegitimately spiritualizing them and their promises.

---

[1] Here and throughout this section I am using the term 'hermeneutic' in the basic sense of a method or approach to the reading of the Bible. Dispensationalism is characterized by a particular hermeneutic, or way (following certain rules or principles) of reading the biblical texts, one which especially stresses the principle of a literal reading.

This emphasis upon a literal hermeneutic is closely linked to the dispensationalist distinction between God's earthly people, Israel, and his heavenly people, the church. It is argued that the prophecies and promises of the Bible that relate to Israel must correspond to Israel as a distinct people. Because Israel is a national and ethnic entity with a literal, concrete identity and history, whatever Scriptural promises refer to her must be equally literal and concrete.[1] Thus, if the Scriptures are to be rightly interpreted, they must always be taken in their literal meaning, unless this proves to be impossible.

I. WHAT IS 'LITERAL'?

In order to evaluate the dispensational hermeneutic of literalism, it is necessary to define more precisely what is meant by a literal reading of the Bible. Opinions vary among dispensationalists themselves as to what it is.

It is interesting to observe that even in the case of Scofield and the classic form of Dispensationalism, the emphasis upon a literal hermeneutic was somewhat qualified. According to him, the historical books of the Bible are not only literally true but often also of allegorical or spiritual significance. An historical event, like the relationship between Isaac and Ishmael, is literally true, but it may also have further meaning and significance (see *Gal.* 4:23–31). However, in the case of the prophetic books of the Bible, Scofield insisted that

> we reach the ground of *absolute literalness*. Figures are often found in the prophecies, but the figure invariably has a literal fulfilment. Not one instance exists of a 'spiritual' or figurative fulfilment of prophecy ... Jerusalem is always Jerusalem, Israel always Israel, Zion always Zion ... Prophecies may never be spiritualised, but are always literal.[2]

[1] See, for example, Ryrie, *Dispensationalism Today*, pp. 86–109, 132–55.

[2] Cyrus I. Scofield, *The Scofield Bible Correspondence School, Course of Study* (7th ed., 3 vols.; no place or publisher given), pp. 45–46 (as

This is a strong statement. It declares that all the prophecies in the Scripture have a literal fulfilment, so that whenever they are not interpreted literally, but figuratively, their meaning is necessarily distorted. However, the statement also concedes, at least with respect to historical passages, that the events recorded may be interpreted also in terms of their spiritual meaning.

Among later dispensationalist authors, further attempts have been made to define what is meant by a literal hermeneutic. Two representative definitions have been given by Charles C. Ryrie in his *Dispensationalism Today*[1] and Paul Lee Tan in his *The Interpretation of Prophecy*.[2]

Ryrie gives the following account of the dispensationalist position: 'Dispensationalists claim that their principle of hermeneutics is that of literal interpretation. This means interpretation which gives to every word the same meaning it would have in normal usage, whether employed in writing, speaking or thinking.'[3] In his exposition of this claim, Ryrie goes on to argue that 'normal usage' is really the equivalent of a grammatical and historical interpretation of the text. It takes words in their normal, plain or ordinary sense. Tan's definition of this hermeneutic is quite similar: 'To "interpret" means to explain the original sense of a speaker or writer. To interpret "literally" means to explain the original sense of the speaker or writer according to the normal, customary, and proper usage of words and language. Literal interpretation of the Bible simply means to explain the original sense of the Bible according to the normal and customary usage of its language.'[4]

---

cited by Vern S. Poythress, *Understanding Dispensationalists* [Grand Rapids: Zondervan, 1987], p. 24).

[1] Chicago: Moody, 1965.

[2] Winona Lake, Indiana: BMH Books, 1974.

[3] *Dispensationalism Today*, p. 86.

[4] *The Interpretation of Prophecy*, p. 29.

THE PROMISE OF THE FUTURE

Like Ryrie, Tan maintains that a literal reading of the biblical texts is equivalent to a grammatical-historical reading, a reading that simply takes the words and language of the text in their ordinary, common and plain meaning.

Despite these variations, the primary claim of Dispensationalism is that the biblical texts should be read in their plain, ordinary, or literal sense, especially when these texts speak of God's earthly people, Israel, and when they make promises respecting Israel. Though the presence of non-literal and figurative language is not completely denied – Scofield even acknowledged the possibility of spiritualizing interpretations of historical events – the first rule for any reading of a biblical text is that it be read in the most literal way possible.

II. Evaluating the Hermeneutic of Literalism
Undoubtedly, dispensationalist authors differ considerably on the subject of a literal reading of the Bible. Variations are evident between the earliest and classic forms of Dispensationalism, and more recent revisionist and progressive forms. However, we will take the two definitions cited as a fair representation of the predominant view among dispensationalists.

When considering these typical definitions of what constitutes a literal hermeneutic, two problems immediately stand out.

Literal and Perhaps Spiritual
The first problem is the tacit acknowledgement that a literal reading of the text need not exclude a spiritual meaning or figurative and symbolical language. In the original position of Scofield himself, a somewhat arbitrary distinction is made between the historical and prophetic texts in the Bible. This distinction is made in order to allow for the possibility that the historical texts may have both a literal and a spiritual meaning. Though Scofield maintains that this is never possible in the case of prophetic texts, there seems to be no

reason why this cannot be the case. Why can historical texts that speak of Jerusalem have a spiritual meaning, while prophetic texts that speak of Jerusalem must invariably have a literal meaning? Furthermore, the possibility of non-literal elements indicates that it is somewhat simplistic and misleading to insist that texts always be read literally.

LITERAL BUT NOT REALLY LITERAL

A second and even more fundamental problem with these definitions is the attempt to identify 'literal' with a grammatical-historical reading of the text, which in turn is identified with taking words in their normal or plain meaning. The problem with this approach is that it begs the question of what 'literal', 'normal', or 'plain' strictly mean. This can be illustrated by considering the meaning of the word 'literal'.

The 'literal sense' is a translation of the Latin *sensus literalis* which means 'the sense of, according to the *letter*'. That is to say, texts are to be read as language and literature according to the rules that ordinarily and appropriately apply to their usage and forms. This means that if the text is poetry, it should be read, according to the letter, as poetry. If the text is historical narrative, recounting events that occurred in a particular time and place, it is to be read as historical narrative. If the text uses forms of speech – symbols, figures, metaphor, simile, comparison, hyperbole, etc. – it is to be read according to the letter, treating such forms in the appropriate manner. The basic idea is that when the biblical texts are read in terms of their literal meaning, they are to be read in accordance with all of the appropriate rules and norms.

For Dispensationalism to begin with a commitment to the 'literal, plain or normal reading of a text' entirely begs the question as to what that sense is. To say that the literal meaning of biblical prophecy and promises must always be the most plain, concrete and obvious meaning, is to prejudge the meaning of these texts before actually reading them 'according to the letter', that is, according to the rules that obtain for the kind of language being used.

It has been common since the time of the Protestant Reformation to speak of a grammatical-historical reading of the biblical texts. This is one that takes the words, phrases, syntax and context of the biblical texts seriously – hence, grammatical – and also takes the historical setting and timing of the texts into careful consideration – hence, historical.

This approach was set over against the common Medieval approach to the biblical texts that distinguished, in addition to the literal or historical meaning of a text, three further levels of meaning: the tropological (moral), the allegorical, and the anagogical (ultimate or eschatological) sense.[1] Against this Medieval fourfold sense of the biblical texts, the Reformers spoke of the *sensus literalis*, the literal sense of the text. This means that a text is to be read according to the rules of language and grammar, and pertinent historical circumstances, in order to discover its literal (and only) meaning.[2]

This demonstrates in principle the illegitimacy of Dispensationalism's understanding of what is involved in a literal hermeneutic. But because this is such an important matter, we will illustrate it more concretely by way of three problem areas: first, the relation between Old Testament prophecy or promise and its New Testament fulfilment; second, the subject of biblical typology; and third, the oft-repeated claim

[1] On the basis of this fourfold sense of the biblical texts, a reference to water could mean literally, a colourless liquid; morally, the need for purity; allegorically, baptism by water; and anagogically, the eternal life in the heavenly Jerusalem. Or, to use another common example, Jerusalem could mean literally, the city in Palestine; morally, the need for heavenly-mindedness; allegorically, citizenship in heaven; and anagogically, the Jerusalem of the new heavens and the new earth.

[2] Speaking against this Medieval teaching of a fourfold sense, the *Westminster Confession of Faith*, chapter 1.9, states that 'the true and full sense of any Scripture . . . is not manifold, but one'.

that non-dispensationalists illegitimately spiritualize the biblical promises regarding the new earth. Each of these problem areas shows how unworkable and unhelpful it is to say that a literal reading looks for the plain or normal sense of the biblical texts.

III. PROPHECY AND FULFILMENT

The first problem area is Dispensationalism's treatment of Old Testament prophecies and their fulfilment. Here the insistence upon a literal reading of the biblical texts, especially the prophecies, actually masks the more basic claim that only earthly or non-spiritual promises can be made to an earthly people. Because the promises to Israel are always and necessarily earthly and literal, they may not be directly applied to the church. Dispensationalism would collapse, as a method of reading biblical prophecies, were it shown that the promises made to Israel in the old covenant find their true and final fulfilment in the new covenant church.

The problem here is that the New Testament repeatedly refers the Old Testament prophecies and promises made to Israel, to the church. Whatever the previous fulfilments of Old Testament prophecy may have been, they reach their ultimate fulfilment in Christ, in whom all the promises of God have their 'yes' and their 'amen' (2 *Cor.* 1:20). This can be illustrated with several examples.

Among the most basic promises in all of Scripture is the promise made by the Lord to Abraham, that 'in you all the families of the earth shall be blessed' (*Gen.* 12:3). This promise is repeated in Genesis 15, where Abraham is promised descendants as numerous as the stars of the heavens (verse 5), and then in Genesis 17, where Abraham is promised a seed and is said to be the father of a multitude of nations (verse 4). In the New Testament account of the fulfilment of this promise, especially in the Apostle Paul's treatment of it in Galatians 3 and 4, it is expressly stated that this promise has been fulfilled in Christ. Not only is Christ the seed of promise, the One in whom these earlier promises to Abraham are fulfilled, but all who belong to Christ, whether Jew or Gentile, are also Abraham's seed. In gathering, through the gospel, believers from every tribe and tongue and people and nation, the Lord's promise to Abraham is literally fulfilled. However, the dispensationalist's view is that this can be at best only a secondary application, not the literal fulfilment, of the promise to earthly Israel. This view contradicts the Apostle Paul's teaching that all Jewish and Gentile believers are the seed of Abraham and co-heirs of the promise.[1]

Similarly, the promises made during the old covenant to King David find their fulfilment in the coming and kingship of Jesus Christ, David's Son and his Lord. In the announcement of Jesus' birth through the angel to the virgin Mary, the angel is recorded to have said to her: 'And behold, you will conceive in your womb, and bear a son, and you shall name Him Jesus. He will be great, and will be called the Son of the Most High; and the Lord God will give Him the throne of His father David; and He will reign over the house of Jacob forever; and His kingdom will have no end' (*Luke* 1:31–33). This passage, when read literally, says that the child to be born is the fulfilment of the Lord's promise in 2 Samuel 7:13–16 (cf. *Psa.* 89:26, 27), the promise that David's Son would be seated forever upon the throne of his father David. However, Dispensationalism in its classic form teaches that this Davidic kingdom is an exclusively earthly kingdom, a kingdom reserved to the period of the millennium (a thousand years) and for the earthly people of God, Israel. Not only does this understanding fail the test of being a literal reading of the biblical descriptions of the promise of a Davidic kingdom (a thousand years is not forever), but it also seems far less a plain reading of the text than the one ordinarily

---

[1] In the previous section dealing with the relationship between Israel and the church, the argument offered for rejecting any sharp separation between them is closely related to this biblical understanding of the fulfilment of the promises to Israel in the new covenant.

adopted by non-dispensational interpreters – that Christ's coming is the beginning of the fulfilment of the promise made earlier to David.

One other biblical promise that illustrates the problem of Dispensationalism's treatment of biblical prophecy is the promise of a restored temple. Ezekiel 40–48 extensively describes the future rebuilding of the temple after Israel's restoration from her captivity. This description speaks in detail of the dimensions of this rebuilt temple, as well as of the variety of sacrifices that will be offered in it, including sin offerings. In the dispensationalist reading of this prophecy, this refers to the literal rebuilding of the temple in Jerusalem during the millennial kingdom. However, this creates a problem of how to interpret the language describing the reinstitution of the sacrificial system, at a time after the coming of Christ and the accomplishment of redemption through his once-for-all sacrifice upon the cross. In the *New Scofield Reference Bible*, it is conceded that this language need not be taken literally: 'The reference to sacrifices is not to be taken literally, in view of the putting away of such offerings, but is rather to be regarded as a presentation of the worship of redeemed Israel, in her own land and in the millennial temple, using the terms with which the Jews were familiar in Ezekiel's day.'[1]

The admission that some elements of Ezekiel's prophecy regarding the rebuilt temple need not be taken literally is fatal, however, to the claims made by Dispensationalism for a literal reading of prophecy. The same reason that leads the dispensationalist to read the language about sacrifices in this passage in a non-literal way – because it would lead to

[1] The *New Scofield Reference Bible*, note on Ezekiel 43:19. This note represents a change from the original *Scofield Reference Bible*, which says: 'Doubtless these offerings will be memorial, looking back to the cross, as the offerings under the old covenant were anticipatory, looking forward to the cross. In neither case have animal sacrifices power to put away sin (Heb. 10:4, Rom. 3:25)' (note on Ezekiel 43:19).

conflict with other portions of Scripture – could equally well apply to other aspects of the prophecy. Indeed, the Word of God does indicate the fulfilment of this prophecy, but not in the literal sense of a rebuilt temple in Jerusalem during the period of the millennium.[1]

These are only some examples of the way Dispensationalism fails to acknowledge the fulfilment of many of the Old Testament prophecies to Israel in the coming of Christ and the gathering of his church during this present age. Rather than allowing the New Testament's understanding of the fulfilment of prophecy to determine its viewpoint, Dispensationalism operates from the prejudice that no promise to Israel could, in the strict sense of the term, ever be literally fulfilled in connection with the church. But this is a prejudice based upon an unbiblical dichotomy between Israel and the church.

IV. BIBLICAL TYPOLOGY AN ACHILLES' HEEL?

A second and related problem area, the interpretation of biblical types and shadows, is in some ways the Achilles' heel of the dispensationalist's literal hermeneutic.[2] Biblical types may be loosely defined as those events, persons, or institutions in the Old Testament, that prefigure or foreshadow

---

[1] The dispensationalist claim that the temple will be rebuilt in Jerusalem during the millennium presents a number of problems: first, even were there no sacrifices reinstituted or perhaps only memorial sacrifices offered, as some dispensationalists have suggested, Christ could not minister in this temple because he is not a priest 'according to the order of Levi' (cf. *Heb.* 7:14); second, Ezekiel says nothing about the rebuilding of the temple during the period known as the millennium; and third, the prophecy of the temple's rebuilding is a prophecy of the dwelling of the Lord in the midst of his people that is described in Revelation 22. Dispensationalism misinterprets this prophecy because it has an improper view of biblical types and shadows in relation to their fulfilment, a subject to which I will turn below.

[2] For a critical evaluation of Dispensationalism's handling of biblical typology, see Poythress, *Understanding Dispensationalists*, p. 111–17.

their New Testament realities.[1] In the instances of such biblical types, the Old Testament type is fulfilled in its typical and symbolical meaning by the New Testament reality. Thus, if it can be shown that many of the historical events, persons, and institutions which were integral to the Lord's administration of the covenant of grace in the Old Testament, foreshadowed events, persons, and institutions in their new covenant reality and fulfilment, Dispensationalism, as a method of biblical interpretation, would seem to be seriously imperilled.

Though many examples of biblical types could be cited, three are especially problematic for Dispensationalism: the temple, Jerusalem, and the sacrifices.

We begin with the typology of the temple because it is with this that we concluded the previous section on prophecy. In the teaching of the Scriptures, the temple (earlier, the tabernacle) of the Lord is the place of his peculiar dwelling in the midst of his people. The temple was the focal point for the worship of Israel, the place where the people of the Lord could draw near to God as their sins were atoned for by means of the sacrifices instituted in the law. Speaking of the tabernacle's significance in the Old Testament, Geerhardus Vos, in his *Biblical Theology*, remarks:

> The tabernacle affords a clear instance of the coexistence of the symbolical and the typical in one of the principal institutions of the Old Testament religion. It embodies the eminently religious idea of the dwelling of God with His people. This it expresses symbolically so far as the Old Testament state of religion is concerned, and typically as regards the final embodiment of salvation in the Christian

[1] T. Norton Street, *How to Understand Your Bible*, rev. ed. (Downers Grove, Illinois: InterVarsity, 1974), p. 107, gives the following useful definition of a biblical type: 'A type can be defined as a divinely purposed, Old Testament foreshadowing of a New Testament spiritual reality.'

state . . . That its main purpose is to realize the indwelling of Jehovah is affirmed in so many words [Ex. 25:8; 29:44, 45].[1]

In its typical significance, the temple was a shadow or type of the reality of the Lord's dwelling with his people. According to the New Testament, this reality is now found in Christ himself (*John* 1:14; 2:19–22; *Col.* 2:9) and in the church as the place of God's dwelling by the Spirit (*Eph.* 2:21–22; *1 Tim.* 3:15; *Heb.* 3:6; 10:21; *1 Pet.* 2:5). Christ and the church are the fulfilment of the symbolical and typical significance of the temple. Moreover, in the final state of consummation, when the Lord dwells forever in the presence of his people in the new heavens and earth, it is expressly taught that there will no longer be any temple for the Lord will dwell in their midst (*Rev.* 21:22).

The dispensationalist insistence that the temple is an institution which pertains, in its literal form, peculiarly to Israel, fails to appreciate its typical significance in biblical revelation. The idea that the temple would be literally rebuilt and serve as a focal point for the worship of Israel during the period of the millennium represents, from the point of view of the progress and unfolding of biblical revelation, a reversion to Old Testament types and shadows. From this point of view, Dispensationalism turns back the clock of redemptive history.

A similar misunderstanding of biblical typology also characterizes the dispensationalist's treatment of 'Jerusalem', or 'Zion'. In the Old Testament, Jerusalem, or Zion, is the city of David, the theocratic king, and symbolises the rule of the Lord in the midst of his people. Jerusalem is the city of the Lord's anointed, the place of his throne and gracious rule among his people. It is the 'city of God' (*Psa.* 46), the place where children are conceived and born to the Lord (*Psa.* 87).

---

[1] Grand Rapids: Eerdmans, 1948 (and UK edition, Edinburgh: Banner of Truth, 1975), p. 148.

It is the city to which the nations, whom the Lord has promised to give to David's Son as his rightful inheritance (*Psa.* 2), will come.

However, in the New Testament, we are taught that Jerusalem is now the 'heavenly Jerusalem'. For this reason, the writer to the Hebrews is able to say to new covenant believers: 'But you have come to Mount Zion and to the city of the living God, the heavenly Jerusalem, and to myriads of angels, to the general assembly and church of the firstborn who are enrolled in heaven' (12:22–23). This is also the reason the Apostle John can report the following vision of the heavenly Jerusalem as it will be at the close of the history of redemption: 'And I saw a new heaven and a new earth; for the first heaven and the first earth passed away, and there is no longer any sea. And I saw the holy city, new Jerusalem, coming down out of heaven from God, made ready as a bride adorned for her husband. And I heard a loud voice from the throne, saying, "Behold, the tabernacle of God is among men, and He shall dwell among them, and they shall be His people, and God Himself shall be among them"' (*Rev.* 21:1–3).

These kinds of passages describe for us the fulfilment of all that the Jerusalem of the old covenant typified and foreshadowed. They confirm the pattern of biblical typology: the literal Jerusalem of the old covenant is typical of the new covenant city of God, the church. The dwelling of the Lord in the midst of his people, the presence of the temple sanctuary, the throne of David – all of these find their fulfilment and reality in the new covenant blessing and consummation witnessed by the Apostle John in his vision on the isle of Patmos.

One further and closely linked instance of biblical typology is that of the sacrifices stipulated in the law of Moses, especially in the book of Leviticus. These sacrifices were symbols and types of the person and work of Jesus Christ, the high priest after the order of Melchizedek, who fulfils and perfects all that they foreshadowed. This is the principal argument of the book of Hebrews, which compares and contrasts the old covenant tabernacle, priesthood and sacrifices to their fulfilment and perfection in Christ. The types and shadows of the old covenant have been abolished, or better, find their reality and perfection in the realities of the new covenant:

> Now the main point in what has been said is this: we have such a high priest, who has taken His seat at the right hand of the throne of the Majesty in the heavens, a minister in the sanctuary, and in the true tabernacle, which the Lord pitched, not man. For every high priest is appointed to offer both gifts and sacrifices; hence it is necessary that this high priest also have something to offer. Now if He were on earth, He would not be a priest at all, since there are those who offer the gifts according to the Law; who serve a copy and shadow of the heavenly things . . . But now He has obtained a more excellent ministry, by as much as He is also the mediator of a better covenant, which has been enacted on better promises. . . When He said, 'a new covenant', He has made the first obsolete. But whatever is becoming obsolete and growing old is ready to disappear (*Heb.* 8:1–6, 13).

The point summarized in this passage and exhibited in the previous examples of biblical types constitutes what is being termed the Achilles' heel of the dispensationalist claim for a literal hermeneutic. Not only does this claim fail to do justice to the New Testament's teaching regarding the fulfilment of Old Testament prophecy, but it also militates against the claim made by the inspired New Testament authors regarding the typological significance of the Old Testament sanctuary, priesthood and sacrifice: the reality of the new covenant renders the shadow obsolete and superfluous. The same principle, moreover, holds for all of the types and shadows of the old covenant administration. Once this principle is conceded, Dispensationalism's insistence upon a literal reinstitution of the types and shadows of the old covenant seems to be in serious conflict with the teaching of biblical typology.

The third problem area that remains to be considered is the dispensationalist claim that a non-literal fulfilment of the biblical prophecies and promises to Israel betrays a spiritualizing that cannot do justice to the biblical texts. According to Dispensationalism, many promises to Israel cannot be accounted for unless they are understood to be fulfilled literally and concretely during the period of the millennium to come.

Among such prophecies, dispensationalists often cite passages like Isaiah 11:6–10 and 65:17–25. Both of these prophecies are treated in the *Scofield Reference Bible* as predictions of the millennium, the one-thousand-year period of Christ's literal reign upon the earth from Jerusalem. This millennial reign represents the resumption of God's peculiar dealings with his earthly people, Israel, after the times of the Gentiles, the parenthesis period of the church, has concluded with the rapture and the following seven-year tribulation. According to Dispensationalism, these prophecies are a compelling proof that the prophecies of the Lord to Israel can have only a literal, concrete fulfilment. The language used in both passages, according to the dispensationalist, can only be understood to refer to a literal millennium or Davidic kingdom on earth.

However, a closer inspection of these two prophecies does not support this claim. In Isaiah 11:6–10, the prophet describes a beautiful picture of the reign of the shoot from Jesse. This reign will be characterized by universal peace and tranquillity. In this kingdom, the Lord declares that 'the wolf will dwell with the lamb, and the leopard will lie down with the kid . . . They will not hurt or destroy in all My holy mountain, for the earth will be full of the knowledge of the Lord as the waters cover the sea' (verses 6, 9).

It is not evident that this describes the millennium of dispensationalist expectation. No mention is made of this being a period that will be limited in time, perhaps a period of one thousand years' duration. More importantly, this passage speaks of a reign characterized by a universal peace and knowledge of the Lord. The millennium of dispensationalist expectation, by contrast, includes the presence of some people who do not acknowledge the Lord, and even a substantial rebellion at its close on the part of many against him – Satan's 'little season'. The description of Isaiah 11:6–10, accordingly, might better be referred to the final state of the 'new heavens and earth' than the millennium. Though this language is legitimately taken to describe the circumstance upon the earth – and not to be spiritualized in a non-earthly sense – it better describes the universal peace and knowledge of the Lord that will characterize the final state in the consummation than the earthly and Davidic kingdom of dispensational expectation.

The second of these prophecies, Isaiah 65:17–25, is somewhat more difficult to interpret. In the *New Scofield Reference Bible*, the first verse, which speaks of the new heavens and a new earth, is taken as a description of the final state, but the remaining verses (verses 18–25) are taken as a description of the millennium.[1] Thus, this passage is taken to be a description of both the final state and the millennium that will precede it. This reading has some plausibility, because verse 20 describes a time when infants will not be cut off after having lived only a few days, and when those who are older will not die prematurely. This verse expressly states that 'the youth will die at the age of one hundred and the one who does not reach the age of one hundred shall be thought accursed'. Because death is mentioned in these verses, dispensationalists argue that it cannot refer to the final state.

---

[1] These verses are given the heading, 'Millennial conditions in the renewed earth with curse removed' (*New Scofield Reference Bible*).

Though this is a difficult passage, it may well be the case that, in this prophetic description of the new heavens and the new earth, this language is being used to describe the final state. If the language is pressed literally, it may seem to conflict with the biblical teaching that death will be no more in the new heavens and earth. But perhaps the language used is simply a way of figuratively or poetically affirming the incalculably long lives that the inhabitants of the new earth will live.[1] It should be observed that these verses also speak of the lives of the inhabitants being 'as the lifetime of the tree' (v. 22), suggesting an extraordinary longevity of life. Perhaps more significantly, these verses say that 'the voice of weeping and the sound of crying' will no longer be heard in Jerusalem, the very language used in Revelation 21:4 to designate the final state. The likeliest reading of these verses, therefore, is that they, from verse 17 through verse 25, describe in the language of present experience, something of the joy, blessedness, and everlasting life that will be the circumstances of God's people in the new heavens and the new earth.[2]

In other words, these and similar texts have an appropriate place within a non-dispensationalist reading of the Bible. It is simply not the case that all non-dispensationalists spiritualize these prophecies and fail to take their description of renewed life on the new earth seriously. One does not have to be a dispensationalist to do justice to the concrete, earthy language used in these prophecies of the new heavens and earth. So long as it is understood that the final state requires

[1] This language and suggestion is that of Anthony Hoekema, *The Bible and the Future*, 1979), p. 202.

[2] Some postmillennialists would regard the description of these verses as referring to the millennium, the golden age that will precede the return of Christ and the final state. See, e.g., Davis, *Christ's Victorious Kingdom*, pp. 37–8. Though this view does not include the dispensationalist understanding of a kingdom reserved to God's earthly people, Israel, it does regard this passage as describing a period whose blessings fall short of the perfection of the final state.

a new heavens and a new earth, the richness and concreteness of the imagery in these biblical passages can be appreciated.[1] Indeed, from one perspective, it could even be argued that to the extent that the dispensationalist millennium falls short of the blessedness of life in the new earth described in these passages, it becomes the more guilty of spiritualizing their language and meaning. So long as non-dispensationalists properly insist upon the restoration of the earth in the final state, they need not concede in the least the charge that they have illegitimately spiritualized the prophecies of Scripture regarding the final state.

Conclusion

The dispensationalist claim regarding a literal interpretation of the Scriptures is really the product of its insistence upon a radical separation between Israel, God's earthly people, and the church, God's spiritual people. Without this undergirding assumption – that God has these two distinct peoples – there is no reason to deny the fulfilment of old covenant promises in the new covenant realities. Nor is there any longer reason to avoid the implications of biblical typology for the dispensationalist system.

Perhaps the most telling evidence against the dispensationalist hermeneutic is to be found in the book of Hebrews. The message of the book of Hebrews is, if I may speak anachronistically, a compelling rebuttal of Dispensationalism. Whereas the book of Hebrews is one sustained argument for the finality, richness and completion of all of the Lord's covenant words and works in the new covenant that is in Christ, Dispensationalism wants to preserve the old arrangements intact for Israel, arrangements which will be reinstituted in the period of the millennial kingdom. However, this would be tantamount to going back to what has been surpassed in

---

[1] I will return to this issue in subsequent chapters on the resurrection (Chapter 13) and the new heavens and earth (Chapter 16).

the new covenant in Christ, reverting to arrangements that have been rendered obsolete and superfluous because their reality has been realised in the provisions of the new covenant. The Mediator of this new covenant, Christ, is the fulfilment of all the promises of the Lord to his people. Thus, to the writer to the Hebrews, any reversion to the old covenant types and ceremonies would be an unacceptable departure from the realities of the new covenant in preference for the shadows of the old.

Though it may seem too severe to some, no other judgement is permitted us respecting the system of biblical interpretation known as Dispensationalism: it represents a continued attachment to the shadows and ceremonies of the old covenant dispensation and also a failure to appreciate properly the finality of the new covenant. Its doctrine of a literal hermeneutic proves not to be literal in the proper sense of the term. Rather than reading the New Testament 'according to the letter', Dispensationalism reads the New Testament through the lens of its insistence upon a radical separation between Israel and the church.

11

What About
Revelation 20?

N O BIBLICAL TREATMENT of the subject of the millennium
can avoid directly addressing the teaching of Revelation
20:1–11, and especially of verses 1–6. This is the one passage
in the Bible that explicitly speaks of the millennium, using an
expression which literally means a 'thousand years', and it
does so no less than six times.[1] George Eldon Ladd has
correctly noted that though the Scriptures may not clearly
teach a millennium in other passages, one passage that
clearly teaches the millennial reign of Christ after his second
coming is sufficient to establish the doctrine. Since he and
other premillennialists are convinced that Revelation 20 is
just such a clear passage, our evaluation of Premillennialism,
whether of the historic or dispensational variety, would
be incomplete and unconvincing without giving special
attention to this passage.

[1] As noted earlier, our English term 'millennium' is actually the
Latin equivalent for the Greek expression used in Revelation 20, a
compound word formed from the words for 'one thousand' (*mille*)
and 'year' (*annus*) in Latin.

Thus far, our evaluation of the two premillennial views, historic and dispensational Premillennialism, has been rather general. We have argued that the central tenet of all premillennialist views, that the return of Christ will precede the millennium, does not enjoy the support of the general teaching of Scripture. We have also evaluated more directly some of the tenets of Dispensational Premillennialism that are unscriptural. However, the key question that must be put to any millennial view remains: Does it do justice to the teaching of Revelation 20? To borrow language from the arena of warfare, the primary battleground in the debates regarding the millennium is the vision of the Apostle John recorded in Revelation 20.

Because of the importance of this passage, our consideration of it will be divided into several parts. We will begin with a summary of how it has been traditionally understood by premillennialists. After this we will take up the question of the relation between Revelation 19 and 20, as this is one aspect of the premillennialist case. We will present several reasons why the vision of Revelation 20 should not be read as though it described events that are chronologically subsequent to the vision in Revelation 19:11–21.

Only after dealing with these preliminary and introductory matters will we turn to consider the most important aspects of Revelation 20. The first of these is the opening section of the vision in Revelation 20:1–3, which describes the binding of Satan so as to prevent him from deceiving the nations during the millennium. The second is the vision in Revelation 20:4–6, which speaks of the saints who 'came to life' and who reign with Christ during the millennium. In this section reference is made to a first resurrection of the believing saints in distinction from an apparent second resurrection of the unbelieving at the end of the millennium. Because of the decisive role this distinction plays in premillennial thinking, this part of the vision will be given special attention.

The Premillennialist Case

Most premillennialists maintain that Revelation 20 presents a clear and compelling picture of the millennium. According to historic and dispensational premillennialists, Revelation 20 constitutes an insurmountable obstacle to any non-premillennialist understanding of the millennium. Before examining this claim in the light of this passage, the main lines of the premillennial case need to be set forth.

I. REVELATION 20 DESCRIBES EVENTS AFTER THE RETURN OF CHRIST
The starting point for the premillennialist understanding of Revelation 20 is the claim that the events depicted in the vision of Revelation 20 follow in time the events depicted in the vision of Revelation 19, especially verses 11–21. The sequence of visions in Revelation 19 and 20 should be, in this view, read chronologically. When read in this manner – the simplest and most straightforward reading, according to the premillennialist – the visions in these chapters of Revelation describe a number of events in series. What the Apostle John is revealing in these chapters is a chronological tale of what will happen in the future. It is as though he were saying, 'first this will occur . . . then this . . . then this.'

The importance of this way of reading the relation between Revelation 19:11–21 and Revelation 20:1–11 for the premillennialist case becomes evident when it is noted that most who hold this view regard Revelation 19:11–21 as a description of the second coming of Christ. When read in this way, the insistence that the return of Christ precedes the millennium seems indisputable because the return of Christ, depicted at the close of Revelation 19, comes immediately before the events of Christ's binding of Satan and reigning with his saints for a thousand years.

Though we will return to the issue of the relation between Revelation 19 and 20 in the following section, it does seem correct to regard Revelation 19:11–21 as describing the second coming of Christ and his victory over all his enemies. There are several reasons for holding this view.

In the vision of Revelation 19:11–16, Christ is described as a conqueror, as the divine warrior who comes to vanquish all his enemies. He is portrayed in these verses as riding upon a white horse and coming to judge and wage war in righteousness (verse 11). His name is called 'The Word of God' (verse 13) and 'on his robe and on his thigh he has a name written, "King of Kings, and Lord of Lords"' (verse 16). Furthermore, the weapon this glorious and conquering Christ uses to destroy and defeat the nations whom he rules with a rod of iron is a sharp sword protruding from his mouth (verse 15). The language used in these verses seems best suited as a description of the return of Christ at the end of the age, when he will destroy both his and his people's enemies (see 2 *Thess.* 1:6–10). The weapon with which Christ will win this victory is not the armies of this world, but the Word of God which is 'living and active, sharper than any two-edged sword' (*Heb.* 4:12).

That this vision depicts the return of Christ is suggested further by the references in Revelation 19 to the marriage supper of the Lamb (19:7–10) and the defeat of the beast and the false prophet (19:17–21). The marriage supper of the Lamb symbolizes the full and intimate communion between Christ, the Lamb, and his blood-bought bride, the church, who will be united at his coming. The destruction of the beast and the false prophet represents the destruction of the Antichrist, whose person and work were earlier described in Revelation 13 and 17. These events coincide with the return of Christ as the divine warrior and symbolize his complete defeat of his enemies at his coming. Within the context of the visions of Revelation, it seems apparent that Revelation 19:11–21 constitutes a symbolic depiction of the second coming of Christ.[1]

---

[1] George Eldon Ladd, 'Historic Premillennialism', in *The Meaning of the Millennium: Four Views*, ed. Robert G. Clouse, 34, adds the

THE PROMISE OF THE FUTURE

If Revelation 19 is a description of the return of Christ, then it is obvious why so much depends upon the relation between its vision and that of Revelation 20. On the premillennialist view that the vision of Revelation 20 follows the vision of Revelation 19, it seems quite natural to regard the sequence of events in the future as one in which the return of Christ will be followed by the millennium of Revelation 20. For this reason, we will return to this question in the next section.

II. THE BINDING OF SATAN IS COMPLETE

Within the context of this understanding of the relation between Revelation 19 and 20, premillennialists believe the description of the millennium in Revelation 20:1–6 clearly supports their position. In these verses, repeated reference is made to a period of one thousand years that commences with the binding of Satan. This period is a literal period during which Christ will reign with his saints upon the earth after his return at the end of the present age. Throughout this period, with the exception of Satan's 'little season' of rebellion at its close, the nations will be subject to Christ's blessed reign and the fruits of his reign will be abundantly evident in the earth. The nations and peoples of the earth will be largely subject to Christ, and the rebellion and disobedience of the nations will be extinguished from the earth.[1]

---

consideration that, were this vision not a reference to the second coming of Christ, the book of Revelation would contain no clear reference to this great event at the end of the age. Many postmillennialists regard the vision of Revelation 19 as a description of that point in history (realized suddenly or gradually over time) when Christ's kingdom will come to ascendancy in the earth, but not a description of Christ's physical return at the end of the age. These postmillennialist interpreters agree that Revelation 19 and 20 should be read as chronologically successive, though they regard the coming of Christ in Revelation 19 as something other than his second coming. See, for example, John Jefferson Davis, *Christ's Victorious Kingdom*, pp. 92–93.

[1] There are, of course, differences between historic and dispensational premillennialist understandings of this millennium, particularly

In the opening verses of Revelation 20, the binding of Satan is described in this way:

> And I saw an angel coming down from heaven, having the key of the abyss and a great chain in his hand. And he laid hold of the dragon, the serpent of old, who is the devil and Satan, and bound him for a thousand years, and threw him into the abyss, and shut it and sealed it over him, so that he should not deceive the nations any longer, until the thousand years were completed; after these things he must be released for a short time.

Premillennialists insist that this description means that, by contrast to his previous freedom to exercise influence and deceive the nations, the binding of Satan will not only curtail but completely exclude any active working of Satan among the peoples and nations of the earth. Christ and his people will enjoy, during the period Satan is bound, an unprecedented period of relief from Satan's wiles. Only at the close of the millennium will Satan be permitted a limited period of rebellion, during which he will once again gather the nations against Christ and the church.

According to the premillennialist, nothing less than a literal millennium, during which Satan is completely bound and prevented from exercising any deceptive influence among the nations, could answer to the description of Revelation 20:1–3. Certainly the amillennialist view that the present age of the church coincides with this millennial period appears unlikely, if not impossible. Satan enjoys at the present time far too much freedom and influence among the nations to permit this period of history to be identified with the

---

in terms of its importance for God's peculiar purposes for Israel. Though most premillennialists believe in a future conversion of many of the children of Israel prior to the millennium, only dispensationalists insist that this represents the resumption of God's distinctive programme for his earthly people, Israel.

millennial binding of Satan depicted in the vision of Revelation 20:1–3.[1]

III. THE FIRST AND SECOND RESURRECTIONS

Perhaps the most vital part of the premillennialist argument from Revelation 20, however, is the reference to a first resurrection in this passage. Here premillennialists believe that they have a strong argument for their position on the millennium. In verses 4–6, the first resurrection is described as follows:

> And I saw thrones, and they sat upon them, and judgement was given to them. And I saw the souls of those who had been beheaded because of the testimony of Jesus and because of the word of God, and those who had not worshiped the beast or his image, and had not received the mark upon their forehead and upon their hand; and they came to life and reigned with Christ for a thousand years. The rest of the dead did not come to life until the thousand years were completed. This is the first resurrection. Blessed and holy is the one who has a part in the first resurrection; over these the second death has no power, but they will be priests of God and of Christ and will reign with Him for a thousand years.

For premillennialists, this description of the coming to life of believing saints who reign with Christ during the

---

[1] Ironically, many postmillennialists echo this criticism of Amillennialism. Many postmillennialists argue that the millennium of Revelation 20 is the golden age that will conclude the present period of history before Christ's return. Only an 'unprecedented period' of Christ's kingly rule, to use a phrase of John Jefferson Davis, can answer to the language of Revelation 20 when it describes the binding of Satan. The alleged pessimism and minimal expectation for Christ's rule in the present age so often characteristic of Amillennialism cannot, in the view of these postmillennialists, be found compatible with the millennium of Revelation 20. See John Jefferson Davis, *Christ's Victorious Kingdom*, pp. 93–95; Mathison, *Postmillennialism*, pp. 179–85.

millennium is of decisive importance. Only believing saints are said to come to life in this way and participate in the first resurrection. By contrast, the rest of the dead remain in the grave and do not come to life until the thousand years are completed. Unlike the saints who are not subject to the second death, the unbelieving who do not enjoy this first resurrection will come to life only to be cast forever into the lake of fire with the beast and the false prophet (verses 13–15). Since a close parallel is suggested between those who come to life in the first resurrection, and those who come to life in the second resurrection, the most obvious and plain reading of the text would be one which takes both resurrections to be bodily resurrections, the one of believing saints before the millennium, the other of the unbelieving after the millennium. This is precisely the view of Premillennialism.

The classic statement of this point, and one that is almost invariably quoted in the literature, remains that of Henry Alford:

> If, in a passage where *two resurrections* are mentioned, where certain *psychai ezesan* [souls came to life] at the first, and the rest of the *nekroi ezesan* [dead came to life] only at the end of a specified period after the first, – if in such a passage the first resurrection may be understood to mean *spiritual* rising with Christ, while the second means literal rising from the grave; – then there is an end of all significance in language, and Scripture is wiped out as a definite testimony to anything.[1]

[1] *The Greek Testament* (Boston: Lee and Shepard, 1872), IV, p.732. Alford does overstate the matter a bit when he says this passage mentions two resurrections. It should be noted that the passage explicitly speaks only of a first resurrection, not of a second resurrection. Though the idea of a second resurrection is certainly implied, a strict reading of the passage requires noting that what distinguishes the beneficiaries of the first resurrection or coming to life is that they are not subject to the second death. Those who come to life at the end of the millennium are subject to the second death. Whether their coming to life is a second resurrection is not explicitly affirmed in the text.

As this statement of Alford illustrates, the premillennialist takes the language of this passage to support the teaching of two resurrections, both bodily in nature, though distinguished as to their timing and benefit. The first precedes, the second follows, the millennium; the first grants millennial blessings and immunity from the second death, while the second is unto judgement and death.

When these various pieces of the premillennialist case are put together, a fairly clear picture emerges of its understanding of the vision of Revelation 20:1–6. After Christ returns and subdues the nations under his feet, Satan will be bound and the millennium will commence. The millennium will be a one-thousand-year period of unprecedented blessedness and well-being upon the earth. The nations and peoples of the earth will be united in obedience to the Lord Jesus Christ. Coinciding with the binding of Satan, believing saints will be raised bodily and granted the privilege of reigning with Christ upon the earth for one thousand years. At the conclusion of the millennium and the little season of Satan's rebellion, a second resurrection of the unbelieving will occur. The unbelieving will be raised to be judged by Christ and consigned to everlasting punishment in the lake of fire.

The Millennium Is Now

We have observed that a key issue in the interpretation of this passage is that of the relation between Revelation 19:11–21 and Revelation 20:1–11. If Revelation 19 is a vision of the second coming of Christ at the end of the present age, and if Revelation 20 describes events which occur after this event, then the primary claim of Premillennialism would seem to be established. For on this understanding, the millennium would commence after the return of Christ.

However, must these visions be read in chronological succession, as premillennialists typically maintain? Or are there reasons to believe that the events depicted in these visions may parallel each other?

Though the premillennial claim on this point has an initial plausibility, there are several reasons, some more significant than others, why they should be read as parallel descriptions of the same time period. A careful study of these visions within the setting of the book of Revelation as a whole suggests that they describe the same period of history, but from differing vantage points.

I. THE RECAPITULATORY STRUCTURE OF THE BOOK OF REVELATION

Students of the book of Revelation have observed that it is structured according to a series of visions, several of which repeat or recapitulate events and periods of history covered in preceding or following visions. Each of these cover events that occur within the period between Christ's first and second coming. This being so, the book can hardly be read as a prophecy of future events in their exact chronological order. The visions recorded overlap a great deal, and often jump from one set of events to another. In spite of the wide range of interpretations of the book, most interpreters agree that it should not be read as a historical novel, a preview of upcoming events listed in their order of occurrence.[1]

[1] As noted previously, a preterist reading of the book says that the events described in its language of vision and prophecy were events occurring or about to occur at the time the book was first written. These events are, from our vantage point, past events, things that have already occurred – hence the term. A futurist reading of the book says that the events described in its prophecy are events yet to occur in the future, primarily in the period just prior to Christ's coming at the end of the age. An historicist reading of the book identifies the events in the visions of Revelation with historical developments throughout the history of the church. An idealist reading of the book says that the visions and prophecy of Revelation refer to events that typify the principles and forces at work in the entire period of history between Christ's first and second comings. See G. K. Beale, *The Book of Revelation*, pp. 44–49. Following Beale, who argues for an eclecticism or 'redemptive-historical form of modified idealism', it is best to read the book of Revelation, not exclusively in terms of one of these approaches, but inclusively in terms of the insights of each. The book,

William Hendriksen, for example, in his overview of the book of Revelation concludes that its structure is one of 'progressive parallelism'. He notes that the book can be divided into seven distinct sections, the first three sections describing events between Christ's first and second comings as they transpire upon the earth, the second four sections describing events between Christ's first and second comings as they transpire in heaven. The first three sections are: the description of Christ dwelling among the seven churches in the world, represented by means of the seven lampstands (chapters 1–3); the vision of the church suffering trial and persecution, represented by the seven seals (chapters 4–7); and the description of the church protected and ultimately vindicated, represented by the seven trumpets (chapters 8–11). In these first three sections of the book, the progress and unfolding of events under Christ's dominion are portrayed from the vantage point of the earth. These sections describe the foreground of history.

However, in the last four sections of the book, events are described from the vantage point of their background, that is, the conflict between Christ and the Antichrist. These four sections are: the description of Christ opposed by the dragon and his helpers (chapters 12–14); the description of the pouring out of God's wrath upon the unbelieving and impenitent, represented by means of the seven bowls of judgement (chapters 15–16); the description of the fall of Babylon and of the beasts (chapters 17–19); and the description of the final defeat of the dragon, including the commencement of the final state (chapters 20–22). According to Hendriksen, the seven sections of the book of Revelation should be read as parallel descriptions of the period between the first and

---

though addressed originally to the circumstance of the church in the first century of the Christian era, certainly speaks of events that will occur prior to the return of Christ and as well of events that are typical of the entire period of history in which we now live.

the second comings of Christ. They parallel and often recapitulate events earlier described in preceding visions. Furthermore, as the book of Revelation proceeds, it progressively emphasizes events that lie upon the furthest horizon of history, just prior to the end of the present age. For this reason, the book concludes with a grand vision of the state of consummation, the new heavens and the new earth.[1]

Whether Hendriksen's analysis of the structure of the book of Revelation is entirely correct in all of its particulars is not so important at this juncture. What is important is that it illustrates a commonly acknowledged feature of the book: that it should not be read as a linear description of end-time events. The simple fact that one vision follows another vision in the book does not mean that it does so chronologically. As is often true throughout the book, the events depicted may well parallel and recapitulate events represented in a preceding vision.

This means that the visions of Revelation 19 and 20 need not be read as though they depicted events in sequence. If other clues in the text suggest that these visions are parallel or recapitulatory, then there is no reason to insist, certainly no reason so far as the structure of the book of Revelation is concerned, to insist that they are in chronological order.

It is important to recognise this general structure of the book of Revelation because it raises the question whether Revelation 20 might be introducing a new vision sequence, a vision whose events parallel and repeat the course of events earlier depicted in other visions. An analysis of the general structure of Revelation alone, however, is insufficient proof that this is in fact the case. The question is, Does the text specifically indicate that Revelation 20 begins a new vision

---

[1] See William Hendriksen, *More Than Conquerors* (1967; repr. Grand Rapids: Baker, 1975), pp. 11–64. Hendriksen's analysis treats Revelation 20 as an introduction of a new vision sequence spanning the period from Christ's first coming to his second coming and the consummation.

sequence in parallel with the vision of Revelation 19? Indeed, it does. Several features of the visions of Revelation 19 and 20 corroborate the thesis that they should be read not in sequence, but in parallel to each other.

At least six such features are of particular significance.[1]

i. The theme of angelic ascent and descent
The vision of Revelation 20 begins with the descent of an angel from heaven in order to bind Satan for a period of one thousand years. In other instances in the book of Revelation where an angel's ascent or descent begins a new vision sequence, the vision portrays the course of events from the present time to the time of Christ's return at the end of the age. For example, similar visions of an angel ascending or descending are found in Revelation 7:2, 10:1 and 18:1. In these instances, the angel's ascent or descent occurs at a time clearly prior to the return of Christ and marks the beginning of a vision whose sequence of events concludes with the coming of Christ in final victory over his enemies. It would not be surprising, accordingly, were the angel's descent in Revelation 20 to be another instance of this pattern. Not only would this be consistent with the structuring of the book of Revelation throughout, but it would also be following a pattern evident elsewhere, in which vision sequences that parallel each other are introduced by the announcement of an ascending or descending angel.

---

[1] In what follows, I am especially indebted to R. Fowler White who has thoroughly examined the relation of the visions in Revelation 19 and 20 and summarized his findings in two studies: 'Reexamining the Evidence for Recapitulation in Rev 20:1–10', *Westminster Theological Journal* 51/2 (Fall 1989), pp. 319–44; and 'Making Sense of Rev 20: 1–10? Harold Hoehner Versus Recapitulation', *Journal of the Evangelical Theological Society* 37/4 (December 1994), pp. 539–51. For an earlier treatment of this relation that anticipates some of White's arguments, see Raymond Zorn, *Christ Triumphant: Biblical Perspectives on his Church and Kingdom* (Edinburgh: Banner of Truth, 1997), pp. 106–7 (previously published as *Church and Kingdom*, 1962).

ii. The discrepancy between Revelation 19:11–21 and Revelation 20:1–3

Secondly, the visions of Revelation 19 and Revelation 20 show an obvious discrepancy if they are read in chronological sequence. In Revelation 19:11–21, especially verses 19–21, we see a vision of Christ's triumph over and destruction of the nations that are opposed to his kingdom. The language used to describe this triumph is vigorous: all the nations are described as taking up arms against Christ and are said to fall without exception by the sword that he wields against them. Christ's victory over the nations is complete and final. They are wholly destroyed at his coming. However, if the vision of Revelation 20 follows in time and sequence the vision of Revelation 19, it seems senseless to speak of the binding of Satan in order to prevent his deception of the nations. Presumably, nations that have been utterly destroyed constitute no viable or continuing threat to the reign of Christ or the deceptive wiles of Satan. What sense does it make to speak of nations being protected from Satanic deception, when those nations which were formerly deceived by Satan have now been completely vanquished?

Premillennialists who recognize this discrepancy might suggest, in order to mute its obvious implications for their view, that the nations of Revelation 20 are survivors of the battle described in Revelation 19. This suggestion, however, presents two difficulties. On the one hand, the language of the nations' defeat in Revelation 19 is too absolute to allow for the notion that some nations survive unscathed. And on the other hand, the terminology of 'the nations' in Revelation typically denotes nations in their opposition to Christ and his church. The nations are the nations in rebellion against the Lord's anointed. However, on this premillennialist construction, the nations of Revelation 20 would actually be the peoples of the earth during the millennial reign of Christ. The nations of Revelation 20 would have a different reference from the nations mentioned just before in Revelation 19.

THE PROMISE OF THE FUTURE
iii. The use of Ezekiel 38–39 in these visions
In the visions of Revelation 19 and 20, the language used is
extensively borrowed from Ezekiel 38–39. This prophecy
describes a great end-time battle between the Lord and the
nations of the north who are opposed to him and his people.
In the description of this great battle upon the mountains of
Israel, reference is made to Gog, prince of Rosh, Meshech
and Tubal, and to Magog.

There are several striking parallels between Ezekiel 38–39
and Revelation 19 and 20. In Revelation 19:17–18, an angel
issues an invitation to the great supper of God. This is almost
an exact quotation of the invitation extended for the
Gog-Magog conflict in the prophecy of Ezekiel (39:17–20).
However, in Revelation 20:7–10, when the Apostle John
describes the great warfare that will conclude Satan's little
season at the close of the millennium, the prophecy of
Ezekiel regarding Gog-Magog is again drawn upon extensively. The nations in rebellion are termed Gog and Magog
(verse 8; cf. *Ezek.* 38:2; 39:1, 6). The weapon used by God to
destroy Gog-Magog is a fire coming down from heaven (verse
9; cf. *Ezek.* 38:22; 39:6). This means that the Apostle John, in
his respective descriptions of the rebellion and defeat of the
nations in Revelation 19 and 20, is drawing upon identical
language and imagery from Ezekiel's prophecy. It seems hard
to believe, accordingly, that the episodes described in these
visions are different episodes in history, separated by a period
of one thousand years duration. A much more plausible reading would conclude that these visions describe the same event
and are to be read as parallel descriptions of the same historical period.[1]

---

[1] Thus, premillennialists, recognizing John's use of the same
prophecy in Ezekiel 38–39 to describe these allegedly distinct episodes,
disagree among themselves whether Ezekiel 38–39 is fulfilled before
and/or after the millennium. See, for example, R. H. Alexander,
'A Fresh Look at Ezekiel 38 and 39', Journal of the Evangelical
Theological Society, 17 (1994), pp. 157–169.

iv. The battle of Revelation 19:19 and 20:8

The visions of Revelation 19 and 20 show a similar parallelism in their description of the battle that will terminate the period of history portrayed in them. In three instances in the book of Revelation, an end-time conflict between Christ and his enemies, a conflict in which Christ is triumphant and the rebellious nations defeated, is described as 'the battle'. Not only is the definite article used, suggesting that this battle represents a final and conclusive defeat of Christ's enemies, but also the language used to describe the nations' revolt and campaign against Christ is virtually identical (see *Rev.* 16:14; 19:19, 20:8).

Interpreters of the book of Revelation readily acknowledge the parallels between the description in Revelation 16:14–21 of the battle on the great day of Christ's second coming and the description in Revelation 19:19–21. The latter battle is regarded commonly as a resumption and conclusion of the battle first described in Revelation 16. Fewer interpreters have noticed the similarities of language in Revelation 20:7–10 in its description of the Gog-Magog revolt. This is likely due to the assumption that the battle of Revelation 20:8 refers to a different battle after the millennium from the battle that occurred before the millennium at the time of Christ's second coming.

If we reckon with the possibility of a parallel description of the same period of history in Revelation 19 and 20, then it is likely that the battle described in these passages is one and the same battle. Rather than positing the reoccurrence of a similar conflict and victory for Christ at the end of the millennium, a conflict that replays the earlier war that concluded history at Christ's second coming, it is more likely that these battles are the same battle, variously described in visions that parallel each other and depict the same historical period.[1]

---

[1] Perhaps this is the place to mention a phrase coined by Jay Adams in his criticism of Premillennialism. Adams uses the phrase 'premillennial

v. The end of God's wrath

When Revelation 19 and 20 are read as two visions in sequence, a further discrepancy is introduced. Just as we noted a discrepancy between the complete destruction of all the rebellious nations in Revelation 19 and their continued presence in Revelation 20 (were these two visions describing events in sequence), so there is a discrepancy between the end of God's wrath in Revelation 19 and the further outpouring of his wrath and judgement yet again in Revelation 20.

Revelation 15:1 contains an important declaration regarding the end of God's wrath: 'And I saw another sign in heaven, great and marvelous, seven angels who had seven plagues, which are the last, because in them the wrath of God is finished.' This verse indicates that the dispensing of the seven bowls of wrath by the seven angels will bring to a close the outpouring of God's wrath upon the wicked in the course of history. The last of these bowls of wrath is described in Revelation 16:17–21, a passage that concludes with the final defeat of Christ's enemies, the nations in the vision of Revelation 19:19–21. The vision of Revelation 19, therefore, represents the completion of the course of history and the finishing of God's wrath upon the nations. The time frame for the fulfilment of the outpouring of God's wrath in Revelation 15:1 is concluded by the vision of Revelation 19.

However, on a premillennialist reading of the visions of Revelation 19 and 20, the battle and pouring out of God's wrath in the vision of Revelation 20 comes one thousand years later than the battle and pouring out of God's wrath in the vision of Revelation 19. Thus, this reading conflicts with

---

diplopia' to describe the double-vision that often characterizes its reading of Scripture in general and the book of Revelation in particular. Because differing visions that describe the same history and events are read as though they described different events in sequence, a doubling occurs (two second comings of Christ or victories at the end of the age, two resurrections, etc.). See Jay Adams, *The Time Is At Hand*, pp. 17–40.

the teaching of Revelation 15:1. It suggests that God's wrath in history is not finished with the events depicted in the vision of Revelation 19. Some one thousand years later would come another and truly last outpouring of God's wrath upon the nations. The deadline set for the completion of God's wrath in history in Revelation 15:1 would be exceeded. For this and the reasons already mentioned, it makes better sense to read the vision of Revelation 20 as a recapitulation of the period of history earlier described in Revelation 19. Both visions would then be describing the same battle at the close of history with the final outpouring of God's wrath upon the nations.

vi. The cosmic destruction of Revelation 19:11–21 and 20:9–11

Finally, another parallel in the visions of Revelation 19 and 20 reflects the influence of Old Testament prophecy. The Old Testament scenes of the Lord's judgements and triumphs among the nations often refer to the involvement of the created universe in these events. Similarly, many of the visions in Revelation of the warfare between Christ and his enemies describe the shaking of the cosmos itself. It is remarkable to notice in a series of such descriptions in the book of Revelation, how this shaking accompanies the coming of Christ as King and the exercise of his judgement upon the nations (e.g., 6:12–17; 16:17–21; 19:11–21; 20:9–11). The last two instances of this association of Christ's coming in victory and the shaking of the earth itself occur in the visions of Revelation 19 and 20.

Again, this would confirm that these visions describe the same end-time event, but from a slightly different vantage point. Since the shaking of the earth at Christ's coming is elsewhere said to be the last instance of such shaking, after which nothing shakeable will remain to be shaken further (*Heb.* 12:26–27), it would not make sense to say that the shaking of the cosmos at Christ's second coming (*Rev.* 19) would still have to be followed by a further shaking of the cosmos at the end of the millennium (*Rev.* 20). A more likely reading would take these two visionary descriptions of this shaking to refer to the end of present history at the second coming of Christ.

These various clues and indicators of parallels between the visions of Revelation 19 and 20 having been considered, it may be helpful to summarize their significance for the understanding of the vision of the millennium in Revelation 20.

The premillennialist position depends significantly upon the claim that the visions of Revelation 19 and 20 are to be read in sequence. Since Revelation 19 is a vision of the return of Christ, and since the millennium of Revelation 20 follows this event, it seems that the premillennial position is the most likely one. However, if the considerations we have summarized in the preceding are correct, the premillennial position is seriously compromised, if not refuted. Not only does Premillennialism enjoy little support from other portions of Scripture, but it also fails to provide a plausible account of the relation between the visions of Revelation 19 and 20. For if these visions are not to be read in sequence but as parallel accounts of the same period of history, then the millennium of Revelation 20 would precede rather than follow the event of Christ's return at the end of the age.

This seems to be the conclusion to which the above considerations lead. Just as the vision of Revelation 19 describes the return of Christ, the complete destruction of all of the nations, the last outpouring of God's wrath at the close of the present period of history, so the vision of Revelation 20 closes with a description of the return of Christ at the close of the millennium, the complete destruction of all the nations, and the last outpouring of God's wrath at the close of the present period of history. The parallels between these visions – in language, symbolism, use of Old Testament prophecy, and content – is so pervasive and compelling as to yield but one likely explanation: they are describing the same period of history, the same episodes and the same conclusion at the end of the age.

This means that in our study of the vision in Revelation 20 of the millennium, we have every reason to believe that the millennium it describes is now. The millennium of Revelation 20 coincides with the period of history prior to Christ's return at the end of the age, prior to the day of Christ's final victory over his and his people's enemies, and prior to the last judgement and all the other events that will accompany the close of this present age.

The Binding of Satan

The vision of Revelation 20:1–6 is divided into two sections. The first, in verses 1–3, describes the binding of Satan for a period of one thousand years. The second, in verses 4–6, describes the reign of the saints with Christ during this millennial period and includes a reference to the saints who participate in the first resurrection and are not liable to the second death.

Now that we have considered some of the broader issues of interpretation relating to Revelation 19 and 20, we are in a position to take up directly the interpretation of the vision itself.

The vision of Revelation 20 begins with a striking portrayal of the binding of Satan:

> And I saw an angel coming down from heaven, having the key of the abyss and a great chain in his hand. And he laid hold of the dragon, the serpent of old, who is the devil and Satan, and bound him for a thousand years, and threw him into the abyss, and shut it and sealed it over him, so that he should not deceive the nations any longer, until the thousand years were completed; after these things he must be released for a short time (*Rev.* 20:1–3).

Though interpreters differ as to how far the details of this vision are to be pressed, the main emphases are little disputed.[1] The Apostle John sees an angel descending from heaven in order to carry out God's will and purpose. The whole vision suggests that this angel's divine authorization and power to carry out his assigned task is invincible and unassailable. He is equipped with the key of the abyss, language which suggests the power to open and to close, to unlock or to lock (see *Rev.* 3:7, *Matt.* 16:19). The abyss is elsewhere described in the book of Revelation as the dwelling place of the demons. Revelation 9:1–6 depicts a bottomless pit out of which demonic locusts swarm forth to afflict those who dwell upon the earth. It is into this place that the angel comes to cast Satan according to Revelation 20. In addition to the key, representing the power to loose or unloose Satan, the angel has in his hand a great chain. Some have suggested that this chain represents the Word of God (see *Rev.* 19:13, 15), though its precise identification remains uncertain.[2] What is clearly represented by the key and the great chain together is that the angel is properly equipped to execute God's purpose to bind and restrict the activities and wiles of Satan.

[1] The hermeneutic or method of reading Revelation that always insists that the text be taken literally (for example, Dispensationalism) runs into obvious difficulties when it comes to the vision of Revelation 20. This vision portrays events in the form of images and symbols, many of which can hardly be interpreted literally. Are the key and chain used by the angel a literal key and chain? Is the abyss a literal place of confinement for Satan in the depths of the earth? Simply to ask these questions exposes the problems of a literalistic hermeneutic. A similar difficulty emerges, as we shall see, with the expression 'one thousand years' in this passage. See Vern S. Poythress, 'Genre and Hermeneutics in Rev 20:1–6', *Journal of the Evangelical Theological Society* 36/1 (March, 1993), pp. 41–54. Poythress helpfully suggests that we read the visions of Revelation at four levels of communication: the linguistic (the textual record itself), the visionary (the visual experience of John), the referential (the historical reference of the vision), and the symbolic (what the vision connotes about its referent).

[2] For example, G. R. Beasley-Murray, *The Book of Revelation* (The New Century Bible Commentary; Grand Rapids: Eerdmans, 1974), pp. 284–5.

The focus of this first section of the vision is fixed upon the actions of this angel in laying hold of Satan who is variously named 'the dragon, the serpent of old . . . the devil'. The angel seizes Satan, casts him into the abyss, and seals it over him. The language of sealing is symbolic of the complete and sovereign control that is being exercised over Satan (cf. *Dan.* 6:17, *Matt.* 27:66). Thus, when Satan is released for a short time after the period of one thousand years, the language of the vision makes clear that this will occur only by the permission and under the complete control of God. This emphasis is underscored by the expression, 'After these things he must be released for a short time'.

The key question for the interpretation of this first section of the vision concerns the exact nature and implications of the binding of Satan. Historic and dispensational premillennialists as well as postmillennialists all concur that this binding must be understood as an action that completely curtails the actions of Satan. The restriction implied in this binding represents an unprecedented limitation upon Satan's activity, one that distinguishes the millennial period from all previous redemptive history. Though premillennialists argue that this millennial period commences after the return of Christ and postmillennialists argue that it occurs before, they agree in their insistence that the binding of Satan during the millennium cannot be identified with the entire period between Christ's first and second advents. The vision of Satan's binding is too powerful in its implications for that to be the case. Who would dare maintain that the present period of history is one in which the millennial binding of Satan is a reality? Is there concrete evidence today of the limitation upon Satan's activity that this vision of his binding requires?

Though this objection initially sounds rather powerful, upon further reflection it loses some of its punch. There are good biblical reasons to conclude that the present period of history – taking the vision of Revelation 20 as a description of the period between Christ's first coming and his second coming at the end of the age – represents the period of Satan's being bound so as not to be able to deceive the nations.[1]

Considering the biblical story of the history of redemption, significant change from the old covenant to the new becomes evident in terms of the nations of the earth. Whereas in the old covenant, the Lord called Abraham from Ur of Chaldees and dealt primarily with the nation of Israel, in the new covenant the gospel is being preached in the whole world (*Matt.* 24:14) and the nations are being discipled (*Luke* 24:47, *Matt.* 28:16–20). This difference in covenant administration does not affect the substance of the covenant of grace – the Lord who created the heavens and earth and all peoples, already in the first promise to Abraham spoke of the blessing that would come to all the peoples and nations – but it does affect the way in which the good news is being preached to all the nations of the earth.

Compared to the extension of the kingdom of God in this present age, prior to the coming of Christ in the fullness of time the nations of the earth remained predominantly under the deception of Satan. Though the Lord's dealings with Israel were never narrowly ethnic, they were restricted in ways that, in the present age, are no longer true.[2] Those who

---

[1] See R. Fowler White, 'On the Hermeneutics and Interpretation of Revelation 20:1–3: A Preconsummationist Perspective', *Journal of the Evangelical Theological Society,* 42/1 (March 1999), pp. 53–66. White argues that the language is that of an 'epic idiom of victory over the dragon'. Such language, found elsewhere in the Scriptures, does not require the literalistic conclusion that Satan no longer has any power or room to carry on his rebellious purposes in history. See Strimple, 'Amillennialism', p. 124.

[2] Contrary to popular opinion, Israel was never an ethnically defined people. Abraham was called from Ur of the Chaldees. Among his descendants, the children of Israel, were many who were gathered from the Gentile nations (such as Rahab and Ruth). Provisions were

are members of the new covenant church of Jesus Christ are apt to forget the greater richness of saving blessing that has been poured out upon the nations of the earth in these last days. The light of the gospel that has shone among the nations of the earth in the present age contrasts vividly with the darkness in which the nations dwelt during the period of the old covenant.

It is vitally important to note that the language describing the binding of Satan in Revelation 20 associates this with a restriction upon his activity such that he 'should not deceive the nations any longer'. This is the one great purpose and effect of Satan's binding, so far as the explicit language of Revelation 20 is concerned. Satan is bound so that he can neither prevent the spread of the gospel among the nations nor effectively deceive them. This vision confirms the teaching that the period between Christ's first coming and his second coming is one in which the gospel of the kingdom will powerfully and effectively go forth to claim the nations for Jesus Christ. It confirms the confidence and authority with which Christ, after his resurrection, commissioned the disciples to go into all the earth and make disciples of the nations. This commission was given in the context of Christ's having been given all authority in heaven and on earth (*Matt.* 28:18). It was also concluded with the promise that Christ would be with his disciples until the end of the age. Consistent with Christ's confident declaration to his disciples that 'they will come from east and west, and from north and south, and will recline at table in the kingdom of God' (*Luke* 13:29), the vision of Revelation 20 declares that the great obstacle to the evangelization of the nations – Satan's deceptive hold over them – has been removed.

---

made in the law for the incorporation of aliens into the people and inheritance of Israel. Nevertheless, it remains true that the Old Testament does not have the same missionary impulse as is found in the New.

Furthermore, if the vision of Satan's binding is interpreted in the broader context of the book of Revelation and the teaching of the Gospels, it corresponds quite closely to the biblical understanding of the present period in the history of redemption.

In an earlier vision in the book of Revelation, the Apostle John saw a great war in heaven that was concluded with the casting down of the dragon, the serpent, to the earth (12:7–12). In this vision, Satan is described as the one who deceives the whole world. But now that Satan has been defeated in heaven and cast down, a loud voice in heaven is heard to say, 'Now the salvation, and the power, and the kingdom of our God and the authority of His Christ have come, for the accuser of our brethren has been cast down . . . And they overcame him because of the blood of the Lamb and because of the word of their testimony, and they did not love their life even to death' (12:10–11). Though the language of this earlier vision in Revelation is different from that used in Revelation 20, it seems to describe the same realities of which the latter vision speaks: Satan's ability to deceive the nations and prevent the coming of the kingdom of God has been effectively destroyed. Now has come the kingdom of God. Now the nations are being discipled. Now the power of Christ's gospel is being revealed in the earth.[1]

[1] Premillennialists typically regard Revelation 12 as referring to a different event and history from Revelation 20. See John F. Walvoord, *The Revelation of Jesus Christ* (Chicago: Moody, 1966), pp. 191–2. Historic and dispensational premillennialists as well differ in their understanding of it. Because the loud voice in heaven goes on to speak of Satan's being cast down to the earth, 'having great wrath', it is argued that the situation is substantially different from that in Revelation 20, where Satan is cast into the abyss. However, the meaning of the two visions, though different in their imagery and symbolism, seems to be identical: Satan has been decisively defeated and rendered incapable of deceiving the nations any longer. Contrary to the claims of premillennialists (and some postmillennialists), nothing in the vision of Revelation 20 demands the conclusion that Satan is no longer

In the Gospel accounts of the preaching and teaching of the Lord Jesus Christ, the language of some passages finds an echo in the vision of Revelation 20. These passages provide the biblical context within which the vision of Revelation 20 becomes clear.

The Gospel of Matthew contains an account of Jesus healing a demon-possessed man who was brought to him. When the multitudes hear of this miraculous healing, they are amazed and wonder whether Jesus might be the Son of David (*Matt.* 12:23). However, the Pharisees, upon hearing of this healing, are reported to have declared, 'This man casts out demons only by Beelzebul the ruler of the demons' (verse 24). In response to this unbelief and blasphemy on the part of the Pharisees, Jesus notes that no kingdom divided against itself can stand. He then claims that his power to cast out demons is a demonstration of the presence of the power and kingdom of God: 'But if I cast out demons by the Spirit of God, then the kingdom of God has come upon you. Or how can anyone enter the strong man's house and carry off his property, unless he first binds the strong man? And then he will plunder his house' (verses 28–29). In this response to the Pharisees, Jesus teaches that the kingdom of God has come and is among them in his person and work. The healing of this demon-possessed man illustrates the presence of the kingdom and confirms that Satan has been bound so that he is no longer able to prevent the plundering of his house. It is interesting to observe that the word used to express the restraint placed upon Satan, 'to bind', is the same word used in the vision of Revelation 20 to describe the binding of Satan.

---

capable of doing any harm. The only thing that is specifically emphasized in the text is that he can no longer deceive the nations. And that is certainly true of the period of history since Christ's first coming and the outpouring of the Spirit at Pentecost. See Beale, *The Book of Revelation*, pp. 658–61.

THE PROMISE OF THE FUTURE

On another occasion in the Gospel accounts, we are told that he sent out seventy disciples, two by two, to go ahead and proclaim the nearness of the kingdom. In the charge given to the seventy, Jesus commissions the disciples to go into the field of harvest which is plentiful and heal those who are sick, and say to them, 'The kingdom of God has come near you' (*Luke* 10:9). When the disciples return from fulfilling this commission, they return with joy, reporting, 'Lord, even the demons are subject to us in Your name' (*Luke* 10:17). In his reply to their report, Jesus says, 'I was watching Satan fall from heaven like lightning. Behold, I have given you authority to tread upon serpents and scorpions, and over all the power of the enemy, and nothing shall injure you' (verse 19). In this and other Gospel passages, Christ's coming and ministry is a concrete realization of the coming and presence of the kingdom of God, a kingdom that plunders and destroys Satan's household and releases those who are captive to sin and the demons. Christ has now been given all authority in heaven and on earth, so that the demons flee before him, the captive are set free, the sick are healed, and the nations discipled.[1]

In another significant passage in the Gospel of John, the coming of Christ is associated with a dramatic curtailment of Satan's activity among the peoples of the earth and the missionary expansion of the church. Predicting his death, Christ declares, 'Now judgement is upon this world; now the ruler of this world shall be cast out. And I, if I be lifted up from the earth, will draw all men to Myself' (12:31–32). This passage speaks of a casting out in judgement of the ruler of this world, and it speaks of the crucified Christ who will draw to himself all men, Jew as well as Gentile, from among

---

[1] In addition, see the following passages that also speak of Satan's defeat before the power of Christ expressed in the preaching of the gospel of the kingdom: *Matt.* 13:24–30; 47–50, *Acts* 2:14–36; 4:23–31, *Rom.* 16:20, *1 Cor.* 15:20–28.

the peoples of the earth. In these ways it parallels the thought of the vision in Revelation 20, that the kingdom of Christ will be realized through the binding of Satan and the gathering of the nations. Furthermore, as was true of the passage in Matthew 12, the language employed to describe Satan's judgement is very similar to that employed in the vision of Revelation 20. In John 12, we read of the 'casting out' of Satan. In Revelation 20, we read of the 'casting down' of Satan.[1]

If it is a standard rule of thumb in reading the Bible that Scripture should interpret Scripture and that the more obscure passage should be interpreted in the light of the more clear passage, the conclusion that best fits this evidence is: the vision of Satan's binding in Revelation 20, so that he is no longer capable of deceiving the nations, is a representation of the events coinciding with the coming of Christ in the fullness of time. Christ has come and won a decisive victory over the evil one. This victory is variously revealed to us in the Gospels and throughout the New Testament. With his victory over Satan's temptations in the wilderness, his declaration and exhibition of the power of the kingdom in casting out demons and plundering the enemy's stronghold, his vanquishing of sin and death upon the cross, his resurrection from the dead, his ascension to the Father's right hand, and his pouring out of the Spirit of Pentecost – in this entire complex of Christ's saving work he has won a decisive victory over Satan. No longer is Satan able to deceive the nations. The promise of Psalm 2, that the nations will be given by God the Father to his Son as his rightful inheritance, is being fulfilled (verses 7–9). Between the time of Christ's first coming and his second coming, the millennial reign of Christ upon the earth is being manifested for all to see.

[1] The verbs used in these passages, *ekballo* in John's Gospel and *ballo* in Revelation 20, are virtually identical, the former simply having the prefix *ek* ('from') added.

THE PROMISE OF THE FUTURE

One of the intriguing features of the vision of Revelation 20 is its reference to a period of one thousand years. For most premillennialists, this language must simply be taken literally as a reference to a distinct period in history after the return of Christ.[1] Particularly within the context of Dispensational Premillennialism with its commitment to a literalistic reading of the Bible, the language of Revelation 20 is regarded as sufficient to prove the error of Amillennialism and Postmillennialism. Because these two views treat the language of one thousand years in Revelation 20 non-literally, as referring to a long period within God's superintendence during which Satan is bound and the kingdom of Christ is manifested, they are charged with wrongly spiritualizing the meaning of this language. Furthermore, if it is objected that this is the only passage in Scripture which speaks of a one-thousand-year period, the premillennialist response is typically that one passage should be more than adequate to make the point. If this passage clearly teaches a literal millennium of one thousand years, who has the right to deny its teaching?

Before looking at the expression 'one thousand years' more directly, two general observations are to be made regarding this premillennialist claim. First, the insistence that the language of Revelation (and of all Scripture) be taken literally betrays a way of reading the Bible that we have earlier contested. A book like Revelation, with its rich symbolism and use of biblical types and figures, gives no obvious reason to take literally the term of one thousand years. If

---

[1] John F. Walvoord, *The Revelation of Jesus Christ*, p. 293, makes a representative comment: 'The expositor is not free to spiritualize the interpretation of the vision but must accept the interpretation in its ordinary and literal meaning. If this is done, there is no alternative to the premillennial interpretation, which holds that at the second coming of Christ, Satan will be bound for a thousand years.'

much of the book is written in language that is clearly not literal, some reason needs to be given why this must be the case in the vision of Revelation 20 with its use of 'one thousand years'. Second, there is reason to pause before conceding the argument of Premillennialism here precisely because no other passage of Scripture speaks of a literal period in history of one thousand years (whether before or after Christ's return). One of the great difficulties in the case for Premillennialism is the relative lack of support for its doctrine of the millennium from other passages in Scripture. This suggests that before we concede as self-evident the claim that one thousand years must mean one thousand literal years, we consider whether Scripture might not support a different reading of this expression.

Those who argue that the thousand years is not to be taken literally often note that it is a perfect cube of ten, ten being a number of completeness. This would suggest, then, that the reference to a one-thousand-year period should be taken as symbolic of a perfect and complete number within the purpose of God. This is a plausible way of reading this language, but it tends to be too abstract. It still remains to ask, Do the Scriptures elsewhere use the number one thousand in a symbolic way which might cast some light upon Revelation 20?

As a matter of fact, the use of the term 'one thousand' in the Scriptures seems quite pertinent to the interpretation of Revelation 20. Though in some instances the number may be quite literal (for example, *Gen.* 20:16, *Ezra* 1:9–10) or possibly literal as well as symbolic (for example, *Judg.* 15:15–16, *1 Chron.* 29:21), in other instances it has a clearly symbolic meaning. In Deuteronomy 7:9, the Lord is described as a 'faithful God who keeps covenant and mercy for a thousand generations with those who love him and keep his commandments'. In the summary of the law given in Exodus 20, a contrast is drawn between the Lord's visiting of judgement upon the third and fourth generations of those who hate him, and his 'showing lovingkindness to thousands' who love him and keep his commandments (*Exod.* 20:5–6). Similarly, in the Psalms we read that the 'cattle on a thousand hills' belong to the Lord (*Psa.* 50:10–11). The Psalmist also speaks of how a 'day in Thy courts is better than a thousand' (*Psa.* 84:10). In the well-known words of Psalm 90, the believer confesses that 'a thousand years in Thy sight are like yesterday when it passes by, or as a watch in the night' (verse 4). Responding to the mockers who mocked the promise of the Lord's coming, the Apostle Peter notes that 'with the Lord one day is as a thousand years, and a thousand years as one day' (*2 Pet.* 3:8).[1]

What these passages indicate is that the number one thousand is often used in the Scriptures to refer to an extensive period of time. The use of one thousand years in Revelation is, when interpreted against the background of this usage of the symbolism of one thousand, likely a reference to a period of fullness, completion and perfection so far as God's redemptive plan is concerned. This expression is not meant to teach that the millennium will be a period of 365,000 days, not one more nor one less. Just as God's faithfulness is perfect and never failing (unto one thousand generations), so the times within his redemptive purposes are perfect and never failing. The most that can be concluded, then, from the use of the number one thousand in Revelation 20 is that the period of Satan's binding will be great and full, not small and empty, of years. That this is the sense of the vision is only reinforced by the contrasting language that describes Satan's season of rebellion as a little season,

---

[1] Perhaps the Lord's rebuke to Elijah, that there were still seven thousand who had not bowed the knee to Baal, could be mentioned here (*1 Kings* 19:18). This number, whether to be taken as a literal reference to seven thousand or not (not one more nor less), clearly has symbolic significance. The Lord is saying to Elijah, 'I have many, many more than your realize, who are faithful' (cf. *Rom.* 11:4).

suggesting that it is a meagre and limited period of time within the will of God.

To summarize: in this first section of the vision of Revelation 20, we have a representation of that period of history between the time of Christ's first coming and his return at the end of age, in which Satan has been bound so as no longer to be able to deceive the nations. The millennium is now, the period in which Christ's kingdom is advancing by his Spirit and Word and the nations are being discipled. This period is not a literal period of one thousand years, but the entire period, perfect, complete and extensive, between the first and second comings of Christ. Compared to the vast expanse and power of the kingdom of Christ, the period of Satan's rebellion at the end of the age prior to Christ's return, will be pathetically small and limited in scope.

The Believer's Reign with Christ

We move on now to take up the second part of the vision in Revelation 20:4–6. This focuses on the reign of the saints with Christ during the millennium. In particular their participation in the first resurrection, so that they are not liable to the second death, is portrayed. Though it may be unsettling to admit, this is even more controversial and difficult to interpret than the first part. We will have to work our way through these verses very carefully.

I. THE IDENTITY OF THE SAINTS

After describing the binding of Satan, the vision of Revelation 20 changes its angle to focus upon a scene in which the saints, those who participate in the first resurrection, reign with Christ during the millennial period.

> And I saw thrones, and they sat upon them, and judgement was given to them. And I saw the souls of those who had been beheaded because of the testimony of Jesus and because of the word of God, and those who had not

worshiped the beast or his image, and had not received the mark upon their forehead and upon their hand; and they came to life and reigned with Christ for a thousand years. The rest of the dead did not come to life until the thousand years were completed. This is the first resurrection. Blessed and holy is the one who has a part in the first resurrection; over these the second death has no power, but they will be priests of God and of Christ and will reign with Him for a thousand years.

Two questions immediately come to mind which must be addressed before considering the meaning of the reference to the first resurrection. The first question is: what is the location or place of the scene that John sees in this vision? Is this a scene of the saints in heaven or the saints upon the earth? The second and related question is: who are these saints whom John sees? Are they the entire number of believers? Or only believers who have died and now reign with Christ in heaven? Or only martyred believers? Only after these preliminary questions are addressed will we turn to the more difficult matter of the meaning of the phrase, 'they came to life and reigned with Christ for a thousand years'.

It is significant that the first thing the Apostle John sees in this vision are thrones. He says, 'I saw thrones, and they sat upon them, and judgement was given to them.' The likeliest location of these thrones is in heaven. Heaven is the place of the throne of God and the Lamb in the book of Revelation. But it is also the place where the saints who have died or who have been martyred have a share in the reign of Christ. In all of the references to 'throne' in the book of Revelation (some 47 instances), only three refer to some place other than heaven (see 2:13; 13:2; 16:10). For example, in Revelation 3:21 we read this promise of Christ: 'he who overcomes, I will grant to him to sit down with Me on My throne, as I also overcame and sat down with my Father on His throne.' Thus, were the thrones of Revelation 20 located on the earth, taking the reign of these saints as a reigning not only over but also upon the earth, this would be inconsistent with the imagery of the book.

Furthermore, the fact that the Apostle John speaks of the 'souls' of those who had been beheaded because of the testimony of Jesus adds to the likelihood that the scene is a heavenly one. This language is reminiscent of that used earlier in the book of Revelation to describe 'the souls of those who had been slain for the Word of God and for the witness they had borne' (6:9). These souls were seen by the apostle under the altar, that is, before the throne of God in the heavenly sanctuary. Though the word 'souls' need not require that these saints are no longer dwelling in the body, the reference to their beheading implies that this is the case.[1] When it is noted further that these saints are contrasted in verse 5 with 'the rest of the dead', it becomes increasingly certain that John is seeing a vision of the saints in glory, those believers who have died and are translated into the presence of Christ in heaven.[2]

Of course, it must be admitted that the location of these saints, whether in heaven or upon the earth, also depends upon the meaning of their participation in the first resurrection. If the first resurrection is a bodily resurrection, as premillennialists typically argue, then it would seem to follow that their reign is from and upon the earth. In the understanding of Premillennialism, the vision of Revelation 20 is a picture of the resurrected saints reigning upon the earth during the entire period of the millennium. Since we have yet to address the difficult question of the meaning of

---

[1] Though this may seem too obvious to require emphasis, I mention it because sometimes the word 'souls' in the Bible, just as in our language, can refer to people who are dwelling in the body (for example, *Gen.* 2:7, *Luke* 1:46).

[2] The fact that later the vision speaks of some who are subject to the second death further confirms that these are believers who have died and who enjoy a blessing subsequent to death from which unbelievers are excluded.

the first resurrection, our conclusion at this point can only be tentative and provisional. However, the natural reading of this vision certainly favours the position that these saints are reigning with Christ in heaven.

The second question – who are these saints? – is also disputed. Premillennialists commonly argue that John sees a vision of all the saints, believers who come with Christ to the earth after the tribulation period as well as believers who are alive at his coming, who reign with Christ upon the earth for a thousand years. Many postmillennialists and amillennialists regard these saints as the saints in glory, especially the martyred saints. However, some amillennialists say that these saints are only the martyred saints who enjoy a peculiar privilege during the millennium of reigning with Christ. Jay Adams, for example, in his study of the book of Revelation, *The Time is At Hand*, argues strongly that 'during the 1000 years, the martyred saints are said to reign with Christ. The fourth verse speaks of a *limited* group; not *all* Christians. The Apocalypse is deeply concerned with the martyrs and their reward.'[1]

However, there are good reasons to take the saints in this vision to include all the saints in heaven, especially, but not only, the martyred saints. Those, like Adams, who would restrict these saints to the martyred saints do so by insisting that the conjunction 'and', be translated in the sense of 'namely'. In this translation, we should read this text to say, 'And I saw thrones, and they sat upon them, and judgement was given to them, namely the souls of those who had been beheaded.'

Though this is a possible reading of the text, it could better be read using 'and' in the sense of 'especially'. Upon this reading, the privileges enjoyed by the saints – judging, reigning with Christ, not being subject to the second death – would be shared by all the saints in heaven. But the martyred saints would be singled out from among them as special beneficiaries of these privileges. Far from being excluded

[1] *The Time Is At Hand*, pp. 88–89.

from these privileges, the martyred saints' enjoyment of them is particularly emphasized. Not only does this reading fit well the natural meaning of the word 'and' in this text, but it is also consistent with a theme that runs throughout the book of Revelation: that those who are faithful to the Lord and their testimony[1] are more than conquerors through Christ (see 2:7, 10–11, 17, 26–28; 3:11–12, 21, etc.). At the same time, this reading does not require that these martyred saints enjoy privileges exclusive to them. They exercise judgement, reign with Christ as priests, enjoy immunity from the power of the second death – but these are privileges known to all those who belong to Christ (see *Eph.* 2:6, *Rev.* 5:9, 10, *Col.* 3:1, *1 Pet.* 2:9, 10, *John* 12).

The scene, then, that opens before the Apostle John is that of the saints in heaven before the throne of God and the Lamb. Among these saints, John singles out for special emphasis those who were beheaded and martyred for their testimony and faithfulness. What he sees is that they all, including the martyred saints, are enjoying during the period of the millennium a most remarkable set of privileges: they are seated upon thrones, they are reigning with Christ, and they are serving as priests of God and of Christ.

II. The First Resurrection

At this juncture in the vision of Revelation 20:1–6 the most contentious issue arises: what is meant by the 'first resurrection' which is enjoyed by the saints whom John sees? In the description of these saints, we read that 'they came to life and reigned with Christ for a thousand years. The rest of the dead did not come to life until the thousand years were completed. This is the first resurrection.'

On the premillennialist reading of Revelation 20, this is taken to be a reference to the bodily resurrection of all the

---

[1] The word for 'testimony' in the book of Revelation is the word *marturia*, from which is derived our word 'martyr'. The martyr is the one who is willing to die for the sake of the testimony concerning Jesus Christ.

saints at the time of the commencement of the millennium. The language used in this passage for the 'coming to life' of these saints, especially the use of the term 'resurrection', is taken to mean a physical resurrection of believers prior to the millennial reign of Christ on the earth. This resurrection is the exclusive privilege of believers and must be carefully distinguished from a second resurrection, the bodily resurrection of the unbelieving and impenitent, which will occur after the millennium in connection with the Great White Throne judgement described in verses 11–15. Believers who participate in the first resurrection are not liable to the second death. However, unbelievers who participate in the second resurrection remain liable to the second death. According to the premillennialist, nothing could more obviously confirm the idea of a literal millennial reign of Christ with his saints upon the earth after his coming at the end of the age. The postmillennialist and amillennialist position that this first resurrection is not a bodily resurrection but a spiritual reality with corresponding privileges and consequences is simply untenable.

Though this premillennialist argument sounds convincing at first hearing, a number of considerations lead to a different conclusion, namely, that the first resurrection is a reference to the life and blessing reserved for the saints, particularly those saints who have died and will be raised on the last day. In this understanding of the passage, the first resurrection is not a reference to the bodily resurrection of saints at the commencement of the millennium, but to a spiritual participation in Christ which brings the blessings of living and reigning as priests with him, as well as immunity from the power of the second death. Among the considerations that support this understanding are the following.

First, were the first resurrection a reference to the bodily resurrection only of believing saints, an event that occurs at the commencement of the millennium, this resurrection would be separated in time by one thousand years from the resurrection and judgement of unbelievers at the end of the age. This separation in time between the resurrection of the just and the unjust, of believers and unbelievers, however, contradicts the teaching of Scripture elsewhere that these events will occur together as parts of one complex and consummating series of events at the end of the age. In John 5:28–29, Jesus Christ is reported to have said to the disciples, 'Do not marvel at this; for an hour is coming, in which all who are in the tombs shall hear His voice, and shall come forth; those who did the good deeds to a resurrection of life, those who committed the evil deeds to a resurrection of judgement.' This passage speaks clearly of an hour in which all who are in their tombs will hear the voice of Christ, the Son of God, and come forth. At a point in time that coincides for all, the just and the unjust alike, a resurrection of life and a resurrection of judgement will occur. In addition to this passage, a number of other Scriptural passages suggest that the resurrection of believers and unbelievers will occur concurrently at the end of the age (see *Matt.* 16:27; 25:31–33, *Acts* 24:15, *2 Cor.* 5:10, *2 Thess.* 1:6–10, *Rev.* 20:11–15).

Second, though premillennialists correctly point out that the terms 'coming to life' and 'resurrection' are most commonly used in the New Testament for a bodily resurrection, this is not always the case. The verb which is translated in verses 4 and 5 as 'came to life' is used in several places for a life that is not a bodily resurrection.[1] In Luke 20, for example, Jesus, speaking against the Sadducean denial of the doctrine of the resurrection, says that God is not the God of the dead, but of the living; for all live to him (verse 38). In several instances in the book of Revelation itself, this verb is used to describe God, who 'lives forever' (*Rev.* 4:9–10), who

---

[1] The translation 'they came to life' could equally well be 'they lived', the latter being less suggestive of the idea of a bodily resurrection than the former. In other words, the translation, 'they came to life', may lend greater credence to the idea that a bodily resurrection is being referred to than is really the case. See Beale, *The Book of Revelation*, pp. 1004–7.

is the 'living God' (7:2), or who 'lives forever and ever' (10:6; 15:7). One especially interesting passage is found in Revelation 13. The vision here first describes the beast, one of whose heads was 'as if it had been slain' (verse 3). Then, in a subsequent description of this beast, we are told that the beast 'who had the wound of the sword . . . had come to life' (verse 14). This description indicates that the living or coming to life of the beast was not a bodily resurrection, but the healing of an (only) apparently fatal wound. Consequently, when the vision of Revelation 20 speaks of the saints who 'lived', this word need not refer to a bodily resurrection.

Third and perhaps most importantly, the New Testament does speak of the believer's fellowship with Christ, which brings the benefits depicted in the vision of Revelation 20: 1–6, as a resurrection which is not of a bodily kind. It is simply not true, as many premillennialists imply in their treatment of this vision, that the language and concept of resurrection in the New Testament must always mean a bodily resurrection. Indeed, the New Testament teaches a doctrine of the believer's being raised with Christ that is fundamental to salvation and itself the ground upon which the expectation of a future bodily resurrection depends. It is intriguing to note that though the vision of Revelation 20: 1–6 seems by its reference to a first resurrection to imply that there is a second resurrection, it does not actually speak of a second resurrection. Only one resurrection is specifically mentioned, and it is particularly defined as the first resurrection because it brings the benefits of the believer's reign with Christ and immunity from the power of the second death. These are the only benefits mentioned in the text. Nothing is said of a bodily resurrection.

Though the privileges enjoyed by the saints whom John sees in this vision are glorious, it should be noted that all believers in union with Christ may be said to live and reign with him as priests of God. Elsewhere in the New Testament the believer's fellowship with Christ is described as a resurrection that brings victory over the dominion of sin and death. This is evident in the well-known words of John 11:25–26, where Christ promises those who believe in him that they will share in his resurrection power and life: 'I am the resurrection and the life: he who believes in Me shall live even if he dies, and everyone who lives and believes in Me shall never die.' Likewise, the Apostle Paul speaks in several places of the believer's incorporation into Christ as a baptism into Christ that involves the believer directly in his death and resurrection. Through this baptism into Christ, the believer enjoys a fellowship with him that is nothing less than a resurrection.

For example, in Romans 6:3–4, we read: 'Or do you not know that all of us who have been baptized into Christ Jesus have been baptized into His death? Therefore we have been buried with Him through baptism into death, in order that as Christ was raised from the dead through the glory of the Father, so we too might walk in newness of life.' Similarly, in Colossians 3:1–3, the Apostle Paul speaks of the believer's resurrection in fellowship with Christ: 'If then you have been raised up with Christ, keep seeking the things above, where Christ is, seated at the right hand of God. Set your mind on the things above, not on the things that are on earth. For you have died and your life is hidden with Christ in God.' In another passage, the link between the believer's fellowship with Christ and his being raised with Christ so as to sit with him in the heavenly places is especially striking: 'But God, being rich in mercy, because of His great love with which He loved us, even when we were dead in our transgressions, made us alive together with Christ (by grace you have been saved), and raised us up with Him, and seated us with Him in the heavenly places, in Christ Jesus' (*Eph.* 2:4–6).

These passages are especially pertinent to the vision in Revelation 20 of the believer's participation in the first resurrection because they clearly teach that all believers, by virtue of their union with or baptism into Christ, have a share in his resurrection and all its attendant benefits. The believer's resurrection in fellowship with Christ brings with it the reality of life from the dead, the assurance of never-ending life, and the blessedness of being given to sit with and reign with Christ in the heavenly places. Thus, none of the blessings or privileges enjoyed by the saints whom John sees in the vision of Revelation 20 are foreign to believers who are joined through faith to Christ.

This means that when John sees the saints in heaven reigning with Christ as priests of God, exercising heavenly prerogatives in fellowship with the exalted and enthroned Son of God, he sees these saints enjoying in a particular and pronounced way those blessings enjoyed by all believers who are united with Christ. These blessings follow from their participation in the first resurrection. Because of their participation in this first resurrection, they are not liable to the power and dominion of death, including the second death of eternal separation from the presence and favour of God.

This way of understanding the reference to the first resurrection in this vision is perfectly consistent with the teaching of the Scriptures. Not only does it remove the difficulty of separating by one thousand years of time the resurrection of the just from the unjust, but it also appeals to an important biblical teaching regarding the resurrection of believers in union with Christ. Even though this baptism into Christ and share in his resurrection is the common benefit belonging to all believers, in the vision of John in Revelation 20 this benefit is seen in its peculiar application to those who have been translated upon death into heavenly glory.[1]

III. 'THE REST OF THE DEAD'

This reading of the vision finds further confirmation in the language at the close of the vision. Revelation 20:1–6

---

[1] It might be objected here that the vision of Revelation 20:1–6 suggests that these benefits and this first resurrection are the exclusive experience of those saints who have died or been martyred for the faith. It would not be correct, then, to identify this first resurrection with an experience common to all believers. In reply to this objection,

concludes with these words: 'The rest of the dead did not come to life until the thousand years were completed. This is the first resurrection. Blessed and holy is the one who has a part in the first resurrection; over these the second death has no power, but they will be priests of God and of Christ and will reign with Him for a thousand years.'

The 'rest of the dead' refers to the unjust and unbelieving. Because they have no part in the first resurrection, they remain subject to the power of the second death. They share none of the privileges enjoyed by the saints. The second death to which they are subject cannot be physical death, the separation of body and soul as the consequence of sin, because they have already suffered this death. It is a spiritual death, that death which results from separation from favour and fellowship with the living God. The first resurrection is distinguished as first because it brings victory, not over physical death (as in a bodily resurrection), but over spiritual death. The second death is second because it means liability to punishment, not in a physical separation of body and soul,

---

I would note that the text requires only that these saints have a particular and special enjoyment of benefits that are, nonetheless, also the property of all believers in Christ. Far from death or martyrdom depriving them of these benefits, they are witnessed coming to life and enjoying these benefits in a most marvellous way in heaven. The position I am defending is similar to, though not identical with, that presented by Norman Shepherd in his article, 'The Resurrections of Revelation 20' (*Westminster Theological Journal,* 37/1 [Fall, 1974), pp. 34–43). Shepherd identifies the first resurrection with the believer's baptismal incorporation into Christ. Shepherd particularly calls attention to the fact that Revelation 20 does not speak directly of a second resurrection. It speaks only of a first resurrection, the benefits of which are associated elsewhere in the New Testament with the believer's baptism into Christ. With respect to the implied second resurrection, Shepherd suggests that it may refer to the resurrection or renewal of the entire cosmos, including believers in their bodily resurrection, at the last day. Though this suggestion does not enjoy direct support from the vision of Revelation 20, it does seem consistent with the teaching of other biblical passages Shepherd cites (for example, *Rom.* 8:18–23, *2 Pet.* 3:13, *Rev.* 21:1, *1 Cor.* 15:42, 50).

but in a spiritual separation or excommunication from God's presence. The term 'second death' seems to confirm, therefore, that the first resurrection is not a physical resurrection.[1] What distinguishes those who partake of the first resurrection is that they are not subject to spiritual death. They are those who live and whose life consists in unbroken communion with God and his Christ. The same cannot be said of the rest of the dead. They remain liable to death, even the second death under the judgement of God.

Thus, the rest of the dead are not mentioned in this vision in terms of their participation in a second resurrection. Nothing in the language of this vision suggests that the second resurrection will be akin to the first as a bodily resurrection. They are simply said to be excluded from the first resurrection of the dead and its benefits, and to remain liable to the power of the second death.

Conclusion

With these pieces of the puzzle of the vision of Revelation 20:1–6 in place, we are in a position to sum up our findings.

Revelation 20:1–6 presents one in a series of vision sequences in the book of Revelation. The vision of the binding of Satan and the reigning of believing saints with Christ for the period of one thousand years is a vision of history between the time of the first and second advents of Christ. This vision does not describe events that will occur after the return of Christ (with which the vision of Revelation 19 concludes), but events that cover the whole period of the history of redemption from the time of Christ's coming in the fullness of time until the time of his return in glory at the end of the age.

The vision of the binding of Satan portrays the world-wide gathering of the nations into the fellowship of Christ. During

---

[1] See Adams, *The Time Is At Hand*, p. 89: 'The "second death" is not physical. Why must the "first resurrection" be? Just as "second" is added to make it clear that physical death is not intended, so "first" is appended to show that a physical resurrection is not in view.'

these last days of fulfilment, the nations are no longer liable to the deceptive devices of Satan but are being discipled by the Spirit and Word of Christ. Revelation 20 offers a behind-the-scenes glimpse of the triumphant gathering of Christ's church from among the nations, a gathering which will not fail of its successful execution. Though Satan may not be absolutely constrained against any activity, he is not able to deceive the nations any longer. Even the 'little season' of Satanically inspired rebellion that will occur prior to the close of the age will issue quickly in frustration and defeat. Nothing can prevent Christ's gathering and building of his church.

Furthermore, echoing a theme which is sounded throughout the book of Revelation, the vision of Revelation 20 also teaches that, far from the death of the saints or the martyrdom of many indicating defeat for the cause of Christ and his kingdom, these saints have a full share in the glory and victory of Christ. Not least among those who share in Christ's victory are the departed saints, especially the martyred saints, who live and reign with Christ as priests of God during the entire millennium. This victory of theirs is not some earthly reign at a near or distant point in history, after the return of Christ and during a future millennial reign, but a present reality.

The vision of Revelation 20 provides the church, then, to which it was first written in the latter part of the first century AD (and the church since until Christ comes again) a great consolation and encouragement in the face of trial and persecution. Those who as believers see history with the eye of faith join the Apostle John on the isle of Patmos and they stand amazed and strengthened in this vision of the saints in glory seated upon thrones in the presence of God and the Lamb.

Only some such understanding of the vision of Revelation 20 can do justice to the particular language used in it, its context and place in the book of Revelation, and indeed, its place in the teaching of Scripture generally.

12

Evaluating Postmillennialism

I N OUR EARLIER SURVEYS of the four primary millennial views, we promised to evaluate each of them from the standpoint of Scripture. So far we have dealt with the views of Historic and Dispensational Premillennialism, considering their unbiblical separation between Christ's second coming and the close of the present age, and also a number of objections against Dispensationalism itself. We turn now to Postmillennialism.

The term 'postmillennial' simply means 'after the millennium', and this position teaches that Christ will return after the millennium at the end of the present age. In this broad sense it covers two distinct millennial viewpoints, which are golden-age Postmillennialism and Amillennialism. Though these two distinct views are commonly termed Postmillennialism and Amillennialism, they share a common conviction that the return of Christ will come after the millennium and conclude the present period of history. We will argue that Amillennialism, when it does not express a pessimistic view of the presence of Christ's kingdom, is the view which most satisfies the biblical teaching.

Defining Golden-Age Postmillennialism

For the purpose of this evaluation, we will use the term Post-millennialism in its narrower sense, to refer to the view that looks for an unprecedented period, or golden age, between the times of Christ's first and second comings. Though variously described by postmillennialists, this golden age will be marked by an unprecedented triumph of the gospel on the earth. The nations will be converted and honour the requirements of the Word of God. Prosperity and peace will prevail in the earth. This unprecedented period will last a thousand years, not in a literal sense but in the sense of a great and expansive period of time. Only at the conclusion of this millennial period will there be a brief period of Satanic rebellion and apostasy, the 'little season' of Revelation 20.

Postmillennialists differ in their opinions regarding the commencement of this golden age. Some suggest that it will commence gradually and increase. As the gospel progressively penetrates the nations and brings about their conversion, the millennium will eventually come to full manifestation.[1] Others suggest that the millennium will commence more abruptly and suddenly with a future conversion of the nations by an unprecedented working of the Spirit through the gospel. Opinions also vary as to the place and service of the civil magistrate in the realization of this millennial kingdom. Complicating matters even further is the tendency today among some postmillennialists to identify the entire period between Christ's first and second advents as the period of the millennium. Though this latter tendency amounts to a position all but indistinguishable from Amillennialism – while perhaps more optimistic in its expectation – it retains the characteristic emphasis upon a coming golden age.[2]

[1] See, for example, Davis, *Christ's Victorious Kingdom*, pp. 65–82; and Gentry, *He Shall Have Dominion*, p. 71.

[2] These last sentences reflect the position most commonly found among reconstructionists or theonomists. The term 'reconstruction'

THE PROMISE OF THE FUTURE

As this feature of a golden age or future period of unprecedented gospel blessing is essential to all postmillennialist views, it will be the focus of our evaluation, which will be presented in a number of questions.

I. WHEN DOES CHRIST BECOME KING?

The first objection to Postmillennialism can be stated by this question: When does Christ become king? Golden-age Postmillennialism suggests that the kingship of Jesus Christ is not so much a present as it is a future reality. The coming of Christ in the fullness of time, though it inaugurated a new period in the history of redemption, did not by itself constitute the great turning point in history so far as the kingdom of God is concerned. Rather, it commenced a series of events which only in terms of subsequent developments

---

refers to a program of rebuilding and reordering of all of life in its various spheres (ecclesiastical, civil, judicial, economic, familial, etc.) according to the teachings of the Word and law of God. The term 'theonomy' refers to an understanding of the continued normativity of the Old Testament civil or judicial law (including its penal sanctions) for the administration of justice by the civil magistrate. Though not all postmillennialists are reconstructionists, most, if not all, reconstructionists are postmillennialists. They are postmillennialists because their expectation for the realization of Christ's dominion in the earth depends upon what they sometimes prefer to call an 'optimistic eschatology'. The complication here, however, is that many of these reconstructionist postmillennialists tend to identify the millennial period with the entire period between the first and second advents of Christ. In that respect, their position is formally similar to Amillennialism. However, because they insist upon the progressive realization of the kingdom of Christ, including a golden age of unprecedented kingdom blessing, their position might better be regarded as a hybrid version of Postmillennialism. For a thorough presentation of this position, see Kenneth L. Gentry, Jr., *He Shall Have Dominion*; idem, 'Postmillennialism', pp. 13–57. In what follows, I am partially dependent upon a good summary and evaluation of this position by Richard B. Gaffin, Jr. ('Theonomy and Eschatology: Reflections on Postmillennialism', in *Theonomy: A Reformed Critique*, ed. William S. Barker & W. Robert Godfrey, pp. 197–224).

lead to the millennial kingdom. However the millennium commences, it does not commence until some time after the great redemptive events attested in the New Testament Scriptures. The birth, life, death, resurrection and ascension of Jesus Christ, together with the outpouring of the Spirit at Pentecost, initiated a chain of events that will eventually lead to the millennial kingdom. But these events did not coincide with the commencement of Christ's millennial reign, which comes later in the history of redemption.

The problem with this construction is that it compromises the testimony of the New Testament that the reign of Christ commences with his first advent and installation at the right hand of the Father. Though the manifestation of Christ's rule may vary throughout history, it is the entire period between Christ's resurrection and his return at the end of the age in which he has all authority (*Matt.* 28:16–20) and exercises kingly dominion on the earth. The preaching of the gospel to all creation and the discipling of the nations – these are the great tasks of Christ's church in this present period of history, and they express his present rule as king.[1]

Consequently, those passages that speak of Christ's king-ship refer to the entire present age subsequent to Christ's ascension and prior to his return at the end of the age. In Philippians 2:9–11, after the well-known description of Christ's humiliation, the Apostle Paul describes Christ's exaltation in these words: 'Therefore also God highly exalted Him, and bestowed on Him the name which is above every name, that at the name of Jesus every knee should bow, of those who are in heaven, and on earth, and under the earth, and that every tongue should confess that Jesus Christ is Lord, to the glory of God the Father.' This description of Christ's exaltation defines his present glory, not one that is reserved to the future in any new or distinguishable sense. In a similar passage, Ephesians 1:22–23, the present dominion

---

[1] See Strimple, 'Amillennialism', p. 61.

of Christ is described in the strongest terms. According to this passage, God the Father has 'put all things in subjection under His [Christ's] feet, and gave Him as head over all things to the church, which is His body, the fullness of Him who fills all in all' (see also *Col.* 1:15–18, *1 Pet.* 3:22). Christ has been seated at the right hand of God 'far above all rule and authority and power and dominion . . . not only in this age, but also in the one to come' (verses 20–21). No suggestion is made that this present reign of Christ is to be divided into non-millennial and millennial phases, each to be distinguished from the age to come. Something quite different is affirmed: Christ's reign both in the present age and in the age to come, with no other age intervening.

As we have already noted, the only passages in the New Testament that might appear to teach a distinction between Christ's present kingship and his kingship during a millennial period in the future are 1 Corinthians 15:22–26 and Revelation 20:1–6. Upon careful study, however, neither of these passages teaches such a distinction.

In 1 Corinthians 15:22–26, we read the following:

> For as in Adam all die, so also in Christ shall all be made alive. But each in his own order: Christ the first fruits, after that those who are Christ's at His coming, then the end, when He delivers up the kingdom to the God and Father, when He has abolished all rule and all authority and power. For He must reign until He has put all His enemies under His feet. The last enemy that will be abolished is death.

This passage teaches that subsequent to his resurrection from the dead, Christ was installed as king and is presently reigning over all things. This present reign of Christ will come to an end when all of his enemies have been brought into subjection under his feet, including the last enemy, death. There is a no suggestion in this passage of an unprecedented period of Christ's millennial reign that will intervene between the present reality of his reign and the final state, when all his enemies, including death, have been defeated. This passage leaves no place for a golden age between the present age and the age to come. Rather, it teaches that the (millennial) reign of Christ encompasses the present period of history, to be concluded only at the time of the final conquest of all of Christ's enemies at the end of the age.

With respect to the vision of the millennium in Revelation 20:1–6, we do not wish to revisit the arguments of the previous chapter, which supported the view that this encompasses the entire inter-advental period. In order to support from Revelation 20 the view of a future golden age in history, two things would need to be proved. The first is that the events depicted in Revelation 19:11–21 refer not to the second coming of Christ, but to a transitional period in history leading up to the beginning of the millennium of Revelation 20. Revelation 19:11–21 seems clearly to refer instead to the return of Christ at the end of the present age. The second is that the events depicted Revelation 20:1–6 must take place after the events recorded in Revelation 19:11–21. But, as we have also previously argued, this has not been proven and is, in fact, quite unlikely.

There is, accordingly, no biblical support for the idea that Christ's kingship will enter a new and distinct phase with the inauguration of a future millennium or golden age. Christ is king now. And he has been king from the commencement of his mediatorial rule at the Father's right hand.

II. Is the Millennium Now or Future?

In reply to the claim that Postmillennialism's golden age compromises the present reality of Christ's reign, some present-day postmillennialists insist that the difference is not one of kind but only one of degree between the present and future manifestation of the kingdom of Christ. Christ is already king, but his reign will become increasingly manifest as the gospel progressively comes to triumph on the earth. Thus, some present-day postmillennialists concede that the millennium is now, that it began with the advent of Christ and will conclude at his coming at the end of the age. According to these postmillennialists, the only basic difference between postmillennialist and amillennialist views is that the former has a more optimistic and biblical expectation of the success of the gospel in this present age than the latter. Typically, those who argue in this fashion criticize the amillennialist for an unbiblical pessimism and lack of confidence in the promised success of the church's discipling of the nations.[1]

Curiously, this argument seems to abandon the traditional postmillennialist claim of a future unprecedented period of gospel blessing that is distinguishable from the remainder of the period between Christ's first and second advents. It abandons the 'chiliasm' of classic postmillennialist expectation: the view that the millennium of Revelation 20 is a distinct period in history that begins some time after the first advent of Christ. This represents a major concession to Amillennialism. Indeed, it leads to a position that is formally amillennialist, at least in its denial of a distinct millennial period in history. Like Amillennialism, this modified Post-

---

[1] The following statement of Norman Shepherd is representative: 'Both post- and amillennialists argue for the unity of the eschatological complex of events, against premillennialists, on the ground that the relevant passages (Matt. 24 and parallels; Rom. 8:17–23, 1 Cor. 15:22–28, 50–58, 1 Thess. 1:4–10, 4:13–18, 2 Pet. 3:3–15) do not allow for the insertion of a millennium between advent and consummation. Amillennialists also espouse the postmillennial timing of the advent, but differ sharply from postmillennialists on the nature of the millennium' ('Postmillennialism', in *The Zondervan Pictorial Encyclopedia of the Bible* [Merrill C. Tenney, gen. ed.; Grand Rapids: Zondervan, 1975, 1976], p. 822). What is interesting about this statement of Postmillennialism is that it is formally amillennialist; that is, it rejects a distinct interim kingdom or millennial period between the advent and consummation. Oddly enough, however, in the earlier section of this article, Shepherd summarizes the postmillennialist position as one which looks for a future period or millennial era which will be an unprecedented time of peace, prosperity and spiritual glory.

millennialism identifies the millennium of Revelation 20 with the whole period between Christ's first and second advents.

Furthermore, with its abandonment of the older post-millennialist idea of a future golden age, this modified view actually undermines the very idea of the millennium as a golden age. If the entire period of history between Christ's first and second advents is the millennium of Revelation 20, the golden age of the millennium no longer seems as golden as first advertised. On this view, Satan's binding coincided with the first advent of Christ and has characterized the history of the church from the first century. How, then, can advocates of this Postmillennialism continue to describe in the most glowing of terms the anticipated glory of a coming millennial era? Does the glory of this anticipated millennium not start to tarnish and fade when it is admitted that it has been a reality since the beginning of the Christian church of the new covenant era? If the millennium includes the nearly two thousand years of the church's history thus far, during which the church has experienced times of great prosperity as well as adversity, then there seems little reason to expect that this pattern will be radically different in the future. Once the idea of a future distinguishable millennium is abandoned, no place remains for an expectation of a coming period of unprecedented blessing.[1]

In some respects, the difficulty faced here by postmillennialists is the same difficulty faced by any chiliast doctrine that argues for a distinct millennial age in the history of redemption. That difficulty is how to account for the need for

---

[1] Gentry, in his article 'Postmillennialism', illustrates this problem rather clearly. In his definition of Postmillennialism, he speaks in chiliast terms of a future time in history which will be 'an extensive era' (pp. 13–14). Later, however, he interprets Revelation 20 to mean that Satan was bound 'judicially in the first century', a binding that 'increasingly constricts Satan throughout the Christian era' (p. 52). In the first instance, the millennium seems to be a future era; in the second, the millennium coincides with the inter-advental period.

such an interim kingdom, a period of the victorious reign of Christ, before the eternal form of the kingdom. This insertion of a millennial age between Christ's first and second advents seems an unnecessary complication in history. A new age intrudes that is neither the present age nor the age to come in the biblical sense of these expressions. Perhaps this is the reason, when some contemporary postmillennialists describe the millennium, they alternate between descriptions that echo what the Bible ascribes to the new heavens and the new earth and descriptions that seem indistinguishable from what has been true throughout the present period of history.

Though these objections are not a sufficient basis on which to reject golden-age Postmillennialism, they do raise serious questions regarding the biblical basis and consistency of this position. Does the Bible anywhere clearly teach that Christ is not presently king in the way in which he will in the future become king during the millennial age? And, if it is conceded that Christ's present kingship is of a piece with his future kingship (because the millennium is now), then what becomes of the expectation for a distinct and unprecedented period in the future?

III. WHAT ABOUT THE SIGNS OF THE TIMES?

The next objection is more specific than those just mentioned. It is expressed in the question: What about 'the signs of the times'? In our previous consideration of the Bible's teaching regarding these so-called signs, we noted that some of them are signs of opposition to Christ and his kingdom and that three of these are particularly important: tribulation, apostasy and the spirit of the Antichrist.

In New Testament teaching, each of these signs of opposition to Christ is, to a greater or lesser extent, a typical feature of the period of history in which the church now carries out her work. In these last days of the preaching of the gospel to the ends of the earth, it is the ordinary circumstance of believers to encounter these signs of opposition.

Though there may be periods or times (even a 'little season' like that described in Revelation 20) during which the believing church will experience great tribulation or apostasy, tribulation and apostasy are nonetheless typical signs of the gospel's presence in this age. The preaching of the gospel of the kingdom will provoke opposition and conflict between the kingdom of God and the kingdom of the evil one. The testimony of Scripture is that these signs will be the invariable experience of the believing church between Christ's first and second advents. A brief synopsis of these signs of opposition to Christ will be sufficient at this point.

Even if the references to great tribulation (*Matt.* 24:21, *Rev.* 2:22; 7:14) were restricted to the circumstances surrounding the destruction of Jerusalem in AD 70 and the first century church, the New Testament contains frequent references to tribulation which relate to the experience of believers throughout the present period of history.[1] In the opening section of Jesus' discourse in Matthew 24, for example, the tribulation described seems to be a general circumstance that will mark the entire period of the church's preaching of the gospel to the nations (*Matt.* 24:8–9). This is clearly asserted in John 16:33, which records Jesus' words to his disciples: 'In the world you have tribulation, but take courage; I have overcome the world.' Similarly, the Apostle Paul forewarns Timothy, 'And indeed, all who desire to live godly in Christ Jesus will be persecuted' (*2 Tim.* 3:12). This tribulation may

---

[1] In handling these references to tribulation and other signs of opposition to Christ's kingdom in this present age, a common strategy of postmillennialists includes the preterist view that these references relate to events in the past, particularly events that occurred in the first century at the time of the destruction of the temple in Jerusalem in AD 70. Many postmillennialists also read many of the signs of opposition to Christ as Satan's 'little season' after the millennium. Neither of these positions as such is untrue. However, postmillennialists tend to downplay the additional evidence in the New Testament for the continued presence of these signs throughout the entire period between Christ's advents.

take many forms, and produces patience (*James* 1:2–4, *Rom.* 5:3–4) and discipline (*Heb.* 12:6) in the Christian life. Whether believers and churches suffer one or more of these forms of tribulation, whether they suffer them to a greater or lesser degree, or even whether in some exceptional circumstances they suffer them hardly at all – the testimony of the Scripture is that this is the ordinary circumstance of believers in this life.

This pattern of teaching is evident also in respect to the signs of apostasy and the spirit of the Antichrist. Even though some passages refer to distinct periods of great apostasy either in the past (for example, *Matt.* 24:24) or the future (2 *Thess.* 2:3, *Rev.* 20), others refer to ongoing apostasy among those who are members of the church of Jesus Christ. In Matthew 24:10–12, Jesus speaks of 'many' who 'will fall away, and betray one another, and hate one another. And many false prophets will arise and lead many astray. And because wickedness is multiplied, most men's love will grow cold.' The Apostle Paul warns Timothy that 'the Spirit explicitly says that in later times some will fall away from the faith, paying attention to deceitful spirits and doctrines of demons' (1 *Tim.* 4:1). Accordingly, the New Testament gives frequent warnings against apostasy (for example, 2 *Pet.* 3:17, *Gal.* 5:4, *Heb.* 6:6, 2 *Pet.* 1:10) as well as assurances of the Lord's preserving grace in keeping his own from falling away (*Jude* 24). Likewise, despite indications of the coming of one who is the Antichrist (1 *John* 4:2–3, 2 *Thess.* 2:3–4, *Rev.* 17:8), the more common emphasis in the New Testament is upon the recurring expression of the spirit of Antichrist, that is, of teaching which is against the truth of the gospel as it is in Christ (*Matt.* 24:23–24, 1 *John* 2:18, 22; 4:2–3, 2 *John* 7).

What relevance does this teaching regarding the signs of opposition to Christ and his kingdom have for an evaluation of golden-age Postmillennialism? It suggests little likelihood, certainly no biblical expectation, that the circumstance of

Christ's church will typically be one of blessedness during the present age. Golden-age Postmillennialism teaches that the millennium will be an extensive period in history during which the nations will be converted, the principles of the gospel and law of God will govern the conduct of people, and undisturbed peace and prosperity will prevail throughout the world. The opposition to Christ and his kingdom of which these particular signs speak will be largely absent. Tribulation, apostasy and the spirit of the Antichrist will be eliminated for the most part during this millennial period. However, the passages we have considered show that a more restrained and temperate view of the prospects for the kingdom and people of God is demanded.

IV. Is A SERVANT GREATER THAN HIS MASTER?

One of the great themes in the Scriptures relating to the Christian life is the theme of suffering and cross-bearing. Believers who are incorporated into Christ not only share in all the benefits of his saving work, but also come to participate in some way in his sufferings. They are united with him in the likeness of his death, and raised with him in newness of life (*Rom.* 6:3–6). Just as he, their Lord and Master, suffered the hostility and unbelief of the world, so will all those who are his.

For this reason, the theme of the believer's suffering in fellowship with Christ was often emphasised in the writings of the great Reformers, Calvin and Luther. Calvin, in his treatment of the Christian life in the *Institutes*, spoke of cross-bearing as a hallmark of the life and pilgrimage of every Christian.[1] Luther likewise described biblical theology as always a theology of the cross, not a theology of glory.[2]

---

[1] Calvin entitles two of his chapters on the Christian life, 'The Sum of the Christian Life: The Denial of Ourselves' (III.vii) and 'Bearing the Cross, a Part of Self-Denial' (III.viii).

[2] Philip Melanchthon, in his first draft of the *Augsburg Confession*, included persecution and suffering as a mark of the true church. The

From this standpoint, triumphalism, the idea that the believer will go from victory to victory in this life, without suffering any distress as a member of Christ, has no place. Just as in the experience of the early church, so in the experience of Christ's church through the centuries, it is only 'through many tribulations [that] we must enter the kingdom' (*Acts* 14:22).

Though this theme is woven like a thread throughout the New Testament's depiction of the Christian life, we will only mention a few key instances by way of illustration.

In the teaching of Jesus in the Gospels, the emphasis upon suffering as an inescapable dimension of discipleship is unmistakable. We have already cited examples of this emphasis in the preceding section. One of the best known passages is Jesus' statement about cross-bearing as a requirement of anyone who would come after him: 'If anyone wishes to come after Me, let him deny himself, and take up his cross daily, and follow Me. For whoever wishes to save his life shall lose it, but whoever loses his life for My sake, he is the one who will save it' (*Luke* 9:23–24; see also *Matt.* 16:24, *Mark* 8:34, *Luke* 14:27). When Jesus prepared his disciples to go to 'the lost sheep of the house of Israel', he warned them of the opposition they would inevitably face: 'Do not think I came to bring peace on the earth; I did not come to bring peace, but a sword. For I came to set a man against his father, and a daughter against her mother, and a daughter-in-law against her mother-in-law; and a man's enemies will be the members of his household . . . And he who does not take his cross and follow after Me is not worthy of Me' (*Matt.* 10:34–36, 39). These frequently stress the disciple's participation in the reproach and shame that was hurled against the Master. No

---

Belgic Confession in Article 29, addressing the difference between the true and the false church, speaks of the false church as one that 'persecutes those who live holily according to the Word of God and rebuke it for its errors, covetousness, and idolatry'.

disciple is worthy of the Master, unless he or she is prepared to assume the suffering service that marked his life. Greatness in the kingdom of God is measured, not by becoming the first, but by becoming the last or the least of all (*Mark* 9:35; compare 10:43, *Matt.* 20:26). Accordingly, Jesus, in the context of his teaching the disciples about his impending suffering, insisted that they too would drink the cup that he was appointed to drink and 'be baptized with the baptism with which I am baptized' (*Mark* 10:39).

Consistent with Jesus' teaching about the suffering service that will mark the lot of all who are his disciples, the apostles themselves often spoke of their participation in the sufferings of Christ. In his extended discourse in 1 Corinthians 3 and 4 on the service of those who are ministers of Christ, the Apostle Paul admonishes the Corinthians for their arrogance and unwillingness to recognize that it is God's preferred method to magnify his power through human weakness: 'For, I think, God has exhibited us apostles last of all, as men condemned to death; because we have become a spectacle to the world, both to angels and to men. We are fools for Christ's sake, but you are prudent in Christ; we are weak, but you are strong; you are distinguished, but we are without honour' (*1 Cor.* 4:9–10). That this is no incidental or unusual feature of the Christian life becomes apparent when the Apostle Paul speaks of his and every believer's readiness to 'know Him [Christ], and the power of His resurrection and the fellowship of His sufferings, being conformed to His death' (*Phil.* 3:10; cf. *Col.* 1:24). In the service of every believer, there is a conformity to the likeness of Christ's suffering, a participation in Christ that inevitably includes the elements of self-denial, shame and loss.

To cite but one other example of this emphasis, the Apostle Paul describes the whole creation in Romans 8 in language which speaks of suffering as an essential feature of this present age. Echoing language used by Jesus in his Olivet discourse regarding the signs of the times (*Matt.* 24:8), this passage speaks broadly of the 'sufferings of this present time' which are 'not worthy to be compared with the glory that is to be revealed to us' (*Rom.* 8:18). 'For the anxious longing of the creation waits eagerly for the revealing of the sons of God. For the creation was subjected to futility, not of its own will, but because of Him who subjected it, in hope that the creation itself also will be set free from its slavery to corruption into the freedom of the glory of the children of God. For we know that the whole creation groans and suffers the pains of childbirth together until now' (verses 19–22). What is most striking about this passage is that the present age is typified by suffering, not only on the part of those who are members of Christ, but also on the part of the whole creation which, like a woman in childbirth, is travailing until the time of her deliverance. Not until the revelation of the sons of God, that is, the close of this present age and the beginning of the age to come, will this circumstance be changed. Therefore, it is an inescapable feature of this interval between the times of Christ's coming and his return in glory that suffering marks the circumstance of believer and creation alike.

The point of these passages is not that every believer and church in this present age will suffer in the same way or to the same extent. Nor do they deny that at many times and in various places the cause of Christ's gospel and kingdom will enjoy the most wonderful success and blessing. No doubt – as believers have already witnessed – nations will be discipled, kingdoms opposed to Christ will topple, and kingdom standards will transform the life of people and nations. The passages cited do not contradict any of these things. They certainly do not teach, for example, that believers who enjoy prosperity and peace must somehow be guilty of unbiblical compromise or accommodation. But they do teach that, in this present age, the believer and the church must always expect and anticipate some fellowship in the sufferings of Christ. The preaching of the gospel and the advance of the kingdom always call forth a counter-gospel, a reaction of unbelief and opposition. And so believers learn obedience through their suffering, just as Christ their Lord and Master did (*Heb.* 5:8). They understand firsthand the meaning of Hebrews 13:12–14, 'Let us go out to Him outside the camp, bearing His reproach. For here we do not have a lasting city, but we are seeking the city which is to come' (compare *Heb.* 12:3).

Golden-age Postmillennialism mutes this biblical teaching about the fellowship in suffering between Christ and his disciples. No matter how it is qualified or described, the millennium of postmillennialist expectation excludes these dimensions of what it means to be a follower of Christ in the present age. Consequently, Postmillennialism betrays a triumphalist theology of glory that prematurely anticipates in history what will be the circumstance of God's people only in the day of their vindication. Only Christ's coming again will bring an end to the trouble that marks out the Christian's pilgrimage in this life as he or she anticipates the city which has foundations, whose builder and maker is God. No more than Abraham or the saints of the past is the believer today able to find rest in this life.

VI. WHAT IS THE FOCUS OF THE BELIEVER'S HOPE FOR THE FUTURE?
The fifth and final objection to be urged against golden-age Postmillennialism is that it alters the focus of the believer's hope for the future. Whereas the New Testament depicts the church in this present age as continually participating in the sufferings of Christ and eagerly awaiting the return of Christ at the end of the age, the postmillennialist view encourages an outlook for the future that focuses on an anticipated period of largely undisturbed blessedness. The expectation and hope of the believer for the future focuses upon the millennium rather than the return of Christ.

But what is the focal point of the believer's hope for the future in the New Testament? What is held out to the believing church as a source of consolation in the midst of the suffering and distress that often mark this present age? Is it the expectation that in the course of history the gospel will so triumph in the earth, the standards of the kingdom of God will be so honoured among the nations, that the result will be a protracted period of millennial blessedness? Does the expectation of a future millennial era serve as a point of reference to comfort believers in their anticipation of the future?

It is not difficult to show that the biblical focus is upon the return of Christ as the great event on the horizon of the future. In Romans 8:22–25, a passage cited earlier, the Apostle Paul speaks of the hope that believers have in common with the whole creation. That hope looks for the day when the sons of God will be revealed and their bodies be fully redeemed. The writer to the Hebrews, in the midst of his encouraging words to those believers in the early church who were in danger of falling away, speaks of the coming of Christ 'a second time for salvation without sin, to those who eagerly await Him' (9:28). Or again, in the words of the Apostle Peter addressed to those who mocked the certainty of the coming again of Christ: 'Since all these things are to be destroyed in this way, what sort of people ought you to be in holy conduct and godliness, looking for and hastening the coming of the day of God, on account of which the heavens will be destroyed by burning, and the elements will melt with intense heat! But according to His promise we are looking for new heavens and a new earth, in which righteousness dwells' (2 Pet. 3:11–13).

In these and other passages, the second coming of Christ is the blessed hope of the believing church (*Titus* 2:13, 1 Pet. 1:3–7). As the believer faces tribulation and distress in this present age, as the church meets with opposition to Christ and his cause, the one great promise that brings unspeakable comfort is the promise of the return of Christ and the final vindication of his cause at the end of the age.

One particularly striking illustration of this expectation is found in a passage that we have considered before,

2 Thessalonians 1. Writing to a church that had known tribulation and persecution from its earliest beginnings (verse 4), the Apostle Paul holds out the promise of rest at Christ's revelation from heaven: 'For after all it is only just for God to repay with affliction those who afflict you, and to give relief to you who are afflicted and to us as well when the Lord Jesus shall be revealed from heaven with His mighty angels in flaming fire, dealing out retribution to those who do not know God and to those who do not obey the gospel of our Lord Jesus' (verses 6–8). In the context of all the troubles and distresses experienced by the believers in Thessalonica, the apostle assures them that when Christ is revealed from heaven, he will deliver them from their enemies. At the coming of Christ, those who trouble them will be troubled and they will enter into the rest promised them in the gospel. Nothing is said about a future millennial era that will end their present distresses or afford them the quietness and rest they so desperately desire. Only the revelation of Christ from heaven will bring them the salvation for which they long. Only then will they have occasion to see Christ 'glorified in his saints' and 'marveled at among all who have believed' (verse 10).[1]

This is the pattern of teaching throughout the New Testament. A contrast is drawn between the sufferings and distresses of this present age and the joy of the age to come. Between this present age and the age to come, there is no

---

[1] The pattern exhibited in this passage and many others is well captured in the language of Lord's Day 19 of the *Heidelberg Catechism*. In answer to the question, 'What comfort is it to you that Christ shall come to judge the living and the dead?', this catechism says, 'That in all my sorrows and persecutions, with uplifted head I look for the very same Person who before has offered himself for my sake to the tribunal of God, and has removed all curse from me, to come as Judge from heaven; who shall cast all his and my enemies into everlasting condemnation, but shall take me with all his chosen ones to himself into heavenly joy and glory.'

millennial age that might draw the attention away from the return of Christ. What fuels the believer's longing is the great event of Christ's return. Nowhere is the expectation of a future millennial age set forth as an occasion for expectancy. Certainly no promise is held out for a period of uninterrupted and undisturbed blessedness in history prior to the revelation of Christ at the end of the present age.

Two Qualifiers

Having raised several biblical objections to golden-age Postmillennialism, two qualifications to these objections need to be mentioned. Without withdrawing or downplaying these criticisms of Postmillennialism, they need to be placed in an appropriate context, lest we conclude that Postmillennialism has nothing to contribute to an understanding of the future of the kingdom.

First, though golden-age Postmillennialism is inconsistent with the biblical emphases we have discussed, we have not argued that this position directly conflicts with the explicit teaching of the Reformation confessions. The only Reformation confession that explicitly condemns some form of golden-age Postmillennialism is the *Second Helvetic Confession*, one of the historic standards of the Swiss Reformed churches, written by Heinrich Bullinger.[1]

This should serve as a caution against any exaggerated criticism of the postmillennial view among those who hold to these Reformation confessions. Many who subscribe to the *Westminster Confession of Faith*, for example, have advocated one or another form of postmillennial teaching. In doing so, they have not contradicted or compromised any part of the biblical system of doctrine summarized in this confession. Though the Reformation confessions are clearly

---

[1] See Chapter 9, note 22, for a quotation from this confession that condemns 'Jewish dreams that there will be a golden age on earth before the Day of Judgement'.

incompatible with Dispensational Premillennialism and, to a lesser degree, with Historic Premillennialism, they are compatible with the two forms of Postmillennialism we have identified as Amillennialism and golden-age Postmillennialism.[1] The debate between amillennialists and postmillennialists, accordingly, is an intramural one. The differences between these views are on the order of differences of theological emphasis within a common confessional bond.

Second, these criticisms of golden-age Postmillennialism should not be misunderstood as an argument for a pessimistic and limited expectation for the gospel of the kingdom in this present age. The objections are aimed at the view that looks for a distinct period in history during which the gospel will prevail upon the earth. This does not mitigate the often legitimate insistence among postmillennialists that we have the greatest possible confidence in the victory of Christ's cause in history.

Too often the position known as Amillennialism has been associated with a pessimistic view of history. In this view, the expectation is often that things will inevitably go from bad to worse throughout the course of history. If the church does not grow in number, or the standards of God's kingdom are not acknowledged in society, the response is often one of resignation and defeat. Expectations for the growth and triumph of Christ's kingdom are diminished. Little interest or attention is given to the claims of Christ as king in all areas of life.

---

[1] As noted earlier, D. H. Kromminga, professor of church history at Calvin Theological Seminary, brought a request to the synod of the Christian Reformed Church in the 1940s regarding Historic Premillennialism. Kromminga raised the question whether his view was in keeping with the Three Forms of Unity, particularly the statement in the *Belgic Confession*, Article 37, which speaks of the number of the elect being 'complete' at the return of Christ. It does seem that the historic premillennialist position is incompatible with the statement to which Kromminga referred in Article 37.

The foregoing criticisms of Postmillennialism should not be misunderstood as an endorsement of this pessimistic and cramped view of the cause of Christ's kingdom during this present age. There are ample biblical arguments for the most robust expectation for the success of the gospel. Christians ought to be people who live under the banner of Christ's commission, 'All authority has been give to Me in heaven and on earth; go therefore and make disciples of all the nations.' They ought to live out of the full expectation that Christ shall have dominion throughout all the earth, that the nations will undoubtedly be given to him as his rightful inheritance. They ought to seek the kingdom of God and its righteousness in every area of Christ's dominion. Nothing less than the bringing of every thought captive to Christ will satisfy. Nothing less than the subjection of all things to the will and reign of Christ will do. The problem with golden-age Postmillennialism is not that it has emphasized these things. The problem is that it has not also provided a balanced account of other biblical themes.[1]

---

[1] I noted previously the notorious difficulty of labelling different millennial views. If I were to label my own position, I would prefer to call it an 'optimistic Amillennialism'. No doubt, many postmillennialists would view this as an oxymoron.

PART SIX

The Future of All Things

13

The Resurrection of the Body

I N RECENT CHAPTERS, we have been occupied with that part of general eschatology that focuses upon the so-called 'signs of the times' and the millennial reign of Christ. These issues relate to the Bible's characterization of the present age, the interval between Christ's first and second advents. They identify the Bible's understanding of how God's redemptive purposes in Christ will unfold prior to the great event on the horizon of all history – the coming again of Christ at the end of the age. Though we have undoubtedly left a number of loose threads in our consideration of these issues, the time has come to take up the last part of general eschatology, namely, the things that will accompany the return of Christ at the end of the age.

The events that we are going to consider are aptly termed 'concomitants of the second advent' by Charles Hodge in his *Systematic Theology*.[1] Though this term is rather abstract, it nicely captures the idea: we are looking at those events that, according to the Scriptures, will accompany Christ's return

[1] Vol. III (Grand Rapids: Eerdmans, 1952), 'Concomitants of the Second Advent', pp. 837–880.

at the end of the age. The Bible teaches that when Christ returns, his reign as king will be consummated by a series of great acts of redemption and judgement. These events will draw this present age to a close and consummate God's purposes in the history of redemption. They will introduce the final and enduring state of God's kingdom.

The events that we will consider are: the resurrection of the dead, the just and the unjust; the final judgement by Christ of all human beings; the eternal punishment of the unbelieving and wicked in hell; and the creation of a new heavens and earth. In this chapter, we will treat the first of these events. We will do so in the light of the Word of God, mindful that especially on these subjects, when we stray from the sure path laid out in the Word, we are bound to go off in directions that are speculative and uncertain.

Biblical Themes regarding the Resurrection

Since we have touched upon this event before, especially in connection with our treatment of the intermediate state, it may be helpful to recall what has been said.

We have noted that the biblical expectation for the future of believers is not primarily focused upon what is often called the intermediate state. Although the Bible teaches that the believer's fellowship with Christ cannot be broken even by death itself, and that at death the believer will begin to enjoy a more intimate fellowship with Christ (2 Cor. 5:1-9), that is not its main emphasis. Much less is it the immortality of the soul. The spotlight of the Bible falls upon the resurrection of the body, that is, the restoration and renewal of the whole person, body and soul, in a renewed state of integrity within the context of a new heavens and earth.

This is, in fact, one of the distinctive features of the biblical view of the future and of the salvation that is obtained for us in Christ.[1] The biblical account of creation records

---

[1] In many dualistic worldviews which sharply distinguish the spiritual and the material (Manichaeism, some forms of ancient Greek philosophy), and in many monistic worldviews that deny the ultimate

that the Triune God created Adam a 'living soul', formed from the dust of the earth (*Gen.* 2:7). Our creatureliness in its wholeness and integrity always includes the body, which was created originally good. Redemption from the curse of God against sin likewise addresses the whole of our need, body and soul. This is the reason the Reformation confession, the *Heidelberg Catechism*, speaks of the believer's comfort in terms of belonging to Christ 'with body and soul'. Redemption does not deny the integrity and goodness of creation; it rather brings the healing and renewal of creation. The same Lord who forgives all our sins is the One who 'heals all our diseases', including that sickness of body and soul that leads to death (*Psa.* 103:3). Thus, no biblical picture of the believer's future may fail to include as a central part the promise of the resurrection of the body.

I. The timing of the resurrection

Though this expectation is commonly acknowledged by Christian believers whose belief is in accord with the teaching of Scripture, one matter often disputed is the timing of the resurrection. As we have seen in previous chapters, Premillennialism teaches two distinct resurrections, one of the just and the other of the unjust. The resurrection of the just will occur at the time of Christ's coming before the millennium, and the resurrection of the unjust will not occur until after.[1]

---

reality of the material world (Gnosticism, Hinduism, Buddhism), the teaching of a resurrection of the body has no legitimate or proper place. The biblical teaching of the resurrection of the body has an appropriate home within the framework of the biblical understanding of creation and redemption, with redemption as a restoration and renewal, and not a denial, of creation.

[1] This is to state the matter perhaps too simply. Dispensational premillennialists speak of at least two additional resurrections: the resurrection of those saints who experience tribulation in the seven-year period between Christ's coming 'for' and his coming 'with' his saints; and the resurrection of the millennial saints at the conclusion of the millennium. See the *New Scofield Reference Bible* (1967), notes on 1 Corinthians 15:52, Revelation 19:19; 20:4, 10.

The most decisive objection against the separation in time of these resurrections is its incompatibility with the common association in the Scriptures of the resurrection of the just with that of the unjust. In one of the few direct references to the resurrection in the Old Testament, Daniel 12:2, we read that 'many of those who sleep in the dust of the ground will awake, these to everlasting life, but the others to disgrace and everlasting contempt'. In this passage, the resurrections of believer and unbeliever are closely linked.

A similar linking is reflected in Jesus' words to his disciples in John 5:28–29: 'Do not marvel at this; for an hour is coming, in which all who are in the tombs shall hear His voice, and shall come forth; those who did the good deeds to a resurrection of life, those who committed the evil deeds to a resurrection of judgement.' Jesus speaks of one great event in which all of the dead will be raised for the purpose of judgement. Though some premillennialists suggest that this reference to an hour might include a long period of time – appealing to the use of 'hour' in verse 25 of the same chapter where it refers to the period in which the spiritually dead shall be brought to life – its meaning in these verses parallels its common meaning in the Gospel of John (see 7:30; 8:20; 12:23; 13:1; 16:21; 17:1). It refers to a distinct period in which God's purposes will be fulfilled. As in other Scripture passages (*Acts* 24:14–15, *Matt.* 16:27; 25:31–33, 2 *Cor.* 5:10), the teaching of this passage affirms that the resurrection of all the dead, believers and unbelievers alike, will occur at a single point of time in the future.

Moreover, the passage most often cited by premillennialists in support of their view of two distinct resurrections, one before and one after the millennium, shows evidence that the resurrection and judgement will include all people, believers and unbelievers. In Revelation 20:1–15, the vision of the final 'great white throne judgement' that will occur after the millennium portrays 'the dead, the great and the small, standing before the throne' (verse 12). These dead include not only the great and small, but also all those 'given up' by the sea, death and Hades. All of these dead are then judged, 'every one of them according to their deeds' (verse 13). As a consequence of this judgement, death and Hades, and 'anyone's name [that] was not found written in the book of life', are thrown into the lake of fire, the second death. The description of the resurrection and judgement given in this vision implies that all people are embraced and only those among them whose names are written in the Lamb's book of life are saved from the lake of fire. Were the vision only describing the resurrection and judgement of those whose names were not written in the book of life, the language describing this vision would be confusing at best, misleading at worst.

In addition to these passages which clearly associate the resurrection of the just and the unjust, other passages teach that the resurrection of believers will occur on the last day, when Christ will be revealed from heaven and the sound of the trumpet will be heard. The implication of this language is that this event will conclude the present age. With the resurrection of the believer, the last great event will be accomplished which brings to a close Christ's work of redemption. In John 6:40, Jesus assures his disciples that he came in fulfilment of his Father's will and purpose, and that it was his Father's will 'that everyone who beholds the Son and believes in Him, may have eternal life; and I Myself will raise him up on the last day'. In the passage which speaks of the rapture, 1 Thessalonians 4:13–18, the coming of Christ and the resurrection of believers are associated with the call of the Archangel and the sound of the trumpet (verse 16; see also *Matt.* 24:31, *1 Cor.* 15:52). According to these passages, when Christ comes and the dead in Christ are raised, this will close the present age and introduce the glory of the age to come (see *Phil.* 3:20–21, *1 Cor.* 15:23).

Often, those who insist upon two resurrections separated in time will appeal to the language of 1 Thessalonians 4:16

and 1 Corinthians 15:23–24. These passages describe a certain precedence and order among the events of Christ's coming, the resurrection of believers, and the coming of the end of the age. According to the premillennialist, this precedence and order confirms the distinction between two resurrections. However, neither of these passages affords a convincing case for this position. When the Apostle Paul in 1 Thessalonians 4:16 speaks of the dead in Christ rising first, he is not drawing a contrast between the resurrection of believers and of unbelievers, but rather between the resurrection of the dead, those who have fallen asleep in Jesus, and the rapture of believers who are still living at the time of Christ's coming. Far from being excluded from the benefit of Christ's coming, those who have fallen asleep in him will have pre-eminence – they will rise first. Furthermore, as we have previously argued, the order described in 1 Corinthians 15:23–24 – 'Christ the first fruits, after that those who are Christ's at His coming, then comes the end' – is not an order that allows for an intervening period of one thousand years between Christ's coming and the end. The events described, though they occur in a definite order, are components of one great complex of events at the end of the age.

II. THE AUTHOR OF THE RESURRECTION

The more important and difficult questions relating to the Bible's teaching regarding the resurrection have to do with its author and nature. Who will be responsible for raising the dead at the end of the age? And, when we read that the dead will be raised prior to the judgement, how are we to understand this event? In what sense will even the unjust be raised from the dead? What will be the nature of the resurrection body?

It must be admitted that the Bible does not provide a complete description to answer all of these and other questions.[1]

---

[1] For example, the Bible says very little about the resurrection of unbelievers other than to affirm that it will occur. That unbelievers will be raised has already been shown from the passages cited above

Some things are clearly taught to encourage and comfort believers. Others remain shrouded in mystery.

Though the Old Testament includes explicit references to the resurrection of believers (*Isa.* 26:19, *Dan.* 12:2), and though the expectation of the resurrection follows from all that the Lord promises his covenant people in the way of blessing,[1] it is only in the New Testament that the full light of the gospel promise of the resurrection shines. This should not surprise us, since the biblical teaching and hope for the resurrection is securely founded upon the great redemptive accomplishments of Christ in his death, resurrection and ascension to the Father's right hand. As believers are united with Christ, they come to enjoy him and all his blessings, most notably victory over death and the sure confidence of the resurrection of the body.

In spite of this clear focus upon Christ's resurrection and the believer's share in it, the New Testament makes it clear that the author of this resurrection is the Triune God, Father, Son, and Holy Spirit. Each Person of the Trinity plays an integral part in the granting of resurrection life to those who belong to Christ. When Jesus responds to the Sadducean

---

(for example, *John* 5:28, 29, *Acts* 24:15). This resurrection is not an act of Christ as Redeemer, but an act of Christ as Judge. Unbelievers are raised in order that they might be judged and consigned to punishment. Believers are raised in order that they might fully share in all the blessings of salvation that are theirs through fellowship with Christ, the Mediator.

[1] See, for example, *Exod.* 3:6 (compare *Matt.* 22:29–32); *Psa.* 16:10; 17:15; 49:15; 73:24, 25, *Prov.* 23:14, *Hos.* 6:1–2, *Ezek.* 37:1–13. Without denying the progressive disclosure of the truth regarding the resurrection, or the radical significance of Christ's victory over death in his resurrection, we see that the great comfort of the covenant of grace, salvation and life in fellowship with the living Lord, already carried the implicit promise of the ultimate defeat of death as the wages of sin. However dim and sketchy may have been their view of it, Old Testament saints are typified in the faith of Abraham who 'was looking for the city, whose architect and builder is God' (*Heb.* 11:10; 13–16, 19).

denial of the resurrection, he ascribes the power to grant resurrection life to God: 'You are mistaken, not understanding the Scriptures, or the power of God. For in the resurrection they neither marry, nor are given in marriage, but are like angels in heaven' (*Matt.* 22:29–30). The Apostle Paul likewise in 2 Corinthians 1:9 describes believers as those who should not trust in themselves but 'in God who raises the dead'. In other passages, the resurrection of the dead is ascribed especially to the power and work of Christ. In John 5, it is the Son of God who together with the Father calls the dead from their tombs and grants them life (verses 21, 25, 28–29). This authority to raise the dead is, according to the teaching of Christ, a pre-rogative granted to him by the Father and a fruit of his saving work (*John* 6:38–40, 44–45; 11:25–26). Furthermore, the Holy Spirit, who applies and communicates the benefits of Christ's saving work, gives believers a foretaste and share in the power of Christ's resurrection. The same Spirit 'who raised Jesus from the dead' dwells in believers and grants life to their 'mortal bodies' also (*Rom.* 8:11). Thus, as believers share in the benefits which are theirs in fellowship with Christ, they are promised the gift of resurrection from the dead, a gift which the Father is pleased to grant through the Son and in the power of the life-giving Spirit.

This, of course, leaves us with the crucial question yet to be answered: what does it mean to be raised from the dead? What is the nature of the resurrection body, so far as this is disclosed to us in the Scriptures? If the return of Christ will be accompanied by the resurrection of the dead, the just and the unjust alike, and if the resurrection of believers in fellow-ship with Christ is a gracious work of the Triune God, it remains to be seen what the Scriptures teach about the charac-ter of this event.

The Nature of the Resurrection Body

We can arrive at an answer to this question in two ways. One way would be to focus upon the accounts of Christ's resurrection to see what they might tell us. Since the believer's resurrection body will be fashioned after the pattern of Christ's glorious body (*Phil.* 3:20–21), this is one legitimate way to proceed. Another way would be to consider those passages that speak directly of the nature of the resurrection body.

Careful study of the accounts of Christ's resurrection and subsequent appearances to his disciples allows us to draw some conclusions regarding the nature of the resurrection body.

The accounts of the resurrection, for example, consistently witness to the fact that the tomb in which the Lord's body was laid was, by virtue of his being raised from the dead, now empty (*Matt.* 28:6, *Mark* 16:6, *Luke* 24:3, 6, *John* 20:1–10). The same body in which the Lord suffered and was crucified is now raised and glorified. The truth of the empty tomb authenticates that the resurrection was not a spiritual event separable from what happened to Jesus' body in the tomb. There is a genuine continuity between Jesus' pre-resurrection and post-resurrection body (not bodies).

Consequently, when the risen Lord appeared to his disciples after the resurrection, they were able (despite their perplexity and initial unbelief at times) to recognize him, identify the marks of his crucifixion, and even enjoy a meal with him (see *Matt.* 28:9, 17, *Mark* 16:9–14, *Luke* 24:11, 16, 31, *John* 20:19–23, 27–29). In the Gospel of Luke, all doubt as to the reality of the Lord's resurrection body is removed when we read the Lord's words of rebuke to his startled disciples who thought that they were seeing a spirit: 'Why are you troubled, and why do doubts arise in your hearts? See My hands and My feet, that it is I Myself; touch Me and see, for a spirit does not have flesh and bones as you see that I have' (*Luke* 24:38–39).

Though we need to beware of the temptation to draw too many hard and fast conclusions from these accounts, it does seem clear that, whatever the differences in the body of Christ before and after the resurrection, there is a substantial and real continuity.[1] In addition to these accounts of the resurrection of Jesus Christ, a few passages speak more directly of the nature of the resurrection body.

In 2 Timothy 2:18, the Apostle Paul alludes to false teachers in the early church who taught that the resurrection had 'already taken place'. These teachers apparently spiritualized the resurrection and were confusing believing people. In Philippians 3:20–21 the Apostle Paul likewise makes an important comment on the resurrection: 'For our citizenship is in heaven, from which also we eagerly wait for a Savior, the Lord Jesus Christ; who will transform the body of our humble state into conformity with the body of His glory, by the exertion of the power that He has even to subject all things to Himself.' This passage not only establishes the important principle that the believer's resurrection body will be conformed to Christ's, but it also contrasts the humble condition of our present bodies with the glorious condition that will be ours in the resurrection. Our present bodies exhibit all the marks of sin and God's curse – they are weak, decaying, fragile, and temporary. Our resurrected bodies will exhibit all of the marks and benefits of Christ's saving work – they will be strong, incorruptible, indestructible, and enduring.

A similar contrast is drawn in 2 Corinthians 5:1–9, where the believer's present body is described as an 'earthly tent'

---

[1] Some of these differences are suggested in the Gospel of John. When Mary Magdalene first recognized the risen Lord and clung to him, John records the Lord's words to her: 'Stop clinging to Me, for I have not yet ascended to the Father.' Subsequently, when the disciples were gathered on the evening of the day of Christ's resurrection and 'the doors were shut . . . for fear of the Jews', Jesus suddenly comes and stands in their midst. Similarly, in the other accounts of Jesus' resurrection appearances, he comes and goes at will. Too much should not be made of these accounts, so far as the nature of Christ's resurrection body is concerned. The circumstances are unique. Christ is in a transitional period between the time of his resurrection and ascension/glorification at the Father's right hand. However, these accounts allow us to see that it is the same Jesus who is now alive. And yet he now exists in the glory and power of the resurrection.

that, after it is dissolved or torn down, is replaced by a 'building from God, a house not made with hands, eternal in the heavens' (verse 1). This passage then goes on to utilize another metaphor. Just as the present body compares to the resurrection body as an earthly tent compares to a heavenly building, so the present body compares to the resurrection body as a being-clothed-with-mortality compares to a putting-on-the-clothing-of-immortality.

However, the one passage which draws the contrasts between the present body and the resurrection body most extensively is 1 Corinthians 15:35–49. Because of the importance of this passage to our understanding of the nature of the resurrection body, we will quote it in full and then make some observations upon it.

> But someone will say, 'How are the dead raised? And with what kind of body do they come?' You fool! That which you sow does not come to life unless it dies; and that which you sow, you do not sow the body which is to be, but a bare grain, perhaps of wheat or of something else. But God gives it a body just as He wished, and to each of the seeds a body of its own. All flesh is not the same flesh, but there is one flesh of men, and another flesh of beasts, and another flesh of birds, and another of fish. There are also heavenly bodies and earthly bodies, but the glory of the heavenly is one, and the glory of the earthly is another. There is one glory of the sun, and another glory of the moon, and another glory of the stars; for star differs from star in glory. So also is the resurrection of the dead. It is sown a perishable body, it is raised an imperishable body; it is sown in dishonor, it is raised in glory; it is sown in weakness, it is raised in power; it is sown a natural body, it is raised a spiritual body. If there is a natural body, there is also a spiritual body. So also it is written, "The first man, Adam, became a living soul." The last Adam became a life-giving spirit. However, the spiritual is not first, but the natural; then the spiritual. The first man is from the earth, earthy; the second man is from heaven. As is the earthy, so also are those who are earthy; and as is the heavenly, so also are

those who are heavenly. And just as we have borne the image of the earth, we shall also bear the image of the heavenly.

Recognizing the complexity and richness of this passage, we nevertheless see several themes relating to the primary question with which the Apostle Paul is concerned – 'with what kind of body do they come?'

First, the apostle uses the metaphor of the seed that is sown and its eventual germination and bringing forth of fruit to illustrate the connection between the present body and the resurrection body. However great the difference between the seed sown and the fruit that it eventually bears, the seed and the fruit are of one kind. The apostle elaborates at some length upon the obvious differences in the kinds of flesh that distinguish various creatures. The resurrection of the body is likened to the dying of a seed in order that it might come to life in the form of its fruit. This means that the resurrection body is of a distinctively human kind. When God raises believers from the dead, their bodies, however new and changed, remain distinctively and peculiarly human, according to their kind.

Second, a series of contrasts are drawn between what the apostle terms this natural or earthly body and the spiritual or heavenly body. These terms do not contrast a body that is made up of 'material stuff' with a body that is made up of 'spiritual stuff', as if to suggest that the resurrection body will be immaterial or non-fleshly. Rather, they distinguish sharply the present body as one which belongs to the present age which is passing away and under the curse of God, and the resurrection body which belongs to the life of the Spirit in the age to come. The distinction is not between material and immaterial, but between two kinds of bodies that answer to the present age and the age to come. The apostle bases his description of these two bodies upon the two respective heads of humanity – the first man, Adam, and the second man, Christ.

What is especially important for our purpose is to note the four contrasts that are drawn between the natural and the spiritual body. The earthly body of this present age is sown perishable; the heavenly body of the age to come is raised imperishable. When death, the final enemy, has been defeated and the consequences of sin and God's curse have been removed, the liability of the body to perishing, to decay and corruption, to dissolution, will be vanquished. The earthly body is sown in dishonour; the heavenly body will be raised in glory. In contrast to the tarnished and dimmed condition of the present body, the resurrection body will be splendid and striking. The earthly body is sown in weakness; the resurrection body will be raised in power. The fragility and vulnerability to destruction of the present body will be replaced by the enduring and indestructible power of the resurrection body. And finally, the present body is natural; the resurrection body is heavenly. All of these contrasts combine to paint a striking picture of the glory of the resurrection body with which believers will be clothed at the last day. This body will be of a human kind, to be sure, but not like anything believers have seen or known in this life – a body no longer ravaged by sin and its consequences, a body that will be a fit and enduring building in which to dwell and enjoy unbroken (and unbreakable) fellowship with Christ and those who are his.

Third, in the closing section of this passage, the apostle bases his description of these respective bodies upon the contrast between the two original bearers of these bodies – the first man, Adam, and the second man, Christ. There is an intimate and close correspondence between the first man, Adam, who is 'from the earth', and the earthly bodies of those who bear his image. Likewise, there is an intimate and close correspondence between the second man, Christ, who is 'from heaven', and the heavenly bodies of those who bear his image. Adam and Christ represent two humanities. The first humanity is under the dominion and liability of sin, meaning it is subject to perishing, dishonour, weakness and death. The second humanity is under the dominion and blessing of salvation, meaning it is the recipient of imperishability, glory, power and never-ending life.

This passage, though in a more extensive and detailed manner, confirms the teaching of the Scriptures elsewhere on the nature of the resurrection. When Christ returns at the end of the age, the dead will be raised. Some, the unjust and unbelieving, will be raised unto judgement. Others, the just and believing, those who belong to Christ, will be raised unto glory. The nature of this resurrection will be like a seed that is sown and dies, and is raised, according to its kind, in newness of life. The resurrection body of believers will be conformed to that of Christ's glory. It will not be wholly dissimilar to the present body, but will have similarity and continuity. It will be the body as it has been raised or glorified, not an altogether new and unrelated body. Furthermore, it will be a real body, material and fleshly, not immaterial and spiritual so as to deny the continuity between the present body and the resurrection body. However, this body will be so conformed to the image and glory of Christ that no vestige of the power and destructive effects of sin will remain. As the apostle so eloquently puts it at the close of 1 Corinthians 15: 'But when this perishable will have put on the imperishable, and this mortal will have put on immortality, then will come about the saying that is written, 'Death is swallowed up in victory. O Death, where is your victory? O death, where is your sting?' The sting of death is sin, and the power of sin is the law; but thanks be to God, who gives us the victory through our Lord Jesus Christ' (verses 54–57).

The Resurrection/Renewal of All Things

Another concomitant of the second advent of Christ is the renewal of all things, the cleansing of this sin-cursed creation and the (re-)creation of a new heaven and earth. Though we will address this subject further in our final chapter, the relation of the resurrection of the body to this renewal of the creation merits brief attention here. The continuity between the pre- and post-resurrection body of the believer finds its counterpart in the continuity between the present and the renewed creation.

In the biblical understanding of the future, the resurrection glory of the believer will coincide with what might be called the resurrection glory of the new creation. Not only do these realities coincide, but they are also closely linked in their significance. If the salvation of believers includes the restoration of body and soul to a state of integrity and wholeness, then it must also include the full restoration of the creation. Just as Adam was originally formed from the dust of the earth and placed within the creation-temple of God in which to serve and glorify the Creator, so also in redemption the new humanity will be restored to a life and service under the headship and dominion of the second Adam, in a newly cleansed creation temple.

For this reason, Romans 8:18–23 describes the creation as being under the same 'slavery of corruption' that afflicts believers in their present bodies of humiliation. The term used to describe the corruption of creation in Romans 8 is used in 1 Corinthians 15:42, 50 to describe the corruption of the body. The creation's present groaning under the power and curse of sin mirrors the groaning of the believer. The creation itself likewise waits eagerly for the revelation of the sons of God, because the redemption of God's children is a redemption in which the creation itself participates. The future liberation of creation from its present corruption and bondage will occur only in conjunction with the believer's liberation from corruption and death. The link between the resurrection of the believer and the renewal of the creation is an intimate one. The renewal of the creation is the only context or environment within which the resurrection glory of believers in fellowship with Christ can be appreciated and understood. Without the glorification of the creation, the glorification of the new humanity in Christ would be an isolated and strange event.

This intimate link between the believer's resurrection and the renewal of the creation allows us to see the unity between individual and general (or cosmic) eschatology. It also joins together the salvation of the church and her members with the great events of cosmic renewal that will accompany Christ's return at the end of the age. Indeed, in a legitimate sense, the justification and sanctification of the believer find their parallels in the justification and sanctification of the heavens and earth in the new creation. Just as the Lord declared the first creation in its state of integrity very good (*Gen.* 1:31), so the renewed creation will be worthy of the same judgement. And just as the first creation was perfect and holy in its consecration to the Lord, so the renewed creation will be one 'wherein dwells righteousness' (see *2 Pet.* 3:10–13). Justified and sanctified saints will dwell in a justified and sanctified creation. A people holy unto the Lord, a royal priesthood, will enjoy fellowship with the Lord in the sanctuary of his renewed creation.[1]

A Recent Debate

Two further issues remain to be addressed regarding the resurrection of the body. The first issue concerns a recent debate within North American evangelicalism respecting the resurrection of the body, a debate provoked by the writings of Murray J. Harris, professor of New Testament Exegesis and Theology at Trinity International University, Deerfield, Illinois. This debate has raised in a fresh way a number of

---

[1] Previously, I noted that Norman Shepherd in his article, 'The Resurrections of Revelation 20' (*Westminster Theological Journal,* 37/1 [Fall, 1974], pp. 34–43), links the first resurrection enjoyed by believers in fellowship with Christ with the implied second resurrection which he takes to be the creation of the new heavens and earth. This linking of two resurrections, one of the believer and the other of the creation itself, is warranted by the teaching of passages like Romans 8:18–23 (compare *2 Pet.* 3:13, *Rev.* 21:1, *1 Cor.* 15:42, 50).

important questions regarding the resurrection of the body. The second issue has to do with some of the pastoral questions that often arise in connection with the biblical teaching regarding the resurrection.

The recent debate regarding the nature of the resurrection body provides an interesting test case on the doctrine of the resurrection.[1] Though a number of parties played a role in this debate, the two most important antagonists were Murray J. Harris and Norman Geisler, Dean of Southern Evangelical Seminary, Charlotte, North Carolina. Not only Geisler charged that Harris' doctrine was heretical; he was also joined by a number of cult-watching groups that compared Harris' views with those of the cults, particularly the Jehovah's Witnesses.

In a number of works on the subject of the resurrection, Harris described the resurrection body of Jesus as being 'immaterial', 'nonfleshly', and 'invisible'.[2] Though Harris

---

[1] For a brief and popular account of the debate, see 'Trinity Prof Attacked for Resurrection Teaching', *Christianity Today*, 36/13 (9 November 1992), p. 62; and 'The Mother of All Muddles', *Christianity Today*, 37/4 (5 April 1993), pp. 62–66. It should be observed that Harris has been exonerated of the charge of heresy by his institution, denomination (Evangelical Free), and a committee of evangelical theologians. In the same issue of *Christianity Today* Harris adds, 'But let me go on record as saying if I were starting over again, there are words that I would not use. One is the word 'immaterial', because it's so open to misunderstanding; and another would certainly be that phrase 'essentially immaterial', because it's like a red flag to a neo-Thomist.' A Reaffirmation statement was issued in 1996 by the Evangelical Free Church of America which basically resolved this long controversy. Norman Geisler has noted that the matter has been resolved, in his estimation, by the EFCA Reaffirmation Statement (see *Christian Research Journal* [Summer 1996], p. 45).

[2] Harris has written extensively on the subject of the resurrection, the following sources being most important: *Raised Immortal: Resurrection and Immortality in the New Testament* (Grand Rapids: Eerdmans, 1985); *Easter in Durham: Bishop Jenkins and the Resurrection* (Exeter: Paternoster, 1985); and *From Grave to Glory* (Grand Rapids: Zondervan, 1990).

maintained that Jesus' resurrection body retains its essential humanity, even becoming visible and fleshly at will (for example, in the accounts of Jesus' post-resurrection appearances to the disciples), he insisted that the glorified body of Christ is significantly different in kind from the pre-resurrection body. The personal identity of Jesus Christ, according to Harris, is not imperilled, but through the resurrection the body of Christ has undergone a significant change. To say that the body of the risen Christ is fleshly or composed of 'flesh and bone' diminished the significance of the glorification that occurred through his resurrection.[1]

Furthermore, based upon his reading of 2 Corinthians 5, Harris argued that believers receive a 'resurrection body' during the intermediate state, while their physical bodies remain in the grave. When Christ returns, all believers, whether living or dead, will undergo a resurrection of the body in which their physical bodies will be transformed or raised from the grave as spiritual bodies like that of Christ.[2]

In his criticisms of Harris' position, Geisler objected to his teaching that believers will receive an interim resurrection body between death and resurrection at the last day, and to his teaching that the resurrection body is non-fleshly or immaterial.[3]

[1] The following statements from Harris' *Raised Immortal* are fairly representative of his view: 'An analysis of the Gospels suggests that the risen body of Jesus was unlike his pre-Easter body in some important respects. To begin with he was no longer bound by material or spatial limitations' (p. 53); 'The Resurrection marked his entrance upon a spiritual mode of existence, or, to borrow Pauline terminology, his acquisition of a 'spiritual body', which was both immaterial and invisible yet capable of interaction with the world of time and space' (pp. 57–8).

[2] *Raised Immortal*, pp. 44, 100.

[3] I am summarizing Geisler's criticism of Harris' view from the following of his writings: *The Battle for the Resurrection* (Nashville: Thomas Nelson, 1989); and 'In Defense of the Resurrection: A Reply to Criticisms, A Review Article', *Journal of the Evangelical Theological Society*, 34/2 (June, 1991), pp. 243–61.

With respect to Harris' suggestion that believers receive an interim resurrection body between the time of death and resurrection at the return of Christ, Geisler claimed that this is inconsistent with the biblical testimony that the resurrection of the body occurs at the time of Christ's return. Geisler also noted that, in the passage to which Harris appealed for his idea of an interim resurrection body, 2 Corinthians 5:1–9, the believer's circumstance at death is one that is variously described as being 'naked' (verse 3), 'unclothed' (verse 4), or 'absent from the body' (verse 8). These descriptions correspond to the common teaching of Scripture that, in the period between death and resurrection at the time of Christ's return, the believer is in a provisional state of fellowship with the Lord awaiting the future resurrection of the body.

With respect to Harris' view of the nature of the resurrection body, Geisler objected particularly to three distinct emphases: that the resurrection body of Christ is immaterial, that it is not numerically identical with his pre-resurrection body,[1] and that it is not a part of observable history.[2] According to Geisler, the biblical testimony and the confessions of the historic Christian church require that we affirm the material, the flesh-and-blood-nature, of the resurrection body. The continuity between the present and the resurrection body, furthermore, requires that we speak of the same body which dies being raised from the dead. When, for example, in 1 Corinthians 15:35–44, we read of the seed which dies and subsequently bears fruit, we can only conclude that there is a numerical identity between the body which is sown in

[1] Though this language tends to be rather abstract and obscure, the point Geisler is making is that the body of the risen Christ is not another body than the one in which he was crucified. Though this body has been glorified through the resurrection, it remains the same (numerically identical) body.

[2] 'In Defense of the Resurrection', pp. 247–8.

dishonour and raised in glory.[1] Furthermore, though it may be true that we do not acknowledge the truth of the resurrection apart from faith – it is not observable to the naked eye – this does not mean that the empty tomb and the resurrection appearances of Christ are non-observable features of some kind of trans- or non-historical reality.

Perhaps the most critical issue that emerged in the context of this debate between Harris and Geisler has to do with the confessions of the historic Christian church. Do these confessions tell us anything about the resurrection and the nature of the resurrection body that might help to clarify this debate and determine whose view lies closer to the truth?

The confessions do provide us with considerable help at this point and generally tend to favour the position espoused by Geisler in this debate. Familiar is the article in the Apostle's Creed that says, 'I believe in . . . the resurrection of the body.' What we often overlook, however, is that the historic language of this Creed was that of the resurrection of the flesh.[2] The language with which we are familiar, though unobjectionable and true in its own right, became the received text of the Creed only in 1543. In the original language of this Creed, the church deliberately sought to oppose any gnosticizing or spiritualizing tendency to minimize the reality of the resurrection. The *Belgic Confession*, one of the great confessions of the Protestant Reformation, affirms that 'all the dead shall be raised out of the earth, and their souls joined and united with their proper bodies in

---

[1] This is what Geisler has in mind when he uses the awkward expression, 'the numerical identity' of the pre- and post-resurrection body. He is not insisting that the body in each instance be made up of the same material 'particles', though this is possible and held by some Christian theologians. He is only insisting that it is the same body, that there is an identity of person, also bodily, between the believer before and after he undergoes the resurrection.

[2] In the Latin versions of the Creed, the term is *carnis*. In the Greek versions, the term is *sarx*. See Philip Schaff, *The Creeds of Christendom*, II:pp. 45–56.

which they formerly lived' (Article 37). In the *Thirty-Nine Articles* of the Church of England, Article 4, 'Of the Resurrection of Christ', declares: 'Christ did truly rise again from death, and took again his body, with flesh, bones, and all things appertaining to the perfection of man's nature, wherewith he ascended into heaven, and there sits, until he returns to judge all men at the last day.'[1] Similarly, the *Westminster Larger Catechism*, in its exposition of the resurrection of Christ, declares the following: 'Christ was exalted in his resurrection, in that, not having seen corruption in death . . . and having the very same body in which he suffered, with the essential properties thereof (but without mortality, and other common infirmities belonging to this life), really united to his soul, he rose again from the dead the third day by his own power' (Q. & A. 52).

A cursory reading of these classic confessional statements regarding the resurrection of the body, particularly the resurrection of Christ, shows their teaching to be that the resurrection body is substantially the same as the present body, at least insofar as it is material, or flesh and blood. The properties belonging naturally to the body remain true of the resurrection body, though all of those features of the 'body of our humiliation' (*Phil.* 3:21) that are owing to sin and God's curse are utterly removed. The viewpoint espoused by Harris, in other words, can find little or no support in the language and viewpoint of the historic confessions of the church. Consequently, the evidence seems to support the argument of Geisler that Harris' position deviated significantly from the orthodoxy of the historic church. To teach that the resurrection body is immaterial, that it is not composed of flesh and blood, that it is not the same or proper body of the dead, now raised in glory, and that it is unobservable and invisible – to teach any one, let alone all, of these emphases, is to

[1] Mark A. Noll, ed., *Confessions and Catechisms of the Reformation* (Grand Rapids: Baker Book House, 1991), p. 214.

compromise in important ways the doctrine of Scripture and the church.[1]

Pastoral Questions regarding the Resurrection of the Body

When we consider the Bible's teaching regarding the resurrection of the body, many pastoral questions arise. Most believers, when they face the reality of their own death or the death of fellow believers, unavoidably confront questions of this kind. Rather than ignore these questions, our treatment of the resurrection of the body will conclude with a consideration of some of them. Asking and answering these questions, of course, poses a great risk of going beyond what is taught in the Scriptures. However, many of these questions may be answered in terms of the Bible's teaching we have summarized and those 'good and necessary' consequences that follow from its teaching.

I. HOW SHOULD WE TREAT THE BODIES OF DECEASED BELIEVERS?

One question that often surfaces in the face of the death of believers is: how should we treat or regard the body of a deceased believer? Sometimes this question arises in the context of considering cremation or other alternatives to burial. On other occasions this question is provoked by the way fellow believers are comforted at a funeral home viewing with such words as, 'this is not your loved one, but only a body'. When this comfort is extended to believers, it is prompted by a genuine desire to assure those who mourn

[1] This being the case, it is troubling to note that even so trustworthy an expositor of biblical truth as J. I. Packer maintained that Harris' view was 'orthodox' and in accord with 'Scripture and with the consensus of the world church'. In this observation, Packer glossed over the language of the confessions that I have cited above, especially the language which speaks of the 'proper' or 'same' body, as well as of the 'flesh and bones' of the risen Christ. This is the language of historic confessional orthodoxy and it is precisely this language that Harris seemed to repudiate.

that death does not disrupt the fellowship we have with Christ, but ushers believers into the presence of the Lord with whom they are now 'at home'. However, it suggests something about the body of the person who has died that may not be altogether consistent with the hope for the resurrection of the body.

Upon the basis of our understanding of the Bible's teaching regarding the resurrection, it would seem to follow that Christians ought to treat the body of a deceased believer with the utmost respect and care. The way we view and handle, even the way in which we lovingly commit, the body of a believer to the grave, should testify to our convictions about the resurrection of the body. We should not be unaware, for example, that the practice of cremation in modern times originally arose out of an unbelieving denial of the resurrection of the body.[1] To say that the body of a believer is only a body, in no respect to be identified with the one who has died, is perhaps misleading. Because our redemption includes the restoration and reintegration of soul and body, the body remains essential to our identity. The comfort which is ours in the face of death is not simply that we go to be with the Lord, but that we anticipate seeing God 'in our flesh' (*Job* 19:26).

Support for this way of regarding the bodies of deceased believers is found in a remarkable statement in the *Westminster Larger Catechism* (Q. & A. 86). Speaking of the communion in glory of Christ and those united to him, this Catechism makes the following affirmation:

> The communion in glory with Christ, which the members of the invisible church enjoy immediately after death, is, in that their souls are then made perfect in holiness, and received into the highest heavens, where they behold the

[1] This comment is not intended to be a wholesale condemnation of the practice of cremation. Though I believe some biblical considerations militate against this practice, the subject is too complex to address adequately here.

face of God in light and glory, waiting for the full redemption of their bodies, which even in death continue united to Christ, and rest in their graves as in their beds, till at the last day they be again united to their souls.

II. WILL THE RESURRECTION BODY BE RECOGNIZABLY OUR OWN?

A question that sometimes arises in connection with the resurrection of the body and the final state is: will the resurrection body be recognizable? Sometimes it is maintained that fellow believers will not recognize one another in the new heavens and earth because this would be incompatible with the unimpaired joy of the final state. The recognition of one another, it is argued, would require the sad remembrance of sins committed in this present life and call attention to the absence of some who were not saved. Such recognition would also distract from the exclusive attachment to Christ, which surpasses all earthly relationships (including marriage and family relationships) as we now experience them. Some appeal to Jesus' teaching that in the kingdom of heaven 'they neither marry, nor are given in marriage, but are like angels in heaven' (*Matt.* 22:30). Does not the language of this passage – they are like the angels – require the conclusion that the resurrection body will be so unlike the present body as to be unrecognizable?

None of these arguments, however, can withstand careful scrutiny. When Jesus speaks, for example, of believers in the resurrection being 'like the angels', the point of comparison given in the context has to do with marriage and marriage relationships. Because there will be neither marrying nor giving in marriage, those who are raised in the resurrection will be in this sense like the angels. This should not be understood, however, to deny the continuing reality of the created difference between male and female. Nor does it require the conclusion that the personal identity of believers, including their bodily form and uniqueness, will be substantially altered. The biblical testimony to the resurrection appearances of our Lord Jesus Christ convincingly demonstrates that he was recognizable to the disciples. To maintain that the resurrection body would not be recognisably or identifiably our own militates against the biblical teaching of continuity between the present and resurrection body. Strictly speaking, were believers in the resurrection unrecognisable to one another in the wholeness of their persons, they would literally cease to be the persons they presently are. This would mean that in the resurrection our persons would not be restored or healed, but replaced by persons whose identity and form is wholly different from those of the present.[1]

Certainly it is difficult to imagine how believers can recognize one another and enjoy fellowship in the eternal state without their joy being impaired by the remembrance of sin in this present life. It is also somewhat difficult to imagine a circumstance in which, though family and marriage relationships in this life are not forgotten or unknown in the life to come, the institutions of marriage and family do not continue as they now exist. These difficulties notwithstanding, there are ample biblical and confessional reasons to insist that in the resurrection a mutual recognition and fellowship among believers and with Christ will be the perfection, not the denial, of this present life.

III. WHAT ABOUT THE RESURRECTION OF BODIES THAT HAVE BEEN UTTERLY DESTROYED?

In the light of a number of my comments in the preceding, some may be asking: what about the resurrection of bodies that have been utterly destroyed? If the resurrection body is in substantial continuity with the present body, if it is the 'self-

---

[1] For a defence of the identity and similarity of the present and future bodies of believers, see William Hendriksen, *The Bible on the Life Hereafter* (Grand Rapids: Baker, 1959), pp. 66–70; J. Aspinwall Hodge, *Recognition after Death* (New York: American Tract Society, 1889); and Charles Hodge, *Systematic Theology*, III: pp. 774–80. Some Bible passages seem to imply that this is the case: *Luke 16:19–31, Matt. 8:11, 1 Thess. 2:19–20, Isa. 14:12.*

same body', to use the language of the *Westminster Confession of Faith*, how can that be in the case of bodies that have been utterly annihilated? Indeed, the decay of the body after death, its return to the dust whence it came, compels the conclusion that, in many cases, the resurrection of the body represents an act on God's part that is tantamount to a new creation out of nothing.

The difficulty this question poses has to do with whether the material 'particles' or constituents of the present body must be identical with those of the resurrection body. Nothing in the biblical doctrine of the resurrection of the body requires that this be the case. It may be the case – after all, it is certainly possible that God could form the resurrection body from the same identical particles as the present body. But this need not be the case in order for a substantial and personal identity to exist between the present body and the resurrection body. We commonly regard our bodies as the selfsame bodies, even though they undergo considerable change through age and infirmities, even being composed wholly of new cells every several years. If our present bodies are one and the same with our bodies many years ago, then it would seem no problem to affirm the resurrection of the proper bodies of those whose earthly bodies have been wholly destroyed.

IV. WHAT ABOUT THE BODIES OF UNBORN CHILDREN, INFANTS OR THOSE WHO DIE PREMATURELY?

Another question that can arise in a pastoral context among believers is: what about the bodies of unborn children, or of infants and others who die prematurely? This question is related to a more fundamental question, namely, are believers justified in being confident of the salvation of their children?[1] However, I will restrict my comments to the issue

---

[1] For an affirmation of the salvation of the children of believing parents, see the *Canons of Dort*, I,17. The *Westminster Confession*

of the resurrection of the bodies of such children. The specific focus of this question is whether children, who die in a state of immature development, physically and otherwise, will be raised bodily in maturity.

If believers may be confident of the salvation of such children, then it follows that they too will share in the resurrection of the body. Since the final state is one of complete perfection and glorification, it must be the case that all who share in this perfection will do so in a state of full maturity. In the final state of God's eternal kingdom there will not be anything like the process of growth and maturation as we now know it. Just as they will neither marry nor be given in marriage, so there will be no distinction between adult and child, at least not as we now experience them. Hard as it may be for us to imagine, we should be confident as believers that we will enjoy fellowship with all the saints, including those children who die under the circumstances mentioned above, in the fullness of mature and perfected life.

---

speaks differently (though not contradictorily) of the salvation of 'elect infants' in Chap. x.3. For a balanced survey of the question of the salvation of children of non-believing parents, see Bavinck, *The Last Things*, pp. 164–6. Bavinck cites sympathetically the saying of Voetius, 'I would not wish to deny, nor am I able to affirm' (*nolim negare, affirmare non possum*). Such caution is preferable to the confident denial or affirmation of this possibility. Why presume to know more of God's purposes of redemption than he has been pleased to reveal? Though God ordinarily saves through the means of grace, and not apart from them, Reformed theologians have been hesitant historically to deny his freedom to save some in an extraordinary manner (see The Westminster Confession of Faith, x.3). For a defence of the doctrine of infant salvation by a conservative Reformed theologian, see B. B. Warfield, 'The Development of the Doctrine of Infant Salvation', in *The Works of Benjamin B. Warfield*, vol. 9, Studies in Theology (1932; repr. Grand Rapids: Baker, 1981, and Edinburgh: Banner of Truth, 1988), pp. 411–44.

v. WHAT ABOUT THE BODIES OF THOSE WITH SEVERE PHYSICAL AND
MENTAL IMPAIRMENTS?

One final question of a pastoral nature respecting the resurrection of the body is: what about the bodies of those with
severe physical and mental impairments? Obviously, this is a
question that many believers cannot but ask, when they and
fellow believers witness the ravages of sin and the curse upon
these bodies of our humiliation.

To this question, we have an answer in the familiar words
of Psalm 103:2–3: 'Bless the Lord, O my soul, and forget
none of His benefits; Who pardons all your iniquities, Who
heals all your diseases.' When the Lord wipes away every tear
from our eye, when he expels from his sanctified creation
every remainder of sin and its curse, when he grants us
bodies like unto the glorified body of the Lord Jesus Christ –
then we may be confident that the resurrection body, raised in
glory, will be beautiful in appearance and form, rid of every
defect and impairment which sin and the curse have brought.
Though it is unwise to speculate carelessly about all the
features of the resurrection body, it seems to follow from the
biblical testimony that these bodies will be altogether lovely
in every appropriate sense. What that means precisely, no
one knows. But that it will be so seems undeniable.

Conclusion

With these pastoral questions addressed, we come to the
close of our consideration of the biblical teaching regarding
the resurrection of the body. Surely we have not been able to
do this teaching justice. The testimony of the Scriptures to
the certainty of the resurrection is clear. However, many
things are not told us that we might like to know. It may even
be that in addressing some of these pastoral questions I have
exceeded the boundaries of what is given to us to know in the
Scriptures.

Perhaps enough has been said, however, to appreciate afresh the hope of which the Apostle Peter speaks in 1 Peter 1:3–5:

> Blessed be the God and Father of our Lord Jesus Christ, who according to His great mercy has caused us to be born again to a living hope through the resurrection of Jesus Christ from the dead, to obtain an inheritance which is imperishable and undefiled and will not fade away, reserved in heaven for you, who are protected by the power of God through faith for a salvation ready to be revealed in the last time.

14

The Final Judgement

M ANY OF US ARE PROBABLY FAMILIAR with the saying, 'There is nothing more certain than death and taxes'. Not only does this saying reveal an almost universal distaste for paying taxes, but it also reveals a grudging recognition that life, at least life in this body, eventually comes to an end. Though people are adept at finding ways to avoid the reality of death – in the United States, the industry dedicated to keeping people looking young takes in billions every year – no one can ultimately deny its certainty. Though taxes can be avoided by legal or illegal means, death cannot be. The evidence for this truth is compelling and inescapable.

However, there is another reality no less certain than death: the reality of the final judgement. The writer to the Hebrews, speaking of the second coming of Christ, remarks: 'And inasmuch as it is appointed for men to die once and after this comes judgement, so Christ also, having been offered once to bear the sins of many, shall appear a second time for salvation without reference to sin, to those who eagerly wait Him' (9:27–28). The final judgement is, like the resurrection of the body, an end-time event that will accompany the return of Christ at the close of this present period of history. Consequently, when Christians affirm their faith in the Apostles' Creed, they speak not only of the resurrection of the body but also of the return of Christ from heaven 'to judge the living and the dead'.

Questions regarding the Final Judgement

In our treatment of the resurrection of the body in the previous chapter, we began by noting several common themes in the Scriptures regarding this subject. In this chapter on the final judgement we will also begin by addressing several general aspects of the Scriptures' teaching, and then turn to a controversial subject – whether we may speak of differing degrees of reward granted to believers in connection with the final judgement.

I. THE TIMING AND NUMBER OF FINAL JUDGEMENT(S)

Among the first questions that arise regarding the Last Judgement are its time and whether there is more than one. Historic and dispensational premillennialists speak of several judgements, which are distinguishable according to their time, place and subjects. Though opinions differ a great deal among representatives of these views, the most common dispensationalist position speaks of four distinct judgements: the judgement of believers at the rapture; the judgement of Israel at the close of the seven-year period of tribulation; the judgement of the nations; and the 'great white throne judgement' at the close of the millennial age (*Rev.* 20:11–15).[1] The first three judgements precede the millennium, and the last follows. These distinct judgements are a necessary part of the premillennialist conception of the future. For instance, because Premillennialism distinguishes between the resurrection of believers before the millennium and the resurrection of unbelievers after the millennium, at least two distinct judgements are necessary.

[1] *The New Scofield Reference Bible*, notes on Matthew 25:32 and Revelation 20:12.

Once it is acknowledged, however, that the return of Christ will occur after the millennium of Revelation 20, no occasion remains for claiming that there will be more than one judgement. Furthermore, once it is acknowledged that the final judgement will occur after the resurrection of the body and in close association with it, then it follows that the final judgement will be a single event in which all are judged, believer and unbeliever alike, Jew as well as Gentile. Just as we have seen that the resurrection will be an event at the end of the age which embraces believer and unbeliever alike (*John 5:25–29*), so the final judgement will include all people. As the Apostle Paul says, 'For we must all appear before the judgement seat of Christ, that each one may be recompensed for his deeds in the body, according to what he has done, whether good or bad' (*2 Cor. 5:10*). When Christ describes the final judgement in Matthew 25, all the nations are judged together and the 'sheep' separated from the 'goats' (*Matt. 25:31–46*).[1]

Though it is evident that the final judgement will occur as a single event after the resurrection, it is not as clear from Scripture whether it will precede or follow the transformation of the creation at the end of the age. Some passages seem to suggest that the judgement will take place before the recreation of the heavens and earth (for example, *2 Pet. 3:7*). However, in other passages the final judgement is simply linked with the end of the present age (for example, *Matt. 13:40–43; 25:31–32, 2 Thess. 1:7–10*), without any indication that it will occur prior to the renewal of all things. In Revelation 20:12, it is suggested that the judgement will immediately follow the general resurrection: 'And I saw the

---

[1] The confessions of the Reformation typically speak of the final judgement as a single event at the close of the age that includes all people who have ever lived. See *Belgic Confession*, Article 37; *Heidelberg Catechism*, Lord's Day 19; *Westminster Confession of Faith*, Chapter xxxiii; and *Westminster Larger Catechism*, Questions 88–90.

dead, the great and small, standing before the throne, and books were opened; and another book was opened, which is the book of life; and the dead were judged from the things which were written in the books, according to their deeds.' In the sequence of Revelation 20, the great white throne judgement is followed by a series of visions which describe the new heavens and earth. Admittedly, as we had occasion to note earlier, the visions of Revelation are not arranged in a neat chronological order. The placement of the visions of the new heavens and earth after that of the great white throne judgement, however, does suggest that this may be the sequence of events at the end of the age: first, the resurrection, second, the final judgement, and third, the transformation of the creation.[1]

A question that sometimes surfaces, to which the Scriptures do not give a direct answer, has to do with the duration of the final judgement. Will the final judgement be a quick and relatively short event, or will it take place over a more extended period of time?[2] On several occasions, the Bible speaks of the final judgement as a day of judgement (see *Matt.* 7:22; 11:22, *2 Thess.* 1:10, *2 Tim.* 1:12). This language, however, should not be pressed to mean a literal period of one day. It may only be a way of referring to the peculiar period that will be marked off for the purpose of judgement. Just as the Scriptures speak of this as the 'day' of salvation (*Heb.* 3:7–19), a day is coming when all will be judged for what they have done in the body, whether good or bad.

[1] However, the sequence given in the *Belgic Confession*, Article 37, seems to be that the final judgement will follow the transformation or renewal of all things.

[2] The Jehovah's Witnesses' publication *Let God Be True* (New York: Watchtower Bible and Tract Society, 1952), p. 286, teaches that the final judgement will encompass the first one thousand years of the new world. There is no biblical basis for this teaching. Neither is there any basis for a related Jehovah's Witnesses' teaching that the final judgement will be based only upon those works done during the millennium.

II. Its necessity and purpose

One question regarding the final judgement is prompted by our earlier consideration of what we termed the 'intermediate state'. Since this state involves a provisional circumstance of blessedness for believers and of distress for unbelievers, it would seem that the final judgement serves no useful purpose for those who have died prior to Christ's return. Though judgement may be necessary for those who are living at Christ's return, this does not seem to be the case for those who have already entered by way of death into a provisional state that anticipates the judgement. What necessity or purpose is served by the final judgement of those who have already been shown to be saved or lost?

The problem with this question is that it treats the final judgement too much in terms of our ordinary understanding of what takes place in a human trial court with its process of reaching and pronouncing a verdict. The final judgement is a work of God, particularly a work of Christ, who has been appointed as judge. As a work of God, it cannot be understood as a process of investigation to determine the guilt or innocence of those judged, but rather as an occasion to pronounce and execute with divine authority the sentence that God alone can pass with perfect justice upon all who are judged. Since God knows all those who are his – indeed, he knows them from eternity (see *Eph.* 1:4, *Rom.* 8:29) – he is not discovering them by means of this final judgement. Rather, he is revealing his power and glory as the One who alone has the prerogative to judge his creatures and to declare their final destiny. In pronouncing and executing this judgement, God not only declares openly the final state of every person but dispenses his judgement and reward in a way that confirms his righteousness.

The descriptions of the final judgement found in Scripture and the confessions confirm this to be its purpose and necessity. A good example of this emphasis upon the final judgement as the occasion for God to manifest his glory in his work of judgement is found in the *Westminster Confession of Faith*, Chapter XXXIII.2:

> The end of God's appointing this day is for the manifestation of the glory of his mercy, in the eternal salvation of the elect; and of his justice, in the damnation of the reprobate, who are wicked and disobedient. For then shall the righteous go into everlasting life, and receive that fullness of joy and refreshing, which shall come from the presence of the Lord; but the wicked who know not God, and obey not the gospel of Jesus Christ, shall be cast into eternal torments, and be punished with everlasting destruction from the presence of the Lord, and from the glory of his power.

III. WHO WILL BE THE JUDGE?

One prominent and clear teaching of Scripture respecting the final judgement is that Christ will be the judge. Among those prerogatives that characterize the rule of Christ at the right hand of the Father is the prerogative to carry out the final judgement. In keeping with this biblical emphasis, the Apostles' Creed speaks of the return of Christ as his coming 'to judge the living and the dead'. The great work in which Christ will be engaged at his coming is the work of judgement, vindicating his people and the cause of the gospel, condemning all their and his enemies.

It belongs to Christ's office as king that he is granted the authority to carry out the final judgement (*Matt.* 28:18, *Phil.* 2:9, 10). In John 5:22–23 we read, 'For not even the Father judges anyone, but He has given all judgement to the Son, in order that all may honor the Son, even as they honour the Father.' Later in the same chapter, Christ closely associates the resurrection of the just and the unjust with his 'authority to execute judgement' (verse 27). At the close of his sermon on Mars Hill, the Apostle Paul declares that God 'has fixed a day in which He will judge the world in righteousness through a Man whom He has appointed, having furnished proof to all men by raising Him from the dead' (*Acts* 17:31). The Apostle Paul also speaks of the day of judgement as one on which all must appear 'before the judgement seat of Christ, that each one may be recompensed for his deeds in the body, according to what he has done, whether good or bad' (2 Cor. 5:10). Similarly, in the familiar description of the final judgement given in Matthew 25, the Lord Jesus Christ speaks of the time 'when the Son of Man comes in His glory, and all the angels with Him' to sit on 'His glorious throne' (verse 31; compare 2 Thess. 1:7–10). In these and other passages, it is unmistakably clear that the One who will judge and sit upon the throne of judgement is Christ himself.

The significance of this truth is captured well in the *Heidelberg Catechism's* answer to the question, 'What comfort is it to you that Christ shall come to judge the living and the dead?' 'That in all my sorrows and persecutions, with uplifted head I look for the very same Person who before has offered himself for my sake to the tribunal of God, and has removed all curse from me, to come as judge from heaven; who shall cast all his and my enemies into everlasting condemnation, but shall take me with all his chosen ones to himself into heavenly joy and glory.'[1] Though the coming of Christ in glory and power to judge the living and the dead is a fearful prospect for the wicked and unbelieving, it is an unspeakable comfort to those who have believed in him. In the day of Christ's coming, the unbelieving and impenitent will be condemned. But the people of God will receive from the judge, who is also the Saviour previously judged in their place, their vindication and rest.

Before taking up the next question, one wrinkle in the matter of who will be the judge invites comment. Some of the biblical descriptions of the final judgement suggest that believers and even the angels who serve the Lord will play a role in it. In 1 Corinthians 6:2–3, the Apostle Paul, in the context of his rebuke to the Corinthians who take fellow believers to court, reminds them that 'the saints will judge

[1] Lord's Day 19, Q. & A. 52.

the world' (verse 2). The vision of Revelation 20 also speaks of the 'judgement' that is given to those who reign with Christ during the millennium (verse 4). Similar descriptions of believers sharing in the work of judgement are found in other passages as well (e.g., *Psa.* 145:5–9, *Matt.* 19:28). What are we to make of these passages? What role do the saints and the angels play in Christ's work of judgement?

It is difficult to be explicit on this matter. Certainly, because Christ is the Mediator and Head of his people, they share fully in whatever honour or glory belongs to him. On the principle that believers are co-heirs with Christ of all things (*1 Cor.* 3:21–23), it follows that they have some part in his work of judgement. What that part might be remains unclear. Nothing that they might do could be done independently of what Christ will do, nor could their activity add something which is lacking in his work. Perhaps it is best to note simply that they share in the victory and glory that belong to Christ in his role as the judge. As to the involvement of the angels, it is best to restrict it to the kinds of things often mentioned in the biblical descriptions of the final judgement: their ministry is auxiliary and subordinate to that of Christ. To the angels is assigned the work of gathering the peoples together for the judgement and executing the judgement that is pronounced (for example, *Matt.* 13:41–2; 24:31; 25:31, *2 Thess.* 1:7).[1]

IV. WHO AND WHAT WILL BE JUDGED?

The fact that believers need not fear the final judgement because it will vindicate their faith and service to the Lord, does not mean that the final judgement will be only of those who are unbelieving and impenitent. The Scriptures teach that all will be judged, the just and the unjust. No one will be spared or excluded from this judgement when the books are opened and the verdict pronounced.

---

[1] On the role of believers and angels in the final judgement, see Bavinck, *The Last Things*, pp. 141–2.

THE PROMISE OF THE FUTURE

A number of Scripture passages refer to a judgement that will include all people who have ever lived. Some of these passages have been noted already in the preceding. For example, in Revelation 20:11–15 general references are made to 'the dead' (verses 12, 13). The language used in this passage to describe the outcome of the judgement suggests that these dead include both believers and others, who, because their names were not written 'in the book of life' (verse 15), are thrown into the lake of fire. According to the teaching of Romans 2:5–6, in the day of the 'revelation of the righteous judgement of God', every person will receive according to his or her works. The well-known description of the final judgement in Matthew 25 describes 'all the nations' being gathered before the throne of the Son of Man. These passages do not limit in any way those who will be judged. No one will be exempt from judgement.

All believers will therefore be subject to judgement. Though it is not one that they need to fear, it is a genuine judgement for them nonetheless. When in 2 Corinthians 5:10 the Apostle Paul speaks of 'we all' who must appear before the judgement seat of Christ, he is referring specifically to believers. Hebrews 10:30 states that 'the Lord will judge his people'. Writing to believers in Rome, the Apostle Paul admonishes them for judging their brothers, noting that 'we shall all stand before the judgement seat of God'. James 3:1 speaks of a more severe judgement to be applied to those believers who are teachers. And in 1 Peter 4:17, believers are even warned that judgement will 'begin with the household of God'. This liability to judgement, however, does not contradict the clear biblical teaching that believers have already passed out of death into life (*John* 5:24). Nor does it conflict with the confidence expressed in Romans 8:1, that there is 'now no condemnation for those who are in Christ Jesus' (*Rom.* 8:1). It simply means that in the day of judgement a verdict and pronouncement will be made regarding all people who have ever lived, including believers.

One question that has arisen has to do with whether all angels will also be subject to judgement. Some Scripture passages suggest that the disobedient or fallen angels will be liable to judgement (*2 Pet.* 2:4, *Jude* 6). These passages omit any reference to a corresponding judgement of the obedient angels, an omission that has led some to conclude that they are exempted from the judgement. However, one passage, 1 Corinthians 6:3, contains an intriguing reference to the judgement of angels. This passage does not specify whether these angels are obedient or disobedient. On the basis of this passage, it seems possible that all angels, obedient as well as disobedient, will be liable to the final judgement.[1] That all angels should be subject to judgement seems to be consistent with the general teaching of Scripture regarding its purpose. In this way, the justice of God's verdicts regarding all of his creatures will be clearly revealed for all to acknowledge.

If all will be judged – believers and unbelievers, (obedient and) disobedient angels – the question that naturally arises is: what will be judged? This question is especially pressing with respect to believers, because if they are to be judged for sins that are already forgiven, does this not suggest a double jeopardy? Why should the sins of believers, washed and blotted out through the blood of Christ, be brought forward at the final judgement in order to play a role in the pronouncement of God's judgement upon them?

The Scriptures are quite vigorous in their teaching that all will be judged for whatever they have done. This includes not only all thoughts, words and deeds, but also the hidden things. 2 Corinthians 5:10 speaks very broadly of the 'deeds

---

[1] The *Westminster Confession of Faith*, chapter xxxiii.1, seems to take the position that only disobedient or reprobate angels will be judged: 'In which day, not only apostate angels shall be judged, but likewise all persons that have lived upon earth shall appear before the tribunal of Christ.' See the *Westminster Larger Catechism*, Q. 90. The *Belgic Confession*, Article 37, says nothing about the judgement of angels, whether obedient or disobedient.

in the body, according to what he has done, whether good or bad'. Nothing is excluded. Matthew 25:35–40 specifically speaks of those things done to 'the least of these My brethren'. Revelation 20:12 speaks of the dead being judged 'from the things which were written in the books, according to their deeds' (compare *1 Cor.* 3:8, *1 Pet.* 1:17, *Rev.* 22:12). God will not overlook in the day of judgement those works done in accord with his will (*Eph.* 6:8, *Heb.* 6:10). Nor will he overlook the idle words spoken (*Matt.* 12:36), or the deeds which are 'now hidden in darkness' (*1 Cor.* 4:5). Just as all are judged, so all that they have done will be subject to judgement.

The more difficult aspect of this question relates to the propriety of a judgement of the works of believers. If believers are not liable any longer to condemnation, and if they are not fearful of the prospect of a final judgement, then it seems implausible that all of their works should be revealed on the day of judgement. Would not the judgement of these works risk bringing shame and embarrassment to believers whose sins are wholly covered and forgiven for the sake of Christ? And would not such shame and embarrassment be inconsistent with the believer's present confidence that his or her sins have been removed as far as east is from west (*Psa.* 103:12)?

In the following section, we will consider one part of the Scriptures' answer to this question: the reward for good works granted in connection with the final judgement. Clearly, if there is greater or lesser reward for works done by believers while in the body – as 1 Corinthians 3:10–15 seems to suggest – then the recognition of sinful and imperfect works, of greater and lesser obedience, will play a role in the final judgement of believers. To be sure, the final judgement is not an occasion for undoing the confidence that believers now enjoy. But that the works of believers will be judged is undeniable and may even serve as a legitimate encouragement for diligence and conscientiousness in fighting against sin in this life.

V. THE STANDARD OF JUDGEMENT

One critical aspect of the final judgement is the standard to be used to confirm the justice of the verdict pronounced. This will be the law and Word of God so far as these have been revealed to those who are judged. The standard will be the same for everyone: what has been revealed to them concerning God's will. However, because of the important difference in the extent and fullness of what has been revealed, the principle that will apply is that greater privilege brings greater responsibility. From those to whom much has been given, much will be required, whereas from those to whom little has been given, less will be required.

The principle of greater or lesser responsibility is set forth remarkably in Matthew 11:20–22. In this passage, Jesus severely rebukes the cities in which he had done many of his miracles:

> Woe to you Chorazin! Woe to you, Bethsaida! For if the miracles had occurred in Tyre and Sidon which occurred in you, they would have repented long ago in sackcloth and ashes. Nevertheless, I say to you, it shall be more tolerable for Tyre and Sidon in the day of judgement, than for you. And you, Capernaum, will not be exalted to heaven, will you? You shall descend to Hades; for if the miracles had occurred in Sodom which occurred in you, it would have remained to this day. Nevertheless I say to you that it shall be more tolerable for the land of Sodom in the day of judgement, than for you.

These words should not be taken to mean that those to whom less has been given bear little or no responsibility for their unbelief and disobedience. All bear the weight of responsibility, full responsibility, to answer for what God has given to them. Some, however, because they have enjoyed a richer privilege and disclosure of God's words and works, are weighed with a greater responsibility. The principle is one of how much more. It is one of the major themes of the book of Hebrews. Because of the greater richness and blessing of the new covenant, disobedience and unfaithfulness in the new covenant situation becomes even more deadly than in the old covenant situation (*Heb.* 2:1–3; 12:25–29).[1]

The question is often raised as to what will happen to those who have not had the opportunity to hear the gospel or be taught from the Word of God? Is it fair that they should be judged according to a standard that is unknown to them?

To answer this question, I would reiterate: the standard of judgement will be the law and will of God so far as these have been revealed. In Romans 1:18–23 and 2:11–16, we are taught that all people, Jews and Gentiles alike, have been given some knowledge of God through the things he has made and the law whose work is written upon their hearts. No one can be excused before God on the basis of a plea of ignorance. To the extent that God has revealed himself to all, to that extent all are responsible and without excuse before him. Speaking to the question, Is it fair that God should judge those who do not have the full light of his Word and gospel?, Carl F. H. Henry gives the following wise answer:

> God's fairness is demonstrated because he condemns sinners not in the absence of light but because of their rebellious response. His mercy is demonstrated because he provides fallen humans with a privileged call to redemption not extended to fallen angels. He continues to extend that call worldwide even while some rebel humans spurn it as unloving and unjust and prefer to die in their sins. *All are judged by what they do with the light they have, and none is without light.*[2]

---

[1] Corresponding to this degree of privilege, the Bible appears to teach that some will be punished more severely than others in hell. See, for example, Matt. 10:15, 11:20–24, Luke 12:47–48. Since little is said in the Scriptures about this gradation of punishment, I will not give it special attention in this or the next chapter on the doctrine of eternal punishment.

[2] 'Is It Fair?' in *Through No Fault of Their Own?: The Fate of Those Who Have Never Heard*, ed. William V. Crockett and James G. Sigountos (Grand Rapids: Baker, 1991), p. 255.

The *Belgic Confession*, one of the confessional documents
of the Protestant churches, summarizes in its last article the
various aspects of the final judgement that we have considered. Since this Article also concludes with a reference to the
reward awaiting the righteous for their good works, a subject
to which we turn in our next section, it provides a fitting
conclusion to our consideration of these aspects of the Bible's
teaching:

> Finally, we believe, according to the Word of God, when
> the time appointed by the Lord (which is unknown to all
> creatures) is come and the number of the elect complete,
> that our Lord Jesus Christ will come from heaven, corpor-
> ally and visibly, as he ascended, with great glory and
> majesty to declare himself judge of the living and the dead,
> burning this world with fire and flame to cleanse it. Then
> all men will personally appear before this great judge, both
> men and women and children, that have been from the be-
> ginning of the world to the end thereof, being summoned
> by the voice of the archangel, and by the sound of the
> trump of God . . . Then the books (that is to say, the
> consciences) shall be opened, and the dead judged accord-
> ing to what they shall have done in this world, whether it be
> good or evil. Nay, all men shall give account of every idle
> word they have spoken, which the world only counts
> amusement and jest; and then the secrets and hypocrisy of
> men shall be disclosed and laid open before all. And there-
> fore the consideration of this judgement is justly terrible
> and dreadful to the wicked and ungodly, but most desirable
> and comfortable to the righteous and elect; because then
> their full deliverance shall be perfected, and there they shall
> receive the fruits of their labour and trouble which they
> have borne.[1]

Degrees of Reward in the Kingdom of Heaven?

A question that has frequently surfaced throughout the history of the church's reflection on the final judgement is: does

[1] *Belgic Confession*, Article 37.

God reward the righteous according to their deeds? And, in so doing, does God reward in greater or lesser degrees those whom he welcomes into the glory of the kingdom of heaven?'

In the preceding discussion of the final judgement, we argued that all people will be judged according to what they have done in the body. This judgement will be exercised according to the standard of God's law or Word so far as these have been revealed. On these matters, there is general agreement and little dissent.

However, within the framework of these common convictions about the final judgement, several questions have been disputed. Will God reward the righteous for what they have done? Will this reward vary in degree, depending upon the nature and extent of the good works of the righteous? Moreover, how is the idea of God rewarding the righteous compatible with the teaching that our salvation is based upon grace alone? Does the idea of reward not require the reintroduction of some notion of 'merit' in the Christian life? And would disparity in degrees of reward not detract from the perfection of blessedness that the people of God are presumed to enjoy in the final state?

I. SEVERAL KEY PASSAGES

In the history of the discussion of these questions, a number of key passages have played an important role.[1]

1 CORINTHIANS 3:14–15:
If any man's work which he has built upon it remains, he shall receive a reward. If any man's work is burned up, he

---

[1] The passages I will be considering are by no means exhaustive of those that have been appealed to in support of the doctrine of differing rewards granted to the righteous. I am restricting my consideration to those that seem the clearest and most important. Other passages that have been appealed to include: *Dan.* 12:3, *Matt.* 5:19; 11:11, *John* 14:2, *1 Cor.* 3:8; 4:5; 15:41, 42. Though these may confirm the teaching of the passages I will consider, they do not by themselves constitute a strong testimony to the notion of differing degrees of reward.

shall suffer loss; but he himself shall be saved, yet so as through fire.

The context for this passage is the labour of those who are ministers or teachers in the church. Utilizing the metaphor of the church as a building, the Apostle Paul describes those ministers who build upon the foundation which is Jesus Christ, some with 'gold, silver, precious stones', and others with 'wood, hay, straw'. The day is coming when these respective works will become evident. They will be shown for what they are in the day of judgement, when they are tested by fire and their character is revealed. The outcome of this testing of the quality of the works of Christ's ministers will be twofold: some will prove to have been built with solid and enduring materials, some will prove to have been built with insecure and fleeting materials. Those whose works are shown to be worthy will receive an appropriate reward. Those whose works are shown to be unworthy will be saved, 'yet so as through fire'.

This passage seems to teach clearly that those whose labour is in the ministry of the Word of Christ will be rewarded variously, depending upon the quality of their works.[1] Though each class of ministers is expressly said to receive salvation, the one is contrasted with the other from the standpoint of a reward for work well done. The one group is rewarded, the other is not – each because of the difference in the kind of work performed.

---

[1] See Craig L. Blomberg, 'Degrees of Reward in the Kingdom of Heaven?' *Journal of the Evangelical Theological Society*, 35/2 (June 1992), pp. 159–72. Blomberg, who argues against the idea of a diversity of rewards in the kingdom of heaven, maintains that this passage 'says nothing about these distinctions among believers' experiences persisting for all time' (p. 165). This is, at best, an argument from silence. However, it also implies that the experience and reward granted believers at the final judgement will somehow be extinguished from the memory and experience of believers in the final state. There is no apparent reason why this should be the case.

THE PROMISE OF THE FUTURE

2 CORINTHIANS 9:6:
Now this I say, he who sows sparingly shall also reap sparingly; and he who sows bountifully shall also reap bountifully.

In this passage, the Apostle Paul is speaking not only of ministers of the gospel but also of all who give generously in support of the Lord's work. In the context of his encouragement to the Corinthians to give freely and abundantly to the needs of others, he encourages them by reminding them of the correspondence between sowing and reaping. If they sow sparingly, they will reap sparingly. If they sow generously, they will reap generously. This 'law of the harvest' applies also to the Christian life. Those who labour in a spirit of generosity and beneficence will reap a correspondingly greater reward.

Now, it could be argued that this passage has reference only to the experience of believers in this life. On this reading, this passage would say nothing about a diversity of reaping in the life to come. However, in a similar passage (*Gal.* 6:8) and others which use the common Scriptural theme of the harvest (for example, *Matt.* 25:24), the time of reaping coincides with the period of final judgement and the ingathering of the full harvest. This passage, therefore, likely speaks of some kind of reaping in conjunction with the final judgement and its outcome for the righteous. Those who sow much will receive a greater reward than those who sow sparingly.

MATTHEW 25:14–30 AND LUKE 19:11–26:
Among the parables of the kingdom in the Gospels, two of them, the parables of the talents and of the pounds, suggest that God grants different gifts to his servants in this life and also in the life to come. Those who are citizens of the kingdom of heaven vary in the extent and nature of their responsibilities and privileges in the service of their king. Similarly, they receive in the day of reckoning correspondingly different rewards for the service they have rendered.

In the parable of the talents, we are told that when a man prepared to go on a journey, he entrusted to his servants his possessions, granting to one five talents, to another two talents, and to still another just one talent (*Matt.* 25:15). After a long time, the man returns from his journey to settle accounts with his servants. In doing so, he grants a greater reward to the man who received the five talents than to the one who received two. By contrast, the man to whom one talent was given, because he had not wisely used what had been given to him, was deprived of all that he had earlier received and cast into 'outer darkness' (verse 30).

In the second of these parables, the parable of the pounds, the unequal distribution of pounds and of subsequent rewards is even more striking. Though each of the nobleman's servants are given ten pounds, in the day of reckoning one servant is rewarded with responsibility for ten cities, and another for five cities; but another is deprived even of the little he was given. This parable clearly emphasizes the right of the nobleman to grant a diversity of gifts and rewards to his servants corresponding to their responsible use of what is entrusted to them.

The language used in these parables for the final reckoning and rewarding of the servants suggests that they are a description of the final judgement at the end of the age. The return of the man from his long journey and the nobleman from a distant country coincide with the end of the age. The context for the parable in Matthew 25 explicitly refers to the final judgement and the separation that will occur between the righteous and the unrighteous. This is also confirmed by the language of harvest used to describe the master's reckoning with his servants upon his return. Thus these parables appear to teach that Christ will distribute a diversity of degrees of reward to the righteous at the final judgement.

MATTHEW 8: 11; 19:28 AND REVELATION 21:14

In addition to those passages that speak directly of a diversity of rewards at the final judgement, other passages teach that in the final judgement and state certain privileges and responsibilities will be granted to some of the righteous but not to others.

For example, in Matthew 8:11, we read that believers will sit down 'with Abraham, Isaac and Jacob in the kingdom of heaven'. When the rich man and Lazarus die, Jesus speaks of Lazarus being 'carried into Abraham's bosom' (*Luke* 16:22; compare *Rom.* 4:11, 12). In the account of the Transfiguration, Moses and Elijah were present (*Matt.* 17:3) as representatives of the prophets of the old covenant. Christ, in his description of the 'regeneration' at the end of the age, declares that the apostles 'will sit upon twelve thrones, judging the twelve tribes of Israel' (*Matt.* 19:28, *Luke* 22:30). Similarly, when in the book of Revelation we are given a description of the foundations of the heavenly Jerusalem, the names of the twelve apostles are inscribed upon them (*Rev.* 21:14).

These passages suggest that the peculiar distinctions and prerogatives that the Lord has granted to his servants in this life are not lost upon the life to come. The role played by the patriarchs, prophets and apostles in the course of redemptive history is remembered perpetually. These distinctions and privileges are not swept away and ignored in the final state so that a flat 'egalitarianism' prevails among the people of God. The richness, diversity, and degree of privilege and responsibility in this life seem to find their correspondence and fulfilment in the life to come.

1 CORINTHIANS 9:25, 1 THESSALONIANS 2:19, 2 TIMOTHY 4:8

If the above conclusion is correct, then it should not surprise us to find a number of biblical passages which speak of a diversity of 'crowns' to be awarded Christ's servants in the day of judgement.

Admittedly, in some of these passages, the crown granted to believers probably refers to the granting of salvation or eternal life, something which is the common reward and joy of God's people (for example, *1 Cor. 9:25, 2 Tim.* 4:8).[1] This is not always the case, however. In 1 Thessalonians 2:19, the Apostle Paul speaks of the Thessalonians as his 'hope or joy or crown', in whom he will glory and rejoice in the presence of the Lord Jesus at his coming. Clearly this cannot mean any proud or arrogant boasting in the presence of the people of God. But it does mean that the Thessalonians will be an occasion for joy and thanksgiving to the apostle when the work he performed among them is recognised in the day of Christ's coming. In James 1:12, we read of the 'crown of life' that will be given to the man who 'perseveres under trial' in the service of the Lord. The Apostle Peter also encourages the elders in the churches by reminding them that, 'when the Chief Shepherd appears, [they] will receive the unfading crown of glory' (*1 Pet.* 5:4). This crown of glory is a special reward for the faithful ministry of those who serve as shepherds of the flock of God.

In this way, the diversity of gifts and callings among the people of God will not go unnoticed in the final judgement by Christ. Each will receive a reward in keeping with the service rendered. The work of the Lord's servants will not be overlooked. Rather, Christ will openly acknowledge and reward his faithful servants as they together enter into the joy of the Lord.

If the passages we have considered teach not only that Christ will reward the righteous at the final judgement for their works, but also that this reward will vary according to the nature and quality of the works, then several questions become rather pressing. The first of these has to do with the controversial matter of grace and merit.

II. A REWARD OF GRACE, NOT MERIT

If Christ rewards the works of the righteous, does this not reintroduce the idea of merit into the Christian life? How can

---

[1] This is Blomberg's understanding of all these passages. See Blomberg, 'Degrees of Reward in the Kingdom of Heaven?', pp. 163–5.

we say that believers are saved by grace alone, apart from any meritorious good works done in obedience to the law, if we say that the good works of believers have their reward and that this reward varies according to the quality of the works performed?

Broadly speaking, at least three approaches to this question could be – and often have been – taken in the history of the Christian church.

One approach insists that because the Scriptures teach the granting of diverse rewards to the people of God (depending upon the quality and extent of their good works), some notion of merit must be appropriate. In the Roman Catholic tradition, for example, a distinction has been drawn between two kinds of merit in the Christian life, each of which is legitimate. The first, or 'congruent merit' (*meritum de congruo*) is a 'half-merit'. In the case of congruent merit, God grants as a reward to the righteous more than their works, strictly considered, deserve. Though the believer, co-operating with God's grace and doing what lies within him or her, performs works of obedience, these works are imperfect and not strictly deserving of the reward God grants to them. The second or 'condign merit' (*meritum de condigno*) is a 'true merit'. In the case of condign merit, the believer's works truly measure up to the requirements of God's law and, by virtue of the working of God's grace as it is infused into believers, genuinely merit the reward that God grants to them. In this understanding, the biblical teaching that God rewards the works of the righteous demands the conclusion that merit plays a legitimate role in the Christian life. God's people, in this respect, receive from God what they deserve or are due.[1]

---

[1] For an exposition of the Roman Catholic understanding of merit, see the entry for 'merit' in *Sacramentum Mundi: An Encyclopedia of Theology*, ed. Karl Rahner *et al.* (Basle-Montreal: Hermann-Herder Foundation, 1969), IV, pp. 11–14. If I may illustrate this distinction between two kinds of merit with a rather crass commercial analogy, it

A second approach opposes the whole idea of a diversity of rewards because it is incompatible with the doctrine of grace. This approach assumes the legitimacy of the argument just presented that if God variously rewards the righteous for their good works, then merit must play a role in the Christian life. So this approach rejects the idea of a diversity of rewards because it requires merit as its corollary and salvation is wholly by grace.

Those who take this second approach frequently appeal to the parable of the labourers in the vineyard in Matthew 20:1–16. This parable, it is argued, clearly shows that there is no place in the Christian life for the idea of a diversity of rewards corresponding to the diversity of works performed by the righteous. In this parable, all of the labourers in the vineyard are rewarded equally for their labour, whether they began work earlier or later in the day. This parable teaches, then, that the law of the kingdom is a law of grace, not of merit. God, according to this parable, subverts the ordinary law of justice by graciously granting the same wages to all of the labourers. The emphasis upon God's grace militates against any suggestion that in the kingdom of heaven, God's people will receive varying rewards according to the nature of their service.

The third approach, and the one favoured here, maintains that the idea of rewards is consistent with the biblical teaching regarding salvation by grace alone, provided the rewards are of grace and not of merit. In this approach, it is readily acknowledged that the believer receives all things from God's

---

is like the difference between paying an employee an hourly wage that is strictly or justly deserved (based upon contractual obligations and the quality of the work performed) or that is more than is strictly or justly deserved (going beyond contractual obligations and exceeding what the quality of the work performed deserves). The difference is that between a just wage and the granting of an additional bonus. The first of these coincides with condign merit; the second with congruent merit.

grace in Christ. Nothing the believer receives from God is deserved, either in the strict or the lesser sense of condign or congruent merit. When God rewards the righteous for their good works, he only adds grace to grace, rewarding believers for those deeds which he himself works in them by his Spirit (*John* 15:1–17). In no sense whatsoever does any believer receive from God what he or she deserves. The Christian who obeys God perfectly – which, of course, cannot be the case – would be no more than an 'unprofitable servant' who had only done his or her duty (*Luke* 17:7–10). That person would not be deserving of any special praise or commendation from God. All of the gifts of God's grace are just that – 'gifts', unmerited favours granted for the sake of Christ.

The wonder of God's grace in the life of the believer includes God's gracious reward of those (still imperfect and undeserving) good works that the believer does by the powerful working of the Spirit. Like a father who loves his children and who accepts not only them but also their works, so the believer's heavenly Father takes pleasure in the deeds of his children. These deeds are acceptable and pleasing to him, not because they strictly merit his praise, but because of his delight in his children and what they have done, however far short this may fall of what his law demands.

To show how God graciously receives us and even deigns to reward our inadequate good works by his grace, I have sometimes used the illustration of my wife's piano students at their annual recital. It is remarkable to observe how parents, in spite of the often clumsy performance of their children at the piano bench, invariably beam with delight at their performance. Do they measure their children's performance by some strict rule of justice? Do they respond like overbearing perfectionists, quick to find fault with every defect in their child's performance? Not at all! They love their children. And because they love them and find them acceptable, they graciously praise and smile upon their less-than-perfect playing. In the same manner the heavenly

Father, who loves and accepts his children for the sake of his Son, Jesus Christ, also delights to graciously reward them for their good works – no matter that these works are themselves the gifts of his grace and of themselves fall far short of deserving anything like the praise they receive from him.

III. AN ENCOURAGEMENT, NOT A MOTIVE

Another question that often arises concerns the proper motivation of the Christian life. Even if we insist that these rewards are of grace rather than merit, the prospect of such rewards must inevitably influence the motives that play a role in Christian obedience. Does the prospect of reward legitimately function in the Christian life as a motive, a moving impulse, for obedience? And if this were the case, would a mercenary[1] or commercial spirit not corrupt the Christian life? Rather than serving the Lord out of gratitude for his grace in Christ, moved by no other impulse than heartfelt thankfulness, the Christian life would degenerate into a selfish pursuit of personal advantage and gain. Thus, one objection to the idea of diversity of rewards is the worry that this will pollute the stream of Christian service with a spirit of self-seeking labour. Here again, the radical teaching of God's grace is threatened by the introduction of the performance-orientated and commercial spirit that so often corrupts contemporary life and culture in North America.[2]

---

[1] Interestingly, the term, 'mercenary', comes from a Latin word for 'reward'. The mercenary is the person who serves for the sake of the reward granted, not for the sake of loyalty or true devotion to the cause.

[2] Blomberg, 'Degrees of Reward in the Kingdom of Heaven?' p. 169, argues vigorously that this is a primary reason why the idea of varying rewards needs to be rejected: 'The good news of the gospel of Jesus Christ ought to liberate believers from all such performance-centered conceptions of the Christian life. An important step in that direction would be to jettison this misguided and discouraging doctrine of eternal rewards that distinguish one believer from another.' That this

Not to minimize in any way the concern expressed by this question, it is interesting to notice that the *Heidelberg Catechism*, after having declared God's rewards to be 'not of merit but of grace', goes on to say that 'it is impossible that those who are implanted into Christ by a true faith should not bring forth fruits of thankfulness' (Lord's Day 24). This *Catechism* seems to show no awareness of a necessary conflict between the teaching that God graciously rewards the good works of his children and the insistence that those good works are the fruits of thankfulness. While acknowledging that good works are rewarded, this confession recognizes gratitude as the only proper motive for Christian obedience.[1] It does not follow, therefore, that any teaching of rewards for good works in the Christian life must lead to an improper emphasis upon rewards as a motive for Christian obedience. That this may occur, no óne would deny. That it must occur, or that it is inherent in the very idea of varying rewards, does not follow.

Perhaps a distinction between motive and encouragement may be helpful here. Though the prospect of rewards may not serve as a motive or the basis for Christian obedience, it certainly might function as an encouragement. The prospect of rewards encourages the believer to understand that no labour is in vain in the Lord. The thankful life of the Christian does not go unnoticed by Christ in the final judgement. Rather, the final judgement will be an occasion to rejoice in work well done and of enduring value. The sacrificial service of an elder, for example, who labours as a shepherd among the flock of God, not because he must or for

---

worry on Blomberg's part has real merit (no pun intended!) is evident from a book which he cites by way of example: Joe Wall, *Going for the Gold: Reward and Loss at the Judgement of Believers* (Chicago: Moody, 1991).

[1] This is the place also to note that the *Heidelberg Catechism*, in its third major section, treats the entire Christian life under the heading of gratitude or thankfulness.

the thought of 'sordid gain', is surely encouraged by the reminder that 'when the Chief Shepherd appears, [the elder] will receive the unfading crown of glory'. Similarly, in many of the trials and difficulties of grateful service on behalf of the Lord and his kingdom, Christians are properly encouraged to know that their service will be graciously and abundantly acknowledged by Christ at his coming.

In these kinds of circumstances, the prospect of rewards for the righteous does not constitute the motive for Christian obedience. The motive is always one of gratitude for God's grace in Christ. However, this prospect does constitute an encouragement in the midst of the Christian life. It reminds the believer that the heavenly Father is not unmindful of his or her service. It is same kind of encouragement children experience when they realize that their accomplishment is something in which their parents take delight.

IV. COMPATIBLE WITH PERFECT BLESSEDNESS?
The prospect of being rewarded at Christ's coming for those good works done while in the body is not only an encouragement for the believer, but also an occasion for rejoicing in God's gracious gifts to others who are co-heirs of God's grace. One question that often arises is whether this is compatible with the state of perfect blessedness in the final state. Would degrees of rewards granted the righteous not suggest the strange, perhaps self-contradictory, idea of degrees of perfection? And how could one believer enjoy the fullest blessedness, knowing that on account of failures in this life, he or she falls short of others in the life to come?

In the history of Christian theology some partial and helpful answers have been given to these questions. We will mention the two most often suggested.

The first is that the final state of God's kingdom will be characterized by a diversity of giftedness, office, and capacity for service and joy that mirrors the diversity known among the people of God in this life. Though no one will fall behind another in the experience of blessedness and joy, the capacity for and quality of these may well differ considerably among God's people. To use a quantitative analogy, one vessel may be larger than another and therefore of greater capacity. However, if each vessel, the larger and the smaller, is wholly filled, then it can be said to enjoy a fullness or perfection commensurate with its capacity. So perhaps it will be in the new heavens and earth. One of the assumptions of this view is that the final form of God's kingdom will not be a strict egalitarianism. Or, to state it differently, this suggestion opposes the contrary assumption that the perfection of blessedness requires a complete similarity of gifts and capacities.

The other suggestion is that the diversity of giftedness, office and capacity for service in the final state of God's kingdom, far from being the occasion for regret among the people of God, will be the occasion for greater joy. On the principle that perfect holiness excludes every possibility for envy or contention among the people of God, this suggestion argues that the greater rewards enjoyed by some among the people of God will only engender further thankfulness among all. Since it is already true in this life that all things belong to all believers, and all believers belong to Christ, and Christ belongs to God (1 Cor. 3:21–23), this principle will presumably also hold in the kingdom to come. How could there then be any sense of loss or impoverishment among the people who belong to Christ, when some are distinguished from others in gifts and rewards? Just as in this life God's gifts, variously distributed among his children, are the occasion for joy and thanksgiving, so it will be in the life to come. The argument that this varied distribution of gifts would occasion jealousy or envy among God's children, fails to regard seriously enough the perfection of holiness that will mark the heart and life of God's children in the final state.[1]

---

[1] Jonathan Edwards, *Works* (1834, repr. Edinburgh: Banner of Truth, 1974), vol. 2, p. 618, uses both of these suggestions in

Conclusion

No doubt some of these questions relating to the granting of a diversity of rewards at the final judgement deserve further consideration. But the general answer to the question of rewards for good works should be clear. The good works of the righteous will not go unnoticed in the day of judgement. They will be recognized and rewarded. This recognition and reward, however, are expressions of God's gracious dealings with his children. They are rewards not of merit but of grace. They represent God's gracious dealings with his children, adding grace to grace. The prospect of such rewards, though an encouragement to God's faithful children, is not the ground or motive for the Christian life; the great motive for all Christian obedience is gratitude for God's grace in Christ. Furthermore, the prospect of these rewards – rather than suggesting an inequality that would diminish the perfect blessedness of the life to come for all the righteous – suggests a further occasion to rejoice in God's goodness. If all things in Christ belong to all believers, whatever gain one may experience in the life to come will only be gain for all the others.

---

considering this question: 'Now most certainly the holier a man is, the more he loves the same degree of the image; so that the holiest in heaven will love that image of God they see in the least holy more than those do that are less holy; and that which makes it beyond any doubt that this superior happiness will be no damp to them, is this, that their superior happiness consists in their great humility, and in their greater love to them, and to God, and Christ, whom the saints look upon as themselves. These things may be said of this, beside what may be said about every one being completely satisfied and full of happiness, having as much as he is capable of enjoying or desiring; and also what may be said about their entire resignation; for God's will is become so much their own, that the fulfilling of his will, let it be what it may, fills them with inconceivable satisfaction.'

15

---

*The Doctrine of
Eternal Punishment*

NOW THAT WE HAVE CONSIDERED two 'concomitants of the
second advent', the resurrection of the dead and the
final judgement, our study brings us to the subject of the final
state. Here, as with many aspects of the Bible's teaching
about the future, we enter territory that is only broadly
described in the Scriptures. Much of what we are curious to
know is not told us; only the important and necessary truths
are. We will attempt to stay with these, resisting the temptation to wander off into uncharted territory.

The Problem of the Doctrine
No one can avoid the obvious fact that one biblical teaching
about the future, namely, the eternal punishment of the unbelieving and impenitent in hell, is today either neglected or
disapproved. In the environment of western post-Christian
and postmodern culture, the doctrine of eternal punishment
is to most people abhorrent and unacceptable. Nothing can
compromise a person's credibility more quickly today than
the discovery that he or she believes the doctrine of hell in

anything like its historic Christian understanding. Indeed, it is hard to imagine a doctrine more at odds with the affection of moderns for the virtues of 'tolerance' and 'openness'.[1] What could be more offensive to modern sensibilities than the conviction that those who do not believe in Christ or repent at the preaching of the gospel are destined to suffer eternally in hell?

A quick glance at recent treatments of the doctrine of hell readily confirms its unpopularity. Authors speak of *Hell on Trial*,[2] *The Other Side of the Good News*,[3] 'On Banishing the Lake of Fire',[4] and *The Problem of Eternal Punishment*.[5] Roman Catholic theologians speak of 'anonymous' Christians (Karl Rahner) or of a larger hope that all will be saved.[6] Even among evangelical authors, alternative views of the final state for the unsaved are being affirmed. The doctrine of hell, never an easy doctrine to affirm, has become the subject of renewed discussion, most of it by those looking for some alternative to the traditional view.

---

[1] The limits of tolerance, ironically, are quickly met, when you affirm or defend the doctrine of eternal punishment. I do not mean to suggest by these comments that it is only today that the doctrine of hell has become an unpopular one. Certainly this doctrine is intrinsically difficult. Indeed, if God has no delight in the death of the wicked (*Ezek.* 18:23), surely the same ought to be true among his children.

[2] Robert A. Peterson, *Hell on Trial. The Case for Eternal Punishment* (Phillipsburg, New Jersey: Presbyterian & Reformed, 1995).

[3] Larry Dixon, *The Other Side of the Good News. Confronting the Contemporary Challenges to Jesus' Teaching on Hell* (Wheaton, Illinois: BridgePoint, 1992).

[4] Chapter 13 of D. A. Carson, *The Gagging of God: Christianity Confronts Pluralism* (Grand Rapids: Zondervan, 1996), pp. 515–36. It should be observed that Carson does not favour 'banishing' the doctrine; he is describing the tendency to do so as one dimension of the contemporary 'gagging of God'.

[5] J. I. Packer, *The Problem of Eternal Punishment* (No. 10 of *Orthos*, a series of papers from Fellowship of Word and Spirit).

[6] For example, Hans Urs Von Balthasar, *Dare We Hope 'That All Men Be Saved'?* (San Francisco: Ignatius Press, 1988).

THE PROMISE OF THE FUTURE

I. THE HISTORIC OR TRADITIONAL VIEW

Due to the unpopularity of this doctrine and the frequent attempts to revise it, even within conservative evangelical contexts, it is necessary to begin with a brief statement of the historic position of the church on the subject of hell. Only against the background of this historic understanding can we evaluate the more common revisions that are being proposed today. What has the orthodox Christian church historically taught regarding the doctrine of eternal punishment, or hell?

The traditional doctrine teaches that all those persons whom God does not save through the work of Christ will be, subsequent to the resurrection and the final judgement, consigned to hell. Hell, though its exact nature and location remain somewhat uncertain, will be a place of unending punishment for God's enemies. Those who have lived in enmity against God will find themselves forever banished from his blessed presence, in a state of conscious awareness of his disfavour. Among the Reformation confessions, the following statements represent well the traditional Christian understanding of hell:

> And therefore the consideration of this judgement is justly terrible and dreadful to the wicked and ungodly, but most desirable and comfortable to the righteous and elect; because then their full deliverance shall be perfected, and there they shall receive the fruits of their labour and trouble which they have borne. Their innocence shall be known to all, and they shall see the terrible vengeance which God shall execute on the wicked, who most cruelly persecuted, oppressed, and tormented them in this world, and who shall be convicted by the testimony of their own consciences, and shall become immortal, but only to be tormented in the eternal fire which is prepared for the devil and his angels (*Belgic Confession*, Art. 37).

> The end of God's appointing this day is for the manifestation of the glory of his mercy, in the eternal salvation of the elect; and of his justice, in the damnation of the

reprobate, who are wicked and disobedient. For then shall the righteous go into everlasting life, and receive that fullness of joy and refreshing, which shall come from the presence of the Lord; but the wicked who know not God, and obey not the gospel of Jesus Christ, shall be cast into eternal torments, and be punished with everlasting destruction from the presence of the Lord, and from the glory of his power (*Westminster Confession of Faith*, XXXIII.2).

Though these confessional statements set a proper standard of sobriety and reserve in what they say about hell, and though their focus remains primarily fixed upon the comfort that God's people derive from the gospel, they clearly affirm a doctrine of eternal punishment. The language used, echoing that of the Scriptures, underscores the horror of hell as a place of unceasing, consciously felt punishment upon the wicked and unbelieving. With an economy of words, these confessions affirm what the orthodox Christian church has always taught respecting the doctrine of hell. Even though they do not attempt any detailed description of hell as a place of eternal punishment, they clearly affirm its reality.

II. IDENTIFYING THE ALTERNATIVES

If this is the shape of the historic doctrine of the church, what are some of the more common alternatives to this doctrine that are being proposed today? The chief alternatives are universalism and annihilationism. Each of these takes various forms, but for our purpose, we will mention only the most important variations among them.

UNIVERSALISM

Universalism is the teaching that, in the end, all human beings will be saved. No human being will ultimately fail to enjoy the fullness of salvation, by whatever means that salvation is obtained. Universalism can take, broadly speaking, one of two forms: pluralistic or Christian.[1] Pluralistic

[1] See Trevor Hart, 'Universalism: Two Distinct Types' (in *Universalism and the Doctrine of Hell*, ed. by Nigel M. de S. Cameron; Grand Rapids: Baker, 1992), pp. 1–34.

universalism teaches that the Christian faith is one of many ways of salvation, each of which has its own legitimacy and integrity. Christian universalism teaches that Christ is the one way of salvation which all will ultimately travel, either in this life or in the life to come.

In its Christian expression, universalism affirms that Christ alone is the Mediator and Saviour of all. No one will obtain salvation apart from the saving work of Christ. However, this saving work is universal in its scope or reach; no one will finally be lost or suffer eternal punishment in hell. All human beings without exception will be saved through the work of Christ. Christian universalism, like pluralistic universalism, is able to accommodate various forms and expressions. Sometimes, for example, those who advocate a Christian universalism will include the provision for a second opportunity for people to be saved after death, or they may speak of a period of purgatory, subsequent to death, during which some are fitted for the enjoyment of salvation as they suffer a temporary punishment for the sins committed in this life.

ANNIHILATIONISM (CONDITIONAL IMMORTALITY)

Annihilationism is the view that while those who are saved enjoy everlasting life in God's presence in the life to come, all those who are lost will ultimately be annihilated. Those who are lost will not suffer unending torment in hell. Rather, the punishment of the wicked will take its final form in their extinction. The punishment of the wicked is eternal in the sense of result, but not in the sense of experience.

Annihilationism takes many forms.[1] It is clearly the most tempting and therefore dangerous alternative to the

[1] Kendall S. Harmon, 'The Case Against Conditionalism: A Response to Edward William Fudge' (in *Universalism and the Doctrine of Hell*, ed. Nigel M. de S. Cameron), pp. 191–224, carefully distinguishes three kinds of annihilationism. The first kind he calls 'conditionalist uniresurrectionism' because it teaches that all people are annihilated at death and only those who are saved are raised to everlasting life (held, for example, by Jehovah's Witnesses, Socinians). The second

traditional doctrine of hell among evangelicals today. In the form called 'conditional immortality' it has captivated an increasing number of evangelical theologians, some of them of considerable ability and influence.[1] As this term indicates, conditional immortality teaches that only those who meet the conditions for benefiting from Christ's saving work – however those conditions are understood – will obtain immortality. All others will be annihilated, either immediately upon death or subsequent to a limited period of punishment after death. In its most common evangelical form, the annihilation of the lost will take place after they have endured some kind of punishment for their sin and disobedience. So far as the doctrine of hell is concerned, conditional immortality denies any doctrine of unending conscious torment of the wicked.

Since this common form of annihilationism, conditional immortality, is the most subtle and dangerous alternative to the historic doctrine of eternal punishment, we will focus upon its arguments in what follows. If the arguments of the more conservative defenders of this view cannot be sustained, then the more radical denials of the doctrine of hell cannot be sustained, either.

---

kind he calls 'conditionalist eventual extinctionism' because it teaches that all human beings are raised, those who are saved to everlasting life, those who are lost to endure a period of suffering before they are annihilated (held by Seventh Day Adventists). The third kind he calls 'immortalist eventual extinctionism' because it teaches that, though all human beings were created immortal, the wicked will be annihilated after they have been raised and experienced a period of punishment. These variations among annihilationists represent different views of man's immortality and of the intermediate state (if one is affirmed). For our purposes, these precise distinctions are not so important.

[1] To mention only a few: Clark H. Pinnock, John R. W. Stott, John W. Wenham, Philip Edgcumbe Hughes, Edward William Fudge, and Stephen H. Travis. For a recent representation of this position, see Clark H. Pinnock, 'The Conditional View', in *Four Views on Hell*, ed. William Crockett (Grand Rapids: Zondervan, 1996), pp. 135–66.

III. THE PRIMARY OBJECTIONS

Among contemporary advocates of conditional immortality, several common objections are expressed to the traditional doctrine of hell. Though these may not be stated in the same way or be given the same degree of importance by different advocates of this position, they tend to recur in their writings.[1]

The first and perhaps most important objection to the doctrine of eternal punishment is the claim that the Bible speaks of the ultimate destruction of the wicked (for example, *Phil.* 3:19, *1 Thess.* 5:3, *2 Thess.* 1:9, *2 Pet.* 3:7). The idea of destruction, it is argued, suggests the annihilation, the 'ceasing-to-be' of the wicked, rather than their continued existence in a situation of torment. In the Scriptures and in our ordinary use of the word, 'destruction' usually means the cessation of the existence of something. Edward Fudge, an influential defender of annihilationism, whose 1982 book, *The Fire That Consumes: The Biblical Case for Conditional Immortality*,[2] was an alternative selection of the Evangelical Book Club, argues that this is the uniform testimony of both Testaments. The destruction of the wicked after the final judgement means simply that they are removed from existence.

A second and related objection appeals to the biblical imagery used to describe this punishment. Just as the language of destruction implies complete cessation of existence, so the imagery of fire implies a process whereby the sinner is completely consumed. Like the burning of the chaff at the return of the judge in Matthew 3:12, so the burning of the wicked at the last judgement will utterly destroy them.

The third objection takes advantage of the apparent ambiguity in the word 'eternal'. In the history of the church, the parallel between 'eternal' life and 'eternal' punishment in a passage like Matthew 25:46 has been a basis for arguing that hell is a place of unending punishment. However, many

---

[1] Though stated in my own words, I am following Carson's delineation of the principal arguments against the doctrine of eternal punishment (*The Gagging of God*, pp. 518–20).

[2] Houston: Providential Press, 1982. The title of the book says it all.

advocates of the doctrine of annihilation maintain that in the case of eternal punishment, this need only mean that the punishment has an unending result or consequence. It does not require the conclusion that the punishment involves an unending awareness of God's judgement. Annihilation is an eternal punishment, but only in the sense that its consequences never end.

In addition to these objections argued from biblical material, others are of a more theological nature. These raise questions about the consistency of the doctrine of eternal punishment with other doctrines clearly taught in the Bible.

One of these theological objections (and the fourth in our list) argues that the doctrine of hell is incompatible with what we know of the love of God. The horrible prospect of God's punishing sinners unceasingly in hell seems repugnant to the love and goodness of God, especially as revealed in the gospel. Those who raise this objection insist that God could not possibly punish the sinner in hell eternally, were he a God of love. Clark Pinnock, a leading evangelical proponent of the doctrine of annihilation, puts this objection in the strongest terms:

> Let me say at the outset that I consider the concept of hell as endless torment in body and mind an outrageous doctrine, a theological and moral enormity, a bad doctrine of the tradition which needs to be changed. How can Christians possibly project a deity of such cruelty and vindictiveness whose ways include inflicting everlasting torture upon his creatures, however sinful they may have been? Surely a God who would do such a thing is more nearly like Satan than like God, at least by any ordinary moral standards, and by the gospel itself . . . Does the one who told us to love our enemies intend to wreak vengeance on his own enemies for all eternity?[1]

[1] 'The Destruction of the Finally Impenitent', *Criswell Theological Review*, 4 (1990), pp. 246–47, 253. John Stott expresses a similar view, but with less hyperbole, in *Essentials: A Liberal-Evangelical Dialogue* (with David L. Edwards; London: Hodder & Stoughton, 1988), pp. 314–315.

The fifth objection to the doctrine of eternal punishment is similar to the fourth; it argues that this doctrine is incompatible with what we know of the justice of God. If justice in its most basic meaning has to do with due proportion or receiving one's due, this objection maintains that an eternal punishment of the sinner in hell would be a punishment that outweighed the crime. The doctrine of hell, it is objected, teaches that a limited offence will receive at the hands of God an unlimited penalty, and this is manifestly unjust. It would be a clear case of the punishment being far more weighty and grievous than the crime committed.

The sixth and last objection argues that it would mar the perfection and glory of the eternal state. To say that God's purposes in history would terminate in part with the eternal punishment of the wicked in hell suggests that the redemptive work of God in history will fall short of bringing about the fullness of blessing and joy. The beauty of paradise regained will be marred by the continued and eternal presence of sinners under the judgement of God. Consequently, the eternal joy and perfection of God's kingdom will have to compete with the jarring reminder of sin and sin's consequences. According to this objection, the consummation of God's purposes in history would then be a little bit like a story without an altogether happy ending. The joy of heaven would be muted by the weeping of hell.

Answering the Objections

Since no teaching of Scripture labours under a more severe burden of proof than the historic Christian doctrine of hell, our approach to the doctrine of eternal punishment will be to answer these common objections. Though it would be possible to argue that the burden of proof lies with those who are departing from the historic consensus of the Christian church – as indeed they are – we will undertake the defence of this consensus against these objections.

I. THE WORD 'DESTRUCTION'

As noted earlier, the most common biblical argument against the doctrine of eternal punishment appeals to the language of destruction. The common terms in the New Testament for 'to destroy' or 'destruction', according to this argument, simply mean to cause to cease to exist, or the state of no longer existing.[1] For example, when Herod plotted to kill the newborn babies in Bethlehem in order to get rid of the Lord Jesus, he is said to have sought to 'destroy' him (*Matt.* 2:13). In his instruction of the disciples, Jesus also spoke of being afraid, not of someone who can only 'destroy' the body, but of the one 'who can destroy both body and soul in hell' (*Matt.* 10:28). The straightforward meaning of 'destruction' seems to be that of an act that causes something or someone to cease to exist. As John R. W. Stott remarks, 'If to kill is to deprive the body of life, hell would seem to be the deprivation of both physical and spiritual life, that is, an extinction of being.'[2] Furthermore, in two passages where a different term for 'destruction' is used (*1 Thess.* 5:3, *2 Thess.* 1:9), the implication seems to be that this destruction involves an annihilation or cessation of the existence of those who experience it.[3]

When this same term is used in the intransitive form, meaning 'to perish' or 'to die', a similar idea is expressed. When something or someone perishes, this is tantamount to its ceasing to be. In Luke 15:17, we read that when the prodigal son came to his senses, he said, 'How many of my father's hired men have more than enough bread, but I am dying here with hunger.' The Apostle Paul, describing the fate of those Israelites who tested the Lord, speaks of their

---

[1] The verb commonly used is *apollumi*, the noun *apoleia*.

[2] D. L. Edwards and John Stott, *Essentials: A Liberal–Evangelical Dialogue*, p. 315.

[3] The term used is *olethros*. Commenting on these passages, Stott (*Essentials*, p. 316) argues that it 'would seem strange . . . if people who are said to suffer destruction are in fact not destroyed'.

being 'destroyed by the serpents' (1 Cor. 10:9). These passages speak of a physical perishing or destruction. However, several passages also speak of an eternal perishing or dying in connection with hell. The well-known verse, John 3:16, describes those who believe in the only begotten Son of God as those who 'shall not perish but have everlasting life'. In describing the judgement upon those who have 'sinned without the law', the Apostle Paul speaks of their perishing without the law (Rom. 2:12). In 1 Corinthians 15:18, the same apostle insists that a denial of the resurrection of the body for believers means that they will have 'perished'. Furthermore, the Lord who is not slow regarding his promise is said not to wish that any should perish (2 Pet. 3:9).

Though this argument appears plausible, it does not stand up well under cross examination. Certainly, as several of the references cited show, the term 'destruction' can be used to describe cessation of existence. But this is not always the case. In other instances, it describes something rather different.

In the well-known parables of the 'lost' coin or the 'lost' son in Luke 15, the term Jesus uses in each case is the same term as the one used for 'to destroy' in the passages cited above. No one would conclude that the coin or the prodigal son ceased to exist. The destruction in these instances is quite different from the idea of annihilation. Likewise, in Matthew 9:17 the term used to describe the 'bursting' or the 'ruining' of the wineskins is the common term for 'to destroy'. The destruction of these wineskins is not their ceasing to be, but their ceasing to be useful for their intended purpose. When the disciples of Jesus rebuked the woman who anointed Jesus with costly ointment, they are said to have declared her excess a 'waste'. Here the term translated 'waste' is the same term translated elsewhere as 'destruction'. Again, we are not to conclude that the ointment ceased to exist – only that it was inappropriately or excessively used in the anointing of Jesus as a sign of the woman's affection.

Due to this diverse use of the terms 'to destroy' or 'destruction', it is much too simplistic to argue from it for a doctrine of annihilationism. Though these words may sometimes be used for the cessation of existence, the real issue is whether it ever has this meaning when used regarding the final state of the unbelieving. If annihilationism is to be demonstrated, then it must be shown that the word 'destruction', when describing the destiny of the unbelieving, must mean their ceasing to be. Moreover, it would also have to be shown that in other biblical passages that speak of the final state of the unbelieving, the idea of ongoing existence and experience is not affirmed.

II. THE LANGUAGE OF A CONSUMING 'FIRE'

A second and similar argument against the doctrine of everlasting punishment also appeals to the language used in the Scriptures to describe this state. Not only do we find several passages that speak of the 'destruction' of the wicked, but we also find several that use the image of a 'fire that consumes'.[1] This language, together with other common images for the final state of the wicked, suggests that the final outcome of God's judgement upon the unbelieving is their extinction or annihilation. As Edward Fudge, perhaps the leading critic of the traditional doctrine of everlasting punishment, puts it in his commentary on Matthew 5:29, 30 ('It is better for you that one of the parts of your body perish, than for your whole body to be thrown into hell'),

> Jesus makes Gehenna the place of final punishment. Here he gives no graphic description of its destruction or even its duration; only this, that those who enter it go from another place, having been discarded and expelled by God. The picture is one of total loss, and it is entirely in keeping with the Old Testament to see that loss as ultimately consummated in destruction by fire.[2]

[1] See Fudge, *The Fire That Consumes*. This argument is the main leg of Fudge's case against the doctrine of eternal punishment.

[2] *The Fire That Consumes*, p. 166.

Just as fire finally consumes its object, so the fire of hell utterly consumes the wicked. To speak of the continued or unending experience of hell neglects to take account of the way fire ordinarily destroys and extinguishes its object.[1]

This argument can be answered at two levels. The first is hermeneutical: is it permissible to take the word fire in such a literal, non-metaphorical way and draw the conclusion that fire, in the nature of the case, must utterly consume its object? The second level is more directly textual: do the texts that employ this imagery lend any support to the position of the annihilationist?

At the first level, the hermeneutical, it would seem that annihilationists fail to take seriously the metaphorical language of the Scriptures in their descriptions of hell. To say that these descriptions are often metaphorical in no way requires a diminishing of the reality of hell. Hell is certainly real. But the descriptions of hell in the Scripture can hardly be pressed literally. For example, the imagery of a consuming fire – imagery that bespeaks God's holy punishment and judgement of the wicked – is frequently coupled with the imagery of the 'worm that does not die' (for example, *Mark* 9:48; compare *Isa.* 66:24). Were we to insist upon a literal fire that consumes, it would seem rather incompatible with a worm working but not liable to death. D. A. Carson, commenting on this feature of the biblical language, notes that 'if the worms do not die, what keeps them alive once they have devoured all the people? The question is ugly and silly, precisely because it is demanding a concrete and this-worldly answer to the use of language describing the realities of punishment in a future world still largely inconceivable.'[2]

[1] See Stott, *Essentials*, p. 316: 'The main function of fire is not to cause pain, but to secure destruction, as all the world's incinerators bear witness.'

[2] *The Gagging of God*, pp. 524–5. Compare William Crockett, 'The Metaphorical View', in *Four Views on Hell*, ed. William Crockett, p. 59: 'The strongest reason for taking them [that is, words used for hell in Scripture] as metaphors is the conflicting language used in the New Testament to describe hell.'

It is simply impossible to press the language regarding hell in the Scriptures in a purely literal manner.[1] To do so creates more problems than the annihilationist is ready to acknowledge. If the literal meaning of fire is that of a force that consumes its object, then that literal meaning also includes the idea of a rapid, quick process. Many annihilationists, however, want to allow for a period of time during which the wicked undergo differing degrees of punishment prior to their eventual annihilation.[2] The idea of a period of time, however, seems rather incompatible with the way literal fire works. Fire burns and consumes its object rapidly. Moreover, once a literal fire has consumed its object, it is no longer able to be sustained or fuelled by that which it consumes. In the biblical imagery and descriptions of the fire of hell, however, the fire is explicitly described as 'eternal' (*Matt.* 18:8). Like the worm that does not die, it is a fire that is never extinguished. Indeed, in Jesus' unforgettable description of hell in Mark 9:47–48, we read of those who are thrown into hell where '*their* worm does not die, and the fire is not quenched' (emphasis mine).

This description shows a close correlation between the working of the worm and the fire on the one hand, and the wicked and the unbelieving on the other. Just as the worm continues to work and the fire is unquenchable, so those upon whom they work continue to experience their effects.[3]

---

[1] For a recent defence of a literal reading of this language, see John F. Walvoord, 'The Literal View', in *Four Views on Hell*, ed. William Crockett, pp. 11–28. Even Walvoord, however, hesitates to insist that the fire of hell is literal, though he insists that it expresses the idea of physical pain.

[2] See Fudge, *The Fire That Consumes*, p. 364, where he speaks of a 'penal suffering culminating in total extinction'. Philip Edgcumbe Hughes, *The True Image: The Origin and Destiny of Man in Christ* (Grand Rapids: Eerdmans, 1989), pp. 398–407, also argues that the unbelieving will experience a real penal suffering in connection with the final judgement and prior to their eventual annihilation.

[3] Carson, *The Gagging of God*, p. 525: 'It is not "*the* worm" but

One additional example of the metaphorical nature of the imagery regarding hell is the language of 'darkness' or 'outer darkness' that is often used in the Scriptures. In Matthew 8:12, Jesus forewarns that the 'sons of the kingdom shall be thrown into the outer darkness; in that place there shall be weeping and gnashing of teeth'. The guest at the wedding banquet who is present without the appropriate wedding garment in Matthew 22 is likewise bound hand and foot and cast into 'outer darkness' (verse 13). This motif of hell as a place of darkness is commonly found in the Scriptures (for example, *Matt.* 25:30, *2 Pet.* 2:17). Darkness represents the absence of the light of God's favour and countenance. To be cast into darkness is to be cast away from the favour and gracious presence of the Lord. Remarkably, in one passage the imagery of an 'eternal fire' and of 'black darkness' are used in the same context to refer to different dimensions of the reality of the eternal punishment of the wicked (*Jude* 7, 13). Now, if we were to insist upon a literal reading of this imagery, the result would be confusing and incoherent. A literal fire and a literal place of darkness cannot be true of the same reality. This illustrates the metaphorical nature of the biblical language; the differing images represent differing dimensions or features of hell. Hell is not only a place where the unbelieving suffer God's holy displeasure (fire), but it is also a place where the unbelieving experience what it means to be excluded or separated from his blessed presence (darkness).

III. AN ETERNITY OF RESULT OR EXPERIENCE?

The second level at which it is argued that the fire of hell is a fire that consumes is more directly textual. Do the biblical texts support the claim of the annihilationist that the wicked are ultimately destroyed or consumed; that they cease to exist after they experience God's judgement? According to

---

"*their* worm", which suggests that it is perpetually bound up with those who are suffering' (emphasis Carson's).

annihilationism, this is the only sense in which the punishment of the unbelieving is unending: it is eternal in the sense of result, but not in the sense of conscious experience of God's displeasure in hell.[1] If the wicked are destroyed or consumed, this has results that endure throughout eternity, but not in the sense of any ongoing awareness of God's judgement.

Several biblical texts, however, militate against this view. These texts speak not only of hell as a place of fire and judgement, but also of the unending nature of these realities. They constitute a compelling basis for the historic doctrine of eternal punishment, against the claims of annihilationists.

One of these texts, Matthew 25:46, is the well-known conclusion to Jesus' account of the final judgement and the separation of the sheep and the goats: 'And these [the goats] will go away into eternal punishment, but the righteous into eternal life.' Not surprisingly, annihilationists attempt to take the language of eternal punishment in this text to mean something other than a temporally unlimited or everlasting experience of God's judgement. This is typically done in one of two ways: either the adjective 'eternal' is taken in a qualitative sense to mean a *kind of* punishment, or it is taken temporally to refer to the ongoing result of God's punishment in the annihilation of the wicked. The first of these interpretations seizes upon the root of the term used for 'eternal' in this text – *aeon,* or 'age'. Jesus is therefore speaking of a punishment that corresponds to the age to come. The obvious problem with this interpretation is that it neglects the inescapable temporal aspect of the coming age, namely, that it is an age having no end or conclusion. In the Gospel of Matthew, this term always has a temporal meaning, referring to an unlimited period of time.[2]

[1] See Fudge, *The Fire That Consumes,* pp. 37–50, 194–6.
[2] See Scot McKnight, 'Eternal Consequences or Eternal Consciousness?' in *Through No Fault of Their Own,* ed. by W. Crockett and J. Sigountos, pp. 151–7, for a discussion of the meaning of this language in Matthew.

The second of these interpretations is well represented by Clark Pinnock: 'Jesus does not define the nature of eternal life or eternal death in this text. He just says there will be two destinies and leaves it there. One is free to interpret it to mean either everlasting conscious torment or irreversible destruction. The text allows for both possibilities and only teaches explicitly the finality of the judgement itself, not its nature.'[1]

Though Pinnock may be correct to say that his understanding of this text is possible, there is a considerable difference between a possible reading of the text and the likeliest reading of it. Three features of the text make the reading of Pinnock and the annihilationist most unlikely. First, the text is preceded in verse 41 by another description of hell: 'Depart from Me, accursed ones, into the eternal fire which has been prepared for the devil and his angels.' This description, like the one provided in verse 46, seems clearly to teach the presence of a fire or a punishment that has no end or conclusion. Second, verse 46 speaks of an eternal punishment, strong language that suggests the experience or felt awareness of God's displeasure. And third, the parallel and contrast in this verse is between an 'eternal' punishment and an 'eternal' life. The straightforward reading of this text indicates in each case an everlasting experience – of punishment on the one hand, of life and blessing on the other.

Another important text in answering the challenge of annihilationism is Revelation 14:10–11. In this text, those who worship the beast and his image are described as being 'tormented with fire and brimstone in the presence of the holy angels and in the presence of the Lamb. And the smoke of their torment goes up forever and ever, and they have no rest day and night, those who worship the beast and his image, and whoever receives the mark of his name.' This text is especially troublesome to the annihilationist position because it speaks emphatically ('forever and ever') of the

---

[1] 'The Destruction of the Finally Impenitent', p. 256.

ongoing torment of the wicked. Those who experience this torment are said to 'have no rest day and night', language that hardly seems compatible with an experience of judgement that terminates in the extinction of those who suffer. The most common way to explain this text on annihilationist assumptions is to introduce a sequence into the experience of the wicked under the judgement of God. This sequence is one first of suffering, then of total annihilation, and then of the 'memorializing' of that annihilation. Fudge, for example, argues that 'torment is meted out according to the mixture of God's cup. Then, as the next image points out, it is forever memorialized in the smoke that remains.'[1] However, this sequence is something that has been introduced into the text in order to avoid its clear implications. Revelation 14:10–11 does not say that the punishment of the wicked occurs in a sequence of steps, beginning with torment and leading to annihilation. It says, in terms that are as clear as they are terrible, that the wicked will experience an unending torment, a torment that will continue without end and without rest, day or night, throughout all eternity. The doctrine of annihilation is opposed to the clear teaching of this passage, a passage that says nothing about a sequence like that proposed.[2] Though it may be convenient to take the various images of this and other texts – of punishment, of fire, of destruction, of exclusion – and order them chronologically,

[1] *The Fire That Consumes*, pp. 297–8.

[2] See Harmon, 'The Case Against Conditionalism', in *Universalism and the Doctrine of Hell*, ed. by Nigel M. de S. Cameron, 213: 'For Fudge, God's final sentence *begins* with banishment, *continues* with a period of conscious suffering, and *ends* with destruction. In fact, not a single New Testament passage teaches exactly this sequence. Instead, some texts speak of personal exclusion, some of punishment, and others of destruction, and these images need to be understood as giving hints at the same eschatological reality. Fudge not only chronologizes these images, but he also emphasizes one to the exclusion of the other two: destruction dominates while punishment and exclusion fall into the background. Indeed, the latter is hardly discussed.'

the biblical texts commonly use these images as diverse ways of referring to the same reality.

Still another important text in this connection is Revelation 20:10–15:

> And the devil who deceived them was thrown into the lake of fire and brimstone, where the beast and the false prophet are also; and they will be tormented day and night forever and ever. And I saw a great white throne and Him who sat upon it, from whose presence earth and heaven fled away, and no place was found for them. And I saw the dead, the great and the small, standing before the throne, and books were opened; and another book was opened, which is the book of life; and the dead were judged from the things which were written in the books, according to their deeds. And the sea gave up the dead which were in it, and death and Hades gave up the dead which were in them; and they were judged, every one of them according to their deeds. And death and Hades were thrown into the lake of fire. This is the second death, the lake of fire. And if anyone's name was not found written in the book of life, he was thrown into the lake of fire.

This text describes judgement at the great white throne, the final judgement of all the dead and the living at the end of the age. It also describes, in terms that parallel those we have seen in other passages, the state of the wicked subsequent to this judgement in hell or the 'lake of fire'.

Like Revelation 14:10–11, Revelation 20:11–15 speaks unmistakably of an ongoing experience of torment. The devil, together with the beast and the false prophet, suffers a torment that is said to be unending. The language could not be more emphatic: 'they will be tormented day and night forever and ever.' Furthermore, all those whose names are not found in the book of life will also be ultimately thrown into the same lake of fire. According to the annihilationist's view, those who are thrown into the lake of fire will eventually be consumed; they will cease to exist. The problem with this reading of the text is that it must posit a sharp difference between the experience of the devil, together with the beast and the false prophet, and all others who are thrown into the same lake of fire, presumably to experience the same punishment or distress. In the case of the wicked generally, this is a fire that will consume them utterly. But it will not consume the devil, for example, since he is said to be tormented 'day and night forever and ever'. A more obvious reading of this text would conclude that all – the devil, the beast, the false prophet, the wicked – will experience the same judgement and destiny. Why would some who are cast into the same lake of fire be utterly consumed by it – assuming that it belongs to the nature of fire to consume – while in the case of others the fire will not have this effect?

IV. INCOMPATIBLE WITH THE LOVE OF GOD?

The biblical arguments mustered against the doctrine of everlasting punishment are, as we have maintained, weak and unconvincing. Though we have not provided a full biblical case for the doctrine of everlasting punishment in the foregoing, we have considered the arguments commonly used to advocate annihilationism as an alternative to the historic Christian doctrine of hell. None of these arguments contributes to a very strong case against this doctrine.

In the case of most advocates of annihilationism, however, the objections to the doctrine of hell are not, in the final analysis, borne out of the interpretation of the biblical texts. Contemporary critics of the historic Christian doctrine of eternal punishment, including those whose theological convictions are generally evangelical, do not argue against this doctrine so much from the Scriptures. Their treatment of the scriptural givens results from a prior and more basic conviction that the doctrine, in its traditional form, is theologically and morally repugnant. According to these critics, fundamental considerations of theology, morality, and human emotion militate against the notion that the God of the Scriptures would everlastingly punish the wicked in hell.

This means that no matter how inconclusive and insubstantial may be the biblical arguments for annihilationism, the primary objections to the doctrine of hell still remain to be considered.

Perhaps the most common – and to many the most compelling – argument against the doctrine of eternal punishment, is the claim that it contradicts what we know from the gospel about the love of God. That God would pour out his wrath and displeasure upon the wicked by excluding them from the reach of his grace seems incompatible with the biblical portrayal of God's abundant love and unfailing mercy. If God so loved the world that he gave his only begotten Son to save the world (*John* 3:16), how is it conceivable that he should punish the wicked everlastingly in hell?

According to this criticism, it seems needlessly cruel and vindictive that God's displeasure with the unbelieving should continue to be revealed throughout the endless duration of the final state. How can this comport with the scriptural testimony, often repeated and nowhere more dramatically manifested than in the Lord Jesus Christ, that his God and Father does not repay us according to our iniquities; that he is slow to anger and abounding in love; and that like an earthly father, he takes pity upon us and remembers that we are dust (*Psa.* 103:8–14)? The repugnance between the remarkable biblical testimony to the tender-heartedness of God's love toward sinners and the idea of the wicked being eternally tormented in hell can only be resolved by denying the latter in favour of the former.[1]

How should we respond to this charge that the doctrine of hell is incompatible with what the Scriptures reveal regarding God's love? Though some aspects of the answer to this question must wait until we take up the issue of God's justice and the doctrine of hell, at least two responses need to be made at this point.

---

[1] For an older and sustained presentation of this argument, see Nels F. S. Ferre, *The Christian Understanding of God* (New York: Harper and Brothers, 1951).

First, though it may seem too concessive at first hearing, we must acknowledge a significant difference between God's love and his wrath. Whereas the former is his natural and delightful work, the latter is his alien and reluctant work (*Ezek.* 23:23, 30–32). God delights to save in a way that must be distinguished from his holy reluctance to punish or to destroy. To be sure, the Scriptures teach that God has purposed from all eternity to save the elect alone (*Eph.* 1:4–6). They also teach that God has chosen not to save others (*Rom.* 9:6–13). However, they do not teach a perfect symmetry or parallel between God's sovereign purposes to save and not to save.

Some of the issues that arise in this connection are complex and difficult. But the doctrine of hell has been needlessly burdened by defenders of the doctrine who neglect this difference between God's joy and delight in the salvation of lost sinners (*Luke* 15:7, 10, 20–32) and his holy reluctance to punish the wicked. When the biblical theme of God's patience with sinners, his desiring that they should turn from their wicked ways and be saved (*1 Tim.* 2:4, *2 Pet.* 3:9), is minimized, the doctrine of hell suffers distortion.[1] Similarly, when professing Christians exhibit nothing of God's love toward his enemies, but rather take a perverse delight in the punishment of the wicked, then God is mocked and his gospel corrupted. Defenders of the biblical doctrine of hell who do not echo the biblical overtures of God's mercy and grace to any and all, who do not share Christ's sorrow over the unbelief of his fellow Israelites (*Luke* 19:41–44), who do not understand the Apostle Paul's agony over the unbelief of his countrymen (*Rom.* 9:2–3; 10:2) – such defenders of the

---

[1] I might add that the doctrine of hell is sometimes burdened by the unexamined assumption that the relative number of the saved is few. One does not have to share W. G. T. Shedd's Postmillennialism to appreciate his oft-quoted observation: 'The circle of God's election is a great circle of the heavens, and not that of a treadmill.' *The Doctrine of Endless Punishment* (1885; repr. Edinburgh: Banner of Truth, 1986), p. 115. Shedd's study remains a classic defence of the doctrine of endless punishment.

doctrine bring disrepute to the grace of God and encumber the biblical teaching about hell.[1]

The biblical doctrine of hell has nothing to do with a divine cruelty or vindictiveness that takes delight in the condemnation of the wicked in the same way God delights to show mercy. Those who through sin and disobedience forfeit any claim upon God's favour should look only to themselves to find the occasion for their punishment in hell. Their exclusion from God's blessed presence is a consequence of their unwillingness to seek him while he was to be found, to call upon him while he was still near (*Isa.* 55:6–7).

Second, this objection to the doctrine of everlasting punishment tends to isolate one feature of the biblical doctrine of God, the attribute of the love of God, from other features such as God's justice or his holiness. In the process, significant dimensions of the Bible's teaching are diminished or rejected outright. The love of God is made the defining attribute that truly expresses God's nature, whereas other attributes are said to be derivative or subordinate. Furthermore, having diminished other aspects of the biblical doctrine of God, the love of God is itself redefined in ways that make it inconsistent with any doctrine of divine punishment or retribution. The love of God becomes sentiment, making no demands upon those to whom it is communicated and imposing no penalty upon those who wilfully refuse it.

In the biblical doctrine of God, however, God's holiness and justice are emphasized as well as his love. Each of these attributes of God's nature discloses who he is, so that it is impermissible to play one attribute against another. God's justice is not incompatible with his love. Rather, these qualities define each other. God is loving in his justice, and just in his loving. He could not be otherwise without ceasing to be

---

[2] J. R. W. Stott expresses this in the form of a challenge (in Edwards and Stott, *Essentials*, p. 313): 'I long that we could in some small way stand in the tearful tradition of Jeremiah, Jesus and Paul. I want to see more tears among us. I think we need to repent of our nonchalance, our hard-heartedness.'

the God he is. To speak of God's love at the expense of his justice would be to deny the biblical view of God in favour of a doctrine that exhibits more affinity to modern notions of love than to the scriptural understanding.

V. INCOMPATIBLE WITH THE JUSTICE OF GOD?

Another related theological objection is that the doctrine of everlasting punishment is unjust. If one of the cardinal rules of justice is that the punishment should fit the crime, then the doctrine of eternal punishment involves a form of punishment that outweighs the crime. For a creature to suffer unendingly under God's displeasure in hell represents a disproportionate meting out of punishment. Annihilationists, though they recognise the need for God's justice to be exercised in the punishment or ultimate destruction of the wicked, typically argue that the doctrine of hell represents a gross disproportion between the limited offence of the sinner and the unlimited consequence that follows. To address this objection, we need to begin with a brief reflection upon the biblical view of justice, particularly the divine attribute of God's justice.

Defining what we mean by justice and, in particular, by the justice of God, is no simple task. One place to begin is with the so-called *lex talionis*, the law of retribution set forth in the well-known words of Leviticus 24:19–20: 'And if a man injures his neighbor, just as he has done, so it shall be done to him: fracture for fracture, eye for eye, tooth for tooth; just as he has injured a man, so it shall be inflicted on him.' The principle enunciated in this passage is one of due proportion or equity between offence committed and punishment exacted. The perpetrator of the offence must, by means of a corresponding punishment, be brought to acknowledge and pay for the offence. It would be wrong or unjust, were the perpetrator to get off scot free without a due admission of guilt and an appropriate punishment suffered. Whether the offence is small or great, justice demands that redress be made in the form of owning up to the offence and suffering the proper consequences.

This rule of justice presumes a standard of right and wrong which, when violated in greater or lesser degree, requires that the wrongdoing be admitted and some form of amends be made. Parents whose children misbehave know well (or should know) that such misbehaviour needs to be pointed out and a suitable penalty be paid. Often the most difficult questions they face concern the appropriateness of the penalty and the fairness of its application in expressing proper restraint and love. But it is irresponsible to overlook the offence or to neglect the discipline which it demands. Similarly, in the administration of justice by the civil authorities, the law distinguishes clearly between different crimes and obligates the courts to assign corresponding penalties. One of the difficulties, of course, that a biblical view of justice faces in the modern age is the tendency to downplay this idea of retribution – imposing an equitable punishment upon the criminal – and to emphasise almost exclusively the role of remedy in the administration of justice. If the only purpose of the judicial system is to restore the offender, then the notions of just recompense and suitable punishment lose their place.[1]

[1] J. I. Packer, in his *The Problem of Eternal Punishment*, pp. 7–8, acknowledges that hell involves divine retribution upon the lost sinner. Remarkably, however, he goes on to suggest that we should generally not 'use vocabulary of punishment at all'. Rather, we should use terms to describe hell that are 'conceptually clear but not emotionally loaded'. Though I have some sympathy for this suggestion – the terms 'punish' and 'torment' can easily be burdened with inappropriate connotations of vindictiveness, cruelty, arbitrariness, and excess – I do not see how it is possible to convey the biblical teaching without using these terms. Even Packer's preferred term, retribution, if it is explained, will have to include a just punishment that corresponds to the crime committed. Even the language used to describe Christ's atoning work as a 'penal' satisfaction makes clear that this language cannot be avoided altogether. One should exercise caution, of course, in using this language. But it can hardly be avoided.

The Doctrine of Eternal Punishment

According to the biblical doctrine of God, one of God's defining attributes is his justice. Because God is just and cannot deny himself, he always deals with human sin in a manner that upholds the strictest rule of justice, including the rule of appropriate retribution. Though this dimension of God's nature often receives short shrift in contemporary theology, the Scriptures are full of references to his unwillingness to permit sin to go unpunished and to his role as the One who will judge all human beings with justice. What human conscience and the rule of law demand by way of acknowledging wrongdoing and suffering its consequences only reflect the justice of God in his administration of the affairs of his creatures.

God is, biblically understood, the supreme lawgiver and the vindicator of the right (*Psa.* 119:137–8; 145:17, *Jer.* 12:1, 1 *John* 2:29). He is the One who maintains righteousness and finally vindicates the moral order he has established (*Psa.* 99:4, *Rom.* 2:6, 7).

This understanding of God's justice underlies the biblical teaching about the final judgement. It also provides the necessary context within which to comprehend the atoning work of Jesus Christ on behalf of his people.

According to the biblical descriptions of God's judgement, all those who are judged will be brought to recognize what they have done, whether it be good or bad. God's justice will serve as a mirror to expose every wrongdoing, even those wrongs that might otherwise be hidden from view. The secret things, including the motives of the heart, will be revealed in the presence of God (1 Cor. 4:5, *Rom.* 2:16).

Each person judged will receive at the hands of God what they have deserved (2 *Cor.* 5:10, *Psa.* 62:12, *Jer.* 17:10). No one will be able to escape this judgement (*Acts* 17:30ff, *Isa.* 29:15–17). All will be called to give an account of their lives and actions (*Matt.* 25:31–46). The purpose of this judging and the exacting of an appropriate penalty will be nothing other than the vindication of God's justice, the revelation of his authority and rule in maintaining the right within his creation (*Rev.* 16:1–7; 19:1–6, *Psa.* 82:1, 8).

This raises an important question for which the biblical understanding of Christ's atoning work provides the answer – how can God be just in pardoning sinners and treating with favour those who have offended against him? Not all who are judged will be required to acknowledge their sin and suffer the just consequences of their offence. All will acknowledge their sin and unworthiness, to be sure; but those who by the working of the Holy Spirit have trusted in Christ and repented of their sins will be openly declared acceptable to God and the recipients of the rewards of his grace. The biblical answer to this question focuses upon the cross of Christ.

Christ, by virtue of his life of obedience and his atoning death, met the demands and the penalties of the law on behalf and in the place of his own people. All those who are beneficiaries of Christ's saving work as their Mediator are restored to favour with God and made acceptable to him. In the biblical view this work involved a perfect marriage or harmony between God's love or mercy and his justice. The work of Christ displays equally the mercy and the justice of God. As the Apostle Paul describes it in Romans 3:21–26:

> But now apart from the Law the righteousness of God has been manifested, being witnessed by the Law and the Prophets, even the righteousness of God through faith in Jesus Christ for all those who believe; for there is no distinction, for all have sinned and fall short of the glory of God, being justified as a gift by His grace through the redemption which is in Christ Jesus; whom God displayed publicly as a propitiation in His blood through faith. This was to demonstrate His righteousness, because in the forbearance of God He passed over the sins previously committed; for the demonstration, I say, of His righteousness at the present time, that He might be just and the justifier of the one who has faith in Jesus.

One interesting consequence of this biblical emphasis upon Christ's atonement as a demonstration of God's justice is what it tells us about the seriousness and gravity of human sin. The common objection to the doctrine of eternal punishment – that the punishment outweighs the crime – would seem to hold with equal force against the justice of Christ's suffering and cross. Why would God be just in exacting an infinite penalty – the death of his own Son – were the offence limited in its seriousness? The justice of God in exacting the price of Christ's atoning death would be imperilled, were some lesser or limited price adequate to meet the need of sinners. To estimate the seriousness of human sin apart from a consideration of Christ's cross and work of atonement would be to call into question the justice of God's provision for our need. Ironically, John R. W. Stott, today a cautious defender of annihilationism, has expressed this point as well as anyone in an earlier study, *The Cross of Christ*:

> The doctrine of substitution affirms not only a fact (God in Christ substituted himself for us) but its necessity (there was no other way by which God's own holy love could be satisfied and rebellious human beings could be saved). Therefore, as we stand before the cross, we begin to gain a clear view both of God and of ourselves, especially in relation to each other. Instead of inflicting upon us the judgement we deserved, God in Christ endured it in our place. Hell is the only alternative. This is the 'scandal', the stumbling-block, of the cross. For our proud hearts rebel against it. We cannot bear to acknowledge either the seriousness of our sin and guilt or our utter indebtedness to the cross.[1]

To state the matter more concisely: that Christ suffered the agony of hell to atone for our sins teaches us that hell is what

---

[1] *The Cross of Christ* (Downers Grove, Illinois: InterVarsity Press, 1986), p. 161. I say 'cautious defender' because Stott does not so much affirm annihilationism as oppose the traditional idea of unending punishment.

we sinners deserve. This penalty for sin was infinite in its price precisely because human sin offends against the infinite majesty and worth of God himself.[1]

One further consideration requires comment. Though it is often assumed that the unbelieving and impenitent cease to sin at the judgement of God, it seems more probable that they continue to sin and live in hostility toward God throughout the final state. When God delivers the impenitent over to hell, he can be said to give them not only what they deserve but also what they perversely continue to desire. To live apart from God and his favour is the epitome of the suffering of hell. But this is precisely what the impenitent sinner seeks even in hell, namely, to live without God. D. A. Carson has argued that the continued sinning of the wicked in hell is the most probable scenario and may even be directly supported by Scripture (*Rev.* 22:10–11; 16:21).[2] If this be the case, the ongoing punishment of the lost will correspond to their ongoing sin and rebellion. On balance, this seems to be a more likely circumstance than that the lost would begin to love God and their neighbour, as the law of God requires. This likelihood cannot be conclusively demonstrated.

---

[1] The *Heidelberg Catechism* in Q. & A. 11 expresses well the infinite seriousness of sin because it is an offence against God: 'God is indeed merciful, but he is also just; therefore his justice requires that sin which is committed against the most high majesty of God, be also punished with extreme, that is, with everlasting punishment of body and soul.' The problem with most denials of the gravity of human sin is that they do not reckon with the infinite worth of the Triune God against whom all sin is ultimately directed. Because God is diminished, sin against him is likewise diminished.

[2] *The Gagging of God*, pp. 533–4. See also D. A. Carson, *How Long O Lord? Reflections on Suffering & Evil* (Grand Rapids: Baker, 1990), p. 102: 'Perhaps, then, we should think of hell as a place where people continue to rebel, continue to insist on their own way, continue societal structures of prejudice and hate, continue to defy the living God. And as they continue to defy God, so he continues to punish them. And the cycle goes on and on and on.'

However, it seems to fit the biblical data better than the contrary assumption that the lost begin to live in full conformity to God's will.

These considerations regarding the law of retribution, the justice of God, the atoning work of Christ, and the likelihood of continuing rebellion on the part of the lost in the final state, together confirm the justice of the doctrine of eternal punishment. Those who contest the justice of hell either fail to estimate properly the gravity of human sin against God or to respect the justice of God in dealing with it. There can be no escape from God's justice: either Christ suffered it for us at the cross or we shall suffer it ourselves.

VI. A BLEMISH UPON THE FINAL STATE OF THINGS?

The last objection to the doctrine of everlasting punishment that we will consider appeals to the glory and perfection of the final state. If God's redemptive and re-creative purposes in Christ find their ultimate fulfilment in the consummation of all things, then the continued presence of the wicked in hell would constitute a blemish upon the otherwise pristine state of the new creation. One articulate proponent of this argument, Philip Edgcumbe Hughes, has pointedly stated this objection:

> The conception of the endlessness of the suffering of torment and of the endurance of 'living' death in hell stands in contradiction to this teaching [that is, the renewal of creation]. It leaves a part of creation which, unrenewed, everlastingly exists in alienation from the new heaven and the new earth. It means that suffering and death will never be totally abolished from the scene . . . To this it must be objected that with the restoration of all things in the new heaven and the new earth, which involves God's reconciliation to himself of all things, whether on earth or in heaven (Acts 3:21, Col. 1:20), there will be no place for a second kingdom of darkness and death. Where all is light there can be no darkness; for 'the night shall be no more' (Rev. 22:5).

When Christ fills all and all and God is everything to everyone (Eph. 1:23, 1 Cor. 15:28), how is it conceivable that
there can be a section or realm of creation that does not
belong to this fullness and by its very presence contradicts
it?[1]

To put the matter a bit more prosaically, these objectors
insist that hell would deprive God's programme in history of
a happy ending. At the end of the day, when all of God's
purposes in Christ will have reached their fulfilment, the
presence of sin and sinners will still remain within the realm
of God's creation. The loose thread of the presence of hell
will mar the beautiful tapestry of God's redemptive purpose
brought to its appointed end.

Of all the objections to the biblical doctrine of hell, this
one is the most difficult to answer, not because it is so
persuasive, but because it is so speculative. For the argument
to work, it has to be assumed that the reality of hell represents a failure on God's part to realise his purposes of grace.
Hell would, on this view of things, be an insuperable
obstacle to the complete victory of God's gracious work
through Christ. The reach and effectiveness of God's grace
would be bounded. The embrace of God's love would be
frustrated at the borders of hell. But are these assumptions
true to the biblical revelation regarding God's purposes and
the triumph of his kingdom?

Contrary to these assumptions, the biblical understanding
of hell includes the conviction that even in the punishment of
the unbelieving and impenitent, God's purposes and justice
will be vindicated. Hell does not represent a limitation upon
the reach of God's purposes or frustrate his redemptive work
in Christ. In the judgement and ultimate punishment of the
lost, God's justice will be fully revealed. Every mouth will be
stopped. No occasion for protest will be found. All will be
held accountable to God, and no one will have reason to

[1] Hughes, *The True Image*, pp. 405–6.

complain against the justice of his judgements (see *Rom.* 2:19–20, 9:17, 22–24). Indeed, all those for whom Christ shed his blood and on whose behalf he made atonement will be saved. Not one will be lost or snatched from his hand. Not one will be overlooked or forgotten. Certainly, not one of his own will fall outside of the reach of his gracious purpose to save (*John* 10:14–18, 27–29).

In the final analysis, this last objection rests upon an assumption that is nowhere set forth in Scripture. It is a disguised form of universalism, since it asserts that all who are not redeemed by the grace of God must be annihilated. However, in the biblical understanding, God's will and purpose are triumphant in both the salvation of his people and in the condemnation of the lost.

Conclusion

The biblical teaching regarding hell and the eternal punishment of the lost is difficult to maintain in the face of the many assaults upon the doctrine today. Whether in the form of benign neglect[1] or open hostility, whether registered by those who repudiate or defend the Christian faith – opposition to the doctrine of hell is all but overwhelming. Even the form in which I have cast my treatment of the doctrine in the foregoing has about it an air of defensiveness. Never in the history of the Christian church has this dimension of the Bible's teaching regarding the future been more obviously on trial.

Rather than close our consideration of this doctrine on a defensive note, however, I would like to conclude with a few general observations.

First, the doctrine of hell is a true test of our willingness to stay within the boundaries of Scripture when it comes to the subject of the last things. At no point in our consideration of

---

[1] See Martin Marty, 'Hell's Sober Comeback', *U.S. News & World Report* (March 25, 1991), p. 56: 'Hell has disappeared and no one noticed.'

the Bible's teaching about the future are we more inclined to allow our own judgements and opinions to take precedence over an exposition of the Bible's teaching and the church's historic understanding. What we do with the subject of hell is a litmus test of our readiness to follow the way set out for us in the Scriptures, even when that way proves at times to be difficult and unpleasant.

Second, the doctrine of hell has immense significance for the manner in which the church proclaims the gospel and addresses those who still live in unbelief and impenitence before God. We do not wish to endorse what is often known as 'Pascal's wager', but it cannot be denied that if the biblical teaching about hell is true, then it is scarcely possible to exaggerate the importance of seeking the Lord while he may be found, calling upon him while he is still near. Though we will not attempt here to explore the ramifications of this doctrine for the Christian believer or the mission of the church, they are transparent and undeniable. The seriousness with which believers 'work out their salvation with fear and trembling', and the urgency with which the church preaches the gospel to the nations – these are a fair measure of conviction regarding the doctrine of eternal punishment. Ironically, perhaps one of the reasons this doctrine is so little believed and confessed is the failure of many ostensibly orthodox Christians to live in a manner consistent with its truth. For it is a practical denial of hell to take a cavalier attitude toward one's own salvation, or to treat with indifference the awful plight of those who are perishing in the darkness of unbelief.[1]

And third, an inappropriate fascination with and literalistic understanding of the biblical imagery for hell have often encumbered the doctrine of hell. Fuelled by the lurid imagery of Dante's poetic descriptions in his Inferno and the preaching of some over-zealous friends of the doctrine of

---

[1] See Robert A. Peterson, *Hell on Trial*, pp. 223–42, for a concise treatment of 'What Difference Does It Make?'

hell, this fascination with the doctrine can easily become an unnecessary stumbling block. We need to remember that the biblical imagery conveys something of the reality of hell, as a place both of punishment and of exclusion from the presence of God's favour. But such imagery ought not to be taken literally. We should not think that it enables us to imagine or begin to comprehend what hell is really like. What we should do is think soberly and carefully about the reality to which this language and imagery points us: the reality of being banished from the blessed presence of God, being under the felt impression of his everlasting displeasure, and being subjected to the perpetual frustration and fury of sinful, but futile, rebellion against his will.

J. I. Packer offers us sage advice along these lines, advice with which we conclude our consideration of the doctrine of hell:

> Do not speculate about the retributive process. Do not try to imagine what it is like to be in hell. The horrific imaginings of the past were hardly helpful, and often in fact proved a stumbling-block, as people equated the reality of hell with the lurid word-pictures drawn by Dante, or Edwards, or C. H. Spurgeon. Not that these men were wrong to draw their pictures, any more than Jesus was wrong to dwell on the fire and the worm; the mistake is to take such pictures as physical descriptions, when in fact they are imagery symbolising realities of possible experience of which we can only say they are far, far worse than the symbols themselves . . . Our wisdom is rather to spend our lives finding ways of showing gratitude for the saving grace of Christ which ensures that we shall not in fact ever go to the hell that each of us so richly deserves, and to school our minds to dwell on heaven rather than on the other place, except when we are seeking, in Jude's phrase, to snatch others from the fire. Let us then labour to be wise.[1]

[1] *The Problem of Eternal Punishment*, pp. 14–15.

16

The New Heavens and New Earth

I N HIS *WEIGHT OF GLORY AND OTHER ESSAYS*, C. S. Lewis compares the insurmountable challenge any Christian faces when speaking of heaven, the final state awaiting the children of God, to a schoolboy struggling with the difficulties of grammar and syntax. Such a schoolboy has difficulty enough with the simplest demands of ordinary prose, but finds the greater challenge of writing poetry beyond his reach: 'The Christian, in relation to Heaven, is in very much the same position as this schoolboy. Those who have attained everlasting life in the vision of God doubtless know very well that it is no mere bribe, but the very consummation of their earthly discipleship; but we who have not yet attained it cannot know this . . . Poetry replaces grammar, gospel replaces law, longing transforms obedience, as gradually as the tide lifts a grounded ship.'[1]

If it is true of hell, the final state of the unbelieving, that no one who hasn't been there knows its reality, then it is likewise

---

[1] (1949; repr. Grand Rapids: Eerdmans, 1979), p. 3.

true that, short of having entered its glory, no one knows what the final state of the blessed will be like. Certainly, no one would be so bold as to think that the reality of heaven could be described in anything more than the most inadequate of words. Here one can only stammer like a little child. When it comes to the subject of the new heavens and earth, we face a dimension of the future of which it may be said without exaggeration, 'Things which eye has not seen and ear has not heard, and which have not entered the heart of man, all that God has prepared for those who love him' (*1 Cor.* 2:9).[1]

However, while acknowledging the unspeakable mystery that is the final state of the people of God, we must also be wary of the false modesty and ingratitude that would prevent our saying anything about something of which the Bible does speak. Not only do the Scriptures provide us with a window upon the glory and splendour of heaven, but they also teach us that believers even now have tasted something of the glory that awaits them (*1 Cor.* 2:10). Consequently, without a consideration of heaven, a study of the promise of the future would be incomplete, for at least two compelling reasons.

First, in keeping with a theme that has recurred throughout our treatment of the future, we must acknowledge that the Bible does reveal, albeit in language that is symbolic and rudimentary, something of the splendour of the final state of believers. Though we must always avoid the temptation to go beyond the limits of what the Scriptures disclose, we may not ignore what they do tell us. Here, as elsewhere, we must honour the limits of Scriptural revelation, while echoing what is told us. To say more about heaven than we are permitted would be proud presumption, to be sure; however, to say less than the Scriptures say would be a false modesty.

---

[1] Perhaps this explains the relative brevity with which many studies of biblical doctrine treat the subject of heaven. Louis Berkhof, for example, in his *Systematic Theology*, devotes only a little more than one page to it.

Second, the newness of life in the Spirit that believers presently enjoy is of a piece with the fullness of immortal life that is yet to come (2 Cor. 5:4–5). As with many other aspects of the Bible's teaching about the promise of the future, the future of the new heavens and earth is a reality whose firstfruits are the present experience of those who share fellowship with the risen and ascended Christ. The great future of the fullness of life in communion with the Triune God, promised to those who already enjoy the beginnings of salvation in this life, is not a complete mystery shut off from all human reflection. Though we know in part, we truly do know something of what awaits the child of God in the life to come. 'For now we see in a mirror dimly, but then face to face; now I know in part, but then I shall know fully just as I also have been fully known' (1 Cor. 13:12). And what we know, even if but dimly, is something on which it is impossible to be silent.

All New Things? Or All Things Made New?

Any reflection upon the Bible's teaching about the final state of the believer must treat an issue raised at the outset of this study. What is the relation between the first creation and the second creation? If one of the great themes of the Scriptures is that 'paradise lost' will become 'paradise regained', what does this tell us about the continuity between God's first creation of the 'heavens and earth' and his work of re-creation? For the Bible speaks not only of 'heaven' as the final state of the righteous, but also of the 'new heavens and the new earth' (2 Pet. 3:13).

I. THE MEANING OF 'HEAVEN'

Christian understanding and popular piety have tended to view the final state in a way that almost suggests a denial of the goodness of creation. Life in the new creation is portrayed in terms that are so unlike life in the present state of creation that all continuity between the present and the future is denied. For example, in a considerable body of

Christian hymnody, the portrait of heaven is so 'spiritualized' and ethereal that life in the renewed creation has a barren, almost sterile, quality. Familiar is the picture of believers dressed in white robes flitting about in an indefinable space, playing harps and singing in a celestial choir. The expectation for the life to come is so radically other than the richness and concreteness of life in the creation as it is now experienced that heaven takes on a surreal, even dreamlike, quality.

Undoubtedly, some of these popular portraits of heaven have been shaped by the imagery of Scripture. But they do not adequately reflect the biblical understanding of heaven and the promise of the life to come. In particular, they often show a failure to understand how the term 'heaven' is used in the Scriptures. The term 'heaven' in the Scriptures is commonly used in at least three ways.[1]

First, the term 'heaven' is often used in conjunction with the 'earth' to describe the fullness of what the Triune God has created. To say that God is the Almighty Maker of 'heaven and earth' is equivalent to saying that he is the Creator of all things. Heaven in this sense is a part of creation, distinguishable from the earth but nonetheless, like the earth, a place that God has created to reveal his glory. In Genesis 1:1, we read that 'in the beginning God created the heavens and the earth'. In the New Testament Gospels, frequent references to the 'heaven and earth' confirm that heaven is a dimension of God's creation corresponding to, but distinguishable from, the earth.[2] In this first use of the term 'heaven', heaven in conjunction with the earth constitutes an essential part of the created world or cosmos.

---

[1] See Millard Erickson, *Christian Theology* (Grand Rapids: Baker, 1985), pp. 1226–7. For a summary of the biblical teaching about heaven in distinction from the earth, see Klaas Schilder, *Heaven: What is It?*, trans. Marian M. Schoolland (Grand Rapids: Eerdmans, 1950), ch. 4, 'The History of Heaven', pp. 39–57.

[2] See, for example, *Matt.* 5:18; 11:25; 24:29, 35, *Luke* 4:25; 16:17.

Second, the term 'heaven' can be used as a synonym for God himself. In the Gospel of Matthew, the kingdom of God is referred to as the 'kingdom of heaven', a usage that probably reflects Matthew's deference to Jewish readers who were reluctant to use the name of God for fear of misusing it. When the prodigal son returns to his father and confesses his sins before him, he says, 'I have sinned against heaven and in your sight' (*Luke* 15:18, 21). In Matthew 21:25, Jesus asks the Pharisees whether the baptism of John was 'from heaven or from man'. And in John 3:27, John the Baptist declares that a 'man can receive nothing unless it has been given him from heaven'. In these passages, heaven is simply another way of referring to God.

And third, heaven in its most significant use in the Scriptures refers to the peculiar place of God's dwelling in the midst of his creatures. Though God fills heaven and earth and cannot be restricted to any particular place, he has purposed to draw near to the creation from his special dwelling in heaven. Illustrations of this use of heaven are not difficult to find in the Scriptures. When Jesus taught his disciples to pray, he taught them to address God as 'Our Father who art in heaven' (*Matt.* 6:9). In conformity with this form of address, he also often spoke to them of 'your Father who is in heaven' (*Matt.* 5:16, 45; 6:1; 7:11; 18:14) and of 'my Father who is in heaven' (*Matt.* 7:21; 10:32, 33; 12:50; 16:17; 18:10, 19). The same idea is expressed by the term 'heavenly Father' (*Matt.* 5:48; 6:14, 26, 32; 15:13; 18:35). Because God's dwelling is in heaven, the Scriptures also speak of Christ's coming 'from heaven', whether it be his first coming or his second coming at the end of the age (*John* 3:13, 2 *Thess.* 1:7). The angels who stand in the presence of God and do his bidding are likewise commonly described as being in or coming from heaven (*Matt.* 28:2, *Luke* 22:43, *Isa.* 6:1–6, *Psa.* 103:19–20).

For a proper understanding of the final state, these uses of the term heaven in the Scriptures are most significant. Just as the totality of creation comprises heaven and earth together, so the work of redemption embraces heaven and earth together. Sin has disrupted the harmony and peace between the Triune God and his creatures, a disruption that encompasses heaven and earth. Even in heaven itself, the enemies of God have rebelled against his gracious rule. Indeed, the rebellion of the creature against the Creator began in heaven and spilled over to the earth.[1] Consequently, when God's work of redemption reaches its consummation, not only will every rebellious creature be cast out of heaven, but the earth itself will be cleansed of every vestige of sin. Heaven and earth, rather than being estranged from each other, will once more be reunited in a new heaven and new earth in which righteousness dwells (*2 Pet.* 3:13).

Though the teaching of the Bible regarding heaven is much richer than this brief sketch suggests, this should suffice to show that redemption's reach is as broad as the creation itself, embracing heaven and earth. The future of the believing community will be one in which the original harmony between heaven and earth is restored. The peace or shalom that mark the life of the renewed creation will be expressed in the reconciliation of heaven and earth. Heaven, the place of God's special dwelling, will come down to the earth and God will dwell in the midst of his people. The promise of the future for believers finds its focus in heaven, but it does not exclude the earth. Rather, all things will be united in Christ, whether things in heaven or things upon the earth (*Eph.* 1:10).

II. ALL THINGS MADE NEW

Consistent with the biblical emphasis upon the reconciliation of heaven and earth, the future state will be one in which all

---

[1] It is therefore not surprising that in the visions of God's triumph in the book of Revelation, heaven is the place where this triumph is first achieved, and only thereafter is it accomplished upon the earth. See, for example, *Rev.* 12:7–12; 20:1–10. The same idea is expressed by the motif of angelic descent from heaven (10:1; 18:1; 20:1), and by the note that the new Jerusalem will come down 'from heaven' to the earth (21:2).

things, whether in heaven or on earth, will have been renewed. The whole creation, heaven and earth, will undergo by the Triune God's working, a process of renewal and transformation. Through this process the creation will be wholly sanctified, cleansed of every stain and remainder of sin. The new heavens and the new earth will be more glorious and resplendent of God's power, wisdom and grace, than the creation at its beginning. Once more, but now in a surpassing way, the creation will be a temple fit for the dwelling of God with his people, a place suitable for the enjoyment of communion and friendship between the Creator and the creature.

One question that naturally arises at this juncture is: will the new creation be radically unlike the present creation? Or will it be substantially like it though having undergone a transformation? To state this question somewhat abstractly, what will be the measure of continuity or discontinuity between the present state of the creation and the final state?

In the history of the church, both of these views have had advocates. Some have argued that the new heavens and earth will be altogether new; the present creation will be destroyed, and a new creation will take its place, one that is quite unlike the present. Others have maintained that the new heavens and earth will be this creation made new, one that is similar in substance to the present.[1] The second of these views – that the new heavens and earth will be substantially similar to the present heavens and earth – seems more likely for several reasons.

First, when we considered the subject of the resurrection of the body, a decision was made in favour of the view of substantial similarity between the present body and the

---

[1] Herman Bavinck, *The Last Things*, p. 156, cites the following as representatives of the first view: Origen, the Lutherans, the Mennonites, the Socinians, Vorstius, the Remonstrants, and 'a number of Reformed theologians like Beza, Rivet, Junius, Wollebius, and Prideaux'. Compare G. C. Berkouwer, *The Return of Christ*, p. 220, n. 18, who lists a number of Lutheran advocates of the discontinuity position.

resurrection body. Now just as the resurrected body represents the transformation of the present body of the believer, so the new creation represents the transformation, not the annihilation, of the present creation. However new and glorious this resurrection body may be, it does not involve a radical breach with what has gone before. Rather, like the seed that must die before it produces fruit, so the dissolution of the body is a prelude to its glorification (*1 Cor.* 15: 35–49). In the biblical understanding, the future of the believer, or individual eschatology, corresponds to the future of the creation, general or cosmic eschatology. The resurrection in newness of life that the believer undergoes parallels the resurrection that the whole creation will undergo at the consummation of all things.

Second, if the new heavens and the new earth will be substantially unlike the present heavens and earth, then we would have to conclude that the Triune God's redemptive work discards rather than renews all things. Though this is a rather general consideration, the teaching that the new creation involves a radically new beginning would suggest that sin and evil have become so much a part of the substance of the present created order that it is unrelievedly and radically evil. The original pronouncement of God regarding the created heavens and earth – that they were 'very good' – would no longer have any validity regarding their now fallen condition. But such an implication seems incompatible with the doctrine of the integrity and goodness of the creation, however much it may have been corrupted and distorted through sin. It would even imply that the sinful rebellion of the creation had so ruined God's handiwork as to make it irretrievably wicked. On such a view of things, the rebellion of Satan and the subsequent fall of the human race into sin would overwhelm God's capacity to restore and redeem the work of his hands.[1]

---

[1] Speaking of this implication, Anthony Hoekema, *The Bible and the Future*, p. 281, remarks: 'If God would have to annihilate the

These considerations notwithstanding, advocates of the view that the new creation will be altogether different from the present creation appeal to a number of passages in the Scriptures that seem to imply this view. In the pronouncements of Old Testament prophecy regarding the new heavens and earth, language is used that seems to imply the destruction and removal of all things. In Psalm 102:26, the old heavens and earth are compared to a garment that wears out and perishes: 'Even they will perish, but Thou dost endure; and all of them will wear out like a garment; like clothing Thou wilt change them, and they will be changed.' The prophet Isaiah describes the wearing away of all the host of heaven as being like a leaf that withers from the vine or the fig tree (34:4). Like the vanishing of smoke, the sky will vanish and the inhabitants of the earth will die (*Isa.* 51:6). When the prophet goes on to speak of the new heavens and earth, he speaks of them as something God will 'create', 'the former things shall not be remembered or come to mind' (65:17; compare 66:22). In a similar way, New Testament passages that describe the work of recreation employ the imagery of perishing or wearing out like a garment (*Heb.* 1:11), of a fire that consumes (*2 Pet.* 3:10), of a changing of all things (*Heb.* 1:12), and of the present order of things passing away (*Matt.* 5:18; 24:35, 2 Pet. 3:10, 1 John 2:17, Rev. 21:1). The implications of these images seem to be that the present world will be extinguished to make way for the introduction of something altogether new.

However, the vivid imagery and language of these passages ought not to be pressed too literally. Though they convey the

---

present cosmos, Satan would have won a great victory. For then Satan would have succeeded in so devastatingly corrupting the present cosmos and the present earth that God could do nothing with it but blot it out totally of existence. But Satan did not win such a victory. On the contrary, Satan has been decisively defeated. God will reveal the full dimensions of that defeat when he shall renew this very earth on which Satan deceived mankind and finally banish from it all the results of Satan's evil machinations.'

thought of a radical renovation or renewal of all things, they do not require the conclusion that this renewal will mean the complete annihilation of the present cosmos. Indeed, some Scriptural passages describing this renewal require the alternative – that this renewal will involve a process of purification and cleansing of the old making all things new, but not all new things. Two of these passages are especially significant and deserve particular attention.

ROMANS 8:18–25

We had occasion to consider this passage earlier in connection with our discussion of the resurrection of this body. We saw that it not only illustrates the analogy between the resurrection of the believer and the resurrection-renewal of the whole creation, but that it also describes the new creation in terms that confirm its substantial continuity with the present creation.

> For I consider that the sufferings of this present time are not worthy to be compared with the glory that is to be revealed to us. For the anxious longing of the creation waits eagerly for the revealing of the sons of God. For the creation was subjected to futility, not of its own will, but because of Him who subjected it, in hope that the creation itself also will be set free from its slavery to corruption into the freedom of the glory of the children of God. For we know that the whole creation groans and suffers the pains of childbirth together until now. And not only this, but also we ourselves, having the first fruits of the Spirit, even we ourselves groan within ourselves, waiting eagerly for our adoption as sons, the redemption of our body. For in hope we have been saved, but hope that is seen is not hope; for why does one also hope for what he sees? But if we hope for what we do not see, with perseverance we wait eagerly for it.

Several features of this passage are relevant to the question of the continuity between the present and the future state of the creation.

First, it reminds us that the introduction of sin into the creation has affected not only the human race but also the whole creation. The curse upon Adam and his posterity is one that includes the creation itself. As the apostle expresses it, the creation has been subjected to 'futility', to 'vanity' or 'pointlessness', because of the sinful rebellion of God's image-bearers. Though we are not told how this futility is to be understood, undoubtedly the cosmos itself has been adversely affected by sin and evil. Without becoming unrelievedly evil, sin has brought distortion and corruption to the entirety of God's handiwork. The fabric of creation has been torn and broken, corresponding to the humiliation and weakness that now affect the human body (1 Cor. 15, Phil. 3:21).

Second, the redemption for which the children of God eagerly wait and the redemption of the creation itself are intimately connected.[1] Individual eschatology and cosmic eschatology are so joined together that what is true for believers holds true for the creation itself. Just as believers who, by the first fruits of the Spirit, eagerly anticipate the fullness of redemption, so the creation itself looks forward to its release from the futility to which it has been subjected. When the children of God are revealed in glory and freedom, a similar glory and freedom will be granted to the creation itself. Its present corruption and distortion will be removed. Its torn fabric will be mended. Remarkably, the language describing the restoration of creation corresponds exactly to the language describing the restoration of the children of God. The same process of renewal that promises the

---

[1] This does not mean, however, that the redemption of the children of God is the only real interest of this passage. For a treatment of this passage that argues against an exclusively 'anthropological-soteriological' reading of it, see John Bolt, 'The Relation Between Creation and Redemption in Romans 8:18–27', *Calvin Theological Journal*, 30/1 (April 1995), pp. 34–51.

transformation the believer's present bodies of humiliation into bodies of glory will transform the creation itself.[1]

And third, the metaphor of childbirth that dominates this passage suggests that the transformation of the creation will be in substantial continuity with its present state. The creation groans, according to this passage, like a woman in childbirth prior to the delivery of her child. Though it may be inappropriate to press this metaphor too far, certainly it requires the idea of a substantial likeness between that which gives birth and that which is born. Like gives birth to like. So the new creation, born of the old, will bear a resemblance and similarity to the original. To suggest that the new creation will be radically other than the former creation would violate the clear implication of this passage.

2 PETER 3:5–13

This passage is also of special importance to the question of the continuity between the present creation and the life to come. The Apostle Peter is answering those 'in the last days' who conclude, because Christ has not returned and the universe continues uninterruptedly, that the promise of his coming is untrue. To this the apostle responds:

> For when they maintain this, it escapes their notice that by the word of God the heavens existed long ago and the earth was formed out of water and by water, through which the world at that time was destroyed, being flooded with water.

[1] John Murray, *The Epistle to the Romans* (NICNT; 1959; repr. Grand Rapids: Eerdmans, 1975), pp. 304–5, makes the following comment on this coincidence of cosmic and individual transformation: 'The creation is to share, therefore, in the glory that will be bestowed upon the children of God. It can only participate in that glory, however, in a way that is compatible with its nature as non-rational. Yet the glory of the children of God is one that comprises the creation also and must not be conceived of apart from the cosmic regeneration – the glory of the people of God will be in the context of the restitution of all things (cf. Acts. 3:21).'

But the present heavens and earth by His word are being reserved for fire, kept for the day of judgment and destruction of ungodly men. But do not let this one fact escape your notice, beloved, that with the Lord one day is as a thousand years, and a thousand years as one day. The Lord is not slow about His promise, as some count slowness, but is patient toward you, not wishing for any to perish but for all to come to repentance. But the day of the Lord will come like a thief, in which the heavens will pass away with a roar and the elements will be destroyed with intense heat, and the earth and its works will be discovered. Since all these things are to be destroyed in this way, what sort of people ought you to be in holy conduct and godliness, looking for and hastening the coming of the day of God, on account of which the heavens will be destroyed by burning, and the elements will melt with intense heat. But according to his promise we are looking for new heavens and a new earth, in which righteousness dwells.

The gist of the apostle's answer to these mockers is clear. The Lord will indeed fulfil his promise, but in his own time and in accord with his desire to grant to all an opportunity for repentance. In his patience and mercy, the world continues as before so that the gospel might be preached and the day of salvation prolonged. No one, however, should misjudge the Lord's patience and conclude that the day of his coming will not arrive. For our purpose, we do not need to go into the question that often captures the attention of interpreters of this passage – whether it teaches that God sincerely calls all to repentance, though he does not choose to save all to whom the gospel is preached. This certainly is the most natural reading of the passage. What interests us is the teaching of this passage about the present and future state of creation.

Two features of this passage speak directly to this issue.

First, the Apostle Peter compares the destruction of the world in the days of the great flood with the future destruction of the world at the 'day of God' (verses 6–7, 10–12). The language of destruction is used in both instances. Though we may be inclined to take this to mean the complete annihilation of all things, this cannot be the case, at least in the first instance. When God's judgement fell upon the world at the time of the flood, the world was destroyed only in the sense that its wicked inhabitants were subjected to judgement and the earth cleansed of its wickedness. The destruction, however, did not involve the removal of all things and the provision of all new things.

And second, the imagery used in this passage to describe the creation of the new heavens and earth suggests a process of refinement and purification, but not of utter annihilation. Imagery drawn from the field of metallurgy – the refining process that produces a pure grade of metal – is used to describe what God will do to create a renewed world 'in which righteousness dwells'. To be sure, the language of this passage speaks of a violent and destructive process: 'the heavens will pass away with a roar'; 'the elements will be destroyed with intense heat'; 'the earth and its works will be discovered'; 'the heavens will be destroyed by burning'; and 'the elements will melt with intense heat'. These descriptions undoubtedly suggest a process of extraordinary power and destructiveness.[1] However, they ought not to be taken to describe a process of annihilation. Rather, they describe a process by which the present creation is purified, refined, and cleansed, all of the impurities of evil and sin removed, and the creation left in a state of pristine purity. Just as the refiner's fire is used to produce the highest and purest grade of gold or silver, so the refining fire of God's judging and sanctifying this sin-cursed creation will yield a new heavens and earth where all is holy and pure. In this process, far from being eliminated, the integrity of the creation is restored, all the unnatural impurities having been removed.

[1] Anyone familiar with the process still used today of producing a high grade of steel from iron ore will acknowledge that the process is a violent and destructive one. This destructiveness, however, aims to remove impurities, not to annihilate.

An interesting confirmation of this reading of the passage may be found in the seemingly odd expression in verse 10, 'and the earth and its works will be discovered'. Many of the later Greek manuscripts use a different verb in this verse, 'burned up', so that it conforms to the language of verse 12 and the idea of the working of fire. However, the word used in the older and better manuscripts conveys the idea of a process that does not so much destroy or burn up, but uncover or lay open for discovery the creation, now in a renewed state of pristine purity. What to us may seem an odd or difficult expression – the earth and its works are 'discovered' or 'found' – is actually just the right expression to convey the idea of a process that does not destroy but restores the creation to a state of integrity. In the same way the process of refining precious metals 'discovers' or 'lays bare' the metal in all of its purity, so God uncovers by removing every impurity the beauty and glory of the created order.[1]

[1] I am indebted for this suggestion to Al Wolters who, in an excellent discussion of this term and passage ('Worldview and Textual Criticism in 2 Peter 3:10', *Westminster Theological Journal*, 49/2, Fall 1987, pp. 405–13), argues that translations of this text have often been influenced by a worldview that denies the continuity between the present and future state of creation. Wolters also suggests that the Apostle Peter's use of this term in two other instances corresponds to this metallurgical use in 2 Peter 3:10: 'It is striking that for the two occurrences of the absolute use in the letters of Peter, the context in both cases evokes the image of a metal's purification in a melting pot or crucible. Could it be that the common Greek verb *heuriskesthai* ["to be discovered", "to be found"] has a precise technical sense in the vocabulary of the smelter and refiner? Its meaning would then be something like "emerge purified (from the crucible)", with the connotation of having stood the test, of being tried and true. In a word, the technical sense would be equivalent to the English "to show one's mettle", an idiom which also originates in the world of metallurgy. A number of passages in extrabiblical Greek authors dealing with the refining of metals use *heuriskoo* in a way which is consistent with this hypothesis.' For a similar treatment of this passage, see Gale Z. Heide, 'What is New about the New Heaven and the New Earth? A Theology of Creation from Revelation 21 and 2 Peter 3', *Journal of the Evangelical Theological Society*, 40/1 (March 1997), pp. 37–56.

2 Peter 3:5–13 confirms, then, the basic idea also expressed, though in different language, in Romans 8. The new heavens and earth will issue from God's sovereign and redemptive work. Though this work is unimaginably powerful, beyond anything within the reach of our present experience, it will involve the renewal of all things, not the creation of all new things. This creation will undergo a process of cosmic sanctification, so that every remainder and vestige of sin will be removed. All of God's renewed creation-temple will be holy unto the Lord (*Zech.* 14:20–21), a place suitable for his dwelling with his people and for their service to him.[1]

Life in the Renewed Creation

Considering the substantial continuity between the present and new creation, it follows that the life to come in the new creation will be as rich and full of activity in the service of the Lord as was intended at the beginning. Just as humankind was originally placed in God's creation-temple to fulfil a particular office and calling, so the new humanity, in union with Christ, the second Adam, will live in unceasing joy in the presence and service of God.

Though there is some danger of speculation in speaking too much of the life to come in the renewed creation, the Scriptures provide some indications of what that life will entail. These indications are often negative, denying to the life to come those features of life which are the result of sin and the curse of God. Nonetheless, the Scriptures do provide something of a portrait of the splendour and beauty of life in the renewed creation.

---

[1] Hoekema, in his treatment of the Bible's promise of a new heavens and earth, argues at some length that this answers the common dispensationalist complaint that Amillennialism 'spiritualizes' the concreteness of the future kingdom (*The Bible and the Future*, pp. 275–9). Ironically, the future millennium of dispensational expectation is in some ways a less literal fulfilment of the biblical promise of the new heavens and earth than that of Amillennialism.

THE PROMISE OF THE FUTURE

I. THE BLESSINGS

The blessings of the life to come for the redeemed people of God will be a consummation of those blessings enjoyed already now in fellowship with Christ. These blessings represent the fruition of the work of redemption already experienced through the indwelling Spirit of Christ. However, in the life to come, these blessings will flower forth in the most beautiful manner. What believers now know and experience only in part will then be theirs in fullness. Those who today can praise God that their 'cup overflows' (*Psa.* 23) will in the life to come drink unendingly from the inexhaustible riches of their inheritance in Christ.

Among these blessings are such things as: perfection in holiness (*Rev.* 3:4, 5; 7:14; 19:8; 21:27); the complete experience of the joy and benefit of adoption (*Rom.* 8:23); the fullness of salvation from sin (*Rom.* 13:11, *1 Thess.* 5:9, *Heb.* 1:14; 5:9); unbroken and unbreakable fellowship with God and his Christ, together with all the saints (*John* 17:24, *2 Cor.* 5:8, *Phil.* 1:23, *Rev.* 21:3; 22:3); conformity to Christ (*Rom.* 8:29, *1 John* 3:2, *Rev.* 22:4); eternal life (*Matt.* 19:16, 29); and the glory of full redemption (*Luke* 24:26, *Rom.* 2:10; 8:18, 21, *2 Thess.* 1:10).[1] Believers who presently bless God for 'every spiritual blessing in Christ' (*Eph.* 1:3), will enter into the perfection of these blessings in the life to come. Every vestige and remainder of sin will be utterly expunged. Every obstacle to fellowship with the Triune God will be removed. No impediment or weight of sin will stand in the way of wholehearted communion and love for God.

Consistent with the completion of the sanctifying work of the Spirit and the enjoyment of the fullness of every spiritual blessing, believers will also enjoy the blessings of freedom from every effect of the curse. Life within the renewed creation will be freed from culpable ignorance and error

[1] I am indebted here to the discussion of Bavinck, *The Last Things*, p. 161. Bavinck cites many more passages from Scripture for these manifold blessings.

(*John* 6:45), from the fear and reality of death (*Heb.* 2:15, *1 Cor.* 15:26, *Rev.* 2:11; 20:6, 14), from every form of futility and frustration, from sickness and affliction, from hunger and thirst, cold and heat (*Matt.* 5:4, *Luke* 6:21, *Rev.* 7:16–17; 21:4), and from all weakness, dishonour and corruption (*1 Cor.* 15:42). Believers will stand in the glory of resurrection bodies in the presence of God and all his people, unbowed by the burden of sin's devastation. The God who forgives all the sins of his people, who heals all their diseases (*Psa.* 103:3), will renew the youth and strength of his people. Believers will know what it is 'to take up wings like eagles' and experience the exhilaration of never growing weary in well doing.

Even though the language is negative, telling us more about what will not characterize the life to come, the vision of John in Revelation 21:1–4 stirs the hearts of God's people in their anxious longing:

> And I saw a new heaven and a new earth; for the first heaven and the first earth passed away, and there is no longer any sea. And I saw the holy city, new Jerusalem, coming down out of heaven from God, made ready as a bride adorned for her husband. And I heard a loud voice from the throne, saying, 'Behold, the tabernacle of God is among men, and He shall dwell among them and they shall be His people, and God Himself shall be among them, and He shall wipe away every tear from their eyes; and there shall no longer be any death; there shall no longer be any mourning, or crying, or pain: the first things have passed away.[1]

Surely no one can adequately describe all that this stirring vision promises God's people. No child of God, however,

[1] Hoekema, *The Bible and the Future*, p. 280, observes that in this passage and in 2 Peter 3:13, the Greek term used for 'new' is *kainos* rather than *neos*, a term meaning new in nature or in quality. This is consistent with the idea that the new creation is 'not the emergence of a cosmos totally other than the present one, but the creation of a universe which, though it has been gloriously renewed, stands in continuity with the present one'.

who has felt deeply the pain and brokenness of sin and the curse – in sinful indifference to God and others, broken relationships, the terror of crippling disease, the boredom and barrenness of life without God, the injustice among people and nations, and so much more – can read these words without being stirred. For they fan into flame an eagerness and longing, like that of a little child who waits expectantly, even impatiently, for the fulfilment of a parent's promise.

One of the blessings of the life to come that must not go unnoticed in the Scriptures is the blessing of communion or fellowship. Though we will later focus upon the epitome of this communion – namely, communion with the living God, dwelling in his presence and looking upon his face – here I would focus only upon the communion among the people of God. Unlike hell, which is a place of utter isolation, separation from God and others,[1] life in the new creation will be marked by friendship and love, perfect fellowship with God and those who belong to him. Though some might be tempted to regard the cessation of marriage to be loss, the beauty of the marriage relationship, of self-denying love between a man and a woman, will be surpassed by the beauty of the marriage between Christ, the bridegroom, and the church, his bride. Whatever loss of brothers, sisters and loved ones that loyalty to Christ may bring in this life, will be more than matched by an increase of spiritual brothers and sisters, not only in this life, but also in the life to come (*Mark* 10:29–30, *Matt.* 12:50, *Heb.* 12:22–24). No words can adequately express what it will be like when all of God's people will dwell together in the most perfect friendship. Petty jealousies, vying for supremacy, bitterness over wrongs committed – these marks of sinful hostility will be

---

[1] See C. S. Lewis, *The Great Divorce* (New York: Macmillan, 1946), pp. 8–9. Lewis, in his imaginative portrayal of hell, describes a place whose streets are empty and whose residents live at an impossible distance from each other – otherwise they would only quarrel!

vanquished and replaced with perfect joy in one another. When the Psalmist exults, 'How good and how pleasant it is for brothers to dwell together in unity' (*Psa.* 133:1), he leads the people of God in singing of what someday will be their experience. The second table of the law will be fulfilled, when all of God's people dwell together in the most intimate and rich communion. The sinful brokenness and division that so often mar the beauty of Christ's bride, the church, in this present age, will give way to the glory for which Christ prayed, when he asked the Father for the oneness of his people, even as he and the Father are one (*John* 17:21).

One question that sometimes surfaces is whether the blessings of the life to come will include the creaturely pleasures of life in the body as we presently experience them.[1] Though the Scriptures plainly teach that in the kingdom of heaven they will neither marry nor be given in marriage, they nonetheless use imagery that suggests that many of the ordinary pleasures of life in the body will characterize life in the new creation. Some of the most common imagery speaks of the saints eating and drinking, enjoying table fellowship with God and others. In the prophetic descriptions of the Old Testament, life in the new heavens and earth is depicted as a rich banquet, lavishly furnished with the best of foods. Isaiah, for example, pictures the day of redemption as one in which 'the Lord of hosts will prepare a lavish banquet for all peoples on this mountain; a banquet of aged wine, choice pieces with marrow, and refined, aged wine' (25:6). This picture is drawn in a context that clearly refers to the final state when 'the Lord God will wipe tears away from all faces, and he will remove the reproach of His people from all the earth' (verse 8). Jesus, on the occasion of the institution of the Lord's supper, spoke of the time when he would drink

[1] For an extended treatment of this and related questions, see Peter Kreeft, *Every Thing You Ever Wanted to Know About Heaven – But Never Dreamed of Asking!* (San Francisco: Ignatius, 1990), pp. 84–132. Kreeft's study is as fascinating as its title suggests.

anew with his disciples from the fruit of the vine in the kingdom (*Matt.* 26:29). Revelation 19:9 speaks of the coming 'marriage feast of the Lamb'. We also are told in the Gospels that Christ, after his resurrection, not only appeared to his disciples but enjoyed eating and drinking with them (*Luke* 24:43, *John* 21:9–14). Do these descriptions support the conclusion that life in the new creation, then, will include also the creaturely pleasures of eating and drinking and the like?

Though some might be inclined to deny this outright, it might be that this denial is borne out of an over-spiritualized view of the final state. If, as we have argued, life in the new creation will be in substantial continuity with life in the present creation, then there is no reason that this might not be the case.[1] Just as our eating and drinking today is to be done to God's glory (*1 Cor.* 10:31), so it may well be in the new heavens and earth that the blessings of food and drink, sanctified through the Word of God and prayer (*1 Tim.* 4:5), will be the occasion for worshipping and serving the living God. It is wise not to be too dogmatic on this question one way or the other. Nevertheless, life in the new creation will undoubtedly be like a rich banquet at which the saints of God will sit down together and enjoy the richest of foods. The joy and happiness that we have known in this life on the occasion of the wedding of a man and woman is but a foretaste of the joy and happiness that will be ours when Christ receives his bride on his wedding day. The wine Christ served at the wedding of Cana is surely a foretaste of that best of wines that he will furnish on that day.

---

[1] Hoekema, *The Bible and the Future,* p. 252, appeals to 1 Corinthians 6:13 ('Food is for the stomach, and the stomach is for food; but God will do away with both of them') to support the claim that 'the digestive functions of the body will no longer be necessary in the life to come'. Hoekema may be correct in his conclusion, but I doubt that this text, in its context, can bear the weight he places upon it.

II. LIFE AS WORSHIP

When describing the blessings of the life to come, we face the danger of losing sight of what is central to every aspect of that life – the worship and service of the Triune God. The blessings enjoyed by the children of God in the new heavens and earth have their meaning only within the context of the worship of God. True life for the child of God is first and foremost a life of worship. So it will be in the life to come.

One prominent way in which this is emphasized throughout the Scriptures is the promise of a Sabbath rest for the people of God. At the conclusion of his work of creation, God himself rested from his creative labours and entered into the enjoyment of his handiwork (*Gen.* 2:2–3). That rest was not a state of inactivity but of active pleasure in the work of his hands and in communion with his image-bearers. For their part, Adam and Eve were placed in a circumstance of peace and joy in fellowship with their God and with each other. All was in a state of peaceful harmony or shalom. The life of the covenant between God and humankind was to be a life of heartfelt service and praise. The dominion which Adam and Eve were to exercise over the creation, under God and in his service, was to flow from a life of worship, an unending and full-orbed offering of themselves in loving obedience to their Creator and Friend, the living God.

Sin, however, radically broke these bonds of fellowship between God and his people. Rather than the whole creation being a temple in which God dwelt in harmony with his covenant children, it became a place of brokenness and disharmony. The Sabbath rest of God and the shalom of his people were disrupted. Humankind's labour became a toilsome burden. The care over the creation assigned to God's image-bearers degenerated into a state of sinful misuse and cultural development in the service of the creature rather than the Creator. Heaven and earth no longer sang in harmony to the praise of the Triune God.

The work of redemption aims to restore fellowship between the Triune God and his covenant people. This restoration promises a renewal of rest and shalom in the relations between God and his people, and between his people and the creation under their care. The ordinance of the Sabbath among the people of Israel was a sign of this renewed fellowship and service. The rest promised Israel in the land that the Lord gave to her was only a prefigurement of that eternal rest that awaited her at the consummation of God's saving purposes in Christ. Canaan was a type of the true promised land, the new heavens and earth wherein righteousness dwells. The writer to the Hebrews emphasizes this theme throughout his epistle. Israel, though promised rest, never entered fully into the promise (*Heb.* 3:11, 18). Joshua, an Old Testament type of the Saviour, Jesus, was unable to bring God's people into the rest promised her. 'There remains therefore a Sabbath rest for the people of God. For the one who has entered His rest [Jesus Christ, the Mediator of the new covenant] has Himself also rested from His works, as God did from His. Let us therefore be diligent to enter that rest, lest anyone fall through following the same example of [Israel's] disobedience' (*Heb.* 4:9–11).[1] The peace, joy and rest that God's Old Testament people enjoyed in their Sabbath day worship and festivals were only a foretaste of what God's New Testament people enjoy in their Lord's Day worship. However, even the Lord's Day, in which the people of God gather for worship and praise, resting in the finished work of the crucified and risen Saviour, remains a promissory note of the Sabbath rest that still awaits them. The worship of the Lord's Day is but a foretaste of the eternal Sabbath yet to come, an emblem of eternal rest.

[1] For a summary of the biblical typology of the land of Canaan in relation to the new earth, and of the motif of Sabbath rest in the Scriptures, see Patrick Fairbairn, *Typology of Scripture* (1845–47; New York: Funk and Wagnals, 1900), I, pp. 329–61; Klaas Schilder, *Heaven: What is It?*, ch. 7, 'Fulfilled Sabbath Rest', pp. 101–18; and Geerhardus Vos, *Biblical Theology*, pp. 138–43.

Though this is a mere sketch of these themes in the Scriptures, it reminds us of what will characterize the life to come. That life will be one wholly devoted to the worship and service of God, an unending Sabbath of peaceful rest and joyful praise. The disruption and brokenness in the relationship between God and his people will be ended. All toil and burdensome labour will give way to gladhearted service of God. The life of God's people will be one of unending, thankful worship. This worship will take place within the setting of the new heavens and earth.

For this reason, in the book of Revelation, the visions of the life to come are full of the imagery of worship and praise. What the prophet Isaiah glimpsed in a vision of the Lord seated upon his throne, surrounded by the seraphim and the host of heaven who unceasingly declare his holiness (*Isa.* 6), John witnessed again and again in his visions of heaven. In Revelation 4, he describes the throne of God in heaven as surrounded by twenty-four elders and the four living creatures. Representing the whole company of the people of God and every living creature, this heavenly assembly falls down before God in worship, saying, 'Worthy art Thou, our Lord and our God, to receive glory and honour and power; for Thou didst create all things, and because of Thy will they existed, and were created' (verse 11). An equally vivid picture of the worship of God is given in Revelation 19: 'And I heard, as it were, the voice of a great multitude and as the sound of many waters and as the sound of mighty peals of thunder, saying, "Hallelujah! For the Lord our God, the Almighty, reigns . . . for the marriage of the Lamb has come and His bride has made herself ready"' (verses 6–7). When the new Jerusalem descends from heaven to earth, the whole creation will become a dwelling place for God in fellowship with his people. There will be no temple there, for the Lord God himself and the Lamb will be in the midst of the people (*Rev.* 21:22). The sanctuary in which God dwells and in which he is served and worshipped will be the new heavens and earth.

No doubt there is a danger in speculating too much about the nature of this creation-temple worship that will characterize the life of the redeemed. However, this worship will surely include the two facets that characterize the worship of God among his people already now. In the Scriptures, the worship of God includes not only the worship of the cultus but also the worship of the whole of life. God's people assemble at specific times and places for official worship. They gather on the Sabbath or the Lord's day for the purpose of entering the sanctuary of God's presence, to offer corporate sacrifices of thanksgiving to him. Such worship includes elements like singing his praise, presenting thank offerings, prayer, the reading and hearing of his Word, and the sacraments. In obedience to God's command and in gratitude for his saving work, God's people gather in worship to acknowledge the Triune God's worthiness to receive the thankful praise of all creation.

This does not exhaust the worship or service of the people of God, however. In the two tables of the law, commanding love for God and for neighbour, the life of God's people is described as a life of worship. As royal priests, believers in union with Christ respond to God's mercy and grace by offering their selves wholly to God (1 Pet. 2:9, Rom. 12:1). No legitimate activity of life – whether in marriage, family, business, play, friendship, education, politics, etc. – escapes the claims of Christ's kingship. In fellowship with Christ, the second Adam and obedient servant of the Lord, the redeemed of God are renewed unto the service of their Creator in every area of life. Though we are not told what life as worship in the new creation will involve, certainly those who live and reign with Christ forever will find the diversity and complexity of their worship of God not less, but richer, in the life to come. Every legitimate activity of (new) creaturely life will be included within the life of worship of God's people.

This helps to answer a frequent puzzle: will the people of God not become weary, perhaps even bored, in a life that has no end?[1] It is difficult to imagine a life of worship, whether in the narrow or broad sense, that never concludes but ceaselessly continues. In a creation that has no night (*Rev.* 21:25) and in which God is perpetually praised, will not God's people find the ways and means to serve God ultimately limited and eventually so familiar as to become contemptible?'

Admittedly, this question, though sometimes asked, is difficult to answer. We lack the imagination necessary to grasp with any adequacy the richness and texture of the life to come. There is so much we do not know about the worship of God's people in the new creation. However, if the Sabbath rest of God's people, far from being an inactive and listless passing of time, is full of activity in the worship of God, we have the beginning of an answer to this puzzle. In our present experience, we know what it is for time to pass with painful slowness. No parent travelling a distance with children on vacation is unaware of the common lament, 'Are we there yet?'. Sometimes time seems to come to a halt, and the movement of the clock seems imperceptible. On the other hand, who has not known the rapid passage of time? When we are engaged in an exhilarating activity time seems to fly by so that we almost lose track altogether of its passing. If we allow our imaginations some freedom, what child of God cannot imagine something of what it will be in the life to come to glorify God and enjoy him forever? No child of God

---

[1] The fear of boredom is reinforced by the bland and unimaginative ideas many have of heaven which were mentioned earlier. Regis Martin, *The Last Things* (San Francisco: Ignatius, 1998), p. 161: 'The reason [so few long for heaven] is that for most people the only idea they have of Heaven is the everlastingly boring one of men and women seated forever on a cloud playing harps and shouting Hosannas.' Martin also quotes Dorothy Sayers' observation about the circumstance of the damned by comparison – 'nothing to do and all eternity to do it in' (p. 149). Written from a Roman Catholic point of view, Martin's study is beautifully written and rich in citations from Christian tradition.

who has experienced something of the unspeakable joy of knowing Christ need fear that the life to come will end in boredom or tiresome repetition. Though the language is poetic and somewhat general, the hymn writer well expressed it – 'When we've been there ten thousand years . . . we've no less days to sing his praise'. The inexhaustible glory and splendour of their God will be more than enough to furnish the praise of God's people in the life to come.[1]

III. A RICH INHERITANCE

Consistent with our argument that the life of the redeemed in the new creation will be rich and diverse, one of the descriptions in the book of Revelation speaks of the rich inheritance that awaits God's people. In Revelation 21, John's vision of the new heaven and earth includes a vision of the nations walking together by the light that is the Lamb. The nations will walk together and, the vision adds, 'the kings of the earth will bring their glory into it [the holy city]' (verse 24). According to this vision, the rich diversity of peoples, together with the works and accomplishments of those who have been among the leaders of the nations, will contribute significantly to the glory and splendour of the new heaven and earth.

Since the language of this vision does not elaborate upon the meaning of this inheritance of God's people, we are left to surmise what it might mean. It has been plausibly suggested that it describes the way the new creation will receive all of the appropriate fruits of human culture and

[1] I am assuming here that time as a succession of moments will continue to characterize the life of God's creatures in the new creation. Only God is by nature eternal, transcending the limitations of created time. Though in popular piety some Christians have the strange (and unorthodox) idea that 'time will be no more' in the final state, this would be a serious denial of the difference between God as Creator and the creation. For a recent discussion of this issue, see Wayne Grudem, *Systematic Theology* (Grand Rapids: Zondervan, 1994), pp. 172–3, 1162.

development that have been produced throughout the course of history. Every legitimate and excellent fruit of human culture will be carried into and contribute to the splendour of life in the new creation. Rather than the new creation being a radically new beginning, in which the excellent and noble fruits of humankind's fulfilment of the cultural mandate are wholly discarded – the new creation will benefit from, and be immensely enriched by, its receiving of these fruits. Far from being an empty and desolate place, the new creation will be enriched with the sanctified fruits of human culture. Nothing of the diversity of the nations and peoples, their cultural products, languages, arts, sciences, literature, and technology – so far as these are good and excellent – will be lost upon life in the new creation. Life in the new creation will not be a starting over, but a perfected continuation of the new humanity's stewardship of all of life in the service of God.

Though some have argued that this reading of John's vision is speculative and unwarranted,[1] the language of Revelation 21:24 can scarcely be read otherwise.[2] The alternative – denying that life in the new creation will be enriched by the

[1] See, for example, Klaas Schilder, *Heaven: What is It?*, pp. 11–12.

[2] For examples of interpreters who read the passage in this way, see: G. B. Caird, *A Commentary on the Revelation of St. John the Divine* (Harper's New Testament Commentaries; New York: Harper and Row, 1966),p. 280; A. Hoekema, *The Bible and the Future*, pp. 285–6; Hendrikus Berkhof, *Christ the Meaning of History* (1966; Grand Rapids: Baker, 1979), pp. 188–92; A. Kuyper, *De Gemeene Gratie* (Amsterdam: Höver & Wormser, 1902), I:pp. 454–94; and Al Wolters, *Creation Regained* (Grand Rapids: Eerdmans, 1985), pp. 57–71. H. Berkhof (p. 191) translates the following representative quote from Kuyper (*De Gemeene Gratie*, I, pp. 482–3): 'If an endless field of human knowledge and of human ability is now being formed by all that takes place in order to make the visible world and material nature subject to us, and if we know that this dominion of ours over nature will be complete in eternity, we may conclude that the knowledge and dominion we have gained over nature here can and will be of continued significance, even in the kingdom of glory.'

presence of these fruits of human culture – seems unlikely and problematic. Life in the new creation will not be a *repristination* of all things – a going back to the way things were at the beginning. Rather, life in the new creation will be a *restoration* of all things – involving the removal of every sinful impurity and the retaining of all that is holy and good.[1] Were the new creation to exclude the diversity of the nations and the glory of the kings of the earth, it would be impoverished rather than enriched, historically regressive and reactionary rather than progressive. To express the point in the form of a question: is it likely that the music of Bach and Mozart, the painting of Rembrandt, the writing of Shakespeare, the discoveries of science, etc., will be altogether lost upon life in the new creation?

To Enjoy God Forever

The *Westminster Shorter Catechism*, one of the better known catechisms of the Reformation, begins with a justifiably famous question and answer: 'What is the chief end of man? Man's chief end is to glorify God, and to enjoy him forever.' If our lives find their chief end in glorifying and enjoying God, it should not surprise us that the epitome of life in the new heaven and earth will consist in the worship and enjoyment of the true God. The life to come, because it will bring the fruition of human blessedness, will consist in finding joy in God, living before his face.

Consequently, one of the most beautiful ways in which the life to come is summarized in the Scriptures is in terms of the believer's vision of God. In the traditional language of Christian theology, the joy of heaven will consist essentially in the contemplation (*visio*), knowledge (*comprehensio*) and enjoyment (*fruitio*) of God.[2] When believers see God in the

[1] See Al Wolters, *Creation Regained*, p. 63, to whom I am indebted for this language.

[2] For a brief summary of this traditional understanding, see Bavinck, *The Last Things*, p. 162.

life to come and know him even as they are known, their joy in God will have no measure or end. Indeed, remove the joy of God's presence and the sight of his face, and all of the blessings of the life to come that we have described would amount to very little. For the confession of every believer is that of the Psalmist, 'Whom have I in heaven but Thee? And besides Thee, I desire nothing on earth' (73:25). The restlessness of the human heart finds no end, unless we find our rest in God (Augustine). The deepest longing and thirst of every image-bearer of God can be quenched only by God himself (*Psa.* 42:1–2; 63:1–2).[1]

When the Bible speaks of the believer's future, it is this enjoyment of God, this 'seeing God face to face' that is most emphasized. Whereas sin has brought shame upon the human race so that we cannot look upon God's face without averting our eyes (*Gen.* 3:7–11, *Luke* 18:13), redemption promises the restoration of direct communion between God and his people. The work of Christ as Mediator, not only in justification but also in sanctification, restores those who are united with him to favour with God (*1 Cor.* 1:30, *Rom.* 8:1, 33). Sanctified by the work of Christ and his indwelling Spirit, Christ's people are enabled to see God (*Heb.* 12:14). When the work of redemption is completed, believers will stand unbowed before God, confident again in his presence that they are acceptable to him (*Heb.* 10:19–22). The smile of God's countenance will shine upon the glorified members of Christ throughout all eternity. The pure in heart will see God (*Matt.* 5:8). Those who have purified themselves even as he is pure, will be like him for they shall see him as he is (*1 John* 3:2).

As with other dimensions of the life to come, this joy of seeing God stands out in the depictions of the new heaven and earth in the book of Revelation. In the last chapter of the

---

[1] For a study of heaven written from the standpoint of the 'heart's deepest longing', see Peter Kreeft, *Heaven: The Heart's Deepest Longing* (1980; San Francisco: Ignatius, 1989).

Bible, John sees a vision of this enjoyment of God. Using language drawn from the picture of paradise in Genesis, he writes,

> And he showed me a river of the water of life, clear as crystal, coming from the throne of God and of the Lamb, and in the middle of its street. And on either side of the river was the tree of life, bearing twelve kinds of fruit, yielding its fruit every month; and the leaves of the tree were for the healing of the nations. And there shall no longer be any curse; and the throne of God and of the Lamb shall be in it, and His bondservants shall serve Him; and they shall see His face, and His name shall be upon their foreheads. And there shall no longer be any night; and they shall not have need of the light of a lamp nor the light of the sun, because the Lord God shall illumine them; and they shall reign forever and ever' (*Rev.* 22:1–5).

Central to this vision of the future is the believer's direct communion with God, basking in the light of his presence and favour, enjoying fellowship with him in the midst of the splendour of the new creation.

That the vision, knowledge and enjoyment of God stand at the centre of life in the new creation is undeniable. But how we are to understand this vision of God is a more difficult matter. In the history of the church, particularly in the Roman Catholic doctrine of the beatific vision and the Eastern Orthodox doctrine of *theosis* or deification, this vision involves an unmediated knowing of God's being. Though Roman Catholic and Eastern Orthodox teaching differ on the nature of this vision of God, common to these traditions is the idea of an immediate participation in God's nature or communion in the divine energy. In the Roman Catholic understanding of the beatific vision, believers will know God as he is in his innermost being.[1] In the Eastern

---

[1] For an exposition of the traditional Catholic doctrine of the beatific vision, see Joseph Pohle, *The Catholic Doctrine of the Last*

Orthodox understanding of deification, believers will become so much like God as to be, in some sense, participants in his divine life. Believers, indeed, will become 'god-like'.[1] Just as God became man in the incarnation, so through mystical union with Christ believers will become partakers of the divine nature. In each view, it is claimed that believers will no longer depend upon any creaturely medium or Mediator in order to see God. The vision of God will be a literal seeing of God as he is in his essential nature. All the limitations presently upon our knowledge will fall away when God is known by us in the way we are known by God.

Those who teach this idea of an immediate vision of and participation in the being of God often appeal to 2 Peter 1:4.[2] In this text, the Apostle Peter declares that God 'has granted to us his precious and magnificent promises, in order that by them you might become partakers of the divine nature,

---

Things: A Dogmatic Treatise (St. Louis: B. Herder, 1917), pp. 34–7. For a classic statement of the doctrine, see *Introduction to St Thomas Aquinas*, ed. Anton C. Pegis (New York: Random House, 1948), pp. 467–77. Speaking of this vision, Aquinas maintains that 'if God's essence is to be seen at all, it must be that the intellect sees it through the divine essence (*per essentiam*) itself; so that in that vision the divine essence is both the object and the medium of vision' (p. 468).

[1] For a representation of the view of Eastern Orthodoxy, see T. Ware, *The Orthodox Church* (Middlesex: Penguin, 1980), pp. 236–42. For a sympathetic treatment of this doctrine by an evangelical theologian, see Daniel B. Clendenin, *Eastern Orthodox Christianity* (Grand Rapids: Baker, 1994), chap. 6, 'The Deification of Humanity', pp. 117–37. Clendenin maintains that Eastern Orthodoxy does not teach a literal fusion with the divine essence. Needless to say, the language of Orthodoxy does not seem to guard sufficiently against this idea.

[2] T. Ware, *The Orthodox Church*, calls this 'the famous text of 2 Peter' that supports the Eastern Orthodox teaching of *theosis* or participation in the being of God. In fairness to the position of Eastern Orthodoxy, it should be noted that this participation is in the divine 'energy' (*energeia*) and not in the divine 'being' (*ousia*) as such.

having escaped the corruption that is in the world by lust'. This text seems to lend support to the view that redemption ultimately involves a separation from the being of this world in order to participate directly in the being of God. Upon first reading, this strange text seems clearly to suggest the idea of an absorption into the being of God himself.[1]

Two considerations, however, lead me to reject the teaching of an immediate seeing of the being of God in the life to come. The first relates to the meaning of the language of 2 Peter 1:4. The second has to do with the broader issue of the difference between God as Creator and all creatures, a difference that renders suspect any teaching of an immediate participation in the being of God.

When it comes to the meaning of 2 Peter 1:4, the key to interpretation lies in the three Greek terms that are commonly translated, 'partakers of the divine nature'. In a recent study Al Wolters has offered a persuasive argument for a different translation of these terms.[2] Wolters notes that the second term used in this phrase is a noun whose common meaning is that of 'partner' or 'companion'. He also argues that the first and second terms, usually translated abstractly as 'the divine nature', ought better be translated concretely as 'of the deity'. Peter is speaking, on this translation of the text, of the promise that the redeemed people of God will become his 'partners' or 'companions'. Based upon a comparative study of the use of this language in other biblical and extra-biblical literature, Wolters concludes that Peter is using covenantal language. The goal of our redemption, consistent

---

[1] See Al Wolters, '"Partners of the Deity"': A Covenantal Reading of 2 Peter 1:4', *Calvin Theological Journal*, 25/1 (April 1990), p. 29, for references to commentators who have noted the strangeness of this text.

[2] '"Partners of the Deity"', pp. 28–44; and 'Postscript to "Partners of the Deity"', *Calvin Theological Journal*, 26/2 (November 1991), pp. 418–20.

with the general teaching of Scripture, is covenantal fellowship with the Triune God. Rather than conveying the strange idea of a commingling of the being of the creature and the Creator, this language conveys the idea of communion between God and those who are his. Redemption will find its consummation in the restoration of perfect friendship between God and his people.

This translation and understanding of 2 Peter 1:4 corresponds to the teaching of Scripture of an unbridgeable difference in being between the Triune Creator and the creature, even the creature bearing God's image. For the creature to know and enjoy God, God must take the initiative and condescend to the level of the creature. Throughout the entire course of creation and redemption, God is the One who comes to us, speaking language we can understand and appearing in a creaturely form within our reach. Accordingly, when God in the fullness of time comes to dwell with us (*John* 1:14), he does so by way of a Mediator, the Word become flesh. The miracle of the incarnation is not that we climbed our way up to God. The miracle is that God came down to us, assuming our flesh and blood. Through all of his acts of condescension, and chiefly through the incarnation of his beloved son, God is able to be known and loved by the creature. However, at no time does the creature know and enjoy God *im-mediately*, that is, apart from any creaturely means of communion. God manifests his power and wisdom, not directly or immediately, but through the means of his handiwork (*Psa.* 19, *Rom.* 1:18–20). God manifests his mercy and grace through the Person and work of Jesus Christ, the Mediator. To see God one must see his glory in the Son (*John* 1:18; 14:9; 17:24).

In the same way, when God's fellowship with his people in the new heaven and earth is complete, God will be God and his people will still be creatures. The people of God will not be absorbed into or partake in an immediate way of the being of God. In order to do so, they would have to cease to be who they are as creatures. Nor will they know God with a perfection that knows no boundaries. Though their knowledge and enjoyment of God will be perfected, untainted by the culpable ignorance of sin, it will not be a knowing that fully exhausts who God is in his incomprehensible greatness. To know God even as he knows himself will ever remain outside of the reach of the creature.

How are we to understand, then, what it will be for God's people to see God? If it does not mean that we become as God is, knowing him as he alone knows himself, then what is meant by the expression, 'They shall see his face'?

Though believers have only a small inkling of what this means, what they do know is full of the promise of the future. To see the face of God means at least this: that believers will dwell in God's presence without any hint of fear or shame. In the new heaven and earth, God will be as pleased with his people – his face will shine upon them – as they are with him. God's joy in his people will be reciprocated by their joy in him. But more than that, God's people will see him without any of the sinful limitations of the present. No sin-induced stupor, no failure of hearing, no blindness of vision will obscure the beauty of God from their knowledge. Though believers will still be creatures, limited in their capacity to know God as he knows himself, their knowledge of God will be pure and undiminished by sin. Though God's majesty, splendour, holiness, love, wisdom, and all that he is, surpass the knowledge of any creature in inexhaustible richness, still believers will see God as they have never seen him before. This seeing will be of one piece with what they have already seen in this life, to be sure (2 Cor. 4:6). But it will be so much richer and fuller as to leave room only for unending praise and thanksgiving.

Such is the great promise of the future for which the children of God wait – to dwell in God's blessed presence, glorifying and enjoying him forever.

Selected Bibliography

With few exceptions, this bibliography lists only works cited in this book.

ADAMS, JAY, *The Time Is At Hand,* 1966; revised edition, Philadelphia: Presbyterian and Reformed, 1976.

ALEXANDER, R. H., 'A Fresh Look at Ezekiel 38 and 39', *Journal of the Evangelical Theological Society,* 17/3 (Summer 1994), 157–169.

ALFORD, HENRY, *The Greek Testament,* Vol. 4, Boston: Lee & Shepard, 1872.

ARENDZEN, J. P., *Purgatory and Heaven,* New York: Sheed and Ward, 1951.

AQUINAS, THOMAS, *Introduction to St. Thomas Aquinas,* ed. Anton C. Pegis, New York: Random House, 1948.

BAHNSEN, GREG L., *No Other Standard: Theonomy and Its Critics,* Tyler, Texas: Institute for Christian Economics, 1991.

BAHNSEN, GREG L., *Theonomy in Christian Ethics,* 1977; 2nd edition, Phillipsburg, New Jersey: Presbyterian and Reformed, 1984.

BARKER, WILLIAM S. and GODFREY, W. ROBERT, eds., *Theonomy: A Reformed Critique,* Grand Rapids: Zondervan, 1990.

BAVINCK, HERMAN, *The Last Things: Hope for This World and the Next,* 1928; new edition, ed. John Bolt, trans. John Vriend, Grand Rapids: Baker, 1996.

BEACH, J. MARK, ed., *Mid-America Journal of Theology, Theme Issue: Preaching* (Vol. 10); Dyer, Indiana: Mid-America Reformed Seminary, 1999.

BEALE, G. K., *The Book of Revelation: A Commentary on the Greek Text, NIGTC,* Grand Rapids: Eerdmans, 1999.

BEASLEY-MURRAY, G. R., *The Book of Revelation,* Grand Rapids: Eerdmans, 1974.

BERKHOF, HENDRIKUS, *Christ the Meaning of History,* 1966; trans. L. Buurman, Grand Rapids: Baker, 1979.

BERKHOF, LOUIS, *Principles of Biblical Interpretation,* Grand Rapids: Baker, 1950.

BERKHOF, LOUIS, *Systematic Theology,* Grand Rapids: Eerdmans, 1939; revised edition, 1941; London: Banner of Truth, 1958.

BERKOUWER, G. C., *Man: The Image of God,* trans. Dirk W. Jellema, Grand Rapids: Eerdmans, 1962.

BERKOUWER, G. C., *The Return of Christ,* trans. James Van Oosterom, Grand Rapids: Eerdmans, 1972.

BLAISING, CRAIG A., & BOCK, DARRELL L., eds., *Dispensationalism, Israel and the Church: The Search for Definition,* Grand Rapids: Zondervan, 1992.

BLAISING, CRAIG A., & BOCK, DARRELL L., *Progressive Dispensationalism: An Up-to-Date Handbook of Contemporary Dispensational Thought,* Wheaton, Illinois: Victor, 1993.

BLAUW, JOHANNES, *The Missionary Nature of the Church: A Survey of the Biblical Theology of Mission,* 1962; Grand Rapids: Eerdmans, 1974.

BLOMBERG, CRAIG L., 'Degrees of Reward in the Kingdom of Heaven?' *Journal of the Evangelical Theological Society,* 35/2 (June 1992), pp. 159–172.

BOCK, DARRELL L., ed., *Three Views of the Millennium and Beyond,* Chapters by Kenneth L. Gentry, Jr. ('Postmillennialism'), Robert B. Strimple ('Amillennialism') and Craig Blaising ('Premillennialism'), Grand Rapids: Zondervan, 1999.

BOETTNER, LORAINE, *The Millennium,* Philadelphia: Presbyterian and Reformed, 1957.

BOLT, JOHN, 'The Relation Between Creation and Redemption in Romans 8:18–27', *Calvin Theological Journal,* 30/1 (April 1995), pp. 34–51.

BONWETSCH, N., 'Montanus, Montanism', In *New Schaff-Herzog*

Encyclopedia of Religious Knowledge, ed. S. M. Jackson *et al.,* Grand Rapids: Baker, 1950, Vol. 8, pp. 485–7.

BRUCE, F. F., *Commentary on Ephesians and Colossians, NICNT,* Grand Rapids: Eerdmans, 1956.

CAIRD, G. B., *A Commentary on the Revelation of St. John the Divine,* New York: Harper and Row, 1966.

CALVIN, JOHN, *Commentary on the Second Epistle of Paul to the Corinthians, CNTC,* trans. T. A. Smail, ed. D. W. Torrance & T. F. Torrance, 1964; Grand Rapids: Eerdmans, 1979.

CALVIN, JOHN, *The Epistles of Paul the Apostle to the Romans and the Thessalonians, CNTC,* trans. Ross Mackenzie, ed. D. W. Torrance & T. F. Torrance, 1960; Grand Rapids: Eerdmans, 1973.

CALVIN, JOHN, *Institutes of the Christian Religion,* trans. Ford Lewis Battles, ed. John T. McNeill, Philadelphia: Westminster, 1960.

CALVIN, JOHN, *Psychopannychia,* in *Selected Works of John Calvin: Tracts and Letters,* eds. Henry Beveridge and Jules Bonnet, Vol. 3, 1851; Grand Rapids: Baker, 1983.

CAMERON, NIGEL M. DE S., ed., *Universalism and the Doctrine of Hell,* Grand Rapids: Baker, 1992.

CAMPING, HAROLD, *1994?* New York: Vantage Press, 1992.

CAMPING, HAROLD, *Are You Ready?* New York: Vantage Press, 1993.

CARSON, D. A., *The Gagging of God: Christianity Confronts Pluralism,* Grand Rapids: Zondervan, 1996.

CARSON, D. A., *How Long O Lord? Reflections on Suffering & Hell,* Grand Rapids: Baker, 1990.

Catechism of the Catholic Church, Liguori, Missouri: United States Catholic Conference, Inc. – Libreria Editrice Vaticana, 1994.

CHAFER, LEWIS SPERRY, *Systematic Theology,* Vol. 4., Dallas: Dallas Seminary Press, 1948.

CHARLES, R. H., *A Critical and Exegetical Commentary on the Revelation of St. John, ICC,* Vol. 2., New York: Scribners, 1920.

CLENDENIN, DANIEL B., *Eastern Orthodox Christianity,* Grand Rapids: Baker, 1994.

CLOUSE, ROBERT G., ed., *The Meaning of the Millennium: Four Views,* Chapters by G. E. Ladd ('Historic Premillennialism'), Herman A. Hoyt ('Dispensational Premillennialism'), Loraine Boettner

('Postmillennialism'), and Anthony A. Hoekema ('Amillennialism'), Downers Grove, Illinois: InterVarsity, 1977.

COOPER, JOHN, *Body, Soul, & Life Everlasting: Biblical Anthropology and the Monism-Dualism Debate*, Grand Rapids: Eerdmans, 1989.

COX, WILLIAM E., *Amillennialism Today*, Philadelphia: Presbyterian and Reformed, 1972.

CROCKETT, WILLIAM, ed., *Four Views on Hell*, Chapters by John F. Walvoord ('Literal'), William V. Crockett ('Metaphorical'), Zachary J. Hayes ('Purgatorial'), and Clark H. Pinnock ('The Conditional View'), Grand Rapids: Zondervan, 1996.

CULLMANN, OSCAR, *Christ and Time*, trans. Floyd V. Filson, Philadelphia: Westminster, 1960.

CULLMANN, OSCAR, *Immortality of the Soul or Resurrection of the Dead?* New York: MacMillan, 1964.

CULLMANN, OSCAR, *Salvation in History*, trans. S. G. Sowers, New York: Harper and Row, 1967.

DAVIS, JOHN JEFFERSON, *Christ's Victorious Kingdom*, Grand Rapids: Baker, 1986.

DEMAR, GARY, *Last Days Madness*, Atlanta: American Vision, 1994.

DIXON, LARRY, *The Other Side of the Good News: Confronting the Contemporary Challenges to Jesus' Teaching on Hell*, Wheaton, Illinois: BridgePoint, 1992.

Ecumenical Creeds and Reformed Confessions: Classroom Edition, Orange City, Iowa: Mid-America Reformed Seminary, 1991.

EDWARDS, DAVID L., & STOTT, JOHN R. W., *Essentials: A Liberal Evangelical Dialogue*. London: Hodder & Stoughton, 1988.

EDWARDS, JONATHAN, *The Complete Works of Jonathan Edwards*, Vol. 2, 1834; Edinburgh: Banner of Truth, 1974.

ELLIS, E. EARLE, *Paul and His Recent Interpreters*, Grand Rapids: Eerdmans, 1961.

ERICKSON, MILLARD J., *A Basic Guide to Eschatology: Making Sense of the Millennium* (First published as *Contemporary Options in Eschatology*, 1977), revised edition, Grand Rapids: Baker, 1998.

ERICKSON, MILLARD J., *Christian Theology*, Grand Rapids: Baker, 1985.

FAIRBAIRN, PATRICK, *Typology of Scripture*, Vol. 1, 1845; New York: Funk and Wagnalls, 1900.

Selected Bibliography

FEINBERG, PAUL D., 'The Case for the Pretribulational Rapture Position' in *The Rapture: Pre-, Mid-, or Post-Tribulational,* Gleason L. Archer, Jr. *et al.,* Grand Rapids: Zondervan, 1984, pp. 45–86.

FERRE, NELS F. S., *The Christian Understanding of God,* New York: Harper and Brothers, 1951.

FUDGE, EDWARD, *The Fire That Consumes,* Houston: Providential Press, 1982.

GAFFIN, RICHARD, Jr., *Resurrection and Redemption: A Study in Paul's Theology;* a revised and updated version of *The Centrality of the Resurrection* (Grand Rapids: Baker, 1978), Phillipsburg, New Jersey: Presbyterian and Reformed, 1987.

GAFFIN, RICHARD, Jr., 'Theonomy and Eschatology: Reflections on Postmillennialism', in *Theonomy: A Reformed Critique,* ed. William S. Barker and W. Robert Godfrey. Grand Rapids: Zondervan, 1990, pp. 197–224.

GEISLER, NORMAN, *The Battle for the Resurrection,* Nashville: Thomas Nelson, 1989.

GEISLER, NORMAN, 'In Defense of the Resurrection Body: A Reply to Criticisms, a Review Article', *Journal of the Evangelical Theological Society,* 34/2 (June 1991), pp. 243–61.

GELDENHUYS, NORVAL, *Commentary on the Gospel of Luke, NICNT,* Grand Rapids: Eerdmans, 1951.

GENTRY, KENNETH L., Jr., *The Beast of Revelation,* Tyler, Texas: Institute for Christian Economics, 1989.

GENTRY, KENNETH L., Jr., *Before Jerusalem Fell: Dating the Book of Revelation,* Tyler, Texas: Institute for Christian Economics, 1989.

GENTRY, KENNETH L., Jr., *He Shall Have Dominion,* Tyler, Texas: Institute for Christian Economics, 1992.

GRENZ, STANLEY, *The Millennial Maze,* Downers Grove, Illinois: InterVarsity, 1992.

GRUDEM, WAYNE, *Systematic Theology,* Grand Rapids: Zondervan, 1994.

GUNDRY, ROBERT H., *The Church and the Tribulation,* Grand Rapids: Zondervan, 1973.

HARMON, KENDALL S., 'The Case Against Conditionalism: A Response to Edward William Fudge', in *Universalism and the Doctrine of Hell,* ed. N. M. de S. Cameron, Grand Rapids: Baker, 1992, pp. 191–224.

THE PROMISE OF THE FUTURE

HARRIS, J. MURRAY, *Easter in Durham: Bishop Jenkins and the Resurrection,* Exeter: Paternoster, 1985.

HARRIS, J. MURRAY, *From Grave to Glory,* Grand Rapids: Zondervan, 1990.

HARRIS, J. MURRAY, *Raised Immortal: Resurrection and Immortality in the New Testament,* Grand Rapids: Eerdmans, 1985.

HART, TREVOR, 'Universalism: Two Distinct Types', in *Universalism and the Doctrine of Hell,* ed. Nigel M. de S. Cameron, Grand Rapids: Baker, 1992, pp. 1–34.

HEIDE, GALE Z., 'What is New about the New Heaven and the New Earth? A Theology of Creation from Revelation 21 and 2 Peter 3', *Journal of the Evangelical Theological Society,* 40/1 (March 1997), pp. 37–56.

HELM, PAUL, *The Last Things: Death, Judgment, Heaven and Hell,* Edinburgh: Banner of Truth, 1989.

HENDRIKSEN, WILLIAM, *I and II Thessalonians, NTC,* Grand Rapids: Baker, 1955; Edinburgh: Banner of Truth, 1972.

HENDRIKSEN, WILLIAM, *The Bible on the Life Hereafter,* Grand Rapids: Baker, 1959.

HENDRIKSEN, WILLIAM, *Israel in Prophecy,* Grand Rapids: Baker, 1974.

HENDRIKSEN, WILLIAM, *More Than Conquerors,* Grand Rapids: Baker, 1967.

HENRY, CARL F. H., 'Is It Fair?' in *Through No Fault of Their Own?: The Fate of Those Who Have Never Heard,* eds. W. V. Crockett & James G. Sigountos, Grand Rapids: Baker, 1991, pp. 245–55.

HILL, CHARLES, *Regnum Caelorum: Patterns of Future Hope in Early Christianity,* Oxford: Clarendon, 1992.

HODGE, CHARLES, *A Commentary on the Epistle to the Romans,* 1835; Edinburgh: Banner of Truth, 1972.

HODGE, CHARLES, *Systematic Theology,* Vol. 3, 1871–2; Grand Rapids: Eerdmans, 1952.

HODGE, J. ASPINWALL, *Recognition After Death,* New York: American Tract Society, 1889.

HOEKEMA, ANTHONY, *The Bible and the Future,* Grand Rapids: Eerdmans, 1972.

Selected Bibliography

HOEKEMA, ANTHONY, *The Four Major Cults,* Grand Rapids: Eerdmans, 1963.

HOLWERDA, DAVID E., *Jesus and Israel: One Covenant or Two?* Grand Rapids: Eerdmans, 1995.

HUGHES, PHILIP EDGCUMBE, *The True Image: The Origin and Destiny of Man in Christ,* Grand Rapids: Eerdmans, 1989.

JEREMIAS, J., 'Har Magedon (Apc. 16:16)'. *Zeitschrift für die neutestamentliche Wissenschaft,* 1 (1932), pp. 73–77.

JEREMIAS, J., 'Har Magedon', in *Theological Dictionary of the New Testament,* Vol. 1, trans. G. W. Bromiley, ed. Gerhard Kittel and Gerhard Friedrich, Grand Rapids: Eerdmans, 1964.

KIK, J. MARCELLUS, *An Eschatology of Victory,* Phillipsburg, New Jersey: Presbyterian and Reformed, 1971.

KLINE, MEREDITH, 'Covenant of the Seventieth Week', in *The Law and the Prophets: Old Testament Studies in Honor of Oswald T. Allis,* ed. John H. Skilton, Presbyterian and Reformed, 1974, pp. 452–69.

KLINE, MEREDITH, 'Har Magedon: The End of the Millennium', *Journal of the Evangelical Theological Society,* 39/2 (June 1996), pp. 207–22.

KREEFT, PETER, *Every Thing You Ever Wanted to Know About Heaven . . . But Never Dreamed of Asking!* San Francisco: Ignatius, 1990.

KREEFT, PETER, *Heaven: The Heart's Deepest Longing,* 1980; San Francisco: Ignatius, 1989.

KROMMINGA, D. H., *The Millennium in the Church,* Grand Rapids: Eerdmans, 1945.

KROMMINGA, D. H., *The Millennium.* Grand Rapids: Eerdmans, 1948.

KROMMINGA, JOHN H., *The Christian Reformed Church: A Study in Orthodoxy,* Grand Rapids: Baker, 1949.

KYLE, RICHARD, *The Last Days Are Here Again: A History of the End Times,* Grand Rapids: Baker, 1998.

KÜMMEL, WERNER, *Promise and Fulfillment,* trans. Dorothea M. Barton, London: SCM, 1957.

KUYPER, ABRAHAM, *Dictaten Dogmatiek,* 2nd ed., Vol. 5, Grand Rapids: J. B. Hulst, no date.

KUYPER, ABRAHAM, *De Gemeene Gratie,* Vol. 1, Amsterdam: Hoever & Wormser, 1902.

THE PROMISE OF THE FUTURE

LADD, G. E., *The Blessed Hope,* Grand Rapids: Eerdmans, 1956.

LADD, G. E., *Commentary on the Revelation of John,* Grand Rapids: Eerdmans, 1972.

LADD, G. E., *Crucial Questions About the Kingdom of God,* Grand Rapids: Eerdmans, 1952.

LADD, G. E., *The Gospel of the Kingdom,* Grand Rapids: Eerdmans, 1959.

LADD, G. E., *The Presence of the Future* (a revised and updated version of *Jesus and the Kingdom,* New York: Harper and Row, 1964), Grand Rapids: Eerdmans, 1974.

LADD, G. E., *A Theology of the New Testament,* Grand Rapids: Eerdmans, 1974.

Let God Be True, New York: Watchtower Bible and Tract Society, 1952.

LEWIS, C. S., *The Great Divorce,* New York: MacMillan, 1946.

LEWIS, C. S., *Weight of Glory and Other Essays,* 1949; Grand Rapids: Eerdmans, 1979.

LINDSEY, HAL, *The Late Great Planet Earth,* Grand Rapids: Zondervan, 1970.

LOCONTE, J., 'Trinity Prof Attacked for Resurrection Teaching', *Christianity Today,* 36/13 (9 November 1992), p. 62.

LOETSCHER, LEFFERTS A., *The Broadening Church,* Philadelphia: University of Pennsylvania, 1954.

MARTIN, REGIS, *The Last Things,* San Francisco: Ignatius, 1998.

MARTY, MARTIN, 'Hell's Sober Comeback', *U. S. News & World Report* (25 March 1991), p. 56.

MATHISON, KEITH A., *Postmillennialism: An Eschatology of Hope,* Phillipsburg, New Jersey: Presbyterian and Reformed, 1999.

McKNIGHT, SCOT, 'Eternal Consequences or Eternal Consciousness?' in *Through No Fault of Their Own,* eds. William V. Crockett and James G. Sigountos, Grand Rapids: Baker, 1991, pp. 147–57.

MOO, DOUGLAS J., *The Epistle to the Romans, NICNT,* Grand Rapids: Eerdmans, 1996.

MORGAN, TIMOTHY C., 'The Mother of All Muddles', *Christianity Today,* 37/4 (5 April 1993), pp. 62–66.

MOUNCE, ROBERT H., *The Book of Revelation, NICNT,* Grand Rapids: Eerdmans, 1977.

MURRAY, IAIN, *The Puritan Hope: Revival and the Interpretation of Prophecy,* Edinburgh: Banner of Truth, 1971.

MURRAY, JOHN, *The Epistle to the Romans, NICNT,* Vol. 1, 1959; Grand Rapids: Eerdmans, 1975.

MURRAY, JOHN, 'The Interadventual Period and the Advent: Matt. 24 and 25', in *Collected Writings,* Vol. 2, Edinburgh: Banner of Truth, 1977, pp. 387–400.

NAISBITT, JOHN, *Megatrends. Ten New Directions Transforming Our Lives,* New York: Warner Books, 1982.

The New Jerusalem Bible, Reader's Edition, Garden City, New York: Doubleday & Company, Inc., 1968.

NOLL, MARK A., ed., *Confessions and Catechisms of the Reformation,* Grand Rapids: Baker, 1991.

PACKER, J. I., *The Problem of Eternal Punishment,* Orthos (a series of papers from Fellowship of Word and Spirit), No. 10.

PATE, C. MARVIN, ed., *Four Views on the Book of Revelation,* Grand Rapids: Zondervan, 1988.

PETERSON, ROBERT A., *Hell on Trial: The Case for Eternal Punishment,* Phillipsburg, New Jersey: Presbyterian and Reformed, 1995.

PENTECOST, DWIGHT, *Things to Come,* Findlay, Ohio: Dunham, 1958.

PETERSON, E., 'Apanteesis', in *Theological Dictionary of the New Testament,* trans. G. W. Bromiley, ed. Gerhard Kittel, Vol. 1, Grand Rapids: Eerdmans, 1964.

PINK, ARTHUR W., *The Antichrist,* Grand Rapids: Kregel, 1988.

PINNOCK, CLARK, 'The Destruction of the Finally Impenitent', *Criswell Theological Review,* 4 (1990), pp. 243–359.

POHLE, JOSEPH, *The Catholic Doctrine of the Last Things: A Dogmatic Treatise,* St. Louis: B. Herder, 1917.

POYTHRESS, VERN, 'Genre and Hermeneutics in Rev. 20:1–6', *Journal of the Evangelical Theological Society,* 36/1 (March 1993), pp. 41–54.

POYTHRESS, VERN, *Understanding Dispensationalists,* Grand Rapids: Zondervan, 1987.

RIDDERBOS, HERMAN, *The Coming of the Kingdom*, trans. H. de Jonste, ed. Raymond O. Zorn, 1950; Philadelphia: Presbyterian and Reformed, 1962.

RIDDERBOS, HERMAN, *Paul: An Outline of His Theology*, trans. John Richard de Witt, 1966; Grand Rapids: Eerdmans, 1975.

RIDDLEBARGER, KIM, 'The Antichrist', *Modern Reformation* (May/June 1994), pp. 4–6.

ROBERTSON, O. PALMER, 'Is There a Distinctive Future for Ethnic Israel in Romans 11?' in *Perspectives on Evangelical Theology*, ed. K. S. Kantzer and S. N. Gundry, Grand Rapids: Baker, 1979, pp. 209–27.

ROSS, ALEXANDER, *Commentary on the Epistles of James and John*, *NICNT*, Grand Rapids: Eerdmans, 1954.

RUSSELL, J. STUART, *The Parousia: A Study of the New Testament Doctrine of Our Lord's Second Coming*, 1887; Grand Rapids: Baker, 1983.

RYRIE, CHARLES C., *The Basis of the Premillennial Faith*, New York: Loizeaux, 1953.

RYRIE, CHARLES C., *Dispensationalism Today*. Chicago: Moody, 1965.

SAUCY, ROBERT L., *The Case for Progressive Dispensationalism*, Grand Rapids: Zondervan, 1993.

SCHAFF, PHILIP, ed., *The Creeds of Christendom*, Vol. 1–3, 1931; Grand Rapids: Baker, 1985.

SCHAFF, PHILIP, AND WACE, HENRY, eds., *A Select Library of Nicene and Post-Nicene Fathers of the Christian Church*, Second Series, Vol. 1, repr. Grand Rapids: Eerdmans, 1976.

SCHILDER, KLAAS, *Heaven: What Is It?* trans. Marian M. Schoolland, Grand Rapids: Eerdmans, 1950.

SHEDD, W. G. T., *The Doctrine of Endless Punishment*, 1885; Edinburgh: Banner of Truth, 1986.

SHEPHERD, NORMAN, 'Postmillennialism', in *The Zondervan Pictorial Encyclopedia of the Bible*, ed. Merrill C. Tenney, Grand Rapids: Zondervan, 1975, 1976.

SHEPHERD, NORMAN, 'The Resurrections of Revelation 20', *Westminster Theological Journal*, 37/1 (Fall 1974), pp. 34–43.

Selected Bibliography

SCOFIELD, C. I:, ed., *The New Scofield Reference Bible,* Editorial Committee: E. Schuyler English, *et al.,* New York: Oxford University Press, 1967.

SCOFIELD, C. I., ed., *The Scofield Reference Bible,* New York: Oxford University Press, 1909.

SPROUL, R. C., *The Last Days According to Jesus,* Grand Rapids: Baker, 1998.

SPYKMAN, GORDON, *Reformational Theology,* Grand Rapids: Eerdmans, 1992.

STEVENS, EDWARD E., *What Happened in 70 AD,* Ashtabula, Ohio: Northeast Ohio Bible Institute, 1981.

STOTT, JOHN R. W., *The Cross of Christ,* Downers Grove, Illinois: InterVarsity, 1986.

STREET, T. NORTON, *How to Understand Your Bible,* revised ed., Downers Grove, Illinois: InterVarsity, 1974.

TAN, PAUL LEE, *The Interpretation of Prophecy,* Winona Lake, Indiana: BMH Books, 1974.

TOFFLER, ALVIN, *Future Shock,* New York: Random House, 1970.

VAN DER WESTHUIZEN, M. J., *De Antichrist in het Nieuwe Testament,* Amsterdam: H. A. Van Bottenburg, 1916.

VAN GRONINGEN, GEORGE, *Messianic Revelation in the Old Testament,* Grand Rapids: Baker, 1990.

VANLANINGHAM, MICHAEL G., 'Romans 11:25–27 and the Future of Israel in Paul's Thought', *The Master's Seminary Journal,* 3/3 (Fall 1992), pp. 141–74.

VENEMA, CORNELIS P., '1994?: Another Misguided Attempt to Date the Return of Our Lord', *The Outlook,* 43/8 (1993), pp. 14–17.

VON BALTHASAR, HANS URS, *Dare We Hope 'That All Men Be Saved'?* San Francisco: Ignatius, 1988.

VOS, GEERHARDUS, *Biblical Theology,* Grand Rapids: Eerdmans, 1948.

VOS, GEERHARDUS, *The Pauline Eschatology,* Princeton: University Press, 1930.

WALDEMAR, MOLINSKI, 'Merit', in *Sacramentum Mundi: An Encyclopedia of Theology,* ed. Karl Rahner, *et al.,* Vol. 4, Basle-Montreal: Hermann-Herder Foundation, 1969.

WALLS, JOE, *Going for the Gold: Reward and Loss at the Judgment of Believers*, Chicago: Moody, 1991.

WALVOORD, JOHN F., *The Millennial Kingdom*, Findlay, Ohio: Dunham, 1959.

WALVOORD, JOHN F., *The Revelation of Jesus Christ*, Chicago: Moody, 1966.

WARE, T., *The Orthodox Church*, Harmondsworth, Middlesex: Penguin, 1980.

WARFIELD, B. B., 'Annihilationism', in *Studies in Theology*, New York: Oxford University Press, 1932, pp. 447–500.

WARFIELD, B. B., *Selected Shorter Writings*, Vol. 1, Nutley, New Jersey: Presbyterian and Reformed, 1970.

WARFIELD, B. B., *The Works of Benjamin B. Warfield*, Vols. 2 & 9, 1929/32; Grand Rapids: Baker, 1981.

WHITE, R. FOWLER, 'Making Sense of Rev. 20:1–10? Harold Hoehner Versus Recapitulation', *Journal of the Evangelical Theological Society*, 37/4 (December 1994), pp. 539–51.

WHITE, R. FOWLER, 'On the Hermeneutics and Interpretation of Revelation 20:1–3: A Preconsummationist Perspective', *Journal of the Evangelical Theological Society*, 42/1 (March 1999), pp. 53–66.

WHITE, R. FOWLER, 'Reexamining the Evidence for Recapitulation in Rev. 20:1–10', *Westminster Theological Journal*, 51/2 (Fall 1989), pp. 319–44.

WOLTERS, A. M., *Creation Regained*, Grand Rapids: Eerdmans, 1985.

WOLTERS, A. M., '"Partners of the Deity": A Covenantal Reading of 2 Peter 1:4', *Calvin Theological Journal*, 25/1 (April 1990), pp. 28–44.

WOLTERS, A. M., 'Postscript to "Partners of the Deity"', *Calvin Theological Journal*, 26/2 (November 1991), pp. 418–20.

WOLTERS, A. M., 'Worldview and Textual Criticism in 2 Peter 3:10', *Westminster Theological Journal*, 49/2 (Fall 1987), pp. 405–13.

YOUNG, E. J., *The Prophecy of Daniel*, Grand Rapids: Eerdmans, 1949.

ZORN, RAYMOND O., *Christ Triumphant: Biblical Perspectives on His Church and Kingdom* (originally published as *Church and Kingdom*, Philadelphia: Presbyterian and Reformed, 1962), Edinburgh: Banner of Truth, 1997.

Glossary of Terms

ADVENT (Latin, *adventus*, 'coming', 'arrival'): The season of the ecclesiastical year when the Christian church prepares to celebrate the birth of Jesus Christ and reflects upon the expectation of his second coming in glory to judge the living and the dead. This designation derives from the basic meaning of the term 'coming', which refers to the past event of Christ's first coming in the fullness of time, and the future event of his second coming at the end of the present age.

THE AGE TO COME: The New Testament equivalent of the Old Testament term, especially in the prophets, 'the latter days'. With the coming of Jesus Christ in the fullness of time, the future is inaugurated, though the fullness of redemption still lies in the future, in the age to come after the return of Christ to judge the living and the dead and establish his kingdom. For this reason, the New Testament speaks not only of the presence of the future, but also of the abiding contrast between 'the present age' and 'the age to come'.

AMILLENNIALISM: One of four major views of the millennium of Revelation 20:1–10. Amillennialism teaches that there is no distinct period in history between the first and second coming of Christ when the kingdom of Christ will be manifest in an unprecedented manner upon the earth. The kingdom of God is now present on earth as the victorious Christ rules his church and all things through his Spirit and Word. The millennium of Revelation 20 is understood to be a description of the souls of deceased believers presently reigning with Christ in heaven. The future and perfected form of the kingdom will be inaugurated only after the second coming of Christ, when the dead will be raised and the final judgement pronounced.

ANNIHILATIONISM (Latin, *nihil,* 'nothing'): The view that some or all human souls will cease to exist after death. Annihilationism takes one of three primary forms: (i) all human beings will cease to exist altogether at death (materialist); (ii) while human beings are naturally mortal, God will grant the gift of immortality to some, those who benefit from Christ's saving work (conditional immortality); and (iii) while all human beings were created immortal, God will destroy those who do not benefit from Christ's saving work (annihilationism proper).

ANTICHRIST (Greek, *antichristos*): The Old and New Testaments contain descriptions of an arch-opponent of God and of his Messiah. In the New Testament, especially the Johannine writings, the presence of anti-Christian teaching and persons is more clearly taught. The disciples are warned that false christs will attempt to deceive even the elect (*Matt.* 24:24, *Mark* 13:22). The Apostle John speaks of many antichrists, and of an Antichrist. In 2 Thessalonians, the Apostle Paul speaks of 'the man of lawlessness' (2:3, 8–9), and in Revelation the Apostle John speaks of the 'beast' (13; 17:10–12). At the time of the Reformation, many identified the Antichrist with the papacy. Idealists regard the figure of the Antichrist as a personification of the presence of evil and rebellion in the period before the return of Christ.

APOCALYPTIC (Greek, *apocalypsis*): The term is derived from Revelation 1:1, which refers specifically to the book of Revelation. *Apocalyptic* commonly refers to biblical and extra-biblical literature which reveals the mysteries of the end times prior to the establishment of the kingdom of God. The word means literally an 'unveiling', or a disclosure of those events in the future that will bring about the coming of God's kingdom in its final form.

APOKATASTASIS (Greek, *apokatastasis*, 'restoration'): This term is found in only one New Testament passage (*Acts* 3:21). This refers to the final restoration of all things at the conclusion of the present period of the history of redemption. In the history of doctrine, this term has come to be used for the teaching – associated with the early church Father Origen – that at the final restoration God will redeem all things and every creature from sin and evil. In this usage of the term, it is synonymous with absolute universalism.

APOSTASY (Greek, *apostasis*, 'falling away'): A deliberate falling away or repudiation of the Christian faith by professing believers. Throughout the history of the Old and New Testaments, apostasy is present. It is one of the characteristic 'signs of the times' marking the present age prior to Christ's second coming. The New Testament also warns of a 'great apostasy' before Christ's return (*1 Tim.* 4:1–3, *2 Thess.* 2:3).

ARMAGEDDON: (Greek, *harmagedon*): A prophetic battleground mentioned only in Revelation 16:16, where the term refers to a confrontation involving the 'kings of the whole world'. Most interpreters believe this battleground to refer to the mountain of Megiddo, an important Old Testament military stronghold (*Josh.* 12:21; 17:11, *Judg.* 1:27, *1 Kings* 9:15). Others believe it may refer to the 'mountain of Israel', Jerusalem. Dispensationalists commonly teach that it refers to a literal battle just prior to the establishment of Christ's millennial kingdom. Others believe it may be a symbolic reference to the final and decisive battle between Christ and his enemies prior to the establishment of God's kingdom at the end of the age.

CHILIASM (Greek, *chilias*, 'a thousand'): In a general sense, it is a synonym for millennialism. In the history of Christian doctrine, the term has come to be used for any millennial view that looks for a future golden age, either of a literal one-thousand-year duration or an extensive period of time, during which Christ's reign on earth will be manifest, the norms of the Word of God will govern men and nations, and peace and prosperity will prevail upon the earth.

CONDITIONAL IMMORTALITY: The teaching that immortality was not a natural endowment at creation but is God's gift to those who believe in Jesus Christ and benefit from his saving work. All those who do not believe in Christ will ultimately be destroyed and cease to exist. Though this teaching enjoyed some popularity in the nineteenth century, it has come to greater prominence more recently among evangelical theologians who find the doctrine of eternal punishment unacceptable for biblical and moral reasons.

THE PROMISE OF THE FUTURE

THE DAY OF THE LORD: In the Scriptures this refers to a future coming of the Lord, primarily in judgement but also in blessing. In the New Testament, the day of the Lord has already come with the advent of Christ and the outpouring of the Spirit at Pentecost. However, a future day of the Lord is still coming at the end of the present age. Sometimes 'the day' or 'the day of God' (2 Pet. 3:12) is used to refer to this future event of the Lord's coming.

DEATH: In biblical teaching, death is the 'wages of sin', the unnatural consequence of human rebellion against God. Death brings about the separation of body and soul, as well as separation from fullness of life in fellowship with God. The redemptive work of Christ brings immortality and life to believers, overturns the consequences of sin and the curse, and includes the reunion of body and soul in the resurrection. The spiritual dimension of death as separation from God is expressed in the Scriptures by the term 'second death'. The second death is a synonym for the 'lake of fire' into which those who are not found in God's book of life are ultimately cast (Rev. 2:11; 20:6, 14; 21:8).

DEGREES OF REWARD: The teaching that believers will receive varying degrees of reward for their faithful service. Two New Testament passages especially speak of such rewards (1 Cor. 3:8–15; 9:16–27). These rewards are not merited in the strict sense, but are the fruits of God's grace in recognizing and crowning the faithful service of his servants.

DISPENSATIONALISM: A view of the history of redemption that was developed through the writings of John Nelson Darby in the nineteenth century and propagated by means of the *Scofield Reference Bible* (1909; revised ed. 1967). The name for this view derives from the Greek term, *oikonomia* ('economy') and expresses one of the most distinctive aspects of its teaching: the history of redemption is divided into seven distinct dispensations or 'economies' in the outworking of God's programme. Two cardinal principles of dispensationalist teaching are: (i) a 'literal' hermeneutic that insists that biblical symbolism and prophecy always has a literal or concrete reference; and (ii) a sharp demarcation between God's earthly people, Israel, and his heavenly people, the church. In keeping with these principles, Dispensationalism teaches that the New Testament church did not begin in the Old Testament but at the day of Pentecost. The present dispensation of the church will be concluded with the rapture and first resurrection of believers at Christ's coming 'for the saints'. Then will commence a seven-year period of tribulation during which the Antichrist will emerge, to be concluded with the battle of Armageddon. After this seven-year period, Christ will return to earth 'with his saints' to begin his millennial reign from Jerusalem, during which God's programme for Israel will resume. Only after the millennium and Satan's little season will the second resurrection of unbelievers take place and the Great White Throne judgement occur.

DUALISM: When applied to the doctrine of man's constitution, the teaching that the human person is composed of two distinct aspects, body and soul. In this sense it is a synonym for dichotomy. Dualism can take at least two forms: (i) the Greek view that speaks of the body as a 'prison-house' of the soul, and of redemption as a release from the body; and (ii) the biblical view which, while permitting a distinction between body and soul and recognizing a bodiless existence in the intermediate state, insists that redemption encompasses the whole person, body and soul. The biblical view is also sometimes called 'wholistic dualism', to maintain the close relation between body and soul and to emphasize the importance of the resurrection of the body to the full redemption of God's people.

THE END OF THE AGE (THE END): The New Testament terms for the great event of Christ's return, which will conclude the present age or period of redemptive history. The end of the age can also be termed 'the last day' (singular). When the expression 'the last days' is used, it may refer to days yet in the future (in the Old Testament) or to the days inaugurated at the coming of Christ in the fullness of time (for example, in *Heb.* 1:2).

EPIPHANY: Literally, a disclosure or manifestation. In the Scriptures this word refers to the appearance of Christ in the fullness of time and his appearance at the end of the age. Liturgically, Epiphany is the festival at which the revelation of Christ at his first coming is celebrated. The feast is celebrated on 6 January in commemoration of the manifestation of Christ to the wise men from the East.

THE PROMISE OF THE FUTURE

ESCHATOLOGY (Greek, *eschatos*, 'last', and *logos*, 'word'): The doctrine of the 'last things' according to the teaching of Scripture. Eschatology is commonly divided into two parts, individual and general (or cosmic) eschatology. Individual eschatology deals with the future of individuals, especially believers, in the state between death and resurrection. General or cosmic eschatology deals with the future of all things, the final judgement, the resurrection of the body, and the final states of heaven and hell. Two different expressions are sometimes used to affirm different aspects of the Bible's teaching about the last things: (i) 'future eschatology' refers to the Bible's teaching about events still to come; and (ii) 'inaugurated (or 'realized', or 'semi-realized') eschatology' refers to the Bible's teaching about events that have already occurred in history, but which anticipate the fullness of redemption when Christ returns at the end of the age.

FINAL JUDGEMENT: The event coinciding with the return of Christ, when he will publicly judge all people and nations according to their works. Though God executes judgements throughout history, punishing in his justice, rewarding in his mercy, the final judgement is the event which will publicly vindicate God's justice in the declaration of appropriate rewards and punishments. Remunerative judgement refers to God's granting of rewards. Retributive judgement refers to his granting of punishments.

FINAL STATE: The eternal destinies of individuals (heaven or hell) or the consummate form of God's kingdom.

FUTURIST: A particular way of reading the book of Revelation and other New Testament prophecies regarding the future. A futurist interpretation takes these prophecies to refer to events subsequent to the New Testament era, at a time in the future just prior to the end of the age.

HADES: The Greek term used to translate the Hebrew 'Sheol'. Though it can be used as a synonym for the grave in the New Testament, it usually refers to the dwelling place of the wicked in the intermediate state (for example, in *Luke* 16:13–21).

HEAVEN: This term often refers to the future home and blessedness that will be the experience of the believer in the final state. However, when the Bible speaks of the final state, it often speaks of the new heaven *and* earth. Heaven is commonly used in three ways in the Bible: (i) in conjunction with the earth, it refers to one part of the creation; (ii) it can refer to God himself, as in the expression, 'the kingdom of heaven'; and (iii) it refers to the special place of God's dwelling in the midst of his creatures.

HELL (GEHENNA) (Greek, *geenna*): The most common term used in the Scriptures to refer to the place of future punishment for the wicked. Whereas Hades is the intermediate state of the wicked, Gehenna is the final and eternal state. The Greek term is a transliteration of the Hebrew expression, *ge hinnom* ('valley of hinnom'), which originally was a site of Baal worship and the wicked practice of child sacrifice to Molech (2 *Kings* 16:3; 23:10). In the prophets, it is used metaphorically for the place of everlasting punishment for the wicked. This is the background for its use in the New Testament.

HISTORICIST: One common way of interpreting the book of Revelation. Historicist interpreters read Revelation as predicting the major movements and developments of Christian history, from the time of its writing until the end of the present age.

IDEALIST: One common way of interpreting the book of Revelation. The idealist views Revelation as a symbolic portrayal of the conflict between good and evil throughout history. Unlike the preterist or the historicist, the idealist does not identify any of the symbols of Revelation with particular historical events.

IMMORTALITY: The state of immunity from death that belongs, strictly speaking, to God alone (1 *Tim.* 6:16), but which he also grants to human beings created in his image. Believers obtain immortality or imperishability through the resurrection of the body (1 *Cor.* 15:53–54). Conditional immortality is the teaching that only those who benefit from Christ's saving work are given immortality. All others are annihilated.

INTERMEDIATE STATE: The state of the righteous and the wicked after death and prior to the resurrection of the body.

THE PROMISE OF THE FUTURE

LIMBUS INFANTUM: In Roman Catholic teaching, the place to which unbaptized infants are consigned after death. It is a perpetual state free from the experience of pain and torment, but falling short of supernatural salvation and the blessedness of seeing God.

LIMBUS PATRUM: In Roman Catholic teaching, the place reserved for the souls of the Old Testament saints who awaited the coming of Christ in the fullness of time. When the Apostles' Creed speaks of Christ's descent into hell, this is interpreted to refer to his going to hell after his resurrection to liberate these saints and bring them with him to heaven.

LITERALISM: A way of reading the Bible, especially biblical prophecy, that insists upon the plain or ordinary meaning of the words. Dispensationalism is characterized by its insistence that the biblical promises to Israel be interpreted in the most 'literal' manner possible. Literalism is to be distinguished from grammatical-historical interpretation, which speaks of the 'literal sense' (*sensus literalis*) of the biblical texts. The literal sense is the sense of the text when interpreted 'according to the letter', that is, according to the appropriate standards of grammar and history.

MID-TRIBULATIONISM: The teaching of some dispensationalists that the church of Christ will go through a three-and-a-half-year period of tribulation before being removed from the earth and the period of great tribulation.

MILLENNIUM (Latin, *mille*, 'thousand', and *annus*, 'year'): The 'thousand-year' period referred to in Revelation 20:1–10, during which Satan is bound and Christ reigns with his saints. The four major millennial views are distinct interpretations of the meaning of the millennium in the history of redemption.

MONISM: When referring to man's constitution, this term designates any view that rejects a distinction between the body and soul. Monism teaches that the human person is a 'living soul', composed of only one substance, who ceases to exist upon death. Monism, therefore, denies the possibility of an intermediate state. If a doctrine of immortality is taught at all, it requires a completely new creation of the human person, not a resurrection of the body.

NEW HEAVENS AND EARTH: The final and consummate state of all things, after God's work of redemption has been completed or realized. Just as the believer will enjoy the resurrection of the body, so the whole creation will be transformed and renewed by God, liberated from its present futility and bondage (*Rom.* 8:18–25).

THE OLIVET DISCOURSE: The passage in the Gospels (*Matt.* 24, *Mark* 13, *Luke* 21:5–36) in which Jesus predicts the destruction of the temple in Jerusalem and the 'sign of his coming and of the end of the age'. Sometimes called the 'little apocalypse', this passage is the subject of considerable debate. Preterists teach that Jesus' prophecy was fulfilled at the time of the destruction of the temple in Jerusalem in AD 70. Others teach that Jesus prophesied not only the destruction of the temple but the signs that would characterize the period of history up to the time of his second coming at the end of the age.

PARADISE: A term, probably of Persian origin, that appears three times in the Old Testament. In the New Testament, it refers to the place of blessedness promised to the thief on the cross (*Luke* 23:43), the third heaven to which the Apostle Paul was elevated (2 *Cor.* 12:4), and the location of the promised tree of life (*Rev.* 2:7).

PAROUSIA (Greek, *parousia*, 'being by', 'presence'): The most common of three general terms for the second coming of Christ in the New Testament. In non–biblical usage, it refers to the arrival or presence of a visiting dignitary.

POSTMILLENNIALISM: The teaching that Christ's return will take place after the period of the millennium of Revelation 20:1–10. In this general sense, the millennial views commonly termed Postmillennialism and Amillennialism are postmillennial. With regard to the four major millennial views, Postmillennialism is the view that teaches a future golden age prior to the return of Christ at the end of the age.

POST-TRIBULATIONISM: The teaching that the church of Christ will not be removed from the world until after the tribulations of the present age are concluded.

THE PROMISE OF THE FUTURE

PREMILLENNIALISM: The teaching that Christ's return will take place prior to the millennium of Revelation 20:1–10. It takes two major forms: (i) Historic Premillennialism; and (ii) Dispensational Premillennialism. Historic Premillennialism, though it teaches a literal millennium on earth after the return of Christ, does not share the dispensational convictions of a sharp distinction between Israel and the church, or of a division of the history of redemption into seven dispensations.

THE PRESENT AGE: A biblical expression which distinguishes the present period of history from the future age to come. Unlike the future age to come, the present age is still marked by the presence of sin, death and evil.

PRETERIST: An interpretative approach to the book of Revelation and the Olivet Discourse that views the events prophesied as events in the past. There are two forms of the preterist view of Revelation: (i) the view that sees Revelation as a prophecy of the destruction of Jerusalem in AD 70; and (ii) the view that sees Revelation as a prophecy of the fall of the Roman Empire in the fifth century AD. Most preterists teach a future return of Christ, final judgement and resurrection. However, some 'full preterists' teach that all of the events of biblical prophecy, including the return of Christ, have already occurred.

PRE-TRIBULATIONISM: The dispensational teaching that Christ will come for the saints to remove them from the world (the rapture) before the seven years of tribulation.

PROGRESSIVE DISPENSATIONALISM: A recent modification of Dispensationalism. Progressive Dispensationalism does not sharply distinguish between Israel and the church as distinct peoples of God, and recognizes an overarching unity in the progress of God's kingdom throughout the history of redemption. Progressive Dispensationalism is a more radical modification of Dispensationalism than the revised Dispensationalism represented by *The New Scofield Reference Bible* of 1967.

PURGATORY: The Roman Catholic and Eastern Orthodox teaching of an intermediate state of penal and purifying suffering. Only those believers who have reached a state of Christian perfection in this life go immediately after death to heaven. All other believers must suffer a period of purgation before entering heaven. This purgation remits the temporal penalty of sin, and its duration depends upon the degree of sin remaining prior to death.

RAPTURE (Latin, *raptus,* 'caught up'): In Premillennialism, this refers to the church being united with Christ at his second coming before the commencement of the millennium of Revelation 20:1–10. Dispensationalists ordinarily teach that the rapture is the event of Christ's coming for his saints before the seven-year period of tribulation preceding the millennium. The main biblical passage upon which this teaching is based is 1 Thessalonians 4:15–17. Postmillennialists and amillennialists identify the rapture with the event of Christ's coming to judge the living and the dead at the end of the age.

THE RESURRECTION OF THE BODY: The biblical teaching that the just and the unjust will be raised bodily when Christ comes to judge the living and the dead at the end of the age (*John* 5:28–29). Premillennialists ordinarily distinguish between a first and a second resurrection: the first resurrection is of believing saints prior to the millennium; the second resurrection is of the unbelieving (and millennial saints who have died) after the millennium.

SHEOL (Hebrew, *Sheol*) : The most common Old Testament term for the dwelling place of the dead. It has three basic meanings: (i) the grave to which all people go after death (for example, in *Gen.* 37:35); (ii) the state of death (for example, in *1 Sam.* 2:6); and (iii) the state to which the wicked go upon death, but from which the righteous are to be delivered (for example, in *Psa.* 49:15).

SIGNS OF THE TIMES: The characteristic signs or marks of the present age prior to the return of Christ. The signs of the times include such events as tribulation, apostasy, Antichrist(s), wars, famine, sickness, and the salvation of 'all Israel'.

SOUL SLEEP (Greek, *psychopannychia*): The doctrine that the soul is in an unconscious state between death and resurrection. The arguments for this doctrine usually include: (i) the biblical euphemism for the death of believers as a falling asleep; (ii) the inseparable unity of body and soul; and (iii) the unwarranted and premature anticipation of the final judgement that an intermediate state of bliss or woe would require. This teaching, however, conflicts with the biblical affirmation of an intermediate state of provisional blessedness for the righteous and woe for the wicked (*Luke* 16:13–21).

TRIBULATION (Greek, *thlipsis,* 'trouble'): The trouble or distress experienced by believers in the present age prior to Christ's coming at the end of the age. This tribulation may take various forms: persecution (*1 Thess.* 1:6), imprisonment (*Acts* 20:23), derision (*Heb.* 10:33), poverty (*2 Cor.* 8:13), sickness (*Rev.* 2:22), and inner distress or sorrow (*Phil.* 1:17). The Bible speaks of a period of 'great tribulation' at the time of the destruction of the temple in Jerusalem (*Matt.* 24:21) and of a period of intensified conflict during Satan's 'little season' at the end of the millennium (*Rev.* 20:7–10). Dispensationalism usually teaches that there will be a seven-year period of tribulation on earth after Christ's coming for his saints and prior to the millennium.

TYPOLOGY (Greek, *tupos,* 'form', 'pattern'): The hermeneutic that interprets New Testament realities as the fulfilment of Old Testament shadows or prefigurements. Biblical types include institutions (for example, the temple), persons (for example, David), and events (for example, the exodus). One common criticism of Dispensationalism is its failure to interpret adequately the relation and continuity between the Old Testament types and their New Testament fulfilments.

UNIVERSALISM: The teaching that all persons will ultimately be saved and no one will be lost or suffer everlastingly in hell. In Christian universalism, all are saved through the redemptive work of Christ. In non-Christian universalism, all will be saved whether through Christ or in some other manner. Conditional immortality is a modified form of universalism, since it denies the doctrine of an eternal punishment in hell.

Index of Persons

Index of Selected Subjects

Index of Scripture References

THE PROMISE OF THE FUTURE

Index of Scripture References

References to the Apocrypha

About the Publisher

The Banner of Truth Trust originated in 1957 in London. The founders believed that much of the best literature of historic Christianity had been allowed to fall into oblivion and that, under God, its recovery could well lead not only to a strengthening of the church, but to true revival.

Interdenominational in vision, this publishing work is now international, and our lists include a number of contemporary authors along with classics from the past. The translation of these books into many languages is encouraged.

A monthly magazine, *The Banner of Truth*, is also published and further information will be gladly supplied by either of the offices below or from our website.

THE BANNER OF TRUTH TRUST

3 Murrayfield Road
Edinburgh, EH12 6EL
UK

PO Box 621, Carlisle
Pennsylvania, 17013
USA

www.banneroftruth.org